The Walker

On Finding and Losing Yourself in the Modern City

Matthew Beaumont

V

VERSO

London • New York

First published by Verso 2020
© Matthew Beaumont 2020
All rights reserved

The moral rights of the author have been asserted

1 3 5 7 9 10 8 6 4 2

Verso
UK: 6 Meard Street, London W1F 0EG
US: 20 Jay Street, Suite 1010, Brooklyn, NY 11201
versobooks.com

Verso is the imprint of New Left Books

ISBN-13: 978-1-78873-891-0
ISBN-13: 978-1-78873-894-1 (US EBK)
ISBN-13: 978-1-78873-893-4 (UK EBK)

British Library Cataloguing in Publication Data
A catalogue record for this book is available from the British Library

Library of Congress Cataloging-in-Publication Data

Names: Beaumont, Matthew, 1972– author.
Title: The walker : on finding and losing yourself in the modern city /
  Matthew Beaumont.
Description: London ; New York : Verso, 2020. | Includes bibliographical
  references and index. | Summary: 'Whether one considers Dickens's
  insomniac night-time perambulations or restless excursions through the
  faceless monuments of today's neoliberal city, the act of walking is one
  of self-discovery and escape, of disappearances and secret subversions.
  Pacing stride for stride alongside literary amblers and thinkers such as
  Edgar Allan Poe, André Breton, H. G. Wells, Virginia Woolf, Jean Rhys,
  and Ray Bradbury, Beaumont explores the relationship between the
  metropolis and its pedestrian life' – Provided by publisher.
Identifiers: LCCN 2020024743 (print) | LCCN 2020024744 (ebook) | ISBN
  9781788738910 (hardback) | ISBN 9781788738941 (US ebk) | ISBN
  9781788738934 (UK ebk)
Subjects: LCSH: English literature – 19th century – History and criticism. |
  Walking in literature. | City and town life in literature. | Pedestrians
  in literature. | Walking – England – History – 19th century. |
  England – Civilization – 19th century. | Modernism (Literature) – Great
  Britain.
Classification: LCC PR468.W35 B43 2020 (print) | LCC PR468.W35
(ebook) |
  DDC 820.9 – dc23
LC record available at https://lccn.loc.gov/2020024743
LC ebook record available at https://lccn.loc.gov/2020024744

Typeset in Sabon by MJ & N Gavan, Truro, Cornwall
Printed in the UK by CPI Group (UK) Ltd, Croydon CR0 4YY

For Jordan and Aleem again;
and for Jake, Ruby, Jasmine and Max

– As I walk, solitary, unattended,
Around me I hear that eclat of the world
                    Walt Whitman, 'As I Walk
                    These Broad Majestic Days'

Contents

Introduction

Lost and Unlost Steps

What are the politics of walking in the city? What are its poetics?

In *Nadja* (1928), André Breton's great surrealist novel, his autobiographical narrator at one point describes bringing a pile of books to a bar where he has made an arrangement to meet Nadja herself, who is fast becoming the object of his strange, not to say obsessive libidinal and spiritual investments. This pile of books includes a copy of *Les pas perdus* (1924), *The Lost Steps*, Breton's first collection of essays, which he no doubt brings, along with the first *Manifesto of Surrealism* (1924), in an attempt both to educate her and aggrandize himself. 'Lost steps?' Nadja exclaims on seeing its title. 'But there's no such thing!'[1]

There's no such thing as lost steps! If one were to search for the principle that epitomizes what, in an echo of the title of a book by the late Marshall Berman, might be called 'modernism in the streets', one could probably find it in this exclamation.[2] It informs the writings of all those authors whose various, sometimes countervailing commitments to walking as a socially and psychologically meaningful activity I examine or reconstruct in this book. Those authors, that is, who consistently sought to make the cities with which they were familiar seem new or strange by traversing them aimlessly, sometimes desperately, on foot, in a state of heightened susceptibility to the relentless stimuli of the streets. But it is also a doctrine that, almost a century later, still resonates in the cities of today.

Certainly, it is the article of faith according to which, as a committed, even devout pedestrian, I like to live. No walk, as far as I am concerned, is ever wasted. In contrast, for example, to a car journey. In a city – especially one dominated by cars, by individualistic rather than collective, private rather than public modes of transport – it is walking that habitually makes me feel alive. It makes me feel both vitally connected to the city's ceaseless circuits of energy and, at the same time, delicately detached from them. Stimulant, then, and narcotic.

In the twenty-first century, in cities that are the site of acutely disorienting cycles of creative destruction, where pedestrians are increasingly inured to the environment they more and more mechanically inhabit, not least because of their dependence on the technology of smartphones and other hand-held devices, we need another modernism of the streets. And we need to celebrate some of those embattled individuals for whom, in the nineteenth and the first half of the twentieth centuries, at the high tide of industrial modernity, this activity was a sort of spiritual imperative; a vocation.

There's no such thing as lost steps … Nadja does a lot of loitering on the streets of Paris, so her reaction to the title of Breton's book, which I take to be spontaneously triumphant rather than merely defensive, is understandable. If you wander around the city, or hang about at street corners, things happen.

Of course, people might think as a result that you're a pimp or a prostitute or some other undesirable, and if you're a woman you'll be especially exposed to demeaning assumptions of this sort; but things still happen. With any luck, in fact, you might encounter a Surrealist, as Nadja does. Or, thirty or forty years later, a situationist. These avant-gardists are committed to the idea that it is the street, above all other venues, that provides what Breton, in the essay that opens Les pas perdus, calls the 'surprising detours' that shape a life in the conditions of capitalist modernity.[3]

'The street, with its cares and its glances, was my true element,' Breton declares: 'there I could test like nowhere else the winds of possibility.'[4] The street, site of the most routine practicalities, such as shopping, is also a social laboratory in which all sorts

of utopian potentialities can be tested. The street is the domain
of the trivial; but – as the etymological origin of this word suggests, derived from the Latin for a place at which three roads
meet, typically at the volatile margins of the city where immigrants of all kinds congregate and circulate – it is also a site of
dynamic social experiment. It is a point of intersection, criss-
crossed with restless feet, bristling with creative possibilities for
collective life.

Breton, it can safely be assumed, agrees with Nadja that
there are no lost steps. For her, as he formulates it in a sentence
that Walter Benjamin later cited as the epigraph to his essay
on 'Marseilles' (1929), the streets are 'the only region of valid
experience' ('la rue, pour elle seul champ d'expérience valable').[5]
And walking, implicitly, is the only valid means of traversing
this region or, better, 'field' of experience (it is surely important,
paradoxically, not to erase the ancient pastoral associations of
this phrase). More specifically, that errant, meandering form of
walking that is often classified as wandering is the only valid
means of traversing this field of experience.

Like other Surrealists, and indeed like other modernists of every
stripe, Breton believed that the footstep, as Michael Sheringham
puts it in a phrase to which I will return, is the 'emblem of the
free everyday'.[6] The footstep is an opportunity to escape the logic
of abstraction, the logic of exchange-value constitutive of those
modes of transport with which, in the industrial metropolis, the
walker must compete, from automobiles to buses to trains. Every
footfall, then, in contrast to the revolution of a set of wheels that
travels along roads or tracks, is an adventure. A flight. It is open
to 'surprising detours'. And it is, at the same time, a faint imprint,
on the pavements and other surfaces of the city, of these necessarily individual escapades.

It is in this sense that the lost steps shaping the essays in Breton's
Les pas perdus are not in fact lost steps at all. They are affirmations of the surrealist's freedom simply to drift through the streets
and through the corridors of nineteenth- and early twentieth-
century French literature, opening himself up to the everyday
excitements of chance experience. The polemics, reviews, and
sketches of comrades associated with Dadaism and Surrealism

that comprise *Les pas perdus* don't go anywhere immediately obvious. They are diversions, meaning both deviations from the predictable or prescribed route and distractions. Recreational distractions that, as deviations from normative expectations, are in some fundamental sense re-creational ...

In so far as Breton's collection, both its title and its surrealist spirit, was subsequently 'modified in the guts of the living', to echo Auden's poem about Yeats, it certainly proved creative and regenerative: the Cuban novelist Alejo Carpentier's *Los pasos perdidos* (1953), *The Lost Steps*, in some respects a post-colonial critique of Surrealism, brilliantly explores not only what it means to get lost in the jungle but also just how difficult it is both to move on foot in the streets of a city and to live according to the 'laws of collective motion' that prevail in them.[7] As individual pedestrians, isn't this what we are all trying to do in our everyday lives? Aren't we fighting, in effect, to coordinate the city's 'laws of collective motion'? Like a conductor who arrives at their podium halfway through the fourth movement of the symphony?

Les pas perdus includes the account of an adventure Breton and Louis Aragon had on a Parisian street when, to absolutely no narrative consequence, they became intrigued by an enigmatic and oddly disorientated woman. This *passante*, the object of those 'cares' and 'glances' apparently legitimated, in a patriarchal society, by the sightlines and the sexual-political dynamics of the street, is a Baudelairean passer-by who unlike Nadja resists with considerable insouciance the Surrealists' more or less predatory attempts to recruit her to their schemes. Refusing to audition for the part of Nadja the two men are effectively hoping to cast, this anonymous woman ignores or, still more gloriously, remains completely unconscious of them: 'Louis Aragon and André Breton,' the piece concludes, 'unable to give up the idea of finding the key to the riddle, searched through part of the sixth arrondissement – but in vain.'[8]

But Breton's article, titled 'The New Spirit' and first published in 1922 in the surrealist periodical *Littérature*, is itself proof that their search was not in vain. For the surrealists, all experiences on the streets take the form of experiments, and no experiments are unsuccessful. Furthermore, if the point of this sketch is that it goes nowhere, Breton himself was clearly confident that he was going somewhere. The essays and fragments collected in *Les pas perdus*, which announce an arrival and a departure, function as important preparatory exercises. After all, the *Manifesto of Surrealism*, representing a signal departure for the avant-garde, appeared in the same year. There are no lost steps.

In French, the phrase *pas perdus*, 'lost steps,' recalls the phrase *salle des pas perdus* – the common, peculiarly rich name for the waiting room of a railway station. At once drearily prosaic and poignantly poetic, it evokes the aimless, restless pacing of those who kill time before the departure of their train, tracing a circular, almost self-cancelling movement that collapses walking into waiting, the active into the passive. But, read with a different inflection, the phrase *les pas perdus* can also mean 'the not lost'. It connotes the unlost (the poet Paul Celan once referred to himself, in a beautiful if painful formulation, as 'unlost amid the losses'[9]).

Breton's essay collection is, then, about an intellectual and spiritual elect: Apollinaire, Duchamp, Jarry, Lautréamont, Rimbaud, Vaché, etc. This elect, moreover, which is comprised of the not-lost, or the sort-of saved, is implicitly recruited from the ranks of those who aimlessly pace the streets in pursuit of adventure. Wanderers. *Fugueurs*. For Breton, and for friends such as Aragon and Philippe Soupault, themselves the authors of fine surrealist novels driven by the logic of what the situationists will subsequently call the *dérive*, or psychogeographic 'drift', people who loiter or pace or wander are precisely not lost.[10] On the contrary, they are preoccupied, consciously or unconsciously, with finding themselves.

And they do find themselves – in contrast, for example, to the inhabitants of that infernal cylindrical *salle des pas perdus* at the centre of Samuel Beckett's *The Lost Ones* (1970), where the tortured relationship between waiting and walking acquires both mathematical and mythical overtones. Beckett's vision is shaped in part by Dante's account of the dead massed on the banks of the Acheron in the third canto of the *Inferno*. Perhaps it is also a recollection of the night he spent in the waiting room of Nuremberg station in 1931, an incident that informed a scene in his novel *Watt* (1953). Certainly, it is a vision of the damned: 'Abode where lost bodies roam each searching for its lost one.'[11]

Breton's more redemptive vision is of the not-damned. Those who like him inhabit the immense *salle des pas perdus* that is the metropolitan city might look like lost bodies, lost souls, but they are secretly the chosen ones.[12] For they discover the marvellous in the everyday, reveal enchantment in the disenchanted spaces of urban life, find redemption in everyday forms of perdition. No doubt there are lost soles in the city, just as there are discarded gloves such as the one Breton's autobiographical narrator fetishizes in *Nadja*; but there are no lost souls. The street redeems everyone. Indeed, its least bourgeois inhabitants, the bohemians, bums and criminals, are for Breton and the other surrealists its saints and martyrs.

In the city, then, for the surrealists and other 'modernists of the street', every aimless step counts – precisely because it cannot be counted. The more aimless the better ... The American novelist Henry Miller, who made the streets of Paris his home throughout the 1930s, offers an almost programmatic statement about the opportunities that open up to those who drift through the city on foot when, on the opening page of his novel *Black Spring* (1936), he announces that 'to be born on the street' – as he himself claims he was because of his origins in working-class Brooklyn – 'means to wander all your life, to be free.' 'It means accident and incident, drama, movement,' he elaborates. 'It means above all dream. A harmony of irrelevant facts which gives to your wandering a metaphysical certitude.'[13]

Here is the early twentieth-century equivalent, in the conditions of the industrial and metropolitan city, of the picaresque hero – an individual for whom, in Miller's words, 'nothing of what is called "adventure" ever approaches the flavour of the street.'[14] 'It takes a heroic constitution to live modernity,' Walter Benjamin writes in 'The Paris of the Second Empire in Baudelaire' (1938).[15] Modernists of the street such as Benjamin and Miller live capitalist modernity heroically by committing to walking or wandering the precincts of the city as if this activity were nothing less than a spiritual vocation. Each accident or incident, relevant or irrelevant, affirms the creativity and freedom of what might, in Baudelairean phrase, be characterized as the walker's kaleido-scopic consciousness.

It is the lost steps, then, that are not lost. For the modernists of the street, lost steps are, paradoxically, unlost, and only the steps that follow a specific, prescribed trajectory are lost. Those who commute on foot, for instance, marching in the morning from station to office and in the evening from office to station, trace lost steps through the city precisely because such steps do not *commute* these commuters, in the literal sense of that verb: they do not altogether change or transmute them. They confirm rather than transform these pedestrians' alienated relations to the city.

The canonical image of these people as the damned, or the undead, is no doubt T. S. Eliot's evocation of the crowd flowing over London Bridge, 'so many, / I had not thought death had undone so many', in *The Waste Land* (1922): 'Sighs, short and infrequent, were exhaled, / And each man fixed his eyes before his feet.'[16] These lines, for all that they reflect Eliot's elitism, his contempt for the mass of people, brilliantly encapsulate the con-tradictory state of concentration and distraction that typifies the commuter's consciousness. Fixated on their feet, or on the piece of pavement in front of them, these commuters have closed themselves off from the 'harmony of irrelevant facts', in Mill-er's phrase, that makes the act of walking both aimlessly and attentively through the streets into an everyday affirmation of individual, even of collective, freedom.

The modernists of the street, for their part, cultivate a com-bination of distraction and concentration that is the inverse of Eliot's commuters'. The modernists of the street, too, are fixated on their feet, in the sense of being actively committed to the cre-ative possibilities with which simply walking about the streets are replete; but this attitude entails seeing their feet, instead, as the fundamental means of opening up their embodied conscious-ness to what Berman, to cite the subtitle of another of his books, captures in terms of 'the experience of modernity'.[17] Their state of distraction, their refusal to focus on any one thing amongst the 'harmony of irrelevant facts', whether this be their feet or the destination to which they are thoughtfully or thoughtlessly travelling, is the precondition for a relationship of profound

openness and receptiveness towards the city, one that effectively
frees them (in Miller's language again) to attend to the acciden-
tal and the incidental, to the dreams and dramas of the street.
Their consciousness is in a state of distraction that, as in a dream,
entails a certain fugitive form of concentration.

Here perhaps is an instance of what Benjamin, groping towards
an understanding of the work of art in the age of technological reproducibility, and thinking in particular of the mentality
inculcated by both cinema and urban architecture in the early
twentieth century, calls 'reception in distraction'.[18] The modernists of the street promote a mode of attention that is neither that
of the bourgeois spectator absorbed by the artefact before which
he stands in contemplation, nor that of the mass of proletarian
spectators seeking escape through the cinema screen. They distinguish 'productive distraction', as Howard Eiland characterizes it
in an article on Benjamin, from '*mere* distraction'; 'distraction as
a spur to new ways of perceiving' from 'distraction as a skewing
of attention, or as abandonment to diversion.'[19] Walking is, precisely, an act of productive distraction. Or it should be.

In contrast to the masses condemned by Eliot in 'Burnt Norton'
(1936), who are 'distracted from distraction by distraction', these
heroes of modernity use their alertness to the intrusion of accidents or random incidents in the street to distract them from
their distraction.[20] Benjamin mentions that G. K. Chesterton,
in his book on Dickens, 'has masterfully captured the man who
roams the big city lost in thought'. Benjamin's point here is that
the pedestrian who is 'lost in thought' is not for this reason necessarily immune to the city's stimulations or provocations. On the
contrary, he is utterly alive to them. Indeed, the most 'revealing
representations of the big city', as Benjamin avers, have come
from 'those who have traversed the city absently, as it were, lost
in thought or worry'.[21] Concentration in distraction.

Distracted consciousness is of course a necessary, if not compul-
sory means of coping with the ceaselessly demanding, stimulating
conditions of city life. It protects us more or less effectively from
what the German sociologist Georg Simmel, in his seminal essay
on 'The Metropolis and Mental Life' (1903), enumerates as 'the
rapid crowding of changing images, the sharp discontinuity in

the grasp of a single glance, and the unexpectedness of onrushing impressions' that constitute 'the psychological conditions which the metropolis creates'. Simmel famously characterizes this psychic defence mechanism in terms of the 'blasé attitude' that – mirroring the levelling effects of exchange-value in the capitalist economy – renders everything 'in an evenly flat and grey tone' and thus safely neutralizes the images and impressions with which the city permanently bombards its inhabitants.[22]

In effect, Simmel is saying that if we don't learn spontaneously to adopt this attitude, if we don't walk about the metropolis in a state of distraction, insulated from the danger of what he nicely terms an attitude of 'indiscriminate suggestibility', we will collapse in the face of its monstrous colourfulness and multi-dimensionality.[23] Constant attentiveness galvanizes us to the point at which, crackling like electricity, our nerve ends finally burn out. It takes a heroic constitution, it still needs to be insisted, to live modernity.

In this specific sense, then, distracted walking is imperative in the conditions of the modern city. The pedestrian must be 'lost in thought,' as Benjamin puts it, if they are to survive its onslaughts. This is why the phrase 'unlost steps', enclosing that uncancelled allusion to the lost, in contrast to cognate formulations like 'found' or 'saved' steps, should be retained if we are to understand the dynamics of walking intrinsic to those writers, including Dickens, Chesterton and Benjamin, who are modernists of the street.

In the twenty-first century, however, the phrase 'distracted walking' has acquired a rather different, frankly unsettling, significance. For today it denotes the widespread practice among pedestrians – sometimes dubbed 'smombies', smartphone zombies – of blundering through the streets and crossing roads while absorbed in their phones. This practice routinely causes fatal traffic accidents. The National Safety Council has for example indicated that in the United States nearly 6,000 pedestrians were struck and killed by motor vehicles in 2017, a number that seems to be rising each year at least in part because of people's dependence on using smartphones in the street.[24]

As the industrial engineers Jun-Ming Lu and Yi-Chin Lo have proposed in a preliminary analysis of what they identify as the 'gaze behavior' of people using smartphones, it is the 'need for multitasking' that has driven this rise in 'distracted walking', a habit that results in 'behavioral changes in body movements, gaze patterns, allocation of attention resource and reaction time to unexpected stimulus'. They further report that 'the impaired situation awareness and the occurrence of inattentional blindness could be also some of the reasons of accidents'.[25]

But, as phrases such as 'impaired situation awareness' and 'inattentional blindness' indicate clearly enough, in spite of their clotted quality, 'distracted walking' has other, less material effects. Most importantly, it insulates the individual pedestrian from the sensorium of the city, impoverishing their everyday experience of its physical and social life by funnelling their attention through the screen. This screen, it might be claimed, serves as little more than a portal into the virtual space of what Guy Debord, in ways that seem startlingly relevant once again, described as 'the spectacle', a regime of commodity relations that he summarizes as '*capital* to such a degree of accumulation that it becomes an image'.[26]

The spectacular virtual space of the smartphone screen, whether it functions as the domain of work or leisure, of production or consumption, or whether it deconstructs precisely this distinction, is structured by the profit motive. The 'addiction to distraction' to which the Frankfurt School thinker Siegfried Kracauer alludes in *The Mass Ornament*, which 'fills [the working masses'] day fully without making it fulfilling', here reaches its apotheosis. 'The form of free-time busy-ness,' Kracauer continues, 'necessarily corresponds to the form of business.'[27] Pedestrians' use of their hand-held devices to send emails or texts, even to purchase products online, conforms exactly to the commodified logic of the society of the spectacle in its latest phase of development. If the *flâneur*, according to Baudelaire, was a 'kaleidoscope gifted with consciousness', then the distracted walker is a smartphone endowed with consciousness.[28]

What are the consequences of this conditioning for the lives of individuals and collectives in cities today? For the city's 'laws of collective motion', in Carpentier's lovely formulation?

The urbanist Adam Greenfield has recently argued that 'when someone moves through the world while simultaneously engaged in some remote interaction,' the two spatial experiences, one actual, one virtual, compete directly with each other. 'Only one mode of spatial experience can be privileged at a given time,' he explains; 'and if it's impossible to participate fully in both of these realms at once, one of them must lose out.'[29] Inevitably, Greenfield insists, it is the actual that in these circumstances capitulates to the virtual.

The example Greenfield offers, though he doesn't use the term, is that of 'distracted walking':

> Watch what happens when a pedestrian first becomes conscious of receiving a call or a text message, the immediate disruption they cause in the flow of movement as they pause to respond to it. Whether the call is hands-free or otherwise doesn't really seem to matter; the cognitive and emotional investment we make in it is what counts, and this investment is generally so much greater than that we make in our surroundings that street life clearly suffers as a result.[30]

Street life suffers ... The community of people on the street, even if this amounts to little more than the sum of those individuals that happen provisionally to be present in its precincts at a particular time, is undermined by the introversion fostered by those virtual spatial experiences delivered by smartphones and other mobile devices. The collective life of the street is thus fatally vitiated.

Certainly, in distracting pedestrians, this technology renders the relatively benign, democratic sort of surveillance once advocated by Jane Jacobs in the interests of making cities safer, which was dependent on what she called the community's 'eyes on the street', almost impossible.[31] In the contemporary city, the eyes on screens often outnumber those on the street. And this redirection of attention makes our surroundings susceptible to malign, undemocratic forms of surveillance.

Staring at a phone, people fail to notice the increasingly authoritarian mechanisms through which the state and various

private interests police their activities as citizens and monitor
and manipulate them as consumers. They become the twenty-
first-century equivalent of what nineteenth-century Parisiens
knew as *les badauds*, those onlookers or 'gawkers' whose gorm-
less attitude to events taking place in the streets was credulous
and irredeemably passive.[32] Except that, where *les badauds* were
senselessly, unreflexively fixated on actual, physical events, and
often spontaneously coalesced into crowds because of the spectacle, distracted walkers are senselessly, unreflexively fixated on
virtual ones, and remain almost completely atomized. No doubt
this makes today's pedestrian monads – who only seem spontaneously to form collectives when, with sociopathic calm, they
stop and use their phones to film some horrifying drama as it
unfolds before them – even more susceptible to more or less
covert forms of manipulation than their Victorian predecessors.

Greenfield usefully lists some of the 'networked information-
gathering devices' that – in addition to CCTV, which is a
comparatively, indeed deliberately, visible presence on the street –
have already been implemented in public space:

> cameras, load cells and other devices for sensing the pres-
> ence of pedestrians and vehicles; automated gunshot-detection
> microphones and other audio-spectrum surveillance grids; adver-
> tisements and vending machines equipped with biometric sensors;
> and the indoor micropositioning systems known as 'beacons,'
> which transact directly with smartphones.

In these and other more or less surreptitious ways, the 'contemporary streetscape', like our homes and our bodies, has become
'comprehensively instrumented'.[33] To distracted walkers, no
doubt, the intrusive devices listed above are more redolent of
a vaguely distant dystopian future than of the hidden matrix of
everyday life, commodified and instrumentalized as it is, in the
present.

Pedestrians' cognitive and emotional investment in the virtual
domain thus has grave social and political, as well as aesthetic,
implications. It desensitizes them to the latest modes of surveillance. Moreover, it also prevents them from perceiving the

insidious ways in which, physically, legally and symbolically, their cityscapes are currently being altered and appropriated by capital. Distracted walkers insulate themselves – to potentially calamitous effect at both an individual and a collective level – not only from its politics but from its economics.

When we use our smartphones as we circumambulate the streets, perhaps simply in order to navigate them with a virtual map, we fail to notice the ways in which public space is covertly being colonized by corporate interests and reinvented as an archipelago of private spaces to which ordinary citizens have at best limited access. Recently, as the urban anthropologist Setha Low summarizes it, and to an accelerating extent, 'the boundaries of what is private or public have become less clear, and increasingly incursions by privatization and other neoliberal practices have been transforming public space, placing it back in corporate or commercial hands.'[34] There is a sense, then, in which the steps traced by distracted walkers in cities today, in so far as they are rendered automatic or semi-automatic by a persistent displacement of mental attention from the physical to the virtual, do entail a serious cost. These footsteps, to paraphrase Sheringham, are emblematic of the unfree everyday as opposed to the free everyday. Truly, they are lost steps.

The philosopher Michel de Certeau, in his famous chapter on 'Walking in the City' from *The Practice of Everyday Life* (1980), outlining a 'rhetorics' of pedestrian spatial practice, provides some of the terms in which, for all that it is a more recent phenomenon, 'distracted walking' might be both understood and, ultimately, combated. 'Distracted walking' is perhaps an extreme, malign instance of what de Certeau – in the course of his attempt to theorize the distinction between authoritarian, aerial perspectives on urban space, on the one hand, and demotic, pedestrian perspectives, on the other – calls at one point the '*opaque and blind* mobility characteristic of the bustling city'.

De Certeau conceptualizes the reinscription of the city that is enacted by footsteps, at the level of the pavement, as a horizontal alternative to the all-seeing or panoptic control of urban space embodied in those 'geometrical' and 'geographical' views of the streets that he associates with the vertical perspective of

corporate buildings such as the World Trade Center. Naturally, de
Certeau was not in a position to understand the extent to which,
in the twenty-first century, the opaque and blind mobility of
pedestrians, in so far as it corresponds to the 'impaired situation
awareness' and 'inattentional blindness' of distracted walkers,
reinforces rather than resists the disciplinary disposition of space.
But his insistence on foregrounding the *'migrational*, or metaphorical, city', which he identifies with walkers, as a means of
disrupting 'the clear text of the planned and readable city', points
to how a kind of 'undistracted walking' might be fostered.[35]

It comes down to cultivating an undistracted way of walking
that mobilizes what de Certeau calls 'surreptitious creativities'.
This self-consciously undistracted walking, alert to the operations of capital and its surveillance mechanisms in the street, and
committed if possible to subverting them, insinuates 'a second,
poetic geography on top of the geography of the literal, forbidden,
or permitted meaning' imposed by the 'functionalist and historical order of movement'. It reinvents urban space not simply by
treading it attentively, or in a state of 'productive distraction',
but by recovering memories and stories of the public, collectively
lived city that private interests seek systematically to eliminate. It
also preserves and reinvents it, of course, by militantly defending
these public spaces when they come directly under threat from
private development. Undistracted walking, to appropriate de
Certeau's words once again, carves creative, subversive spaces,
equivalent to 'ellipses, drifts, and leaks of meaning' in discourse,
from 'the accepted framework, the imposed order'.[36]

'Haunted places are the only ones people can live in,' de Certeau
concludes, adding that, because they accommodate memories
and secrets, these places invert 'the schema of the *Panopticon*'.
Instead of distracted walking, then, we need a kind of walking
that creates and cultivates these haunted places. In a double sense,
we need to *haunt* the streets of the city in order to preserve and
protect and reinvent them. In order to make them accountable
to those who inhabit them rather than those who seek to mone-
tize them, we need both to frequent them as familiar places and,
like spectres, to disturb them and make them seem unfamiliar. If
they are to remain our homes – the word 'haunt', incidentally,

is related to the Old English *hām*, meaning 'home' – the streets need to be rendered unhomely. We need to be committed to what Virginia Woolf, in a justly famous essay of that title from 1930, called 'Street Haunting'.[37]

In the fight for the city's future, we need to function like ghosts. In this way, through undistracted walking, we might be able to redeem all those lost steps we currently trace through the city while reasserting the value of those unlost steps that the modernists of the street promoted. Let's haunt the streets …

It is from a conviction that the politics of walking, along with its aesthetics or poetics, have recently acquired a renewed sense of urgency and importance – principally because of the distracted forms it frequently seems to take – that this book returns to the pedestrian practices of, roughly, the second half of the nineteenth and first half of the twentieth centuries.

The Walker explores a series of texts, arranged for the most part chronologically, in which more or less canonical authors, from Poe and Dickens in the early 1840s to Ray Bradbury in the early 1950s, explore the significance of solitary walking, especially in a metropolitan setting. They offer what Susan Sontag, writing about Robert Walser, author of 'The Walk' (1917), refers to in a felicitous phrase as 'portraits of consciousness walking about in the world'.[38] The book's premise, then, is that the different kinds of walking these writers represent in their prose fiction and non-fiction have a good deal to tell us about the experience of modernity, specifically capitalist modernity, that has shaped everyday lives over the last century and a half; and that continues to shape our everyday lives.

I regard all of these authors as modernists of the street (even though only Ford Madox Ford and Virginia Woolf are commonly classified as 'modernists'). They are modernists of the street because, like Breton and Benjamin, they are committed to the idea that, in a society in which individuals who travel by foot seem increasingly outdated, the pedestrian's experience is peculiarly symptomatic of certain social tensions. The walker, for these authors, is a sort of 'indicator species' – a term biologists use to designate an organism whose health reveals the qualitative

conditions of life that prevail in a given environment. The pedestrian's experience is for them of diagnostic value in their ongoing
attempt to understand the ways in which capitalist modernity
both alienates and oppresses people and, conversely, offers them
unprecedented opportunities for escaping or transcending that
alienation or oppression in creative, experimental forms.

This book – which takes as its starting point Raymond Williams's claim that 'perception of the new qualities of the modern
city had been associated', at least since the Romantics, 'with a
man walking, as if alone, in its streets' – centres on the solitary
male walker.[39] This privileged individual, effectively the male
writer as walker, is the dominant metropolitan archetype in the
literature on the 'experience of modernity' that I discuss. But this
is not to imply that the solitary male walker is the only archetype.
In spite of its excessively casual tone, the important qualification
Williams makes in the statement I have cited – 'as if alone' –
evokes the spectral presence on the streets of all those others who
silently accompany him, either because they walk with him or
because their activities, their labours, constitute the material and
social conditions of the city in which he walks.

In particular, Williams's cryptic, perhaps euphemistic qualification, 'as if alone,' invokes the presence, or absence, of women
walking in the streets. Their absent presence. Lauren Elkin has
forcefully pointed out that 'if we tunnel back, we find there always
was a *flâneuse* passing Baudelaire in the street.'[40] Certainly, there
are numerous examples, in the later nineteenth and earlier twentieth centuries, of female writers and their heroines taking to the
streets as observers of the urban scene, from Charlotte Brontë and
Elizabeth Gaskell, via Amy Levy, to Djuna Barnes and Dorothy
Richardson. And feminist critics, in reshaping our understanding
of the metropolitan streetscape, have rightly insisted on shifting
them from its background, where they have so often been rele-
gated, to its foreground.[41]

But, as Erika Diane Rappaport reminds us, there is no denying
that, as distinct from a man's, 'a woman's freedom to "walk
alone" in the city was constrained by physical inconveniences and
dangers as well as by social conventions that deemed it entirely
improper for a bourgeois lady to roam alone out-of-doors'.

When the *flâneuse* 'walked in and wrote about' the streets in this period, 'she stepped out of her prescribed role into male territory.'[42] The *flâneuse* – as distinct from women who, for professional or social reasons, simply in order to travel from here to there, passed through the streets of the metropolis – is not a common phenomenon. But her painful, paradoxical sense of simultaneously being both too invisible and too visible in the city streets was characteristic of all women in these fundamental circumstances.

It must be added, though, that the male territory to which Rappaport refers is by no means homogeneous or socially uniform – except, no doubt, in so far as it marginalises female pedestrians. For, as the writers I discuss here testify, many male pedestrians of the period, far from feeling entitled in the streets, find them distinctly hostile, for a range of different reasons. From Dickens's Master Humphrey to Woolf's Septimus Smith, they are the city's internal exiles, even if their sense of unbelonging is from the start far less fraught, far less freighted with histories of exploitation and oppression, than that of women, or of men and women of colour.

It is the male territory on which this book concentrates, then, even when, as in the chapter on *Mrs Dalloway*, I examine Woolf's more or less systematic critique of the sexual politics of the Baudelairean archetype of a man walking, as if alone, in the city's streets. It does so principally in order to reconstruct a series of relatively deviant kinds of walker, taken from the nineteenth and twentieth centuries, who offer to displace the still persistent paradigm of the *flâneur*. In a sense, like Woolf in *Mrs Dalloway* when she portrays Peter Walsh on the streets of the capital, I offer an immanent critique of the *flâneur*; that is, operating on the familiar terrain of the male, middle-class walker, I seek to expose the points at which, surfacing or erupting in more or less psychopathological symptoms, its internal contradictions render this archetype unsustainable. My *flâneur* is in flight from the city to which he is fatally affiliated.

The *flâneur* glorified by Baudelaire was never the comfortable, complacent bourgeois stroller that had been so fashionable in the 1840s in those illustrations and journalistic sketches known as

the *Physiologies*. As late as 1867, the French historian and journalist Victor Fournel was presenting *flânerie*, which he sketched
in terms of 'drifting along, with your nose in the wind, with both
hands in your pockets, and with an umbrella under your arm,
as befits any open-minded spirit', in positively seraphic terms. In
'The Painter of Modern Life' (1863), however, Baudelaire was
already emphasizing the *flâneur*'s restless, unsettled experience of
both the life of the metropolitan street and his own skin.[43]

As Benjamin recognized, Baudelaire's conception of this archetype was closer to that of his hero Edgar Allan Poe, for whom
'the *flâneur* was, above all, someone who does not feel comfortable in his own company', than to the one purveyed by the
contemporary illustrated periodical press.[44] This can be seen in a
poem like 'Le Soleil', from the *Tableaux Parisiens* section of the
second edition of Baudelaire's *Les Fleurs du mal* (1861), where
the impoverished poet describes venturing out alone ('Je vais
m'exercer seul') in search of the poetry of the city's streets: 'duel-
ling in dark corners for a rhyme / and stumbling over words like
cobblestones.'[45] Like the French language, the French capital is in
this poem a distinctly hostile environment. So is the poet's own
body. By this point, racked by debt, Baudelaire was addicted to
laudanum; mentally and physically ill. Here, the writer as walker
is haunted and hunted.

My book pursues a series of prose writers and their characters, many of them indebted to the example of Baudelaire, whose
experiences of walking dramatize a relationship both to the metropolitan city and to themselves that is disturbed and troubled.
It stages a sequence of crises for the pedestrian, and especially for
the *flâneur*. In a sense, the book presents a series of profiles of
certain types of pedestrian as they attempt to come to terms with
the experience of modernity in the streets. Like Balzac's *Théorie
de la démarche* (1833), one of the first 'theories' of walking, it
tries to capture some of the variations of the human gait, in the
belief that they can communicate a good deal about the embattled conditions of everyday life under capitalist modernity since
roughly the time the French novelist was writing.[46]

The walkers examined here all experience modernity in terms
of what, in the final substantive chapter of this book, which

is about the contemporary city, I characterize in terms of 'not belonging'. They are some of modernity's anti-heroes. They are pedestrians who drift, loiter or aimlessly wander in the city; who collapse in the face of its immensities or accidentally stumble in its streets; who malinger in it after long illness; who mysteriously disappear from its precincts or, more dramatically still, are forced abruptly to flee from those that administer or police it. The book's conviction is that those most attuned to the contradictions of metropolitan modernity, those who live them at the level of the pavement, are best placed to grasp not only the city's alienating but its liberating possibilities. This is what it means to be a modernist of the street.

'And every single fellow had a different way of walking,' James Joyce wrote in *A Portrait of the Artist as a Young Man* (1916) [47] If we attend carefully to some of these different ways of walking, I want to contend, and to the different ways in which, historically, they have been represented, in terms of narrative form as well as content, then we might be able to test both the different forms of alienation characteristic of capitalist modernity and the limits of this alienation, the possibilities of finding a certain freedom from it. In addition, we might come to understand what it means, in historical perspective, to walk distractedly and undistractedly. We might be able to ascertain which steps are lost and which are unlost.

How can we preserve the *flâneur*'s alertness and attentiveness to his environment, in our own efforts to cultivate a state of concentration-in-distraction on the streets, without reproducing the *flâneur*'s privilege and thus forgetting our sense of discomfort? It is doubtless the case, in the era of 'distracted walking', that we need to be both for and against the *flâneur*. We need to emulate the *flâneur*'s perceptiveness as someone who, like a skilled semiotician, patiently reads and interprets the city streets and the activities taking place there. Roland Barthes, who asserts that 'when I walk through the streets, I apply ... one and the same activity, which is that of a certain *reading*', is exemplary in this respect.[48] But we also need to recognize that, because of his prerogatives as a middle- or upper-middle-class white writer, he remains an outdated paradigm, and that it is therefore necessary to refuse his sense of entitlement. We need to decide what is living and what is dead in the tradition of *flânerie*.

'Of the two hundred and fifty-four and a half persons whose gait I studied,' Balzac declares (revealingly enough, he jokes that he has counted 'a man without legs only as half a person'), 'I have not found one who moved gracefully and naturally.'[49] Perhaps, in capitalist society, we should not expect to find anyone who moves gracefully and 'naturally' (whatever that might mean). Obviously, there are today descendants of the early nineteenth-century *flâneur* who have the money, time and social entitlement to stroll along the more prosperous shopping streets of capital cities, with, as Fournel might put it, their nose in the wind and both hands in their pockets. But the mass of people are condemned by the economic and social pressures of capitalism, especially in a climate of precarity like the present one, either to rush from one place to another because they are compelled to do so by the time-discipline of the marketplace, or to saunter and wander simply because they cannot find full or fulfilling employment.

In such a city, built on barbaric social inequalities, most people's bodies are in one way or another contorted by the labour they perform, whether they work in factories, fields or offices, and this makes it almost impossible for them to move 'gracefully and naturally'. In this respect, it is of course moralistic to denounce the bent postures and blind motions, as well as the compulsion to check their smartphone screens, that is characteristic of distracted walkers. Everyone is to some extent the victim of a disciplinary regime that distorts their bodies, their selves, even when they perform the fundamental, indeed primal activity of walking.

Ultimately, then, we must look to some sort of post-capitalist society, however remote the prospect, to restore a graceful, 'natural' movement, through its liberating possibilities for everyday life, to the superficially simple activity of walking. Footsteps as the embodiment, not merely the emblem, of the free everyday ... It was to this future, trivial though its emphasis might at first seem, that Benjamin's friend, the philosopher Ernst Bloch pointed. Bloch insisted, in characteristically complicated prose, on 'the recognition of the human right to "walk upright" [as] essential to the program of a socialist society and the humanity of its living praxis'.[50]

What Bloch called the 'upright gait' (*aufrechter Gang*), which he identified with the tradition of natural law, was for him the pre-eminent sign of a society committed to affording its citizens a dignity that is at the same time 'respected in *persons* and guaranteed in their collective'. Bloch's slogan, in outlining what might be called his orthopaedic politics, was '*uprightness as a right*'.[51] It should be ours, too.

In the meantime, before we finally restore this right to ourselves as a collective, perhaps we should each individually strive to cultivate an upright gait, and an undistracted mode of walking, that are proleptic of this future. To trace unlost steps through the metropolitan city in the name of an unlost society.

1

Convalescing

Edgar Allan Poe's
'The Man of the Crowd'

In his 'Meditations of a Painter', composed in 1912, the Italian painter Giorgio de Chirico narrated the mysterious but at the same time perfectly ordinary experience that had inspired his famous sequence of metaphysical cityscapes, commencing with the *Enigma of an Autumn Afternoon* (1910):

> One clear autumnal morning I was sitting on a bench in the middle of the Piazza Santa Croce in Florence. It was of course not the first time that I had seen this square. I had just come out of a long and painful intestinal illness, and I was in a nearly morbid state of sensitivity. The whole world, down to the marble of the buildings and the fountains, seemed to me to be convalescent. In the middle of the square rises a statue of Dante draped in a long cloak, holding his works clasped against his body, his laurel-crowned head bent thoughtfully earthward. The statue is white marble, but time has given it a gray cast, very agreeable to the eye. The autumn sun, warm and unloving, lit the statue and the dark façade. Then I had the strange impression that I was looking at all these things for the first time, and the composition of my picture came to my mind's eye.[1]

This is a classic modernist epiphany. Life itself, condemned to a state of deadening repetition, especially in the routine spaces

of the city, is apprehended as if for the first time. Earlier in the
'Meditations', de Chirico cites Schopenhauer's dictum that, in
order to have 'immortal' ideas, 'one has but to isolate oneself
from the world for a few moments so completely that the most
commonplace happenings appear to be new and unfamiliar, and
in this way reveal their true essence'.[2]

In the incident in the Piazza Santa Croce, the everyday is
redeemed by what de Chirico calls 'the enigma of sudden revelation'.[3] Several of his canvases from the 1910s revisit this 'primal
modern scene', as Marshall Berman might put it.[4] In *The Mystery
and Melancholy of a Street* (1914), to take one example, a sudden
silence seems to have descended on the city, softly flooding the
most commonplace sights with some unidentifiable spiritual significance. The end of an ordinary day assumes the form of an
ominous interruption. It is as if a mysterious curfew has been
imposed on the city, less because of some specific threat of
destruction than because of a generalized anxiety about death.

This city, as Walter Benjamin might have put it, 'looks cleared
out, like a lodging that has not yet found a new tenant';[5] or like
one from which an old tenant has for nameless reasons been
expelled. Its unsettling atmosphere is objectified in the sinister
silhouette that falls across the piazza from the right-hand side
of the composition, menacing the fragile, fairy-tale innocence of
the child that scampers up the street with a hoop. With its blank
colonnades and its baked, eerily featureless surfaces, the city is at
once a desert and a labyrinth. The poet John Ashbery, an admirer
of de Chirico, has suggestively referred to his 'agoraphobia-
inducing piazzas'.[6]

In *The Mystery and Melancholy of a Street*, as in other paintings by de Chirico at this time, the city has become the implausible
setting for what Marx once referred to, at least according to
Benjamin, as 'socially empty space'.[7] Looking at it, the spectator experiences a creeping sense of agoraphobic panic, one that
perhaps mimics de Chirico's fear of fainting in the street, which
he documented in his memoirs, and his neurotic habit, as a consequence, of sticking close to walls as he gropes through the city.
'In the noisy street,' he reflects in the 'Meditations', 'catastrophe
goes by.'[8] So too, it seems, in the silent street.

The Mystery and Melancholy of a Street 1914 (oil on canvas) by Giorgio de Chirico.

The dreamlike stasis of *The Mystery and Melancholy of a Street* evokes the faint, residual delirium of someone recovering from, say, an intestinal illness. The city de Chirico imagines in this composition is a physiological phenomenon, a physical extension of the painter's embodied consciousness. Its colonnades, streets and open spaces, in contrast to contemporary cities celebrated for their arterial freedom, themselves seem susceptible to a kind of intestinal inhibition that impedes uncomplicated movement, notwithstanding the absence of human throng. The city itself is in a state of preternatural sensitivity.

So, the painting depicts what Benjamin called 'the infirmity and decrepitude of this great city'.[9] But it also depicts the city's capacity to be regenerated or reborn through the contractions that gently convulse it.

⤳

Though often overlooked, the most striking aspect of de Chirico's autobiographical anecdote in the 'Meditations' is the emphasis on his convalescent state, and on the concomitant fact that the 'whole world' feels to him as if it, too, is convalescent.

In addition to de Chirico's personal experience of recovering from intestinal illness, it is surely possible to detect the celebrated influence of Nietzsche on his thinking in this respect. As a young man, de Chirico was a fanatical reader of Nietzsche, and he consciously applied to painting what he called the 'Nietzschean method', which involved 'see[ing] everything, even man, in its quality of *thing*'.[10] This is an aesthetic in which 'metaphysical revelation', to frame it in the art historian Ara Merjian's terms, 'sits within the limits of physical reality.'[11] The convalescent – for whom 'all things have a new taste', as Nietzsche puts it in *Twilight of the Idols* (1889), and who waits in expectancy – is perhaps the ultimate embodiment of the Nietzschean method.[12] For the convalescent, the enigmatic thingness of the things to which he relates is readily apparent.

It is reasonable to assume that, in affirming convalescence as a regime of the senses, de Chirico was recalling the regenerative role played by the convalescent in Nietzsche's philosophy. In *Human, All Too Human* (1878), for example, Nietzsche details what he calls 'another step onward in convalescence'; that is, the moment when 'the free spirit again approaches life, slowly, of course, almost recalcitrantly, almost suspiciously.' He opens himself up to 'feeling and fellow-feeling', and to the world around him:

> He almost feels as if his eyes were only now open to what is *near*. He is amazed and sits motionless: where *had he been*, then? Those near and nearest things, how they seem to him transformed![13]

Nietzsche's description reads like a snapshot of de Chirico on that clear autumnal morning when he sat on a bench in the middle of the Piazza Santa Croce in Florence. Or, more precisely, de Chirico appears to be acting out Nietzsche's prescription.

Perhaps the painter was also thinking of a crucial section on the concept of the 'eternal return' in *Thus Spoke Zarathustra* (1885), where Nietzsche devoted a section to 'The Convalescent'.

There, Zarathustra's animals coax him from the cave where he has lain for 'seven days, with heavy eyes', telling him, in a beautiful formulation, that 'all things want to be [his] physicians!' When in the course of his conversation with the animals Zarathustra recalls his sickness, and his 'disgust at man', they interrupt him: 'Speak no further, convalescent!' they command, 'but go out to where the world awaits you like a garden.'[14] In the Piazza Santa Croce the city waits for de Chirico like a garden, even if in its fallen state it is at once a desert and a labyrinth.

In a later retrospective account of the factors that shaped his 'Pittura Metafisica', entitled 'Some Perspectives on My Art' (1935), de Chirico confirmed that the important canvases he painted in Paris between 1912 and 1915, which were shaped by a visit to Turin in 1911, 'owe[d] a great deal to Friedrich Nietzsche, whom I read passionately at the time'. 'His *Ecce Homo* [1888],' de Chirico specified, 'written in Turin shortly before he succumbed to madness, greatly helped me understand the city's peculiar beauty.' The peculiar beauty of Turin, he continued, resided in its autumnal quality:

> Autumn, as it revealed Turin to me and as Turin revealed it to me, is joyful, although certainly not in a gaudy, dazzling way. It's something huge, at once near and distant; a great peacefulness, great purity, rather closely related to the joy felt by a convalescent finally cured of a long and painful illness.[15]

De Chirico had previously identified convalescence with the melancholic atmosphere and muted affects of autumn – the season's distinctive *Stimmung* – in his elusive novel *Hebdomeros* (1929). There he declares that 'summer is a malady, it's all fever and delirium and exhausting perspiration', whereas 'autumn is convalescence, after which *life* begins (winter)'.[16] As his evocation of the 'clear autumnal morning' in the Piazza Santa Croce indicates, de Chirico's paintings are autumnal in this precise sense. They consciously evoke the space and time of convalescence, a delicate state of suspension and transition between two opposed modes of being. Convalescence is a heightened condition of openness or receptiveness to the world, in which traces

of fever dissolve in a consciousness characterized by a feeling of
preternatural calm.

Either from fear or from a reckless happiness, the child in
The Melancholy and Mystery of a Street dances a little desperately up the street with her hoop. She is a displaced, perhaps
idealized image of the convalescent painter's frail openness to
re-experiencing the concussions and the percussive rhythms of
the city. In 'Some Perspectives on My Art', de Chirico portrayed
the artist's experience of an 'inspiration' or 'revelation' as 'like a
child being handed a toy': 'The likeness between the joy of the
artist touched by a revelation and that of the child surprised by a
present depends, I believe, on the fact that both joys are pure.'[17]

In the literature on convalescence as an aesthetic, if I can
put it like that, which dates back to the Romantics, and specifically to Coleridge in a rural context and Baudelaire in an
urban one, the convalescent's experience of his or her environment is often compared to that of the child. Such a delicate,
almost helpless responsiveness or susceptiveness to life, and
to its forgotten sensations, has something of the child's brittle
innocence: 'I had the strange impression that I was looking at
all these things for the first time,' de Chirico comments on his
convalescence.

The 'nearly morbid state of sensitivity' evoked by de Chirico
in his 'Meditations of a Painter', associated as it is with the aftermath of a long illness, situates the artist within a tradition that I
want to characterize, in a deliberately Baudelairean formulation,
as that of the convalescent as hero of modernity. As de Chirico's
anecdote announces, the convalescent, and particularly the male
convalescent, who is for social reasons less physically restricted
than the female, less confined to the domestic domain, is in spite
of his infirmity and decrepitude not necessarily confined to the
sickroom.

I am especially interested in the moment when the urban convalescent, notwithstanding his frail nerves, takes his first, reckless
steps in the city from which he has been temporarily exiled, and
experiences a sense of freedom at once tentative and abrupt. The
streets, which the convalescent approaches cautiously, still a little
feverishly, at first perhaps as an observer who must half-protect

himself from the impact of the city, are the site of his groping re-engagement with everyday life.

Occupying some indeterminate space between health and illness – even, in his residual feverishness, between reason and unreason – the convalescent is at once acutely sensitive to his environment and oddly insulated from it. 'The body after long illness is languid, passive, receptive of sweetness, but too weak to contain it,' wrote Virginia Woolf in *Jacob's Room* (1922).[18] The convalescent is both alive to the life that continues around him, and dead to it. He is at the same time calm and restless, contemplative and thoughtless.

In *Sons and Lovers* (1913), D. H. Lawrence also narrated an epiphanic moment in which the whole world seems convalescent. 'In convalescence,' the narrator comments, after describing an attack of bronchitis, 'everything was wonderful.'[19] The world has been renewed. As in de Chirico's contemporaneous moment of revelation, the distinctive state of convalescence releases the young protagonist Paul Morel's sense of the pictorial qualities of everyday sights, albeit in the country rather than the city. Seated in bed in his sickroom, he abstractedly concentrates on the wintry view through the window, where snowflakes cling to the pane for a moment and are gone.

In convalescence, as in the Baudelairean conception of spleen explored by Benjamin, 'time is reified: the minutes cover a man like snowflakes.'[20] From Paul's convalescent perspective, the land suddenly comes to seem like a landscape; that is, detached from its instrumental functions, the countryside is spontaneously rendered aesthetic. In this scene, the architrave effectively functions as a picture-frame, and the deep snow outside acts as a blank canvas: 'Away across the valley the little black train crawled doubtfully over the great whiteness.'[21] In de Chirico's paintings from this period, too, black trains that creep against the background are symbolic of an industriousness, indeed an industrialism, from which the convalescent feels gratefully exempt.

In the context of an urban convalescence, the aesthetics of the city and its anaesthetics are inseparable. The convalescent is thus an excellent instance of what Benjamin called 'the law of the dialectic at a standstill' – a social being whose immobility itself incarnates the characteristic ambiguities of everyday life in a metropolitan city.[22] As someone cautiously emerging from the state of isolation associated with sickness, and experiencing in consequence a process of more or less reluctant re-socialization, he is a graphic instance of the metropolitan relationship between the individual and society, the private and the public.

As an aesthetic archetype, furthermore, the convalescent is precisely situated on the cusp of Romanticism and Modernism, both of which, I am assuming, are politico-cultural responses to capitalist modernity. Convalescence is one of the means by which, in an industrial society and in the increasingly uniform, utilitarian culture associated with it, the subject's body obeys the injunction, characteristic of both Romanticism and Modernism, to 'make it new'. In this respect it also represents a revolt, albeit a passive one, that is characteristic of the aesthetics of romantic anti-capitalism; in other words, it is a redemptive reaffirmation of 'the repressed, manipulated and deformed subjectivity' manufactured by capitalism.[23]

There are of course a number of other, superficially more plausible candidates, throughout the nineteenth and early twentieth centuries, for the Baudelairean role of hero of modernity. The most famous of these, and still the most popular, is the *flâneur* (whose affinities to the commodity, repeatedly emphasized by Benjamin, are all too often forgotten by those that celebrate him). As a social archetype, the convalescent has a certain amount in common with the *flâneur*: both of them, for example, tend to perambulate the city at a distinctly dilatory pace; and for both of them, as Benjamin puts it, 'the joy of watching is triumphant'.[24] Like his cousin the *flâneur*, the convalescent inhabits what Fredric Jameson has called 'the bereft condition of the anti-hero who has no motivation at all'.[25] The convalescent – who does not patrol the marketplace; who, in Benjaminian terms, looks about but does not seek a buyer – is the *flâneur*'s poor relation. More precisely, perhaps, he is his poorly relation.

The convalescent is significant because, above all in Baudelaire and Poe, he provides an alternative account of the relationship between the metropolis and mental life in the nineteenth century, one in which the immobility of the urban subject is as important as his mobility.

'It is strange that while so much has been written for the invalid in the time of sickness, there are but few books which deal with the special needs of Convalescence.'[26] So argued the Rev. S. C. Lowry in *Convalescence: Its Blessings, Trials, Duties and Dangers: A Manual of Comfort and Help for Persons Recovering from Sickness* (1845), a book that explores convalescence as a spiritual, no less than physical, condition.

The same statement holds true about contemporary scholarship on the culture of modernity, and this too has helped to make the convalescent almost invisible in the nineteenth and twentieth centuries. Sickness, and its role in nineteenth-century literature and culture, has been discussed ad nauseam, so to speak. Athena Vrettos, for example, who has devised a 'poetics of illness', asserts convincingly enough that 'fictions of illness make their appearance in multiple and shifting areas of Victorian thought.' Symptomatically, though, her narrative of these 'somatic fictions' abruptly shifts 'from disease to health', and in so doing completely effaces the importance of convalescence.[27] There is at present no poetics of convalescence.

So how can convalescence be defined, if at all, in a technical sense? In the opening decades of the nineteenth century, when its impact on literature became apparent, a number of French medical students wrote dissertations on convalescence as part of their final examination.[28] One of these, which I have chosen almost at random, can therefore function as a preliminary definition. In his thesis presented at the Faculty of Medicine in Paris on 3 August 1837, Hyacinthe Dubranle makes this statement:

> Convalescence … is an intermediary state between the illness that it succeeds and the condition of health that it precedes. It begins at the stage when the symptoms that characterize the illness have disappeared, and it finishes at the stage when the free and regular exercise of the functions that constitute health is fully restored.[29]

This definition is manifestly problematic, because like all definitions of convalescence it cannot make sharp distinctions between this transitional phase and the phases that precede and succeed it. Is it possible, one might ask, to identify the moment when the symptoms of the disease disappear? Or when the free and regular exercise of those functions that constitute healthiness is fully restored? It is, however, useful enough; and not least because, in making obvious the difficulty of providing a precise definition at all, it implies that convalescence is a diffusive condition, one that spontaneously undoes an uncomplicated opposition between disease and health.

If, on the one hand, convalescence simply occupies the neutral border territory through which the patient must travel in order to escape from disease, on the other, the convalescent state stealthily colonizes health itself, sometimes comprehensively. What the great Romantic essayist Charles Lamb, in the mid-1820s, depicted as 'this flat swamp of convalescence, left by the ebb of sickness, yet far enough from the *terra firma* of established health', has a habit of surreptitiously encroaching on *terra firma*.[30]

The effects of an illness are often especially difficult to eradicate once the patient has resumed ordinary life, once he or she has resumed their role in the production process, even if these effects manifest themselves mainly in the form of psychosomatic anxieties. In the early nineteenth century, when time became increasingly industrialized and commodified, labour was significantly reshaped by emergent forms of temporal discipline associated with the proliferation of clocks and watches. 'Not the task but the value of time when reduced to money is dominant', as E. P. Thompson has explained; 'Time is now currency: it is not passed but spent.'[31] In this context – one in which invalids were invalidated – sickness could not be countenanced. Individuals therefore frequently had to live with illness, accommodating it to everyday life, adapting it to the demands of the production process, in order to sustain themselves.

Prematurely forced by economic necessity to make regular if not necessarily free use of their physical and mental functions, many people were – and are – arrested in an almost perpetual state of transition from sickness to health, from health to sickness.

These people, more or less forced to participate in a society in which they feel perpetually unfit, are at once hypochondriac and heroic. Convalescence is in this sense a chronic rather than an acute phenomenon, and it might even be identified as one of those almost existential conditions characteristic of the historical process of industrial modernization.

Life in the metropolitan city is itself ineradicably febrile. 'The resistance that modernity offers to the natural productive élan of an individual is out of all proportion to his strength,' Benjamin writes in 'The Paris of the Second Empire in Baudelaire' (1938); and 'it is understandable if a person becomes exhausted and takes refuge in death.' For this reason, he argues, 'modernity must stand under the sign of death'.[32] It might equally be said to stand under the sign of convalescence. The experience of modernity is one of being suspended between vitality and exhaustion, life and death.

If convalescence is a state of transition from sickness to health, then in narrative terms this process is not automatically a 'comic' one, in the sense of providing formal or official resolution. To the extent that sickness offers temporary respite from the disciplinary demands of industrial capitalism, convalescence promises not so much the social reintegration that, like marriage, it signals in the plot of the nineteenth-century novel, as a form of disintegration instead.[33] Reintegration and disintegration go together for the convalescent.

So, in his essay 'The Convalescent' (1825), which dramatizes the narrative of convalescence as a tragicomic one, Lamb provocatively celebrates sickness. His mischievous claim is that, in the 'regal solitude' of his sickbed, the patient enjoys positively autocratic privileges which he should only reluctantly give up. In the kingdom of the sick, according to Lamb, all citizens are monarchs. 'How the patient lords it there! What caprices he acts without controul [*sic*]! How kinglike he sways his pillow,' Lamb exclaims.[34] The sick man is thus paradoxically 'disalienated'.[35] 'How sickness enlarges the dimensions of a man's self to himself!' continues Lamb in ecstasies of self-afflation. The convalescent, in contrast, is like a despot who has been violently deposed: 'from the

bed of sickness (throne let me rather call it) to the elbow chair of
convalescence, is a fall from dignity, amounting to a deposition.'[36]

Specifically, Lamb complains that, as a convalescent, he has
once more been made susceptible to the pressures of labour. The
convalescent therefore feels his body, after a delightful interval
of enforced unproductivity, being gradually instrumentalized and
commodified again. Lamb insists that, paradoxically, because he
must divest himself of 'the strong armour of sickness', robust
health makes him vulnerable.[37] Under capitalism, our bodies are
reified, although we are habitually forced to forget this fact. In
the ambiguous state of convalescence, however, when we are
uncomfortably poised between the health that qualifies us for
the production process and the sickness that should disqualify
us from it, we are briefly made conscious of the alienation of our
physical lives from our mental or spiritual lives.

The incontrovertible evidence for the relapse into a state
of alienation decried by Lamb is of course the article on 'The
Convalescent' itself, which he offers his editor – who has impatiently requested publishable copy from him – in the deliberately
self-reflexive flourish of the final paragraph. Lamb's essay thus
reinscribes his convalescence as an abrupt fall back into labour,
which in a tone of satirical contempt he calls 'the petty businesses
of life'.[38] It describes a brutal transition from a prelapsarian state,
the domain of use-value, to a postlapsarian state, the domain
of exchange-value. Ironically, however, it is the delicate nervi-
ness of the convalescent, his euphoric sensitivity even, which has
made it possible for Lamb to produce this clever, supremely self-
conscious effusion for publication in the first place.

Lamb complains that convalescence 'shrinks a man back to his
pristine stature', using 'pristine' in its strict sense to mean original, primitive or ancient.[39] He employs this adjective to evoke
the almost primordial helplessness of the convalescent when, as
if in some painfully mundane re-enactment of Adam's deposition
from Eden, he is violently forced back into the everyday conditions of an advanced civilization. If human beings themselves,
as Freud allegedly argued, are born prematurely, then the convalescent, once he or she inhabits the streets again, is in effect
prematurely reborn as an urban subject.

In the psychoanalyst Jacques Lacan's allusion, in the essay on 'The Mirror Stage', to the 'real *specific prematurity of birth* in man', he discusses the 'relation between the organism and its reality' in the infant's initial development. This is a complicated process of mutual accommodation 'between the *Innenwelt* and the *Umwelt*', between individual consciousness and the environment. The infant's neo-natal months are characterized by what Lacan calls 'signs of uneasiness and motor unco-ordination'; and the 'mirror stage' itself is among other things the process by which these signs of 'foetalization' come to disappear and the infant assumes instead, as he writes in terms that might almost have been taken from Wilhelm Reich, 'the armour of an alienating identity'.[40]

The convalescent, it could be said, is also 'foetalized', because he has not fully acquired the character armour that can equip him to cope once more with reality, especially the reality of the city. He must sit quietly on a bench, like de Chirico; observe the street from the protective safety of a café; or cautiously circumambulate the city at night. It is as if his battered carapace is still too soft to resist the countless shocks of urban life.

The trope that Lacan employs to summarize the infant's prematurity is that of 'dehiscence', a predominantly botanical term meaning to open up, to gape, to burst.[41] The convalescent, whose pores have only recently opened up, rendering him painfully responsive to his environment, is dehiscent too, though in a potentially redemptive sense. His 'small hungry shivering self' – to take an image from George Eliot's novel *Middlemarch* (1872) – cannot completely insulate itself from the constant concussions, the perpetual compulsions and repulsions of metropolitan life in an industrial society. At the same time, however, it is exquisitely sensitive to the almost imperceptible aesthetics of the quotidian, so that consciousness, in Eliot's language again, is 'rapturously transformed into the vividness of a thought'.[42]

The Rev. Lowry is interested in convalescence as a spiritual condition, one that is specific to 'the transition period between the storm and tempest and the ordinary voyage of life'; and, in contrast to Lamb, he identifies it, potentially at least, as a state of redemption. For him, in the accelerated conditions of industrial modernity, it represents the possibility of rebirth. Lowry is conscious nonetheless of the individual's susceptibility, in this uncertain state, to what he calls 'the dangers of convalescence' – namely, indifference, shallowness and worldliness. His particular concern is that, once the patient returns from 'the cloistered seclusion' of the sickroom to 'the busy duties of life', the repentant attitude he has acquired thanks to illness will be fatally lost. 'We live at a fast rate these days,' he notes, 'and sometimes amid all the engrossing occupations and harassing competitions of life, our souls seem to stand a poor chance.'[43]

But if convalescence is susceptible to the spiritual perversion that is inseparable from 'worldliness', according to Lowry, then it is also 'a golden opportunity for *definite conversion* to God'.[44] The former, it should be noted, is for him implicitly associated with urban life, the latter with rural life. In this vision of convalescence, the extent to which it might redeem the patient can be measured by the aesthetic and hence spiritual intensity with which his relationship to nature is reinvented, and made transcendent: 'The flowers seem to glow with a lovelier radiance, the fields are clothed with a brighter green. The carol of the birds, the rustle of the leaves, the murmur of the stream, fall upon your ears with a fresh meaning.'[45]

The ideal convalescent, as Lowry's onomatopoeic diction no doubt clumsily indicates, is as supremely sensitive, as open to redemptive experience, as a pastoral poet. Lowry's anti-capitalism, it might be said, is reactionary, rural and romantic.

The idea of convalescence as an aesthetic disposition probably originates in Samuel Taylor Coleridge's *Biographia Literaria* (1817). There, the convalescent's experience of his environment is often directly compared to that of the child, because the convalescent's openness to unexpected or half-forgotten sensations has something of the fragility and vulnerability, as well as the creativity, of a child.

For Coleridge, convalescence also has an innate poetic intensity. In the first volume of the *Biographia*, he characterizes genius as the capacity 'to combine the child's sense of wonder and novelty with the appearances which every day, for, perhaps, forty years, had rendered familiar'. The 'prime merit' of genius, he continues, and 'its most unequivocal mode of manifestation', is 'so to represent familiar objects as to awaken in the minds of others a kindred feeling concerning them, and that freshness of sensation which is the constant accompaniment of mental, no less than of bodily convalescence'.[46]

In convalescence, then, the whole world is made strange. In this state even the most ordinary individual relates to life like a Romantic poet. Coleridge – at times an almost full-time convalescent himself, especially when living in Highgate, outside London, in the final, drug-addicted decades of his life – captures precisely the state in which I am interested when he refers, rhapsodically, to 'the voluptuous and joy-trembling nerves of convalescence'.[47]

For Charles Baudelaire, the most important proponent of convalescence as an aesthetic disposition emblematic of modernity, the convalescent is in contrast an urban poet, albeit one indebted to the Coleridgean tradition. Convalescence, as he argues, 'is like a return towards childhood,' for 'the convalescent, like the child, is possessed in the highest degree of the faculty of keenly interesting himself in things, be they apparently of the most trivial'.[48]

Baudelaire primarily derives his interest in convalescence, which to him seems inseparable from a state of rapturous, febrile curiosity, from Edgar Allan Poe, and specifically 'The Man of the Crowd', a short story first published in *Graham's Magazine* in December 1840. This strange fantasia set in London, where Poe had lived and been educated between 1815 and 1820, is the pre-eminent instance of urban convalescence in literature. Poe himself, incidentally, probably derived his theoretical interest in the convalescent from Coleridge, whom he read with passionate attention, and whose conception of convalescence he deliberately urbanizes and modernizes.[49]

The narrator of 'The Man of the Crowd' first recalls the convalescent state he has recently inhabited in the story's second paragraph. It was in the ambiguous condition of the convalescent, he explains, that he obsessively pursued an enigmatic old man he happened to glimpse in the street; an old man that, in the end, mentally and physically defeated by this pursuit, the

narrator identifies in hopeless or triumphant tones as 'the type
and the genius of deep crime'. I reproduce this paragraph in full:

> Not long ago, about the closing in of an evening in autumn, I sat
> at the large bow window of the D— Coffee-House in London. For
> some months I had been ill in health, but was now convalescent,
> and, with returning strength, found myself in one of those happy
> moods which are so precisely the converse of *ennui* – moods of the
> keenest appetency, when the film from the mental vision departs
> … and the intellect, electrified, surpasses as greatly its every-day
> condition, as does the vivid yet candid reason of Leibnitz, the mad
> and flimsy rhetoric of Gorgias. Merely to breathe was enjoyment;
> and I derived positive pleasure even from many of the legitimate
> sources of pain. I felt a calm but inquisitive interest in everything.
> With a cigar in my mouth and a newspaper in my lap, I had
> been amusing myself for the greater part of the afternoon, now
> in poring over advertisements, now in observing the promiscuous
> company in the room, and now in peering through the smoky
> panes into the street.[50]

This is an exact description of convalescence as an aesthetic: a
state of unpredictable, half-repressed euphoria in which, because
he is temporarily exempt from the routine demands of everyday
life in the city, the individual's 'electrified' intellect, like his senses,
becomes preternaturally attuned to experience.

The convalescent is painfully sensitive to his environment
and at the same time feels oddly distanced from it. The film has
departed from his mental vision but he nonetheless peers at the
life of the city through 'smoky panes'. His empty, appetitive mood
is at once the opposite of boredom and oddly characteristic of its
restless calm: it is 'the converse of *ennui*', or its obverse. His consciousness processes the shocks of urban life, the traffic on the
roads and pavements, as concussions that seem almost exquisite
because he can remain detached and half-insulated from them.

Poe's urban fable locates his convalescent on the margins of a
mass of people. Detached from the 'dense and continuous tides of
population' that flow past the café as the evening closes in, and
from the rhythms of routine production they collectively embody,

his convalescent describes his fascination with the people he sees commuting home. He is soon lost in contemplation of them: 'At this particular period of the evening I had never before been in a similar situation, and the tumultuous sea of human heads filled me, therefore, with a delicious novelty of emotion' (84).

Initially he examines in the abstract the mass of human forms that pass him. He is particularly interested in those that seem unconfident on the street, those that 'were restless in their movements, had flushed faces, and talked and gesticulated to themselves, as if feeling in solitude on account of the very denseness of the company around' (85). These are the people for whom everyday life in the city is a kind of sickness or fever.

Then Poe's convalescent examines the passers-by in more concrete detail, as if they inhabit some grimy aquarium. Sliding down 'the scale of what is termed gentility', as the light thickens, he classifies their physiognomies, their clothes and step, carefully sifting through the aristocrats, businessmen, clerks, artisans, 'exhausted labourers', pie-men, dandies, conmen, pickpockets, beggars and prostitutes (85). From the café he sees innumerable drunkards – their countenances pale, their eyes a livid red – who clutch at passing objects 'with quivering fingers' as they stride though the crowd (87).

It is 'thus occupied in scrutinizing the mob', his forehead pressed against the glass beside his seat, that the convalescent glimpses the 'decrepid old man' whose *physiologie* he is completely unable to taxonomize (87–8). He stumbles into the street, his curiosity heightened by the snatched sight of a diamond and a dagger beneath the old man's cloak, resolving in a moment of heated decision to follow him. 'For my own part I did not much regard the rain,' he notes, 'the lurking of an old fever in my system rendering the moisture somewhat too dangerously pleasant' (88). Convalescence itself is a 'dangerously pleasant' state.

Poe's narrator then records the man's mysterious movements as he roams the city, throughout the night and into the day, in an apparently futile attempt to understand what motivates him; but finally only tracks him back, on the evening of the second day, to the coffee house from which they had first set out. The old man, who appears completely unconscious of the narrator, seems to be more than human – as if his labyrinthine path through the streets had traced not the arbitrary trajectory of an individual but the secret form or logic of the corrupt, decrepit metropolitan city itself. So, the convalescent abandons his pursuit, making this declaration of defeat: '*He is the man of the crowd*. It will be in vain to follow; for I shall learn no more of him, nor of his deeds' (91).

The old man incarnates the industrial capitalist city in its anti-heroic rather than heroic form. In 'On Some Motifs in Baudelaire' (1939), composed exactly one hundred years after this short story was first published, Benjamin decides that he cannot finally identify Poe's 'man of the crowd' as a *flâneur*, mainly because in him 'composure has given way to manic behavior'. Instead, according to Benjamin, he exemplifies the destiny of the *flâneur* once this intrinsically urbane figure has been 'deprived of the milieu to which he belonged' (a milieu, he implies, that London probably never provided).[51]

The same might be said of Poe's convalescent, in whom composure must compete with a positively monomaniacal mood. Indeed, it might be argued that 'The Man of the Crowd' allegorizes the process by which, in the hectic conditions of a metropolis like London in the mid-nineteenth century, the *flâneur* splits apart and produces two further metropolitan archetypes, one almost pathologically peripatetic, the other static to the point of being a sort of cripple.

The former is the nightwalker, a disreputable, indeterminately criminal type who hypostasizes that half of the *flâneur* characterized by a state of restless mobility. The latter is the convalescent, who hypostasizes the half of him characterized by a state of immobile curiosity. For Poe, these characters are spectral doubles.

What about Baudelaire? The French poet's discussion of 'The Man of the Crowd' is contained in the third section of 'The Painter of Modern Life' (1863), his encomium to the artist Constantin Guys, 'a passionate lover of crowds and incognitos' (5). He portrays Guys as someone whose genius resides in a childlike curiosity, suggestive of 'the fixed and animally ecstatic gaze of a child confronted with something new, whatever it be' (8).

Like the child, who actually 'sees everything in a state of newness', and who is consequently 'always *drunk*', Guys is exquisitely susceptible to impressions (8). For him, 'sensibility is almost the whole being' (8). Ordinarily, Baudelaire emphasizes, adults can only recover this spontaneously poetic disposition temporarily, during a period of convalescence. Guys, however, positively personifies this disposition, because he is 'an eternal convalescent' (8). 'Imagine an artist who was always, spiritually, in the condition of that convalescent,' Baudelaire commands his reader, 'and you will have the key to the nature of Monsieur G' (7).

Baudelaire identifies Poe's convalescent as his inspiration for this claim:

> Do you remember a picture (it really is a picture!), painted – or rather written – by the most powerful pen of our age, and entitled *The Man of the Crowd*? In the window of a coffee house there sits a convalescent, pleasurably absorbed in gazing at the crowd, and mingling, through the medium of thought, in the turmoil of thought that surrounds him. But lately returned from the valley of the shadow of death, he is rapturously breathing all the odours and essences of life; as he has been on the brink of total oblivion, he remembers, and fervently desires to remember, everything. Finally he hurls himself headlong into the midst of the throng, in pursuit of an unknown, half-glimpsed countenance, that has, on an instant, bewitched him. Curiosity had become a fatal, irresistible passion! (7)

It is immediately apparent from this paragraph that Baudelaire's principal interest does not lie in the drama described by Poe's narrative. Instead, he seems more interested in the scene in which the story is initially set. He insists on representing Poe's narrative, in fact, as a relatively static picture, as if he is himself examining the convalescent through a frame.

Perhaps it is most accurate to state that Baudelaire reconstructs the story as a sort of diptych. In the first panel, the convalescent is passively seated in the coffee house. As he observes the street life through the pane of glass, he simultaneously introjects the scenes outside, assimilating them to his consciousness, and projects his consciousness onto the scenes outside, assimilating his consciousness to them. He is 'pleasurably absorbed in gazing at the crowd, and mingling, through the medium of thought, in the turmoil of thought that surrounds him'. The convalescent 'rapturously breath[es] in all the odours and essences of life', making the surface of his body seem absolutely porous, even as the solid pane of glass that he sits beside has apparently been rendered completely permeable.

In the second panel, Baudelaire's description captures Poe's protagonist, as if in a photograph, in the act of flinging himself into the street – like the Baudelairean protagonist who, according to Benjamin, 'plunges into the crowd as into a reservoir of energy'.[52] He is freeze-framed, so to speak, as he 'hurls himself headlong into the midst of the throng'. The convalescent thus metamorphoses into a nightwalker.

The second of these portraits is in effect an image of the convalescent as hero, actively seeking to satisfy his feverish curiosity, even if it could be ultimately fatal to do so (as if Baudelaire had resolved to stalk the seductive widow he wistfully describes in his famous poem 'À une passante' [1855]). Baudelaire's convalescent is thus spared the humiliating defeat that Poe visits on his convalescent at the end of 'The Man of the Crowd', when he is forced to admit that he has failed to identify the figure he has so assiduously pursued through the metropolis, at least as an individual.

Poe's spectral convalescent, more spiritually decrepit than Baudelaire's and less rapturous, is not as deeply indebted to the Coleridgean tradition, even though Baudelaire probably encountered this tradition through the mediation of Poe. But, like Poe's convalescent and in contrast to the *flâneur*, Baudelaire's convalescent remains terminally peripheral to the life of the street. The *flâneur*, according to Baudelaire, in the same section of 'The Painter of Modern Life', is situated 'at the centre of the world' even though he also 'remain[s] hidden from the world' (9). In this respect, as in others, he is like the commodity, so pervasive as to be invisible. The convalescent, Baudelaire implies, on the contrary resists the performative aspect of the *flâneur*'s life in the streets and refuses the spectacular logic of the marketplace.

☙

It is implicitly Poe, however, and not Constantin Guys, who embodies in the end the spirit of convalescence for Baudelaire. Baudelaire had first referred to what he so evocatively describes as 'convalescence, with its fevers of curiosity' in 'Edgar Poe: His Life and Works' (1853).[53] In this piece, which subsequently reappeared as the introduction to his translations in the *Histoires extraordinaires* (1856), Baudelaire locates the 'single character' that populates Poe's numerous narratives as 'the man of razor-sharp perceptions and slackened nerves'. He concludes that 'this man is Poe himself' (91).

This description perfectly captures the constitution of the convalescent, who is acutely sensitive to the life of the streets but at the same time oddly anaesthetized to it. The poetics of convalescence that are perceptible in Poe, and which Baudelaire elaborated, make him absolutely central to the process by which Romanticism, in nineteenth- and twentieth-century literature, became urbanized. Poe is for Baudelaire one of the patron saints of metropolitan modernity because, as 'the writer of the nerves', he too is a perpetual convalescent (90). In the urban sensorium described by Poe and Baudelaire, the sick are too sensitive to cope with the shocks of everyday life, and the healthy are constitutionally insensitive to its secret aesthetics.

Paul de Man grasps the importance of the convalescent for Baudelaire when, in a discussion of him and Nietzsche in 'Literary History and Literary Modernity', he offers this compelling claim:

> The human figures that epitomize modernity are defined by experiences such as childhood or convalescence, a freshness of perception that results from a slate wiped clear, from the absence of a past that has not yet had time to tarnish the immediacy of perception (although what is thus freshly discovered prefigures the end of this very freshness), of a past that, in the case of convalescence, is so threatening that it has to be forgotten.[54]

The convalescent are not necessarily confined to a sickroom, or to some bucolic refuge, in spite of their infirmity and decrepitude. They embody the experience of modernity. Indeed, it might be said that to be absolutely modern, as Rimbaud demanded, one must be convalescent.

2

Going Astray

Charles Dickens's
The Old Curiosity Shop

In 'Night Walks', an article published in his periodical *All the Year Round* in 1860, Charles Dickens describes how, in the aftermath of his father's death in 1851, he took to the streets at night. He went out in order not to have to lie in bed suffering, as he puts it in understated tones, from an 'inability to sleep'. This 'disorder', he reflects, 'might have taken a long time to conquer, if it had been faintly experimented on in bed; but, it was soon defeated by the brisk treatment of getting up directly after lying down, and going out, and coming home tired at sunrise'.[1]

In this sentence from the article's opening paragraph, Dickens gently mocks the bracing regime of exercise he prescribed himself. He hints that, in an ironic inversion, his nighttimes acquired the routine character of life in the city in the daytime. Getting up from bed, going out, coming home. It is a comically abbreviated description of a day's commute – one that is roughly contemporaneous with perhaps 'the first commuter in literature', Mr Wemmick in *Great Expectations* (1860–61).[2] Except that it doesn't simply invert the logic of the diurnal routine ('getting up directly after lying down, and going out, and coming home tired at sunrise'). It redoubles it; making it seem even more desperate, in spite of the light mood, because it leaves no room at all for sleep, for the restorative pleasures of home so cherished by Wemmick. The image of Dickens getting up directly after lying

down at night evokes a daily existence of unsustainable alienation, its comedy darkened by the relentless grind of labour in
an industrial society.

Dickens's nightwalking after his father's death, when he suffered from surfacing anxieties about his finances as well as from
grief and a sense of filial guilt, is both a prescription and a neurotic compulsion. Cure and poison. For, if it is therapeutic, it also
reinforces an almost psychotic sense of solitude. Nightwalking is
a ghastly, sometimes horrifying parody of the comforting, regular
life that, in the opening paragraph of 'Night Walks', he pretends
that it simply mimics; albeit an oddly liberating one.

In the somnambulant conditions of the nightwalk, the city
cannot be dissociated from the individual's imagination. The
metropolis and mental life collapse in on one another. Initially,
in the couple of hours after midnight, Dickens's own restlessness,
his inability to rest, is mirrored by what he calls 'the restlessness
of a great city, and the way in which it tumbles and tosses before
it can get to sleep' (71). This restlessness, a collective restlessness,
eventually fades, and London does indeed 'sink to rest', as he puts
it (72). But he remains terminally restless. 'Walking the streets
under the pattering rain,' he reports, he 'would walk and walk
and walk, seeing nothing but the interminable tangle of streets'
(72). In this state of confused, repetitive solitude, which has the
logic of a nightmare, everything is tainted. Everything becomes
part of some gigantic pathetic, or neurotic, fallacy. The world is
restless even when it is at rest. 'The wild moon and clouds were
as restless as an evil conscience in a tumbled bed' (73).

Dickens, in spite of his respectability in the early 1850s (or
because of it, since he cannot escape the memories of his finan-
cially bankrupt father's lack of respectability), is an archetypal
nightwalker.

What is a nightwalker? The singular, solitary individual who more
or less aimlessly traverses the city on foot at night, or loiters in
its darkened precincts, has from at least the seventeenth century
figured in the popular imagination as a social renegade (in this
sense, he is the direct descendant of the so-called 'common nightwalker' who, because he infringed the mediaeval city's curfew,

was criminalized by statute in the late thirteenth century).[3] Consciously or unconsciously, the nightwalker refuses the logic of the diurnal city, the ceaseless traffic of its commodities and its commuters.

The nightwalker feels at home instead, partly at least, in the state of homelessness afforded by emptied, darkened streets. *Dickens*, after all, discovered a lonely sense of community in the cold depths of the London night, among men defined by 'a tendency to lurk and lounge; to be at street-corners without intelligible reason' (75). 'My principal object being to get through the night,' he wrote, 'the pursuit of it brought me into sympathetic relations with people who have no other object every night of the year' (71). Getting through the night ...

It must of course be added, though, that the nightwalker only feels at home in the nocturnal city, if indeed he does feel at home in it, because he is a man. As my deliberate use of the male pronoun has already implied, the archetypal nightwalker is a man, since men are free, or comparatively free, from the moral opprobrium and physical danger to which women who walk the city at night are exposed. Apart from prostitutes, or streetwalkers, forced onto the pavements at night in order to commodify their bodies, there are for this reason few female nightwalkers in the nineteenth century.

But if female nightwalkers are completely unacceptable in bourgeois society, male nightwalkers are seen as distinctly disreputable. To walk at night is to yield to, or embrace, an outlaw status. It is an outlaw status, however, of the most quotidian kind; one to which any man, given the requisite circumstances, might capitulate, or to which any man might aspire. Night in the city, like the urban crowd, according to Walter Benjamin, is 'the newest asylum for outlaws' and 'the latest narcotic for those abandoned'.[4]

In contradistinction to those who, from necessity, find themselves travelling from one place to another after dark, perhaps because they are compelled either to make a journey or to perform some professional duty (to travail, that is, in two distinct senses), walking at night is a kind of vocation. The nightwalker's ambition is to lose and find himself in the labyrinth of the city. Like

Thomas de Quincey, one of the great Romantic nightwalkers, he experiences the city as a form of phantasmagoria. In its tenebrous spaces he confronts the limits of his subjectivity. Every nightwalk is thus a fugue or psychogenic flight; an escape from the self and, at the same time, a plunge into its depths.

In 'Night Walks', Dickens recalls wandering near Bethlehem Hospital and pursuing a 'night fancy' in sight of its walls: 'And the fancy was this: Are not the sane and the insane equal at night as the sane lie a dreaming?' (76). At night in the city, according to Dickens, there is a democracy of dreamers, one in which there is almost no distinction between the thoughts of people asleep in bed and those of the semi-somnambulant nightwalkers who haunt the darkened streets like the undead.

Nightwalking, it might be said, takes place in the realm of the unnight, a liminal zone between the waking and sleeping city, and between the waking and sleeping state of mind. In the final paragraph of 'Night Walks', Dickens refers to 'the real desert region of the night' in which, to his persistent surprise, the 'houseless wanderer' finds himself almost completely alone (80). The time of night that most accommodates the nightwalker, 'houseless' as he is, and restless, is when respectable people are not only curtained off from the city in their more or less comfortable domestic interiors, their sitting rooms or bedrooms, but when they are helplessly deep in sleep. It is the time of night when the city is almost entirely deserted.

In 'The Heart of London', an article printed in *Master Humphrey's Clock* in 1843, Dickens discriminates between two phases of the night. The first of these, the social night as it might be called, is the night of 'lights and pleasures'; the second, the asocial or anti-social night, is one of 'guilt and darkness'.[5] It is with the second of these phases that Dickens associates nightwalking. In the night of guilt and darkness, the night that refuses to be domesticated, the nightwalker, loitering in the streets, incarnates the unconscious drives shaping the dreams of those that sleep.

It is in this night, to echo the title of an article Dickens once wrote about getting lost in London as a child, that one is at risk of going astray.[6]

❧

At the beginning of the article on 'Night Walks', as I have already noted, Dickens jokily characterizes nightwalking as a 'brisk treatment' for his inability to sleep.

In this context, 'brisk' primarily means fresh, stimulating, tonic in its effect. But it also, secondarily, applies to the action of nightwalking itself. We know that in general Dickens did walk at an extremely rapid pace, often covering twenty miles at a time, to the consternation of people who accompanied him on outings; so at one level this is probably an objective description. On another level, however, it seems to function ironically, since although he admits in 'Night Walks' to traversing 'miles upon miles of streets' (80), his prose implies that he moves at a relatively dilatory pace, in a desultory way. He gives the impression, most strongly, of wandering.

What is wandering? To wander, according to the *OED*, means 'to move hither and thither without fixed course or certain aim; to be (in motion) without control or direction; to roam, ramble, go idly or restlessly about; to have no fixed abode or station'. This more aleatory form of ambulation, comparatively aimless, and open to chance happenings, is characteristic of the nightwalking tradition. So, it is almost as if Dickens is half-ashamed to admit how quickly he navigated through the city at night, in case this disqualifies him from his renegade status as a nightwalker.

Briskness is incompatible with wandering. One cannot wander briskly, just as one cannot saunter and hurry at the same time (though it might be claimed that this is precisely the paradoxical form of perambulation that Charlie Chaplin's Tramp, a character self-evidently indebted to Dickensian precedents, achieved – he both imitates the 'abrupt movements' of machines and the broader economic processes they enact, as Benjamin remarks of the figure of the clown, and artfully parodies and resists them).[7]

'Brisk', a word which first crops up at the end of the fourteenth century in the Old Welsh form *brysg*, 'used of briskness of foot', as the *OED* states, implies industriousness, purposefulness, busyness. In short, it means business. George Eliot, for example, refers in her historical novel *Romola* (1862–63) to 'the brisk pace of men who had errands before them'.[8] In the nineteenth century, as industrial capitalism increasingly remoulded people's everyday experiences and perceptions, the apparently natural, spontaneous action of walking came to seem more and more culturally determined, more and more alienated.

For expanding numbers of people, the simple activity of travelling from A to B, from home to work, was subjected to the mechanical rhythms of factory production. The logic of capitalism, its profit motive, valorised 'briskness of foot'. Lounging, by contrast, became unacceptable. The slogan 'Down with dawdling!' sponsored in the factories of the late nineteenth century by F. W. Taylor, the American apostle of 'scientific management', surely echoed through the factories of the mid-nineteenth century, too.[9] People's most ordinary mode of perambulation was reshaped by the discipline of capitalism. Business required busyness, briskness.

In one of the founding texts of capitalist theory, *An Inquiry into the Nature and Causes of the Wealth of Nations* (1776), Adam Smith argued that the division of labour, the parcelling out of the tasks of production to different workers, or groups of workers, helped to prevent the pernicious habit of 'sauntering'. According to Smith, sauntering was typical of a rural economy, in which the labourer ambled in his or her own time between several tasks, all of which he or she was responsible for executing:

> The habit of sauntering and of indolent careless application, which is naturally, or rather necessarily acquired by every country workman who is obliged to change his work and his tools every half hour, and to apply his hand in twenty different ways almost every day of his life; renders him almost always slothful and lazy, and incapable of any vigorous application even on the most pressing occasions.[10]

In an emergent capitalist economy, where profit levels might be affected by the frittering of time, sauntering was by definition unproductive. Lounging, by the same token, was a positively flamboyant rebuke to the principle of productivity. Only briskness of foot was acceptable.

In his *Principles of Political Economy* (1848), John Stuart Mill cited Smith's critique of sauntering, and declared that, in the intervening seventy years, this habit had in effect become an anachronism. Building on Smith's argument, he claimed that factory workers would feel positively refreshed by walking swiftly between the tasks they had to perform.[11] Hurrying was good for the individual's state of physical and moral health, not merely for the state of the economy. According to this logic, those who had no reason to hurry, the unemployed for example, felt disqualified from a system that prioritized purposeful, purposive movement. Here is 'the horror of not being in a hurry' that, in a haunting formulation, the philosopher Theodor Adorno once evoked.[12]

To a hitherto unprecedented extent, walking became a self-conscious activity in the nineteenth century. Honoré de Balzac registered this shift when in his *Theory of Walking* (1833) he observed: 'Isn't it really quite extraordinary to see that, since man took his first steps, no one has asked himself why he walks, how he walks, if he has ever walked, if he could walk better, what he achieves in walking?' He insisted that these questions were 'tied to all the philosophical, psychological, and political systems which preoccupy the world'.[13] And, it might be added, its economical systems. In the conditions of capitalist society, walking acquired a kind of political economy. The way one walked, as well as when and where one walked, took on socially significant meanings. People's gaits became legible in terms of their position within the division of labour. Hurried or brisk walking, to polarize rather crudely, marked one's subordination to the industrial system; sauntering or wandering represented an attempt, conscious or unconscious, to escape its labour habits and its time-discipline.[14]

Dickens sketches both these kinds of walking, in the guise of Boz, in articles printed in 1835. In 'The Streets – Morning', he describes clerks commuting through London on foot who have no time to shake hands with the friends they happen to meet, because 'it is not included in their salary.'[15] And in 'The Prisoner's Van', by contrast, he celebrates a more dilatory pace of life: 'We have a most extraordinary partiality for lounging about the streets,' he boasts. 'Whenever we have an hour or two to spare, there is nothing we enjoy more than a little amateur vagrancy.'[16]

The character of Dick Swiveller in *The Old Curiosity Shop* (1840–41) provides an additional sense of this vagrant disposition.

His name is of course evocative of evasive movement (though it also implies a certain nervous rapidity). And it is this that Thomas Hood emphasized when he discussed him in a mainly positive review of the novel for the *Athenaeum* in 1840. Hood characterizes Swiveller as a quintessential drifter:

> There are thousands of Swivellers growing, or grown up, about town; neglected, ill-conditioned profligates, who owe their misconduct not to a bad bringing up but to having had no bringing up at all. Human hulks, cast loose on the world with no more pilotage than belongs to mere brute intelligence – like the abandoned hulls that are found adrift at sea, with only a monkey on board.

Hood identifies him, furthermore, as 'an estray', or someone who has strayed like an animal – 'lax, lounging, and low, in morals and habits, and living on from day to day by a series of shifts and shabbiness'.[17] A 'swiveller', from this perspective, is a slippery, spivish sort of saunterer. And he thus resists what Paul Carter, in a different context, has called 'the ideology of the straight line'.[18]

Dickens was acutely conscious of the emblematic distinction between hurrying and sauntering in industrial society when, in his journalistic sketches of the 1860s, he adopted the persona of the Uncommercial Traveller. As he explains in the introductory piece, the Uncommercial Traveller 'travel[s] for the great house of Human Interest Brothers', 'figuratively speaking', and has 'rather a large connection in the fancy goods way'.[19] He is a collector of human curiosities, who accumulates not in order to sell but solely out of interest (the idea of 'curiosity', here and in *The Old Curiosity Shop*, is in part an attempt to de-commercialize the concept of 'interest'). He celebrates use-value over exchange-value. He therefore constitutes an innate challenge to the culture of what, after Thomas Carlyle, was called the 'cash nexus'.[20]

This is evident in the Uncommercial Traveller's means of movement, his mode of transport. Even though the steam train has rendered many pedestrian journeys outmoded, he walks almost everywhere. 'As a country traveller,' he confesses, 'I am rarely to be found in a gig, and am never to be encountered by a pleasure train, waiting on the platform of a branch station.' More importantly, perhaps, his manner of walking is scandalous. For if he sometimes feels obliged to hurry purposefully, he far prefers to saunter purposelessly, 'wandering here and there'.[21]

As the Uncommercial Traveller observes: 'My walking is of two kinds: one, straight on end to a definite goal at a round pace; one objectless, loitering and purely vagabond.' 'In the latter state,' he adds, 'no gipsy on earth is a greater vagabond than myself; it is so natural with me, and strong with me, that I think I must be the descendent, at no great distance, of some irreclaimable tramp.'[22] Nightwalking is walking of this objectless, loitering, vagabond kind.

It is in the light of these reflections on the semiotics of walking that I want to re-examine *The Old Curiosity Shop*. This is a novel that 'almost universally' continues to be thought of as 'a text of notorious sentimentality, morbid and uncontrolled, embarrassing and absurd by turns', as John Bowen has authoritatively stated; and it is in consequence still relatively overlooked by critics.[23]

Published as a weekly serial in *Master Humphrey's Clock*, *The Old Curiosity Shop* was initially conceived as nothing more than a sketch, in a single issue of the miscellany, of the narrator Master Humphrey's encounter with Little Nell, a thirteen-year old girl, in a London street at night. The periodical proving both unpopular and unprofitable, Dickens feared that its 'desultory character', as he put it in the Preface to the 'Cheap Edition' of the novel in 1848, risked undermining his hitherto intimate relationship with his readers.[24]

He therefore extended and reshaped this story, developing Nell's narrative to the point at which it subsumed the weekly publication completely, thus saving it from financial collapse. Daringly, and a little desperately, Dickens also discarded his first-person narrator – in spite of the fact that 'Personal Adventures of Master Humphrey: *The Old Curiosity Shop*' was one of the titles he had recently considered for this tale.[25] Master Humphrey is unceremoniously expelled from the narrative at the end of Chapter 3, when he announces, abruptly and a little confusingly, that he is leaving the other characters to 'speak and act for themselves' (33). (Improbably, Dickens eventually reintroduces

Master Humphrey to the narrative in the form of the Single Gentleman, who is the brother of the Old Man.)

The picaresque plot of *The Old Curiosity Shop* is motivated by the fact that Nell's grandfather, the Old Man, has been gambling in order to support her, and has consequently become indebted to Daniel Quilp, a violent, dwarfish usurer. It is in order to escape Quilp that Nell and her grandfather steal out of London early one morning, in sunshine that transfigures 'places that had shewn ugly and distrustful all night long' and 'chase[s] away the shadows of the night' (119), and commence their journey to some resting place in the countryside where they can forget about their past, and about the city:

> The two pilgrims, often pressing each other's hands, or exchanging a smile or cheerful look, pursued their way in silence. Bright and happy as it was, there was something solemn in the long, deserted streets, from which, like bodies without souls, all habitual character and expression had departed, leaving but one dead uniform repose, that made them all alike. (120)

This flight from a dead city, which famously ends in Nell's death, is structured as a pilgrimage. Later in this chapter, in fact, Nell explicitly compares herself and her grandfather to John Bunyan's Christian (122). So this is a pilgrim's progress; and walking thus serves a spiritually as well as socially symbolic function in *The Old Curiosity Shop*.

In spite of the eventual success of *The Old Curiosity Shop*, the intensive demands of producing a weekly publication had a corrosive effect on Dickens. In the late autumn and winter of 1840, depressed by his relative unproductiveness, he took 'long walks at night through the streets of London to restore his spirits'.[26] The composition of this novel was itself, then, shaped by nightwalking. This compulsive activity appears however not to have provided much relief. As an antidote, it had a positively toxic effect. 'All night I have been pursued by the child,' he told his friend John Forster on one occasion in November, alluding to Little Nell; 'and this morning I am unrefreshed and miserable. I don't know what to do with myself.'[27]

The Old Curiosity Shop is all about pursuing the child. Almost every character in the novel, it transpires, pursues the child (and she 'provides a vehicle for the fantasies of each character that desires, or is curious about her', in Audrey Jaffe's formulation[28]). And the reader, too, pursues her. But, from the reverse perspective opened up by Dickens's comment to Forster, the innocent Little Nell acquires a slightly demonic character. She seems more like 'the implacable and dreaded attendant' that haunts Barton in Sheridan Le Fanu's 'The Familiar' (1872), to cite a slightly later instance of a narrative with a plot centred on pursuit at night.[29]

Master Humphrey is one of those individuals who, albeit not in especially obvious ways, pursues the child. He is a character whose oddness has often been overlooked, perhaps because he is superficially less peculiar than so many of Dickens's characters. Scholars of Victorian fiction have tended either to ignore him or to take him at face value as a benign, if rather eccentric, geriatric.[30] He is a far darker character, though, and not least because he is a nightwalker. In a double sense, he is the novel's most curious character.

Some critics have implicitly recognized this. Bowen, for example, has pointed out that he 'links the archaic and the modern in his nocturnal city strolling'.[31] I intend to unravel his identity a little more intensively. In so doing, I hope to provide an alternative introduction to the novel; and, in a sense, the introduction to an alternative novel. This alternative novel might be called 'The Old Cupiosity Shape' – for such is the phrase with which, in *Finnegans Wake* (1939), James Joyce casually and deftly excavates the book's hidden channels of desire.[32] Master Humphrey is the old cupiosity shape at the heart of *The Old Curiosity Shop*. Its libidinal secret.

At the start of *The Old Curiosity Shop*, Master Humphrey reflects on 'that constant pacing to and fro, that never-ending restlessness, that incessant tread of feet wearing the rough stones smooth and glossy' that typifies life in the metropolis (9). He paints the city as a sort of secular purgatory:

Think of a sick man in such a place as Saint Martin's Court, listening to the footsteps, and in the midst of pain and weariness obliged, despite himself (as though it were a task he must perform) to detect the child's step from the man's, the slipshod beggar from the booted exquisite, the lounging from the busy, the dull heel of the sauntering outcast from the quick tread of an expectant pleasure-seeker – think of the hum and noise always being present to his sense, and of the stream of life that will not stop, pouring on, on, on, through all his restless dreams, as if he were condemned to lie, dead but conscious, in a noisy churchyard, and had no hope of rest for centuries to come. (9)

For the sick man, the activity of physiognomizing people's footsteps, as it might be called, of identifying their relationship to the city, whether it is 'lounging' or 'busy', lazily sauntering or briskly hurrying, becomes a sort of urban mania. The restlessness of London, embodied in the constant, repetitive movement of feet on pavements, shapes the sick man's 'restless dreams', troubling the distinction between the sane and the insane that Dickens subsequently, more deliberately, deconstructs in 'Night Walks' when he describes wandering by the walls of Bedlam.

Indeed, it seems plausible that the nameless man in St Martin's Court is sick precisely because of his obsession with the sound of footsteps; that this febrile attempt exhaustively to classify passing feet is not some palliative response to the sickness, nor even a symptom of it, but the sickness itself. Perhaps, then, it is a mental state rather than a physical one. The man in St Martin's Court is at rest, but he is no less restless for all that; in fact, he is probably more restless as a result of his immobility. Like the nightwalker, he is one of the urban undead, for it is 'as if he were condemned to lie, dead but conscious, in a noisy churchyard, and had no hope of rest for centuries to come'.

This is the urban mania that Alfred Tennyson subsequently explores in his poem *Maud* (1855). In the fifth section of the poet's extraordinary 'monodrama', 'the mad scene' as Tennyson called it, the speaker pictures himself dead and buried 'a yard beneath the street', listening to the horses' hooves and the footsteps above him: 'With never an end to the stream of passing feet, / Driving, hurrying, marrying, burying ...'[33] This is a poem freely scattered with invective against the corrupt practices of mid-nineteenth-century capitalism, so in the gerunds that end the line I have cited, which reproduce what Dickens calls the 'hum and noise' of passing feet, it is possible to detect an implicit association of hurrying and marrying, and indeed burying, with busy-ness. With business. And, by extension, with buying – a word buried in the word 'burying'.

Both the speaker of *Maud* and the man in St Martin's Court, immobilized and entombed as they are, embody a protest, conscious or unconscious, against the rhythms of commerce that drive the life of the metropolis. If sauntering and lounging constitute a muted form of social protest in the conditions of industrial capitalism, then the state of physical paralysis imagined by the speaker of *Maud* represents a pathological refusal of its logic.

As I demonstrated in the previous chapter, another important, contemporaneous representation of this urban mania, or one closely related to it, is the convalescent narrator in Edgar Allan Poe's 'The Man of the Crowd' (1840).

Recall the plot of Poe's mysterious short story. Recovering from an illness, the narrator sits beside the window of a coffee shop in London and watches the passers-by, regarding 'with minute interest', as Poe writes, 'the innumerable varieties of details, dress, air, gait, visage and expression of countenance'.[34] In spite of his sedentariness, he is at this point still a slightly feverish physiognomist of life in the city. Then he suddenly sees a man who fascinates him, because he seems completely unreadable, resistant to physiognomic assessment, and he rushes out into the street, tailing him through the labyrinthine streets of London, throughout the night. As Benjamin puts it, 'Poe purposely blurs the difference between the asocial person and the *flâneur*.'[35] The narrator has become a nightwalker – that is, the neurotic as opposed to neurasthenic incarnation of this urban mania – obsessed with people's perpetual transit through the spaces of the metropolis.

The curiosity that drives the narrative of *The Old Curiosity Shop*, the interest that Master Humphrey takes in Little Nell when he meets her in the streets of London at night, is itself the consequence of a kind of convalescent state. If he distances himself from the 'sick man' about whom he fantasises, he does so because of an uncomfortable proximity to him. For Humphrey is himself a cripple, one who has suffered from some unnamed 'infirmity' since childhood, as he testifies in the first chapter of *Master Humphrey's Clock*. It is presumably partly for this reason that for many years he has 'led a lonely, solitary life'.[36]

Humphrey lives, so he informs us, in an old house in a 'venerable suburb' of London that was once a celebrated resort for 'merry roysterers and peerless ladies, long since departed':

> It is a silent, shady place, with a paved courtyard so full of echoes, that sometimes I am tempted to believe that faint responses to the noises of old times linger there yet, and that these ghosts of sound haunt my footsteps as I pace it up and down. (5)

This courtyard full of the echoes of older footfalls is of course sequestered in a quiet suburb. And the elderly narrator seems quite sane, albeit a little quaint. But Humphrey's footsteps, in this urbane sentence, and the footsteps that haunt them, are indelible symptoms of an urban mania – as the unsettling image of him perpetually pacing this confined space implies. There is evidently some kind of secret kinship, perhaps even an identity, between Humphrey and the sick man he subsequently mentions, who inhabits another courtyard, St Martin's Court, although the former's obsessiveness is far less intense than the latter's, and his infirmity more chronic than acute.

For the frail Humphrey, as for Baudelaire's convalescent, 'curiosity has become a compelling, irresistible passion.'[37] It impels him into the city's streets. In fact, the 'Curiosity Shop' of the title refers not merely to Nell's grandfather's home, stuffed with 'heaps of fantastic things', but to the city itself (19). In *Master Humphrey's Clock*, the eponymous narrator announces that he has lived there 'for a long time without any friend or acquaintance'. He goes on:

> In the course of my wanderings by night and day, at all hours and seasons, in city streets and quiet country parts, I came to be familiar with certain faces, and to take it to heart as quite a heavy

disappointment if they failed to present themselves each at its accustomed spot. (10)

For him, implicitly, faces are curiosities, just as 'the inanimate objects that people [his] chamber' have acquired anthropomorphic qualities (9).

But if he likes to amble around the lumber-room that is the city, Humphrey manifestly isn't completely comfortable in it. Embattled because of his disability, he does not feel at home in the crowd. He is no *flâneur*. In contrast to the hero of the *Physiologies* of the 1840s, who revels in being 'at the very centre of the world' but at the same time 'unseen of the world', Humphrey is, unenviably, in the inverse position: he is a socially marginal figure who is nonetheless the object of public fascination.[38]

Humphrey is, in fact, 'a misshapen, deformed old man', as he himself puts it in *Master Humphrey's Clock* (7). And when he first moved to the venerable suburb he presently inhabits, he informs us, he was variously regarded as 'a spy, an infidel, a conjuror, a kidnapper of children, a refugee, a priest, a monster': 'I was the object of suspicion and distrust – ay, of downright hatred too' (6). We are told that at that time he was known as 'Ugly Humphrey' (7). So, according to his neighbours, who identify him with the feudal, the foreign and the folkloric, he is outside the pale of modernity.

The identities initially ascribed to Humphrey by his suspicious-minded neighbours – spy, infidel, conjuror, kidnapper of children, refugee, priest, monster – might be the consequence of his eccentric nocturnal habits as much as of his peculiar physical condition. He is the victim of popular prejudices about men of slightly odd appearance who walk about the metropolis at night because they do not feel at home in it during the day. He is a 'sauntering outcast', like one of the archetypes whose footsteps the sick man in St Martin's Court hears outside his window.

But Humphrey feels half at home at least in the city at night, when there is nobody around to monitor his 'objectless, loitering, purely vagabond' mode of walking, as the Uncommercial Traveller had put it.

࿒

In *Master Humphrey's Clock* Humphrey claims to walk in both
the country and the city, during both the day and the night. But
in the opening sentence of *The Old Curiosity Shop* he admits to
a preference for the nocturnal city: 'Night is generally my time
for walking' (7).

He adds that he 'seldom go[es] out until after dark', except in
the countryside (where he likes to 'roam about fields and lanes
all day'); and continues:

> I have fallen insensibly into this habit, both because it favours
> my infirmity and because it affords me greater opportunity of
> speculating on the characters and occupations of those who fill
> the streets. The glare and hurry of broad noon are not adapted
> to idle pursuits like mine; a glimpse of passing faces caught by
> the light of a street-lamp or a shop window is often better for my
> purpose than their full revelation in the daylight; and, if I must
> add the truth, night is kinder in this respect than day, which too
> often destroys an air-built castle at the moment of its completion,
> without the least ceremony or remorse. (7–8)

Refusing the 'hurry of broad noon' and the brisk rhythms of
business, Humphrey prefers 'idle pursuits', like rambling, and
speculating about 'those who fill the streets', even when they
aren't filled. The city at night, a place and time in which there are
fewer people about to police a loitering mode of perambulation,
permits him to wander and wonder at the same time. Master
Humphrey is most comfortable walking in the time of 'guilt and
darkness', the asocial phase of the night identified by Dickens
in 'The Heart of London' a couple of years later. It is a space of
fantasy, where – in contrast to the daytime city – 'air-built castles'
can be erected and maintained.

Humphrey's narrative begins, then, with an anecdotal account
of his encounter with Little Nell, the incident that constitutes the
novel's primal scene:

> One night I had roamed into the city, and was walking slowly on
> in my usual way, musing upon a great many things, when I was
> arrested by an inquiry, the purport of which did not reach me,

but which seemed to be addressed to myself, and was preferred in a soft sweet voice that struck me very pleasantly. I turned hastily round and found at my elbow a pretty little girl, who begged to be directed to a certain street at a considerable distance, and indeed in quite another quarter of the town. (9)

After this paragraph, Dickens delays a fraction before reassuring us of the innocence of Nell's inquiry, and of her innate goodness, and we have to suppress an impulse to mistrust her soft sweet voice. We momentarily suspect that Little Nell has attempted to hustle Master Humphrey. As Catherine Robson notes in her perceptive reading of the novel, 'Nell is alone walking the streets, perilously close to Covent Garden, London's traditional red-light district, when she "solicits" Master Humphrey.'[39]

Is this adolescent girl in the street at night a child prostitute? One of the most visible forms of prostitution in the nineteenth century, as Judith Walkowitz has reminded us, was that of 'the isolated activity of the lone streetwalker, a solitary figure in the urban landscape, outside home and hearth, emblematic of urban alienation and the dehumanization of the cash nexus'.[40]

No doubt it is because of the risk his readers might make precisely this association that Dickens decided to amend his first draft of the story. Originally, he specified that, when she meets the narrator, Nell is a 'young female, apparently in some agitation', and that she is 'looking archly'. He also indicated that she has diamonds to sell. In the amended text she is simply a 'pretty little girl' who, in spite of the secret that compels her onto the streets at night, is smiling.[41] In this manuscript version, the opening of *The Old Curiosity Shop* remains disconcertingly close to a depiction of the encounter between an old male nightwalker and a young female streetwalker.

But Dickens does not fully erase the traces of such an encounter even in the final version of the novel. 'I have lost my road,' Nell announces in the ensuing dialogue, in a sentence that – like the phrase going or gone astray – is freighted with moral associations (9). It is designed gently to hint once again that she might be a fallen child, or at the least a potentially corruptible one – perhaps in order to transmit an added frisson of excitement to the reader.

For if young girls walking alone in the city's streets were not necessarily prostitutes, they were, in the popular imagination at least, potential prostitutes, vulnerable to predatory pimps.

Dickens had himself reflected on the criminalization of young girls in an article for *Bell's Life in London* of November 1835. There, he watches two sisters being placed in a prisoner's van on the street, and sermonizes as follows: 'Step by step, how many wretched females, within the sphere of every man's observation, have become involved in a career of vice, frightful to contemplate; hopeless at its commencement, loathsome and repulsive in its course; friendless, forlorn, and unpitied, at its miserable conclusion.'[42] Nell, parented by a grandfather who is deeply in debt and fatally addicted to gambling, is perhaps taking her first steps along this path.

Henry Mayhew's *London Labour and the London Poor* (1851), to give another, slightly later example, included a quotation from the opening address of 'The London Society for the Protection of Young Females, and Prevention of Juvenile Prostitution', founded in 1835. The lecture at one point discusses those who trap, or 'trepan', girls of between eleven and fifteen in order to prostitute them:

> When an innocent child appears in the streets without a protector, she is insidiously watched by one of these merciless wretches and decoyed under some plausible pretext to an abode of infamy and degradation. No sooner is the unsuspecting helpless one within their grasp than, by a preconcerted measure, she becomes a victim of their inhuman designs.[43]

An association with criminalized or victimized young girls on the city's streets, then, and with the contemptible, rapacious men who exploit them, flickers uneasily at the corners of our consciousness as we read of Humphrey's encounter with Nell at the start of *The Old Curiosity Shop*.

Dickens does not directly identify Nell and Master Humphrey with the social outcasts that people Mayhew's taxonomies and his own journalistic sketches. But at the beginning of *The Old Curiosity Shop* we can nonetheless briefly glimpse an alternative London – the dystopian London, perhaps, that he will explore more fully in mature novels such as *Bleak House* (1852–53) and *Our Mutual Friend* (1864–65), with their persistent concern for repressed secrets. We can consequently glimpse an alternative novel, too. The one invoked by Joyce when he rechristens it The Old Cupiosity Shape.

After all, when Humphrey agrees to take Nell back to her grandfather, he grows fearful that, if she herself recognizes the way home, she will take her leave of him. So, he leads her there by a curiously circuitous route: 'I avoided the most frequented ways and took the most intricate, and thus it was not until we arrived in the street itself that she knew where we were' (10). This is at the very least an odd, slightly sadistic way of proceeding. In a strict etymological sense, it is a seduction, a leading away.

I am not proposing that Master Humphrey is a paedophile (the 'kidnapper of children' or 'monster' for which his neighbours once took him), simply that he might not be what he seems. He too is a collector of curiosities, of human ones, as I have observed; and he too, it seems, is reluctant to relinquish his hold on such curiosities. In Joycean terms, he assumes the shape of 'cupiosity', a curiosity darkened by libidinal desire.

An insidious, subtle sense of moral and psychological danger is therefore squandered when Humphrey suddenly disappears from *The Old Curiosity Shop*. Like the clock with which he is associated, Humphrey himself contains a deep, dark, silent interior in which secrets are concealed – as his roaming in the streets of the capital at night in the seminal scene of *The Old Curiosity Shop* seems to imply. Perhaps this is the reason Dickens dismisses him from his role as the narrator of Nell's story. Perhaps it is Humphrey's darkness, rather than his cumbersomeness, that prompts Dickens to expel him.

We have to wait until sixteen years after Dickens's death for a revision of the opening chapter of the *Old Curiosity Shop* that teases out the disquieting subtext of the novel to which I have adverted. In Robert Louis Stevenson's *The Strange Case of Dr Jekyll and Mr Hyde* (1886), the latter is introduced in the following description of a violent nocturnal encounter between a man and a young girl:

> All at once, I saw two figures: one a little man who was stumping
> along eastward at a good walk, and the other a girl of maybe eight
> or ten who was running as hard as she was able down a cross
> street. Well, sir, the two ran into one another naturally enough at
> the corner; and then came the horrible part of the thing; for the
> man trampled calmly over the child's body and left her screaming
> on the ground.

Here, in the shape of Mr Hyde, who is 'pale and dwarfish' and gives an 'impression of deformity', Humphrey is transformed into Quilp.[44]

Stevenson's reinterpretation of the primal scene of *The Old Curiosity Shop* reveals that Humphrey and Quilp have been doubles all along, like Jekyll and Hyde. Quilp, according to this reading, is Humphrey's evil conscience, his unconscious.[45] In his description of the first appearance of Hyde in *Dr Jekyll and Mr Hyde*, Stevenson replays the opening sequence of *The Old Curiosity Shop* at an accelerated speed, as if he is turning a phenakistoscope, and the repressed sexual energies of Dickens's novel explode into violence as a result.

These energies bubble back up, irrepressibly, in two of the most significant and challenging late modernist novels, Joyce's *Finnegans Wake* and Vladimir Nabokov's *Lolita* (1955). In these experimental fictions, the obscene unconscious of Dickens's novel becomes visible. The protagonist of *Finnegans Wake* is another Humphrey – Humphrey Chimpden Earwicker. But if his first name echoes that of Master Humphrey, his second and third names bear traces of Quilp's character. For Quilp, who is more than once identified by Dickens with a monkey,[46] is a compulsive eavesdropper, or earwigger (as in Chapter 9, where he spies on Nell and her grandfather, who are having the conversation during the course of which they decide to leave the city and 'walk through country places' [79]).

These distant associations become more meaningful in the context of a novel that centres on a mysterious moment of obscenity visited by Humphrey on his daughter in a park. For Joyce's Humphrey does indeed appear to have paedophile tendencies.

In the 'Anna Livia Plurabelle' section of *Finnegans Wake*, two washerwomen analyse the stains on Humphrey's underwear and decide that they are evidence of sexual impropriety, in particular his desire for young girls. Later on, Humphrey calls out in Danish, 'I so love those beautiful young girls.'[47] Humphrey Chimpden Earwicker thus threatens to expose or 'out' Dickens's Humphrey. In Joyce's own words, 'to anyone who knew and loved the christlikeness' of the 'cleanminded' Humphrey, 'the mere suggestion of him as a lustsleuth nosing for trouble' seems preposterous. But, once the suspicion has been raised in relation to *The Old Curiosity Shop*, this is precisely the suggestion that lingers around the narrator.[48]

In *Lolita*, the ultimate novel about illicit relations between an ageing man and a young girl, Nabokov too seems to invoke *The Old Curiosity Shop*, leaving Dickens's Humphrey even more exposed by the company he is forced to keep in subsequent literary history. This connection is in part mediated through *Finnegans Wake*, for Humbert Humbert's name echoes that of Joyce's Humphrey, who is also known as 'Mr Humhum'.[49] Nabokov's Humbert at one point refers to himself as 'a humble hunchback abusing [him]self in the dark' – a formulation which might even serve as a cynical description of Master Humphrey in the opening chapter of *The Old Curiosity Shop*.[50]

More specifically still, the mystery of Master Humphrey seems to haunt the passage in which Humbert describes arriving in Briceland, where he plans to seduce or rape Lolita in an inn called 'The Enchanted Hunters'. Only moments before their arrival, he has kissed her 'in the neck', a gesture that stings her into calling him a 'dirty man':

> Dusk was beginning to saturate pretty little Briceland, its phony colonial architecture, curiosity shops and imported shade trees, when we drove through the weakly lighted streets in search of The Enchanted Hunters. The air, despite a steady drizzle beading it, was warm and green, and a queue of people, mainly children and old men, had already formed before the box office of a movie house, dripping jewel-fires.[51]

A queue of children and old men in a town containing curiosity shops ... In the United States in the 1950s Humphrey and Nell end up outside a cinema 'dripping jewel-fires'; or, like Humbert and Lolita, inside the Enchanted Hunters.

If Dickens's Humphrey can be identified with the sick man in St Martin's Court mentioned in *The Old Curiosity Shop*, who is mesmerized by the 'hum and noise' of feet pacing the streets of the metropolis, then he too is a Mr Humhum. He is the ancestor of both Joyce's Humphrey and Nabokov's Humbert. A 'lustsleuth'. These are the vermiculations of Master Humphrey, whose mysterious character becomes modified in the guts of Stevenson, Joyce and Nabokov. From the perspective of the nightwalking scene with which *The Old Curiosity Shop* starts, the 'cupiosity shape' secreted in Dickens's supposedly sentimental novel eventually resolves itself into the even darker visions of their experimental fictions.

3

Disappearing

Edward Bellamy's
Looking Backward

'What if one person woke up one day and was another person?' the film-maker David Lynch once asked.[1] As his films *Lost Highway* (1997) and *Mulholland Drive* (2001) testify, with their abrupt narrative and psychic displacements, Lynch has long had an interest in so-called fugue states.[2]

Dissociative or psychogenic fugue is a rare psychological condition in which, as a result of an amnesiac episode precipitated for example by a traumatic incident, the patient experiences a loss of identity. Individuals who suffer from the condition, which was first diagnosed in the late nineteenth century, often find themselves in unexpected places, even far from home, with no explanation as to how they arrived there. The fifth edition of the American Psychiatric Association's *Diagnostic and Statistical Manual of Mental Disorders (DSM-5)* (2013), in its section on dissociative disorders, refers to 'dissociated travel' and 'the perplexity, disorientation, and purposeless wandering of individuals with generalized amnesia'.[3] But if psychogenic fugue entails a loss of identity, it can also involve the acquisition of a different, entirely unfamiliar identity. In some cases, people disappear from their everyday lives and reappear as ... other people.

Edward Bellamy's novel *Looking Backward* (1888) was the most successful utopian fiction published in the late nineteenth century. In his negotiations both with the utopian city in which he arrives and the dystopian city to which he appears to revert near the end of the novel, and which he traverses in panic on foot, Bellamy's time-travelling protagonist betrays the characteristics of someone undergoing a psychogenic fugue. He thus represents an important precursor to the *fugueur* recently celebrated by Iain Sinclair. In *London Orbital* (2003) and elsewhere, Sinclair affirms that he finds 'the term *fugueur* more attractive than the now overworked *flâneur*'. In an attempt to characterize his circumlocution of the M25 motorway that encircles London, which he undertook in response to 'the increasing lunacy of city life', he remarks that fugue is 'a psychic commando course'.[4]

Its 'key image', Sinclair argues, is a lost picture by Vincent Van Gogh – *The Painter on the Road to Tarascon* (1888). This painting, subsequently emulated by Francis Bacon in a series of tenebrous studies, is the haunted and haunting self-portrait of a solitary man on a road who is 'tracked by a distorted shadow.'[5] It was painted, it so happens, in the year that *Looking Backward* was published. This novel is in part the study of a fugitive in time and space, one who closely resembles the figure of the *fugueur* that appears in *fin-de-siècle* diagnoses of mental illness.

In Bellamy's bestseller, an inhabitant of Boston named Julian West, who suffers from chronic insomnia, falls into a deep sleep one night in 1887, thanks to the assistance of a mesmerist, and wakes up one day in the year 2000. The United States, it transpires, has in the meantime evolved quite naturally and peacefully into a socialist society. Published during the most prolific epoch in the history of utopian thought, the book had a profoundly influential effect on the development of utopia as a literary and political discourse, principally because it located its state-socialist society at a point in historical time rather than geographical space.

'*Looking Backward* was written in the belief that the Golden Age lies before us and not behind us, and is not far away,' Bellamy declared in the Postscript to the book's second edition.[6] The final clause of that sentence, 'not far away', seems ambiguous, for if it means that the origins of the Golden Age lie in the nineteenth century rather than some far-distant future, then it also means that it can be found in the United States rather than some far-distant island. The utopian tradition that commenced with Thomas More's *Utopia* (1516) had of course generally located the ideal society in unmapped space; Bellamy's formal contribution to this tradition was to cement its association with unmapped time, by projecting the ideal society into an imaginable future.

In his review of *Looking Backward* from 1889, the British Marxist William Morris claimed that 'it is the serious essay and not the slight envelope of romance which people have found interesting'.[7] Like a number of subsequent critics, he implied, first, that the book's essayistic and romantic elements are its sole formal components; and, second, that the latter can be dismissed as of merely incidental importance. More recently, for example, Krishan Kumar has remarked that, of all the utopian fictions discussed in his compendious, authoritative account of *Utopia and Anti-Utopia in Modern Times*, 'Bellamy's is in fact the least interesting, considered as literature.'[8]

Bellamy himself, despite his comparative commercial success as an author of ghost stories and romances, seems to have sanctioned this assumption. In an article of 1890, he observed that, in recasting the manuscript of *Looking Backward* after devising the idea of the 'industrial army', which he identified as 'the destined corner-stone of the new social order', he retained 'the form of romance' only reluctantly and 'with some impatience, in the hope of inducing the more to give it at least a reading'.[9]

Kumar has pointed out that, in adopting this attitude, Bellamy was 'rejecting his own past as a romancer and story-teller'. 'He was self-consciously taking on a new, more purposive role, as social critic and prophet,' he concludes; 'but in doing so he ensured that, once his ideas had been generally absorbed, or were no longer considered interesting, there was little to attract a later generation to the book.'[10] This is a misrepresentation of *Looking Backward*, a novel that is in fact possessed of considerable psychological depth. In retrospect, Bellamy's finest achievement is perhaps his rendering of the protagonist's psychology – that is, the aspect of the book that has been most consistently overlooked in scholarly accounts of it.

Indeed, *Looking Backward* can be productively interpreted as a kind of case history in the psychology of the utopian imagination,

one that centres on the fugue states experienced by the protagonist as he traverses the streets of the city of the future on foot.
Ultimately, in fact, the novel implies that utopian dreaming itself
induces a kind of fugue state.

If *Looking Backward* comprises both the essay form and the
romance form, to apply Morris's terms, then these might be
described as torn halves that do not completely add up.[11] But
Bellamy's utopia is all the more compelling because of this subtle
inconsistency. Its most interesting ideas are lodged in the inter-
stices of the text, those passages that describe West's experiences
on the cusp of present and future, for example, or that depict him
as susceptible still to the nightmare of the past.

At the ragged edges of the 'envelope of romance', in Morris's
formulation, another sort of novel can be glimpsed, one that is
unsettling and psychologically suggestive. In this respect, Bellamy's utopia is continuous rather than discontinuous with his
previous fiction in which he speculatively explores abnormal psychological states.[12] In *Miss Ludington's Sister* (1884), for instance,
Bellamy speculates about 'the immortality of past selves', imagining an alternative state of being in which both one's 'past and
future selves' are immediately, perpetually present: 'The idea of
an individual, all whose personalities are contemporaneous, may
there be realized, and such an individual would be by any earthly
measurements a god.'[13]

If the political aspirations of *Looking Backward* have dominated its reception, it should in addition be understood as a
protracted meditation, in the conditions of metropolitan modernity, on the idea of multiple personality, as this is articulated
through a fugue state, especially in the form of 'bewildered
wandering'. Julian West – whose name superficially evokes the
purposive, pioneering travel associated with the injunction to
'Go West, young man, and grow up with the country'[14] – turns
out to embody a mobility of the most errant and apparently purposeless kind.

At the core of the pre-eminent utopian dream of the late nineteenth century, then, in spite of the supremely rationalist social
and political principles it dramatizes, lies the dystopian nightmare of an urban subject whose solitude is a kind of psychosis

and whose unpredictable movement in both space and time signifies some radical instability.

The critical consensus about *Looking Backward*, which insists
that, like most utopian fiction of the late nineteenth century,
it is emotionally flat and lacking in affect, thus falsifies Bellamy's achievements. The book's protagonist, for example, does
not make an untroubled transition to the society of 2000, as
the critics have conventionally assumed. In fact, West suffers
something like a trauma in time-travelling to the future – one far
more severe than that experienced by the Time Traveller in H. G.
Wells's *The Time Machine* (1895), who is afflicted by a kind of
motion sickness that is distinctly upsetting to the nerves but not
permanently damaging.

West's psychology is a disturbed one that raises fascinating
questions about the stability of the human subject under the
peculiar temporal conditions of utopian imagining. Bellamy
reinvented the utopian form in part by conceptualizing it as the
psychological portrait of an individual who effectively becomes
dislocated from time; from both the present he half escapes and
the future to which he is half assimilated. It is a study, in sum, of
time out of joint. 'That story of another world', writes the narrator of one of Bellamy's short stories, 'has, in a word, put me out
of joint with ours.'[15] Throughout his fiction, he is fascinated by
the psychology of disjointedness, and of divided consciousness.

In an intriguing article on 'The Insomnia of Julian West', Tom
Towers once argued that the 'chronic insomnia' from which
Bellamy's protagonist suffers in the late nineteenth century
'becomes the comprehensive symbol of the totality of Julian's
sense of social and psychic disturbance'. His emphasis on the
hero's damaged psyche is original and persuasive, but the article
makes a misleading assumption that the damage is spontaneously repaired once West has appeared in the utopian society
of the twenty-first century: 'Julian seems reborn into a new self-
hood, making him for the first time at peace with himself and
his world.'[16]

The opposite is the case: old neuroses cling to him, nightmar-
ishly, and new ones suddenly emerge. Sleep, for example, remains

a problem even after his reappearance in utopia. On his first night in 2000, it is in a state of 'dread' that West anticipates the moment at which he must be alone in the bedroom he has been allotted by the Leetes, his hosts in this socialist society, because he fears that the 'mental balance' that he has maintained in the presence of these 'friendly strangers' will collapse:

> Even then, however, in the pauses of the conversation I had had glimpses, vivid as lightning flashes, of the horror of strangeness that was waiting to be faced when I could no longer command diversion. I knew I could not sleep that night, and as for lying awake and thinking, it argues no cowardice, I am sure, to confess that I was afraid of it. (28)

West has been poised, semi-consciously, above a psychological abyss, and he suspects that when he has to confront his existential situation alone, he will plummet into it. He is like one of those cartoon characters who, having scuttled unawares over the edge of a cliff, defy gravity until they look down.

Terrified that the 'horror of strangeness' will finally overwhelm him, West therefore defers the moment when he must go to bed, questioning Dr Leete about the society of the future until three o'clock in the morning. At that point, in a tone that is at once benign and slightly threatening, Leete tells him that he is his patient as well as his guest, and administers a 'dose' that will ensure 'a sound night's sleep without fail' (28). And West does indeed sleep deeply.

It is when he wakes up the next morning, once the effects of the narcotic he has taken have lifted, that he first experiences a profound psychological crisis. As Philip Wegner has pointed out in an eloquent reading of the novel, in this passage 'Bellamy evokes the condition of a subject literally pulled from the flow of history.'[17] At first, West lies quite contentedly in bed, because he has no recollection of the fact that he has travelled through time (it is a 'blank' in his memory [45]). But when he realizes that he is in an unfamiliar bedchamber he starts up from the couch and stares wildly about the apartment:

I think it must have been many seconds that I sat up thus in bed staring about, without being able to regain the clew to my personal identity. I was no more able to distinguish myself from pure being during those moments than we may suppose a soul in the rough to be before it has received the ear-marks, the individualizing touches which make it a person. Strange that the sense of this inability should be such anguish! But so we are constituted. There are no words for the mental torture I endured during this helpless, eyeless groping for myself in a boundless void. No other experience of the mind gives probably anything like the sense of absolute intellectual arrest from the loss of a mental fulcrum, a starting point of thought, which comes during such a momentary obscuration of one's identity. I trust I may never know what it is again. (45)

This condition, perhaps momentary, seems to last 'an interminable time', and West leaps from his bed and fights for his sanity in the face of 'apparently irretrievable chaos' (46). In a state of severe mental dissociation, he reflects on the likelihood that he has suffered a schizoidal split: 'The idea that I was two persons, that my identity was double, began to fascinate me with its simple solution of my experience' (46). Here is a first glimpse of the fugue character of his experience in the city of the future.

West subsequently attempts to restore his precarious sense of equilibrium, shattered as it is from his sense of being cast into 'a boundless void', by putting on his clothes and leaving the Leetes' house, though it is scarcely light outside: 'I found myself on the street. For two hours I walked or ran through the streets of the city' (46). In this scene, Bellamy situates a state of non-being in a specifically urban frame, dramatizing the protagonist's loss of self in terms of an agoraphobic reaction to the unfamiliar, the alien city.

Here, the space of the city is susceptible to a sort of psychosis. 'So far as my consciousness was concerned,' he explains, 'it was but yesterday, but a few hours, since I had walked these streets in which scarcely a feature had escaped a complete metamorphosis' (47). He experiences the city as an impossible palimpsest, in which the past merges with the present, the nineteenth century with the twenty-first, 'like the faces of a composite photograph' (47). His mind cannot compute the competing claims of these opposing dystopian and utopian cities – 'it was first one and then the other which seemed the more unreal' (47) – and threatens to implode.

Then, all of a sudden, West finds himself back at the Leetes' house, on the site of his home in the nineteenth century, as if his feet have instinctively saved him from some complete psychological collapse in the vast, empty spaces of the city. Once there, he drops into a chair and makes a final, concentrated attempt to resist the city's colonization of his mental space:

> I covered my burning eyeballs with my hands to shut out the horror of strangeness. My mental confusion was so great as to produce actual nausea. The anguish of those moments, during which my brain seemed melting, or the abjectness of my sense of helplessness, how can I describe? (47)

In so far as it is experienced from the inside rather than the outside, as psychological rather than social space, the city of the future provokes an agoraphobic reaction. Its 'miles of broad streets' which stretch in every direction, its 'large open squares', its 'public buildings of a colossal size', are suddenly threatening, oppressive (22).

The large-scale geometric space embodied in utopian Boston provides precisely the kind of environment that, in the late nineteenth century, kindled panic among individuals prone to agoraphobia. Kathryn Milun has argued that agoraphobia emerged 'during a period of massive migration from country to city, together with the construction of monumental architectural forms that accompanied both metropolitan growth and the rise of the modern nation-state'. 'Nineteenth-century agoraphobics experienced the gigantic squares and boulevards introduced into their cities as hostile environments,' she goes on to claim. 'They perceived these monumental spaces as "empty" and experienced intense anxiety that caused them to retreat to the curb, to their homes, and even to bed.'[18] Agoraphobics, as Milun emphasizes, were often people who, because they had migrated from rural communities, felt overwhelmed by the gigantism of urban society.

Bellamy's protagonist, in spite of his name, is a migrant through time rather than space; but the pathological effect on him is the same.

West is rescued from his agoraphobic collapse, in the first place at least, by the appearance of Dr Leete's daughter Edith, who coaxes the visitor out of his psychotic or phobic state. But the descriptive intensity of the episode is such that, despite his superficially successful assimilation to the Boston of the future thereafter, he never seems fully to escape the threat of some relapse.

The novel's poetic as opposed to political force, in fact, depends on the idea established in this scene that his identity is in some sense doubled; and that, as someone who is simultaneously a product of the nineteenth and the twenty-first century, he is doomed to inhabit the historical equivalent of what Bellamy once described in another context as a 'Jekyll–Hyde existence'.[19]

Doubleness is indeed something like an obsession of Bellamy's in his shorter fiction, where the past and future are often placed in unsettling tension with the present. Stories like 'The Old Folks' Party' (1876) and 'A Midnight Drama' (1877), for all the quaintness of their romance plots, are probing, experimental investigations into what he describes in the latter as the 'odd feeling of being double'.[20] In the former, six young friends stage a fancy-dress party at which they must make themselves up as their future selves; that is, as they imagine they will look in fifty years' time. This game produces 'a singular effect': 'They began to regard every event and feeling from a double standpoint, as present and as past, as it appeared to them and as it would appear to an old person.'[21] As in *Miss Ludington's Sister*, then, past, present and future selves are rendered co-existent.

Read from the perspective of these examples of Bellamy's speculative fiction, *Looking Backward* can even be interpreted as an attempt to infuse the utopian form with psychological realism. It is a laboratory test of what, in 'The Old Folks' Party', he had called 'the fragile tenure of the sense of personal identity'.[22] West does not become magically adjusted to the conditions of Boston in 2000. Plausibly enough, he remains maladjusted. Like Hamlet, he would no doubt count himself a king of infinite space were it not for the fact that he has bad dreams.

These dreams – specifically the nightmare about returning to the nineteenth century in Chapter 28, the book's final chapter, which like West the reader initially assumes is proof that Boston in 2000 was no more than a dream or fantasy – set out the limits of his social assimilation. In phantasmagorical prose, they stage the return of the repressed, dramatizing West's constitutional inability to escape the pull of the dystopian past from which he has ostensibly escaped.

In the hallucinated reconstruction of historical Boston that appears in the book's final chapter, the neo-classical geometries of the vision of the city characteristic of the utopian tradition are shockingly disordered by the chaotic energies of the gothic form. 'Up to this point the story has been told in limp and lacklustre prose,' as Samuel Haber rather ungenerously puts it, 'but now the tone becomes frantic and feverish.'[23] Consequently, the phrase 'hysterical Boston' might better describe this chapter's febrile image of a city of the late 1880s. For here Bellamy's protagonist becomes a terrified pedestrian adrift in an urban environment that seems increasingly alienating and strange, despite (or perhaps because of) its sickening familiarity.

In this scene, he must confront what Marshall Berman has called 'phantoms in the street and in the soul'.[24] The presence of masses of more or less animalized people induces a sense of panicked claustrophobia; a claustrophobia that is merely the obverse of West's agoraphobia. In the dream, the labyrinthine streets of tenement districts are 'thronged with the workers from the stores, the shops, and mills' (188). The rookeries through which he drunkenly reels disgorge atavistic children in a state of advanced degeneration: 'swarms of half-clad brutalized children filled the air with shrieks and curses as they fought and tumbled among the garbage that littered the courtyards' (189). In effect, West thus undergoes a further, even more intense psychotic episode, one that is inseparable from his experiences as someone walking alone in the city.

Even the novel's final tableau – in which, having gratefully awoken from his bad dream and confirmed that his presence in twenty-first-century Boston is after all 'reality', he kneels before Edith in the Leetes' garden with his 'face in the dust' – ultimately seems ambiguous (194). For if, on the one hand, it is an emblem of courtly love, and hence entirely consistent with the novel's romance elements, on the other hand it is an image of what West earlier referred to as 'abjectness' (47).

Bellamy thus dramatically redefines the narrator of utopian fiction, presenting him as someone terminally troubled by existential doubt and psychic uncertainty. In Bellamy, the protagonist of utopian fiction is genuinely agonistic.

Bellamy's conception of the utopian imagination is shaped by contemporaneous developments in psychology; and this helps explain the power of his novel, which is far more than simply an ideological blueprint for a state-socialist future. More particularly, though, he implicitly characterizes Julian West as suffering from a specific psychological disorder dating from the late nineteenth century. This singular condition, in which the afflicted individual suddenly abandons his identity and unconsciously begins to inhabit another one, came to be diagnosed as 'psychogenic fugue'.

As the word *fugue* suggests, derived as it is from *fugere*, the Latin for 'to flee', it entails a flight from the self. The *OED* defines *fugue*, in its psychiatric meaning, as:

> A flight from one's own identity, often involving travel to some unconsciously desired locality. It is a dissociative reaction to shock or emotional stress in a neurotic, during which all awareness of personal identity is lost though the person's outward behaviour may appear rational. On recovery, memory of events during the state is totally repressed but may become conscious under hypnosis or psycho-analysis. A fugue may also be part of an epileptic or hysterical seizure.

In the United States, the first recorded case of fugue occurred in 1887, the year in which Bellamy completed *Looking Backward*. On 17 January 1887, a carpenter in his early sixties called

Ansel Bourne, who lived in the settlement of Greene, on the Con-
necticut border, travelled to Providence, the capital of Rhode
Island, removed his savings from the bank, and vanished. In spite
of all efforts to reconstruct his movements, there seemed to be
no trace of him at all. The man's spouse, whom he had married
after the death of his first wife in 1881, had no idea of his where-
abouts. She had only recently persuaded Bourne, an itinerant
preacher for almost thirty years, to cease travelling from home
and take up professional carpentry, perhaps in order to prove
his commitment to domestic life. It was this apparently settled,
and comparatively parochial, existence that his disappearance
violently ruptured.

Bourne had become a preacher in the first instance as the
result of a dramatic, indeed damascene, conversion. One day
in October 1857, while journeying by foot to Westerly, Rhode
Island, he experienced an acute physiological collapse. His
sight, hearing and capacity for speech abruptly shut down,
though he remained conscious. This blind, deaf and dumb
state persisted for almost a month. It ended, in the convenient
presence of a Christian minister and his congregation, at the
precise moment that Bourne, finding he could still inscribe
messages on a slate and interpreting the situation as a divine
judgement on his sinfulness, recorded his resolution to commit
himself to God. His senses were instantaneously restored.
Bourne was born again.

In consequence, Bourne briefly became the object of medical
and religious debate in the local press. Most of the commentators in this Puritan community interpreted his experience as a
miracle; his doctor, however, diagnosed it as the effect of some
mental disturbance. It is possible, as some specialists subsequently
believed, that he was epileptic. The social anthropologist Michael
Kenny, who has reconstructed Bourne's case, speculates that he
was 'a repressed, isolated, sometimes depressed individual'. Interestingly, he adds that 1857 'was a year of major disturbance in
national life', and that this might have been 'another factor': 'The
stock market had crashed disastrously, leaving behind the wreck
of individual fortunes, the failure of banks, and widespread
apprehension about what the future would hold.'[25]

But what of his disappearance? Almost two months after the fateful journey to Providence, on 14 March 1887, Bourne's nephew, who lived in that city, received a telegram informing him that his missing uncle could be found in Norristown, near Philadelphia. When Bourne's nephew reached Norristown, however, he discovered, to his obvious consternation, that his uncle had been living for some six weeks as a shopkeeper in Newton, New Hampshire, under the name Albert John Brown.

A few days earlier, it transpired, Bourne had woken to find himself in an unfamiliar bed. The last thing he remembered was being in Providence two months earlier. To his astonishment, his neighbours in Newton insisted that he was a respectable businessman called Brown who had recently moved there and set up the variety store he occupied. He regularly attended church, they informed him, and sometimes visited Philadelphia to replenish his stocks of confectionery and stationery.

According to Richard Hodgson, who recorded these details in an article on 'Double Consciousness' published in the *Proceedings of the Society for Psychical Research* in 1892, the man 'appear[ed] to his neighbours and customers as a normal person'; albeit one, so he surmised, who had been 'in a somnambulistic condition all the while'.[26] Bourne's, or Brown's, neighbours – these names, it is noticeable, are virtually anagrammatic of one another – nonetheless became increasingly suspicious. But he does not seem to have deliberately, elaborately deceived them.

Bourne could not have been an imposter, it seemed, because he 'had total amnesia for the period of Albert Brown's existence', as Kenny has confirmed.[27] The man had alternately inhabited two distinct, apparently incommensurable selves. In sum, he had both a Bourne identity and a Brown identity. (The title of *The Bourne Identity* [1980], Robert Ludlum's novel about an amnesiac special agent attempting to reconstruct his identity, subsequently made into a celebrated series of films, is evidently a deliberate, albeit obscure, allusion to the case of Ansel Bourne.)

In contrast to the representatives of the religious community that shaped the terms in which Bourne's collapse was interpreted in the late 1850s, the self-appointed experts who pronounced on him in the late 1880s were in no doubt that he was suffering from

a medical rather than a spiritual condition. 'In the last years of
the century,' Jessica Lieberman has observed, 'the pious imagination of New England Protestantism was insufficient to explain
his amnestic transformation.'[28] As Hodgson's article suggests, an
emergent post-Darwinian psychology instead explored the case
as an instance of double consciousness. Bourne was apparently
afflicted by a divided self.

The most prominent professional psychologist to take an
interest in the case was William James, then in the process of
completing *The Principles of Psychology* (1890). In his chapter
on 'The Consciousness of Self', where he cautiously classed this
case 'as one of spontaneous hypnotic trance, persisting for two
months', James described hypnotizing Bourne in order to reconstruct his experiences as Brown.[29] Under a trance, according to
James, Bourne readily reverted to being Brown; but in this state,
conversely, he registered no knowledge of the life of Bourne.

Adopting a slightly disappointed tone, James recorded that
'the whole thing was prosaic enough; and the Brown-personality
seems to be nothing but a rather shrunken, dejected, and amnesiac extract of Mr Bourne himself'. 'I had hoped by suggestion,
etc.,' he concluded, 'to run the two personalities into one, and
make the memories continuous, but no artifice would avail to
accomplish this, and Mr Bourne's skull to-day still covers two
distinct personal selves.'[30] Here, then, is what Bellamy called a
'Jekyll–Hyde existence'.

Across the Atlantic, at almost exactly the same time as Bourne's
enigmatic peregrination, a number of analogous cases characterized by dissociated identities, all of them entailing arbitrary if
oddly purposeful journeys, most of them on foot, were being
examined by French psychologists. Philippe Tissié documented
the first of these, which also coincidentally came to light in 1887,
in a medical thesis entitled *Les aliénés voyageurs*. It concerned
a young working-class man from Bordeaux, Albert Dadas,
who travelled compulsively, in an apparently amnesiac state,
sometimes reaching locations as distant as Constantinople and
Moscow. Another Albert, then, but one who was born 'Albert',
so to speak, unlike Bourne, who became Albert, or had the name
Albert thrust upon him.[31]

Dadas 'traveled obsessively,' writes Ian Hacking in *Mad Travelers*, 'bewitched, often without identity papers and sometimes without identity, not knowing who he was or why he traveled, and knowing only where he was going next.'[32] So he too laboured under what might be called a Bourne identity, a condition which can be summarized in terms of dissociative or psychogenic fugue.

The comments on his condition in the late 1880s – most influentially, those of the famous neurologist Jean-Martin Charcot, who referred to it in a lecture of January 1888 as a case of *automatisme ambulatoire* – initiated what Hacking has forcefully described as 'the fugue epidemic of the 1890s'.[33] This epidemic emanated from France into Italy, Germany and Russia, where it was analysed under various names, including *determinismo ambulatorio*, *Wandertrieb* and 'dromomania'. Some psychologists argued that fugue was a hysterical condition, others that it was an epileptic one; Charcot, for his part, sometimes spoke of 'hystero-epilepsy'.[34]

In explaining the social conditions in which fugue emerged, Hacking points out that the late nineteenth century is the epoch in which mass tourism, as pioneered by the travel company Thomas Cook and Son, first made its appearance. 'Popular tourism,' he argues, 'was one part of the ecological niche in which a new type of mental disorder, and behavior, was able to locate itself.' Fugue, according to this intriguing argument, was a pathological symptom of the compulsion to travel that characterized the *fin de siècle*. Recapitulating the point, Hacking claims that fugue is thus 'a mirror of tourism'.[35]

It might equally be asserted that, in the late nineteenth century, fugue is a mirror of utopianism (itself perhaps a mirror of tourism at this time, as the example of Jules Verne implies); or, more accurately, that utopian literature, at the height of its popularity as a mass form, mirrors the logic of fugue. Utopianism, it could be said, is the temporal equivalent of ambulatory automatism.

In late nineteenth-century utopian literature, the protagonist disappears from one life and reappears in another, like a *fugueur*. He is an *aliéné voyageur*. But if fugue involves the patient's displacement in space, utopia involves the protagonist's displacement in time. He slips from the present into the future, crossing

an ontological as well as an existential border. He is not simply
an alienated traveller, he is an alien traveller, a time traveller;
in short, he is an alien, albeit one from inner space rather than
outer space. 'I should expect *fugueurs* to occur in the ephemeral
popular writing of the 1890s,' Hacking has written, 'but I do not
know of any.'[36] It is in utopian fiction that they materialize, in
half-disguised form.

Utopian consciousness, divided between the present and the
future, ostensibly describes a political as opposed to a pathological dissociation. In both contexts, however, those of political and
psychological flight, the crucial event, to formulate it in Lynch's
terms, is the moment when the individual wakes up one day and
discovers that he or she is another person. This is the narrative
constitutive of utopian fiction.

Take W. H. Hudson's *A Crystal Age* (1887). In this novel, contemporaneous with *Looking Backward*, the narrator falls from
a rock on a botanical expedition into a ravine and on regaining
consciousness discovers that he is in a strangely wild landscape
populated by beautiful, androgynous human beings. Or, take
Elizabeth Corbett's *New Amazonia* (1889). The narrator, in this
example, falls asleep in her study as she is fantasizing about
Annie Besant's first speech as prime minister, and wakes up to
find she is standing in a beautiful garden, in a feminist arcadia,
beside a distinctly decadent young man who can recall only that,
before being transported into the future, he had been smoking
hashish in Soho.[37]

In the context both of time travelling and mad travelling,
the subject is structured by a 'Jekyll–Hyde existence'. 'Yes, I
had gone to bed Henry Jekyll, I had awakened Edward Hyde,'
Jekyll states in *Dr Jekyll and Mr Hyde* (1886), Stevenson's
celebrated novel about an individual with a skull that covers
two distinct personal selves.[38] Like the *fugueur*, as I have suggested, the utopian protagonist disappears from one life and
reappears in another.

Sometimes, as in Morris's *News from Nowhere* (1890–91), he
returns to his former life, uncomfortably enough, and attempts to
piece together the experiences he has had in a dream state. After

coming to consciousness in his bed in 'dingy Hammersmith' at
the end of the narrative, Morris's protagonist William Guest
reflects that 'all along, though those friends were so real to me, I
had been feeling as if I had no business among them: as though
the time would come when they would reject me, and say, as
Ellen's last mournful look seemed to say, "No, it will not do; you
cannot be of us …".'[39]

At other times, as in *Looking Backward*, the utopian protagonist vanishes and is never seen again. Julian West also recalls one
of the 'mad travellers' investigated by Charcot, a man called Mén,
whose first *fugue* was in May 1887, but who disappeared completely in June 1890, 'despite vigorous inquiries by the police'.[40]
For Julian's journey into the future is a fugue from which he
doesn't return. The same might be said of the Time Traveller in
Wells's novel, at the conclusion of which the narrator admits that
he might have to 'wait a lifetime' for him to return: 'The Time
Traveller vanished three years ago. And, as everybody knows
now, he has never returned.'[41]

The chronological coincidence of the emergence of fugue
and the resurgence of the utopian imagination – of compulsive
wandering and compulsive wondering, so to speak – is certainly
striking. As I have emphasized, Bellamy's book was completed
in the year both that Ansel Bourne disappeared and the case of
Albert Dadas came to be documented. And if the 1890s was, as
Hacking puts it, 'the golden decade for fugue', then the same
can be said of utopian fiction.[42] For although a utopian consciousness, or structure of feeling, is broadly characteristic of the
final three decades of the nineteenth century – the period shaped
by the Long Depression – it is during the late 1880s and early
1890s in particular that the publication of most utopian fiction
is concentrated.[43]

If Bourne's first physiological collapse in 1857 was precipitated
in part by social disturbance, and the 'widespread apprehension
about what the future would hold' that accompanied it, as Kenny
suggests, then similar conditions lie behind what I am diagnos-
ing as West's fugue in 1887 (it just so happens that Bellamy's
protagonist was born in 1857, as he announces in the book's
opening sentence). Boston in 1887 is racked by 'disturbances of

industry', according to West (9); and because his forthcoming
marriage is contingent on moving into a house that, as a consequence of 'a series of strikes', is only half-built, he is particularly
susceptible to what he calls 'the nervous tension of the public
mind' (11).[44]

It is to this socially divided city that West doubles back in
the dream he describes in Chapter 28, the dystopian dream that
he erroneously interprets as reality, and hence as proof that the
socialist society he thought he inhabited was actually a utopian
dream. This chapter effectively documents another fugue; or,
more precisely perhaps, the experience of a *fugueur* who suddenly
finds himself among the scenes of his former life again. West's
initial impulse, on finding himself in late nineteenth-century
Boston once more, as he assumes, is to leave his house and desperately pound the streets: 'A dozen times between my door and
Washington Street I had to stop and pull myself together, such
power had been in that vision of the Boston of the future to make
the real Boston strange' (182).

It is an episode of ambulatory automatism. Shocked that he
has 'so suddenly become a stranger in [his] own city', he stands
at the 'busiest point' in Washington Street and laughs aloud, 'to
the scandal of the passers-by' (183). He then drifts about the
city in an increasingly febrile state, convinced that the people
he encounters are 'all quite dead', their bodies 'so many living
sepulchres' (189). At nightfall, staring in the street at the faces
of the inhabitants of the poorest district of nineteenth-century
Boston, he is 'affected by a singular hallucination': 'Like a waver-
ing translucent spirit face superimposed on each of these brutish
masks I saw the ideal, the possible face that would have been
the actual if mind and soul had lived' (189). West's fugue state
momentarily merges with his non-fugue state, the utopian vision
coalescing with the dystopian one.

But if this revelation almost succeeds in running his dissociated
identities into one, to use James's formulation, he subsequently
suffers an attack of amnesia. He has 'no clear recollection of anything', in fact, until he finds his feet 'obeying some unconscious
impulse' and leading him to his nineteenth-century fiancée's family
home (190). There, he interrupts a dinner party, denouncing the

guests' plutocratic lifestyle, and sermonizing about his social dreams, in the voice of a prophet:

> With fervency I spoke of that new world, blessed with plenty, purified by justice and sweetened by brotherly kindness, the world of which I had indeed but dreamed, but which might so easily be made real. But when I had expected now surely the faces around me to light up with emotions akin to mine, they grew ever more dark, angry, and scornful. Instead of enthusiasm, the ladies showed only aversion and dread, while the men interrupted me with shouts of reprobation and contempt. 'Madman!' 'Pestilent fellow!' 'Fanatic!' 'Enemy of Society!' were some of their cries ... (192)

Finally, he is physically ejected: '"Put the fellow out!" exclaimed the father of my betrothed, and at the signal the men sprang from their chairs and advanced upon me' (192). Rather than feeling enmity for his accusers, though, West is overcome by violent, uncontrollable compassion for them, which makes him seem even less socially acceptable, even less sane.

Indeed, he suffers something that closely resembles a nervous breakdown. 'Tears poured from my eyes,' West recounts. 'In my vehemence I became inarticulate' (193). It is at this point, in an abrupt transition, that he realizes he has dreamed the entire episode while asleep in the Leetes' house in utopian Boston: 'I panted, I sobbed, I groaned, and immediately afterward found myself sitting upright in my bed in my room in Dr. Leete's house' (193). His secondary fugue – it might be understood as a fugue within a fugue – is thus concluded.

In the end, the connections between fugue and the utopian imagination are not simply a matter of coincidence; nor of the structural analogies between these two kinds of flight, the one spatial, the other temporal. I have already alluded to the fact that, in the novels and short stories that Bellamy published before *Looking Backward*, he demonstrated a persistent interest in abnormal psychological states.

A compelling example of this is 'The Blindman's World', first printed in the *Atlantic Monthly* in 1886. In this tale, a professor of astronomy realizes to his astonishment that, during a fit of somnambulism, he has produced a description of a trip to Mars, one that he apparently made in a mysterious cataleptic state from which he has been recuperating, though he has no recollection of it. The sheets of paper that he subsequently finds on his desk 'contained the longed-for but despaired-of record of those hours when I was absent from the body,' he states: 'They were the lost chapter of my life.'[45] So Bellamy manifestly had an interest in something like ambulatory automatism before 1887.

But it is also possible to speculate, more specifically, that he became conscious of the case of Ansel Bourne, since it transpires that, among the plot outlines contained in his unpublished notebooks, there is one that centres on what is in effect a psychogenic fugue. This tale, which was presumably never written, is entitled 'A Mysterious Disappearance':

A Mysterious Disappearance: Let story be narrated in first person at Franksville. Have friend, a fine fellow [called Noakes], who is sick and married, with a pretty baby, prosperous, ordinary sort of fellow. I meet him and know him for a year. I see some curious epileptic symptoms about him that is all. I leave him and go to Indianapolis. I then get board in an interesting family of a 'grass widow' [a woman separated from her husband]. Her husband mysteriously disappeared some years previous. Left her with these children. Supposed to be drowned. I go away. A newspaper account of return of her husband. Afterwards go back to see grass widow, find my friend Noakes installed as her husband. He does not know me from Adam. I ask him questions about Franksville. He evidently knows nothing about it. I guess the truth. What shall I do? I go back and tell his wife the truth. She overwhelmed. Long after he comes back to her but she will not live with him. Would it be wrong? They are different persons.

I take Noakes back to his legal wife. He does not know her but accepts my word that he is her husband, and there reposed him with her, a broken-hearted man.[46]

This outline is obviously prompted by contemporaneous debates about double consciousness. Like James and his associates, including Hodgson, who hinted that, during his time in Norristown, Bourne probably suffered from 'post-epileptic partial loss of memory', Bellamy notes that Noakes had 'some curious epileptic symptoms about him'.[47] Noakes consists of 'different persons', each one living a separate life with a separate wife. In James's formulation, Noakes's skull 'covers two distinct personal selves'. Like Noakes, West consists of 'different persons', though these are shaped not by geographical but historical displacements. *Looking Backward* thus also recounts a mysterious disappearance.

Bellamy's troubled protagonist even exchanges one girlfriend for another, replacing Edith Bartlett, his fiancée in 1887, with Edith Leete, his lover in 2000. In fact, fortuitously, albeit a little uncomfortably for the reader, it transpires that the latter is the former's great-granddaughter; and it is therefore tempting to imagine that the novel's central female characters are susceptible to the logic of a fugue-like doubling too. When West and Edith Leete declare their love to one another in the penultimate chapter, he describes it as 'a double miracle', because his old love, Edith Bartlett, has been 'reëmbodied for [his] consolation' (177).

Here, certainly, is what West, with some understatement, calls a 'confusion of identities' (177). For, if West feels his identity has been split and doubled by the historical displacement he experienced in time-travelling to the future, then so too does Edith Leete. Even more peculiarly, perhaps, since she is positively haunted by her lover's relationship with her antecedent. 'What if I were to tell you that I have sometimes thought that her spirit lives in me, – that Edith Bartlett, not Edith Leete, is my real name', she admits to him, in slightly plaintive tones. 'I cannot know it; of course none of us can know who we really are; but I can feel it' (177). Edith is an individual with two identities, two surnames, 'Leete' echoing and elongating the 'lett' in 'Bartlett', just as 'Brown' had reconfigured 'Bourne'.

It is finally not impossible that West's surname – in addition to its invocation of the pioneer spirit – has a symbolic resonance that has since been lost. In an item entitled 'A Missing Preacher', printed three days after Ansel Bourne's disappearance in 1887, the Providence *Bulletin* reported that he 'may have started for the West'. 'Bourne's fugue,' Lieberman comments in light of the newspaper's speculation, 'was an extreme form of self-liberty; it was the great escape: going West, finding a new life unfettered by the chains of the past – even if that past included personal identity and its constitutive memories.'[48]

> To 'Go West' in this new context, then, would be to escape the limits of individualism, to contest the boundaries of singular consciousness, to conquer the divide between life and death. ... Unable to cope with his own world, he takes flight into the alternate reality of another man.[49]

In his utopian fugue, Bellamy's protagonist also redefines what it means to 'Go West'. He does so in the language of socialism, a language that fits the longings of modern man. He too escapes the limits of individualism, contests the boundaries of singular consciousness, and conquers the divide between life and death. In Boston's utopian future – the alternative reality to which, unable to cope with his own world, West abruptly takes flight – he too finds a new life unfettered by the chains of the past.

So, what conclusions can be inferred from the comparison I have drawn between the utopian imagination and fugue in the 1880s?

First, I think, that utopian fiction becomes more sophisticated at this time because it is shaped by contemporaneous developments in psychology, which enable Bellamy in particular to rethink the mental or existential processes that time travelling, or social dreaming, entail.[50] In rethinking these processes, he imparts a psychological depth to the utopian form that makes it difficult to dismiss *Looking Backward* as a paper-thin romance redeemed only by its political importance. Instead, in this utopia, psychopathology is placed – to take a formulation from Fredric Jameson – 'in the service of collective drama'.[51]

Second, that in the late nineteenth century, utopianism cannot be dismissed as escapism, as its detractors have reflexively insisted. For it is more accurately a form of escape, a flight from the present that, far from leaving it intact or even reinforcing its limits, as escapism does, challenges its ontological unity. If one can meaningfully inhabit two selves, then perhaps one can meaningfully inhabit two histories.

This appears to be Morris's conviction at the conclusion of *News from Nowhere*, when his protagonist Guest reluctantly fades back into the nineteenth century from which he had fled in his dream. 'Or indeed *was* it a dream?' he asks, as he lies in bed in his house in Hammersmith. 'If so, why was I so conscious all along that I was really seeing all that new life from the outside, still wrapped up in the prejudices, the anxieties, the distrust of this time of doubt and struggle?'[52] He is cursed, or blessed, with a double consciousness, one that makes him half an inhabitant of the future, necessarily, as he fights for social revolution in the present. Utopia is from this perspective no more a non-place than the alternative identity inhabited by a *fugueur* is a state of non-being; it is simply an alternative political consciousness.

In a discussion of *The Time Machine*, Robert Philmus has commented that 'Wells designed the fiction to be precisely what its title says it is: a time machine – i.e., a vehicle for transporting its readers ... outside their "temporal" mindset so that they might examine assumptions which they – and human beings as a rule – tend to accept unthinkingly because those assumptions ordinarily remain unconscious.'[53] *Looking Backward* is in this respect a time machine too; and a space machine – though its travels are in inner space.

Like all late nineteenth-century utopian and science fiction, it is a machine for displacing the reader's political imagination, and for putting consciousness to flight. In Bellamy's hands, utopian fiction effectively becomes an 'art of the fugue'.[54]

4

Fleeing

H. G. Wells's
The Invisible Man

'The man's become inhuman, I tell you,' comments one character as the forces of justice close in on the fugitive known as the Invisible Man: 'He has cut himself off from his kind.'[1] H. G. Wells's fourth novel, *The Invisible Man* (1897), is a strange tragicomedy that describes the apparently inexorable process whereby its hero, or anti-hero, a bitter but brilliant scientist called Griffin, who has invented an ingenious means of rendering himself invisible, aspires initially to superhuman status, but collapses finally into an abject, subhuman state.

The Invisible Man, a criminal condemned to fleeing his pursuers on foot, whether they take the form of an urban mob or an armed police battalion, is another exemplary instance – like the Man of the Crowd, and like many of the other figures reconstructed in this book – of a casualty of modernity who is forced to negotiate his outsider status in part through the politics and semiotics of walking. Chased through the streets of London, where he is reduced to a state of homelessness, pursued along the lanes and roads of southern England, the Invisible Man becomes a scapegoat who must bear the sins of the society from which he has been excluded.

For Griffin, imperceptible both to the traffic on the roads and the pedestrians bustling about their everyday business on the pavements, the city streets become a battlefield through which,

in order to protect himself, he must carefully plot his route. 'I
walked to avoid being overtaken,' he observes at one point, in his
retrospective narrative of events. 'Every crossing was a danger,
every passenger a thing to watch alertly' (101). If, in the first
instance, invisibility offered the sort of social privileges associated with *flânerie*, promising to fulfil certain voyeuristic pleasures
with impunity, then soon enough it proves far from liberating.
In the form of the Invisible Man, the *flâneur* finds himself brutally excluded from the urban space to which he assumed he had
unlimited access.

A physicist and former chemist, Griffin is no more than 'a shabby,
poverty-struck, hemmed-in demonstrator, teaching fools in a provincial college' when he first apprehends that it might be possible
to make the 'whole fabric' of his body, including in the end his
blood, completely colourless and transparent (83). As he himself
points out, he is 'almost an albino', 'with a pink and white face
and red eyes', and this lack of skin pigmentation makes it easier
for him to decolourize his tissues (71): '"I could be Invisible," I
said, suddenly realising what it meant to be an albino with such
knowledge' (83).

In addition, Griffin's albinism reinforces his embattled sense
of being a social outsider. In the nineteenth century, after all,
albinos were exhibited at carnivals and fairs, and classed among
degenerates. They were for example among the 'living curiosities'
displayed by P. T. Barnum in North America and Britain from
the late 1850s to the early 1890s. 'What is it that in the Albino
man so peculiarly repels and often shocks the eye, as that sometimes he is loathed by his own kith and kin!' Herman Melville
had exclaimed in *Moby Dick* (1851) – 'this mere aspect of all-
pervading whiteness makes him more strangely hideous than the
ugliest abortion.'[2] Because of his albinism the Invisible Man is
already cut off from his kind.

Sick of confronting a sense of personal, professional and social
impotence, Griffin is driven, in his dream of making himself
invisible, by what Friedrich Nietzsche, exactly a decade before
the publication of *The Invisible Man*, identified as *ressentiment* –
the vindictively resentful attitude fostered in the individual as a

result of the negation of the self that, as opposed to the 'noble morality' of 'the masters', is characteristic of 'slave morality'.[3] In this respect, his spiritual condition anticipates that of the eponymous character of Wells's later novel *The History of Mr Polly* (1910), who hates 'the whole scheme of life', which he regards as 'at once excessive and inadequate of him'; and who consequently falls, each day, 'into a violent rage and hatred against the outer world'.[4] But Griffin is far more malicious than Mr Polly; he is sociopathic. At one point, in order to fund his research, he steals from his own father, who then kills himself because he is secretly in debt.

Like the Underground Man in Fyodor Dostoevsky's *Notes from the Underground* (1864), the Invisible Man is a sick, spiteful individual who derives a perverse strength from what the former describes as 'the poison of unfulfilled wishes that have turned inwards'.[5] But if Griffin internalizes his unfulfilled wishes he also externalizes and, in effect, sublimates them. He alchemizes the poison. Frustrated in his professional ambitions, Griffin 'find[s] compensation in an imaginary revenge', to frame it in terms of Nietzsche's formulation – his dream of becoming an invisible Übermensch.[6]

After discovering 'a general principle of pigments and refraction', Griffin devotes himself to his obsessive scientific labours in the laboratory he has surreptitiously set up in a cheap apartment in central London; and devises an elaborate method that makes it possible, 'without changing any other property of matter,' as he puts it in his retrospective narrative, 'to lower the refractive index of a substance, solid or liquid, to that of air – so far as all practical purposes are concerned' (80).[7] 'Wounded by the world', the Invisible Man thus sets out to dominate it through his command of experimental science, and so to make himself one of the 'masters of the world'.[8]

Once he has performed the painful metamorphosis that follows his secretive experiments, Griffin gives full expression to his contempt for 'the common conventions of humanity' and the 'common people' who embody them (104). Inspired by his *ressentiment*, the Invisible Man's vengeful and destructive actions, which culminate in his announcement that he will launch a Reign of Terror, ensure that he quickly becomes universally feared. He proclaims 'the Epoch of the Invisible Man', while rumours of his terroristic campaign spread across the nation (119).

In this respect, he is a precursor to Rud, the protagonist of *The Holy Terror* (1939), Wells's later, comparatively underrated novel about the rise and fall of a totalitarian dictator in England, who is told by his intellectual mentor that 'to make a new world, the leader must be a fundamentally destructive man, a recklessly destructive man.' At the same time, though, this leader must cultivate a superior attitude to the common people and maintain a certain mysterious distance from them, thereby acting the part of 'an invisible Great Man'.[9] Griffin, like Rud, is a Holy Terror: 'He dreams of a reign of terror!' (113).

In response to the Invisible Man's attempt to implement this terroristic dream, the police impose 'a stringent state of siege' across an area of several hundred square miles surrounding the place in the countryside to which he has fled (116). But it comes too late for one man 'of inoffensive habits and appearance', whom in 'a murderous frenzy' Griffin beats to death with an iron rod: 'He stopped this quiet man, going quietly home to his midday meal, attacked him, beat down his feeble defences, broke his arm, felled him, and smashed his head to a jelly' (116). This is not the 'judicious slaying' Griffin boasted of making when he insisted on establishing his Reign of Terror; it is a 'wanton killing' (110). If he is sociopathic, he is almost psychopathic too. Even the insane moral code to which this monomaniac adheres has collapsed.

Having been driven outside the city's boundaries, the Invisible Man is hunted through the surrounding countryside and brutally killed. This is, in effect, a sacrificial ritual of social purification collectively performed by the community. The novel's protagonist, or antagonist, fulfils the classic function of the scapegoat, whom Terry Eagleton categorizes, in his study of tragedy, as 'a holy terror', a 'guilty innocent'.[10] 'As if by irresistible gravitation towards the unpleasant,' explained one of Wells's most appreciative contemporaries, the campaigning journalist W. T. Stead, when he came to recapitulate its remorseless plot, 'the invisible man passes through a series of disastrous experiences, until finally he goes mad and is beaten to death as the only way of putting an end to a homicidal maniac with the abnormal gift of invisibility.'[11]

If the reader, like Stead, recognizes the inevitability of the Invisible Man's sacrifice, they ultimately feel a certain compassion for him too. Fear and hatred of the scapegoat, as expressed by the characters he encounters in the course of his flight, are in the end transformed by his death into pity; and this identification with the scapegoat, in Eagleton's formulation, ultimately articulates 'horror not of it but of the social order whose failure it signifies'.[12]

Like the pioneering science fictions that Wells published before and after it, *The Invisible Man* exploited topical scientific debate as the basis for an enduring myth about the moral and social consequences of those Promethean aspirations that, at both an individual and collective level, were shaping and reshaping industrial capitalist society. In his review in the *Bookman*, Clement Shorter recognized this when he pointed to the grim 'pessimism' permeating its moral claim that, as he put it in deliberately understated tones, 'scientific experiment never makes the world any better or happier.' He also observed, with considerable relish, that Wells writes 'horrible little stories about monsters'.[13]

The Invisible Man is, in the first instance, a critique of scientism (as the late nineteenth-century conviction that scientific method alone holds the key to understanding the universe later came to be called). It built in particular on contemporary scientific debates about the invisible inspired by the German physicist Wilhelm Röntgen, who in 1895 accidentally discovered X-rays, sometimes known at this time as the 'photography of the invisible'.[14] In *The Invisible Man*, as one critic has underlined, Griffin 'acts out the nightmare that X-rays created in the Victorian imagination', applying it for purely individualistic purposes that quickly become collectively destructive.[15]

To appropriate Marx's allegorical image of the bourgeois class itself in the nineteenth century, he resembles 'the sorcerer, who is no longer able to control the powers of the nether world which he has called up by his spells'.[16] A descendent of the scientist at the centre of Mary Shelley's *Frankenstein* (1818), then, like his close cousins the Time Traveller and Dr Moreau, Wells's anti-hero is thus a distinctly 'Modern Prometheus'.[17]

If Wells's novel is a critique of scientism, it is also an anatomy of power, especially in the conditions of industrial and metro-politan modernity. At the moment the Invisible Man first grasps a scientific means of altering the refractive index of his body's fabric in order to make it completely transparent, he glimpses 'a magnificent vision of all that Invisibility might mean to a man. The mystery, the power, the freedom' (83). The Invisible Man's dream of escaping both the social and technical constraints of his time and the limits of the human form itself, in pursuit of an impossible power and freedom, is of course an ancient one.

John Sutherland, who has pointed to the plentiful presence of 'the invisibility motif' in popular literature of the nineteenth century, especially ghost stories and what he calls '*elixir vitae* fantasies', notes that the 'primeval origins' of the Invisible Man plot 'are buried deep in pre-literate myth and infantile fantasies of omnipotence'.[18] It is a staple feature of fairy tales, such as *Jack the Giant-Killer*, as well as of Greek legends, including the story of Perseus, who uses the helmet of invisibility given him by Athena in order to elude the vengeful Gorgons after he has killed their sister Medusa. But as a means of anatomizing power – both its dynamics and its ethics – the invisibility motif also has an ancient literary and philosophical provenance.

'An Invisible Man is a man of power,' Griffin states at one point (43). In composing *The Invisible Man*, Wells undoubtedly recalled an important episode in Plato's *Republic*, a philosophical work that acted, he later said, as 'a very releasing book indeed for my mind' when he first encountered it as an adolescent in the early 1880s.[19] In Book II of the *Republic*, Glaucon recounts the legend of Gyges, a shepherd who discovers a magic ring, in order to argue that if an individual suddenly acquires the gift of invisibility, and in effect becomes free to act with impunity, he will be unable to resist the temptation to 'go about among men with the powers of a god'.[20] Here, more explicitly than in other ancient versions of the legend, the metaphorical value of invisibility pivots on the moral implications of using and abusing power.

In *The Invisible Man* Wells was probably also thinking of Christopher Marlowe's *Dr Faustus* (c.1594), which at one point presents something like a dramatization of Glaucon's provocative claim. There, Faustus impishly abuses the Pope and his Cardinals after Mephistophilis has rendered him invisible. 'Sweet Mephistophilis,' Faustus cajoles his master, 'so charm me here / That I may walk invisible to all, / And do what e'er I please unseen of any.'[21] Here, in a sense, is the apotheosis of the Baudelairean *flâneur*, whose passion is 'to see the world, to be at the centre of the world, and yet to remain hidden from the world'. In Baudelaire's words, he is 'a *prince* who everywhere rejoices in his incognito'.[22]

As this reference to Baudelaire intimates, Wells deliberately embedded this Faustian dream of freedom, mobility and divine potency in the specific conditions of industrial and metropolitan capitalist society at the end of the nineteenth century. For, in attempting to emancipate himself from his physical form, Griffin presses to an apparently utopian extreme the social or spiritual condition that Georg Simmel, identifying the individual's attempt to preserve their autonomy 'in the face of overwhelming social forces' as the central challenge of 'modern life', classified in terms of the 'intellectualistic' mentality characteristic of the metropolis:[23]

> The metropolitan type of man – which, of course, exists in a thousand individual variants – develops an organ protecting him against the threatening currents and discrepancies of his external environment which would uproot him. He reacts with his head instead of his heart. ... Intellectuality is thus seen to preserve subjective life against the overwhelming power of metropolitan life.[24]

Before Griffin realizes that, in practice, his invisibility will also constitute a disability, forcing him to go naked and defenceless on foot among the streets of the city, he momentarily seems to have redeemed the alienated condition of what Wells, in a phrase that was fashionable at the *fin de siècle*, refers to in the novel as the 'urban brain-worker' (21). This is the metropolitan archetype famously diagnosed as 'neurasthenic' by the American psychologist George Miller Beard in the 1880s; one whose relationship to his body, as a result of being imbricated in modern forms of urban labour, has become more alienated and attenuated the more his mental life has been developed over and above his physical activity.[25]

Wells had himself faced precisely this existential challenge when, impoverished and unemployed, he moved to London in 1888 and, as he testified in his *Experiment in Autobiography* (1934), found accommodation costing four shillings a week in 'a partitioned-off part of an attic' on Theobald's Road in Holborn, a far-from salubrious region of the capital at the time. In this 'period of stress', fruitlessly seeking jobs with 'scholastic agents', he 'ate at irregular intervals and economically', and was forced to find 'light, shelter and comfort' in the Reading Room of the British Museum. Wells discovered at this juncture that, although over the previous five years his brain had 'acquired as much, decided as much and was exercised as much as if it had been inside the skull of a university scholar', it was now 'so occupied with the immediate struggle for life, so near to hunger and exposure and so driven by material needs' that it seemed not to be developing at all.[26] In Simmel's terms, his 'intellectualistic' mentality provided both a refuge from this fraught situation and a retreat farther into it.

Wells openly explored the embattled relationship of the metropolis and mental life in his fiction of the Edwardian period. In *Tono-Bungay* (1909), for example, Wells's narrator, whose travails are manifestly based on his own youthful experiences, discovers with a shock, on arriving in London as a young man bursting with scientific ambition, that a metropolitan existence, in contrast to a provincial one, is necessarily anonymous and atomized, and that on the streets he is little more than a nonentity:

> I did not realise all this when I came to London, did not perceive how the change of atmosphere began at once to warp and distribute my energies. In the first place I became invisible. If I idled for a day, no one except my fellow students (who evidently had no awe of me) remarked it. No one saw my midnight taper; no one pointed me out as I crossed the street as an astonishing intellectual phenomenon. In the next place I became inconsiderable.[27]

As pedestrians, especially in the era of the rise of the automobile, individuals remain no more than unnoticed components of the mass of people. The most corrosive everyday condition of the narrator's alienation – as had been the case for the Invisible Man little more than a decade earlier – is a sense of being universally unnoticed and unseen.

'Wells, who knew from his unemployed period what it was like to wander London as an invisible man,' as one of his recent biographers has written, 'rejoices imaginatively at the revenge Griffin takes on an unappreciative world yet still makes it clear that his *alter ego* is a dangerous psychopath.'[28] Griffin transmutes the lonely condition of anonymity and invisibility in the streets of the metropolis, as he struggles to maintain his sense of intellectual potential, into something positive, glorifying his nonentity. He redeems his social invisibility in the form of physical invisibility. His powerlessness becomes the source of his power. In *The Invisible Man*, Wells thus literalizes the metaphor he later used to describe the narrator of *Tono-Bungay*.

But if, after successfully conducting his experiment on himself, Griffin briefly experiences a sense of evolutionary superiority over the rest of his species, as an *Übermensch* who appears almost to have transcended the limitations of bodily existence, his body itself promptly takes revenge on him for this attempt to escape its constraints. To put it in terms of *The Time Machine* (1895), Wells's first novel, the primitive Morlock in him takes revenge on the over-civilized Eloi. Dystopian realities irrupt into his utopian aspirations.

On first leaving the apartment where he has conducted his experiment, Griffin momentarily feels 'as a seeing man might do, with padded feet and noiseless clothes, in a city of the blind' (92). Seconds later, though, he realizes that – naked as he is so as not to betray his existence with clothes – it might not be so easy to 'revel in [his] extraordinary advantage' (92). The embattled *flâneur* is suddenly forced to struggle for existence in the face of hostile forces that threaten to drive him to a state of extinction.

On the busy streets of central London, his back is jabbed by a heavy basket, his ear grasped by a cabman, and his shoulder blade bruised by the shaft of a hansom cab; finally, his feet are

trampled by a stream of pedestrians. In the wintry conditions
of the capital, he then contracts the first of several persistent
colds, which as well as proving debilitating are inconvenient
because, comically, his sneezes reveal his hidden presence to
passers-by or, more fatally, to his pursuers. Thereafter, as Simon
James points out, Griffin's 'dreams of a bodiless existence as pure
mental abstraction' founder on his need for food; and his 'meg-
alomaniacal plans of world domination are compromised by his
simple needs to eat, sleep, and protect himself from the British
climate.'[29]

In *The Invisible Man*, Griffin reanimates and personifies a
Platonic dream of becoming pure intellect. Wells's novel therefore
dramatizes in tragicomic form its protagonist's doomed desire to
deny that his corporeal frame fatally impedes his intellectual and
spiritual ambitions. In striving to escape his body, the Invisible
Man imprisons himself in it. In trying to become superhuman,
he becomes subhuman. Fleeing on foot in the polluted streets of
the metropolis, he accumulates 'dirt about [his] ankles, floating
smuts and dust upon [his] skin' (101). Rain and fog, he realizes,
will not obscure him as it obscures ordinary people. Rain will
make him 'a watery outline, a glistening surface of a man – a
bubble' (101).

More devastatingly still, he intuits that he 'should be like a
fainter bubble in a fog, a surface, a greasy glimmer of humanity'
(101). He is a mere silhouette of a man, as empty, insubstantial
and vulnerable as an oily bubble of air.

The Invisible Man is in part, then, a cautionary tale about the fatal
dialectic of, on the one hand, intellectual and spiritual aspiration,
and, on the other, social and psychological alienation, that makes
and unmakes modern human identity. In this sense, the short fictions that it most closely resembles are not so much Wells's recent
'scientific romances' as the celebrated, near-mythical accounts of
the crisis or collapse of the bourgeois ego published at the *fin de
siècle* by Robert Louis Stevenson and Joseph Conrad – respectively, *The Strange Case of Dr Jekyll and Mr Hyde* (1886) and
Heart of Darkness (1899). For the metaphor of an Invisible Man
proves an extremely potent one for reconstructing the acutely

alienated, over-developed states of consciousness that interested Wells's contemporaries.

Take Stevenson's novel. There, it is Dr Jekyll's excessive faith in 'the trembling immateriality, the mist-like transience of this seemingly so solid body in which we walk attired' that, in a tragic irony, ends up affirming the beastly materiality of his body in the form of Mr Hyde. A decade later, it is as a result of this same antimony that Griffin dramatically 'cut[s] himself off from his kind' (114). Wells, indeed, appears deliberately to allude to *Dr Jekyll and Mr Hyde* in *The Invisible Man*. The scene in the latter where, because of Griffin's savage cruelty, 'a little child playing near [a] gateway was violently caught up and thrown aside, so that its ankle was broken' (115), irresistibly recalls the one in the former where Hyde, stumping along a street, callously collided with 'a girl of maybe eight or ten who was running as hard as she was able down a cross street' and 'trampled calmly over the child's body and left her screaming on the ground'.[30]

There is no more indisputable proof of the inhumanity of either of these monstrous men than their vindictively violent treatment of these anonymous children. *The Invisible Man* brilliantly captures the experience of becoming-inhuman, as it might be called, which is a consequence, as in the case of Dr Jekyll, of simultaneously aspiring to a condition that is more than human and lapsing into one that is less than human.

If Griffin hopes that, by becoming invisible, he will transform himself from a nobody into a somebody, he ultimately realizes that he has merely transformed himself into a 'nothingness' (33). Conrad, who subsequently dedicated *The Secret Agent* (1907) to Wells, and who probably based the terrifying character of the Professor in this novel on Griffin, instinctively grasped that *The Invisible Man* was about the competing impulses that, in both reaching beyond the body and relentlessly relapsing into it, tear apart the subject at the turn of the twentieth century.[31]

In a letter to Wells from December 1898, Conrad emphasized that what had impressed him about *The Invisible Man* was that it had contrived 'to give over humanity into the clutches of the Impossible and yet manage to keep it down (or up) to its humanity, to its flesh, blood, sorrow, folly'.[32] Like the protagonists of

Stevenson's and Conrad's roughly contemporaneous fables, the Invisible Man is divided between a dream of the impossible and the everyday reality of the desiring, grieving, sickening body. Conrad's hesitation between 'up' and 'down' in this expressive but syntactically rather complicated sentence is symptomatic of the competing, contradictory relationship between the superhuman and the subhuman in Wells's novella.

What of *Heart of Darkness*? Kurtz, the horrifying character at its centre, is in the narrator Marlow's account one of those rare, remarkable men who has stepped over 'the threshold of the invisible'. He is, moreover, 'hollow at the core'.[33] In spite of *The Invisible Man*'s initially light, playful tone, its narrative too finally derives its force from an apprehension of the emptiness and horror at the heart of the individual subject's sense of self. Indeed, paradoxically, it is precisely its refusal to reproduce the intricate operations of consciousness, in contrast to novels published by Henry James and others at this time, that it mimes so effectively the 'crisis of interiority' that was such a significant feature of the *fin de siècle*.[34]

The novel's commitment to surface over depth, narrative over characterization, thus registers Wells's sense of the crisis of interiority at the level of form as well as content. Rachel Bowser is right to argue both that *The Invisible Man* 'invites the reader to interrogate the promise of deep interiority as offered by realist fiction', and that its protagonist's experiences 'expose the fiction of authentic interiority'.[35]

Wells returned to the horror of formlessness, the horror of emptiness, in *The History of Mr Polly* a little over a decade later. There, in a provincial context as opposed to the colonial one explored by Conrad, his narrator reports that, as a result of a peculiarly petty commercial rivalry, 'Mr Polly felt himself the faintest underdeveloped simulacrum of man that had ever hovered on the verge of non-existence.' Mr Polly, it should be noted, is a reader of Conrad ('Conrad's prose had a pleasure for him that he was never able to define, a peculiar, deep-coloured effect'). It is only when he acts heroically in a house-fire which he himself has started, in an attempt to commit suicide, that he feels alive; and that the empty space inside him for a moment seems to be filled. One of his neighbours, not realizing he is an arsonist and agreeing with the popular consensus that he 'ought to have a medal', declares 'that Mr Polly had a crowded and richly decorated interior' – a deliciously suburban celebration of an individual's inner life. 'It was as if he regretted past intimations that Mr Polly was internally defective and hollow,' comments the narrator.[36]

From the perspective afforded by the late nineteenth- and early twentieth-century novel's forensic concerns with what might be characterized, in the terms of Conan Doyle's contemporaneous detective fiction, as 'The Case of the Disappearing Subject', the Invisible Man is one of those whom T. S. Eliot subsequently designated 'Hollow Men'.[37] In Eliot's poem of that name – which takes the first of its epigraphs, '*Mistah Kurtz – he dead,*' from *Heart of Darkness* – he delineates this condition of desolation in these sad, if not despairing tones: 'Shape without form, shade without colour, / Paralysed force, gesture without motion.'[38] The Hollow Man, Eliot's archetype of emptiness, has in Wellsian terms lowered his refractive index to the zero degree.

As Griffin instinctively understands when he imagines himself walking on the streets of the anonymous city in the rain and fog, he is finally no more than the 'glistening surface of a man', a 'greasy glimmer of humanity' (101).

Echoing Eliot's description of Marlowe's strange play *The Jew of Malta* (c.1590), Bernard Bergonzi once classified *The Invisible Man* as a 'tragic farce', and compared its protagonist to Barabas, Marlowe's homicidal anti-hero, because he is 'both farcical and murderous'.[39] It is a useful attempt to explicate the concept of the 'grotesque romance', which is the subtitle of Wells's novel.

To this end, it might also be productive to conceptualize *The Invisible Man* in terms of Northrop Frye's category, in his *Anatomy of Criticism*, of the 'demonic parody', which he outlines as part of his account of the archetypes that shape the 'apocalyptic conception of human life'. 'In the sinister human world one individual pole is the tyrant-leader, inscrutable, ruthless, melancholy, and with an insatiable will,' Frye argues; 'the other pole is represented by the *pharmakos* or sacrificial victim, who has to be killed to strengthen the others.' He concludes that 'in the most concentrated form of the demonic parody, the two become the same'.[40] The Invisible Man, a character from this generic tradition, is at once a 'tyrant-leader' and a 'sacrificial victim'.

Frye's categories certainly capture the novel's unstable compound of humour and horror; but they probably don't give shape to the development or displacement *The Invisible Man* describes, over the course of its structure, from the comic to the tragic. For there is an irreversible darkening of the book's mood about two thirds of the way through the narrative, at the precise point at which the Invisible Man, in his doomed attempt to solicit assistance from a former university acquaintance, a sober-minded professional scientist called Dr. Kemp, who will shortly betray him to the police, commences in his own voice to recount the events that have led to the present, catastrophic situation.

From this moment on, when the action shifts for a time from Sussex to central London, and from the present to the past, Griffin comes to seem increasingly tragic. Then, when the plot reverts again to the present, and to the ever more frenzied efforts of the Invisible Man to escape the forces of justice that are closing in on him throughout the countryside, the sense of tragedy deepens. No longer a tragic farce, it is finally a grimly farcical tragedy.

There are hints of this tragedy, though, which hinges on Griffin's horrifying nihilistic condition, well before that point. It is intermittently present in the somewhat comic scenes set in and around the rural communities of South-East England in the first eighteen chapters of *The Invisible Man*. From the instant Griffin falls 'out of infinity into Iping village', as the narrator puts it with superb economy of expression, a sense of the void, of non-being, intrudes on the ordinary and the everyday (14).

The appearance of the stranger, whose head is wrapped in white bandages, whose eyes are screened by 'inscrutable blank glasses', and whose mouth and jaws are covered by a white cloth, is from the start unsettling as well as ridiculous (7). He is a 'strange man', as the title of the opening chapter indicates, as well as a stranger; 'an unusually strange sort of stranger' (13). An alien.

The local clock-mender, Mr Henfrey, encountering him in the parlour of the pub soon after his appearance in Iping, comments that he is 'like a lobster' (10). Mrs Hall, Griffin's landlady, insists that he looks 'more like a divin' 'elmet than a human man!' (8). That night, moreover, she has a nightmare about 'huge, white heads like turnips, that came trailing after her, at the end of interminable necks, and with vast black eyes' (13). Not a 'human man', then, but an inhuman man. It is the Invisible Man's grotesque physical appearance, however absurd in its associations, that conducts the creeping horror that overtakes the book.

And it is above all the intimations of empty space beneath the Invisible Man's peculiar surface appearance that prove horrifying. When Mrs Hall delivers a tray of food to Griffin's bedroom, where he has ensconced himself with his scientific equipment the day after his arrival, she suddenly notices he has removed his spectacles and failed to replace them: 'they were beside him on the table, and it seemed to her that his eye sockets were extraordinarily hollow' (16). Here is the Hollow Man.

Later that afternoon, the carter Mr Fearenside reports that, when his suspicious dog bit Griffin, for a second he 'seed through the tear of his trousers and the tear of his glove' (18). Instead of the pale pink flesh he expected to see, he explains, there was nothing: 'Just blackness' (18). This is a glimpse into infinity in Iping. Fearenside rationalizes this experience by determining that, far from being the albino the reader knows him to be, Griffin is in fact a black man – 'I tell you, he's as black as my hat' (18). Or, on further reflection, that he is 'a piebald' or 'a kind of half-breed' (18). Griffin's identity as an outsider, ironically underpinned by his albinism, is cemented by these racialized associations, which are erroneous but revealing.

Fearenside fails of course to understand that the blackness beneath the stranger's clothing is in fact that of blank space (the association of blackness and blankness is subsequently underlined when the narrator describes the Invisible Man as 'staring more blackly and blankly than ever' [29]). Mr Henfrey had himself unconsciously mimed or replicated the emptiness of the Invisible Man's interior when, in Chapter 2, he mended the clock in the parlour where Griffin, mysteriously muffled in his disguise, sat by the fire on taking refuge in the pub. Henfrey, the narrator reports, not only took off the hands and face of the clock, but 'removed the works' (12).

Is a clock without its face, hands and works still a clock? Is a
man whose face, hands and body are invisible still a man? This
is the metaphysical question that Wells implicitly poses at this
point. In the meantime, as Henfrey pretends to tinker with the
clock, he looks up at Griffin and is promptly paralyzed by the
sight of 'the bandaged head and huge blue lenses staring fixedly'
at him: 'It was so uncanny to Henfrey that for a minute they
remained staring blankly at one another' (12). In a double sense,
the Invisible Man has a blank look.

It is in this chapter that Mrs Hall too first intuits, in addition to
his strangeness, the stranger's monstrous blankness. On entering
the parlour in order to warn her guest that the clock-mender is
about to interrupt his privacy, she catches Griffin at a moment
when, thinking himself alone, he has lowered the white cloth
that covers his invisible mouth and chin. The room is dark, her
eyes are dazzled by the lamp that she has just lit, and he quickly
screens himself again; 'but for a second it seemed to her that
the man she looked at had an enormous mouth wide open – a
vast and incredible mouth that swallowed the whole of the lower
portion of his face' (10).

This terrifying, self-cannibalizing mouth is a fragment of infinity that takes a ravenous bite out of the everyday. Like the mouth
in Edvard Munch's *The Scream*, first painted in 1893, it threatens
to contort or warp the world of which it is part (in Lacanian
terms, it denotes the presence of the Real). The holes in Griffin's bandaged head, like the 'vast black eyes' of the 'huge, white
heads' about which Mrs Hall had dreamed one night, are portals
or tunnels into the void (13). The bandages conceal nothing less
than the Invisible Man's non-being. Nothing less than nothing.

Mr Cuss, the Iping village doctor, who is 'devoured by curiosity', according to the narrator, and consequently desperate to see
what lies beneath the stranger's bandages, is shocked to discover
that nothing at all keeps the Invisible Man's sleeve 'up and open':
'There was nothing in it, I tell you.' 'I could see right down it to
the elbow,' he adds, 'and there was a glimmer of light shining
through a tear of the cloth' (23). It is as if he fears that he will
himself be devoured by this void. The vacant sleeve is a tear in
the fabric of the universe.

A couple of chapters later – in 'The Unveiling of the Stranger' – it becomes impossible for the inhabitants of Iping to suppress their glimpse into nothingness. Exasperated by Mrs Hall's repeated complaints about his inexplicable activities, especially at night, Griffin resolves to shock both her and the other local people assembled in the public bar into silence: 'Then he put his open palm over his face and withdrew it. The centre of his face became a black cavity' (33). He has removed his false nose.

Performing a grotesque striptease, he takes off his disguise piece by piece – hat, spectacles, false hair, and bandages. 'Everyone began to move. They were prepared for scars, disfigurements, tangible horrors – but *nothing*!' The residents of Iping scramble to escape. 'For the man who stood there shouting some incoherent explanation was a solid, gesticulating figure up to the coat-collar of him, and then – nothingness, no visible thing at all!' (33). His entire head is a black cavity.

Beneath the bandages and clothes that constitute the Invisible Man's concession to the everyday functioning of symbolic reality in society there is only the void. There is nothing behind the veil of appearances. Once he has stripped naked in order to elude his pursuers, and so reduced himself to a 'voice coming as if out of empty space', it is only his speech that protects him and others from a direct, traumatic encounter with the emptiness of his being (35). With the Real.

But, at the same time, this disembodied voice adverts to the empty space from which – as in the sound emanating from the recently invented phonograph – it appears to come. In Chapter 9, when Griffin first encounters the vagrant Thomas Marvel, a fellow itinerant or tramp whom he forces to become a reluctant sorcerer's apprentice, the narrator refers to the Invisible Man throughout as 'the Voice'. 'The voice as a fetish object,' the philosopher Mladen Dolar has written in an enigmatic but suggestive sentence, 'consolidates on the verge of the void.'[41] Or, as the narrator of *The History of Mr Polly* puts it, 'on the verge of non-existence'.[42]

At the end of the novel, shortly before Griffin's gruesome demise, a rumour circulates through the countryside about a disembodied voice, heard by a couple of labourers, which 'drove up across the middle of a clover field and died away towards the hills': 'It was wailing and laughing, sobbing and groaning, and ever and again it shouted' (118). In this strange acoustic image, the Invisible Man's voice seems to slide or dissolve into the void.

It is probably in Chapter 9 – when, after escaping Iping, he recruits Marvel to assist him in his attempt merely to subsist or survive – that the reader of *The Invisible Man* starts to perceive Griffin not simply as someone to be feared but someone to be pitied.

'I am just a human being – solid, needing food and drink, needing covering too,' he appeals to the tramp, who is sitting beside a road on the South Downs contemplating his ill-fitting boots. 'But I'm invisible' (42). If his motives for persuading Marvel to help him are in one sense cynically self-serving, in another they are a matter of the most fundamental human survival. 'I was wandering, mad with rage, naked, impotent,' he confesses (42).

Griffin on the Downs thus echoes King Lear on the Heath. In Lear's terms, the Invisible Man is 'the thing itself'; 'a poor, bare, forked animal'. He is 'unaccommodated man', like all those whom Shakespeare's protagonist hails as having 'houseless heads and unfed sides'.[43] Griffin claims at least that the reason he stopped to communicate with Marvel, when he could have murdered him, is because he felt a sense of solidarity with his rootless condition: '"Here," I said, "is an outcast like myself"' (43). Both men, aimlessly travelling on foot, are fugitives from society.

As the allusion to Shakespeare's tragedy implies, the Invisible Man is portrayed more and more as a tragic anti-hero. The decisive shift from the farcical to the tragic, in Chapter 19, occurs when Griffin begins to narrate his past experiences to Kemp in his own voice. From this point, he is pitiful as well as both ludicrous and atrocious. Of course, when he confesses that he stole from his father in order to fund his necromantic research into invisibility, and that this precipitated his father's suicide, it transmits a shock. But, if he appears to have been a sociopath during this period, his description of the emotional dissociation he experienced nonetheless elicits sympathy from the reader.

He describes in Chapter 20 how, rousing himself from his obsessive scientific labours in order to attend his father's miserable, shabby funeral, 'I was like a man emerging from a thicket, and suddenly coming on some unmeaning tragedy' (84). Here is Griffin, once again, as a Hollow Man; as someone whose capacity for feeling has been almost completely emptied out, someone whose humanity has been almost completely erased. It is not merely that his parent's death, and the social rituals that commemorate it, seem meaningless; he himself, he intuits, is meaningless. *The Invisible Man* itself is in this sense not so much an unmeaning tragedy as a tragedy of unmeaning. A tragedy of meaning, and embodying, nothing.

'He was certainly an intensely egotistical and unfeeling man,' Wells's narrator later remarks of the Invisible Man (118). In Chapter 20, it is Griffin's startling lack of sympathy, ironically, that secures the reader's empathy. His apparently callous account of returning to his former home, his father's house, in a 'place that had once been a village and was now patched and tinkered by the jerry builders into the ugly likeness of a town', is oddly moving (84). He is a casualty, here, of the relentless forces of capitalist modernization.

Griffin is a man who, profoundly alienated from the everyday conditions of industrial capitalist society to which he feels condemned, in part because of the 'frightful disadvantages' under which he must pursue his unorthodox scientific research, is suffering from an acute state of anomie (82). 'I remember myself as a gaunt, black figure, going along the slippery, shiny sidewalk, and the strange sense of detachment I felt from the squalid respectability, the sordid commercialism of the place' (84). This cold-blooded 'black figure', whose albino features have been obliterated by the gloom, is transformed soon after the funeral into an almost bloodless, transparent figure. Ingesting 'drugs that decolourise blood', he undergoes 'a night of racking anguish'. Finally, he informs Kemp, 'I became insensible, and woke languid in the darkness' (89). It is an existential alchemy. Griffin's insensibility, it might be said, in addition to his social nonentity, is the basis of his invisibility.

Griffin's identity as an outcast, which his temporary accommodation in an unfurnished room in a slum on Great Portland Street confirms, is dramatically reconfirmed as soon as he leaves this lodging once he has successfully conducted his experiment on himself. Naked on the muddy roads around Oxford Street, on a freezing cold January day, he first assumes the form of that poor, bare, forked animal which will later implore Marvel for assistance in the Sussex countryside. 'I was now cruelly chilled,' he explains to Kemp, 'and the strangeness of my situation so unnerved me that I whimpered as I ran' (93).

Leaving the 'ghost of a foot' in the mud, feeling increasingly desperate, Griffin is chased through Bloomsbury in his bare feet by a group of inquisitive boys. Homeless, he is at the mercy of the elements and of the city's hostility to outsiders: 'My sole object was to get shelter from the snow, to get myself covered and warm, then I might hope to plan. But even to me, an Invisible Man, the rows of London houses stood latched, barred, and bolted impregnably' (96).

So he conceals himself in a department store, Omniums on Tottenham Court Road, for the night. In the metropolis, there is no one to whom he can appeal for help. 'I knew too clearly the terror and brutal cruelty my advances would evoke' (96).

The Invisible Man in effect converts the 'terror and brutal cruelty' that other pedestrians employ as a defensive strategy into his own offensive strategy. Later in his act of narration, which lasts for several chapters, Griffin announces to Kemp his intention of implementing a Reign of Terror, a 'brutal dream of a terrorised world' (115). Then, when he realizes that, even though he has taken his former friend into his confidence, Kemp has betrayed him to the police, he is forced to flee again. 'He is mad,' Kemp declares; 'inhuman' (113).

It is Kemp who supervises the manhunt with which the narrative concludes. This professional scientist, the source of Griffin's *ressentiment*, directs the police to 'set a watch on trains and roads and shipping' (113). And he issues a proclamation that presents the Invisible Man not simply as 'a legend' but 'as a tangible antagonist, to be wounded, captured, or overcome' (115). As the plot accelerates, mounted police enforce a curfew throughout the countryside. In a twenty-mile circle around Port Burdock, where Griffin is assumed to be in hiding, groups of 'men armed with guns and bludgeons' set out with dogs 'to beat the roads and fields' (116).

The narrator refers to them as 'men-hunters'; and he concludes with some compassion that, though Griffin was soon 'active, powerful, angry and malignant again', 'he was a hunted man' (118).

According to the philosopher Grégoire Chamayou, there are two kinds of manhunt, 'a hunt of pursuit and a hunt of expulsion', but these distinct operations have a complementary relationship: 'hunting human beings, tracking them down, often presupposes that they have been previously chased out, expelled, or excluded from a common order.'[44] The Invisible Man's identity as the object of a manhunt that seeks to capture or kill him is predicated on his prior social exclusion – as an albino, as a dissident scientist, and as a sort of man without content.[45]

For a time, the Invisible Man manages to reverse the apparently implacable logic of the manhunt. He besieges Kemp's home in a bid for revenge, before chasing him through the countryside on foot. Sprinting desperately along the hill-roads, Kemp hears the 'swift pad of his pursuer' behind him (129). In the end, however, it is Griffin who is entrapped by his pursuers, even though at this point he remains invisible.

The final chapter is entitled 'The Hunter Hunted'. At the climax of the narrative, a 'heap of struggling men' consisting of navvies, police constables and a tram conductor savagely wrestles the invisible form of Griffin to the ground. 'Kemp clung to him in front like a hound to a stag, and a dozen hands gripped, clutched, and tore at the unseen.' Savagely beaten, and bleeding badly from a wound inflicted by a spade, the Invisible Man emits 'a wild scream of "Mercy, mercy!" that died down swiftly to a sound like choking' (130).

At the culmination of this manhunt, a mob encircles 'the thing unseen', which is held fast by its 'invisible arms' and 'invisible ankles' (130). Griffin's mouth, which Kemp feels with groping hands as he kneels beside him, is wet with blood: the Invisible Man is dying.

Suddenly, an elderly woman screams and points; and, 'faint and transparent as though it was made of glass, so that veins and arteries and bones and nerves could be distinguished,' the people assembled perceive 'the outline of a hand'. It becomes increasingly 'clouded and opaque'. Then the rest of the Invisible Man's body gradually materializes: 'First came the little white nerves, a hazy grey sketch of a limb, then the glassy bones and intricate arteries, then the flesh and skin, first a faint fogginess and then growing rapidly dense and opaque' (131).

It is an eerie metamorphosis; a coming to life in death. The monstrous terrorist who has menaced the nation, as a tyrant both superhuman and subhuman, can finally be seen in his entirety, and in his humanity. 'When at last the crowd made way for Kemp to stand erect, there lay, naked and pitiful on the ground, the bruised and broken body of a young man about thirty' (131). He really is nothing more than the poor, bare, forked creature he had claimed to be when he first encountered Marvel. Once he has been covered with a sheet, he is lifted from the ground and carried into a nearby pub. 'And there, on a shabby bed in a tawdry, ill-lighted bedroom, ended the strange experiment of the Invisible Man' (131).

In his sordidly commonplace experience of dying, this homeless, hunted, battered man is wholly emblematic of the ordinary humanity he dreamed of transcending. This is what Arnold Bennett meant when, in his review of Wells's novel, he remarked that 'the last few pages are deep tragedy, grotesque but genuine.'[46]

The pathos of the painful process of becoming-human described in the final paragraphs of *The Invisible Man* is reinforced rather than undermined by his anomalous physical appearance: 'His hair and brow were white – not grey with age, but white with the whiteness of albinism' (131). His albino features signify, as we have seen, his outsider status, but at the Invisible Man's death they are also symbolic of a redemptive purity. Indeed, as his age and his 'broken body' indicate, Griffin is implicitly Christ-like at the end.

'Cover his face!' a nameless man cries out after he has died, in a revealing addition Wells made to the first American and second British editions of *The Invisible Man*, both published in 1897. The man's exclamation is an attempt to shield the children present from the ghastly expression of 'anger and dismay' that contorts the dead man's features (131). But it also echoes the scene in St Mark's Gospel when, after Christ's arrest and shortly before his crucifixion, the high priest of the Sanhedrin pronounces him guilty and rends his clothes: 'And some began to spit on him, and to cover his face, and to buffet him' (Mark 14:63, 65).

Here, Christ is performing the ancient role of the scapegoat: the deformed, polluted creature that is sacrificed in order ritually to cleanse and purify the community from which it has been expelled. Griffin too performs the tragic role of society's scapegoat. 'The whole point of the scapegoat', Eagleton has insisted, 'is its anonymity, as a human being emptied of subjectivity and reduced to refuse or nothingness.'[47] The Invisible Man – who aspired to a state of nothingness, in the form of invisibility, and has been reduced to nothingness, as his shabby death indicates – is precisely this human being emptied of subjectivity. His social function at the end of the narrative is to constitute the non-being that symbolically secures the community's sense of belonging. In an atomized industrial society defined by what he had referred to as 'sordid commercialism', Griffin's identity as an alien is in the end the precondition for a renewed sense of social cohesion (84).

Like Dracula, then, and like Frankenstein's demon, the Invisible Man 'serves to displace the antagonisms and horrors evidenced *within* society *outside* society itself', to adapt Franco Moretti's formulation. 'Professing to save the individual,' Moretti continues, the society that destroys the monster 'in fact annuls him'.[48] *The Invisible Man* represents a forensic attempt, in the specific conditions of the *fin de siècle*, to investigate the meanings of this annulation, or annihilation, or nihilation, of the individual subject.

In 'The First Wells' (1946), an essay by Jorge Luis Borges on 'the excellence of Wells's first novels', the ones written before he 'resigned himself to the role of a sociological spectator', the great Argentine modernist insisted that 'not only do they tell an ingenious story but they tell a story symbolic of processes that are somehow inherent in all human destinies.' Borges singled out *The Invisible Man* as especially important among these scientific romances.[49]

Above all, Borges seems to have valued this novel for its evocation of the individual's fundamental emptiness, futility and isolation. Although he misremembered its details slightly, he summarized the novel in these haunting terms: 'The harassed invisible man who has to sleep as though his eyes were wide open because his eyelids do not exclude light is our solitude and our terror.'[50] Almost forty years later, in 1985, not long before his death, Borges reaffirmed that 'Wells's fictions were the first books that [he] read', and concluded his reflections on *The Invisible Man* in these terms: 'In Wells, the poignant is as important as the fabulous. His invisible man is a symbol – one that will last a long time – of our solitude.'[51]

The condition of solitude and terror evoked by Borges is that of an individual compelled to stare into the void lodged like an irreducible fragment at the core of his being. It is a long way from the 'Perils of Invisibility' imagined by W. S. Gilbert, in the innocuous comic ballad of that name from 1870, which probably served as one of Wells's sources.[52] The perils of invisibility explored by Wells involve not simply physical vexation, or even social exclusion, but existential or spiritual annihilation. For Griffin, the *flâneur*'s princely incognito, which he had hoped to exploit with impunity, is replaced by the pauper's experience of precarity and radical non-entity.

The Invisible Man finally enacts the state of being, or non-being, experienced the previous year by the narrator of Wells's short story 'Under the Knife' (1896). This man speculates about his physical and metaphysical status, after apparently experiencing his own death, in the moment immediately before he starts to return to life:

> Were there other souls, invisible to me as I to them, about me in the blackness? or was I indeed, even as I felt, alone? Had I passed out of being into something that was neither being nor not-being? … Everything was black and silent. I had ceased to be. I was nothing. There was nothing, save only that infinitesimal dot of light that dwindled in the gulf. I strained myself to hear and see, and for a while there was naught but infinite silence, intolerable darkness, horror, and despair.[53]

Darkness, blackness, nothingness … This is the undead condition that the Invisible Man too inhabits. Except that he inhabits it not in abstract space but in the concrete conditions of metropolitan modernity at the end of the nineteenth century.

5

Wandering

G. K. Chesterton's
The Man Who Was Thursday

In the autumn of 1893, G. K. Chesterton enrolled at University College, London, in order to study at the Slade School of Fine Art, dominated at the time by the baleful influence, as he perceived it, of the American painter J. M. Whistler.

This was undoubtedly the unhappiest period of Chesterton's life, as he testified both in his *Autobiography* (1936) and, far more obliquely, in *The Man Who Was Thursday* (1908), a novel that is among other things a bizarre, dream-like allegory of the diabolism and nihilism that beset him as a student. In the mid-1890s, Chesterton experienced something like a spiritual or psychological collapse, one that was inseparable from his rejection of both Impressionism, the aesthetic then fashionable at the Slade, and the relativist philosophical implications it seemed to entail. What were these philosophical implications, precisely? Impressionism, the narrator of *The Man Who Was Thursday* declares, 'is another name for that final scepticism which can find no floor to the universe'.[1] Existential and epistemological doubts are thus intertwined.

Chesterton's dedicatory verse to his old school-friend E. C. Bentley, at the beginning of *The Man Who Was Thursday*, is a melancholy description of the spiritual sclerosis that he thought crippled society at the end of the nineteenth century. 'The world was very old indeed when you and I were young,' Chesterton intones, like a man who has himself aged prematurely because he has been fatally contaminated by the climate of decadence (xxxix). The Dedication is in part a re-inscription of Matthew Arnold's 'Dover Beach' (1867), a poem which had mourned the retreating roar of the 'Sea of Faith' on the 'naked shingles of the world', and, in muted apocalyptic tones, evoked 'a darkling plain / Swept with confused alarms of struggle and flight, / Where ignorant armies clash by night'.[2]

In the opening lines of the Dedication, Chesterton recalls the storm cloud of the 1890s, in rhetoric that is Ruskinian as well as Arnoldian, and paints an atmosphere of 'aimless gloom', illuminated only by the ghastly luminescence of the white streak that famously surmounted Whistler's dark head of hair. The prevailing mood of pessimism is 'a sick cloud upon the soul' (xxxix).

The *fin de siècle* that the Dedication depicts – in which 'Science announced nonentity and art admired decay' – is a nightmarish morality play in which Chesterton and Bentley have become trapped. 'Crippled vices', among them Lust and Fear, encircle these innocents 'in antic order' (xxxix). 'This is a tale of those old fears, even of those emptied hells,' he continues (xl). Nonetheless, the Dedication testifies to the fact that, thanks in part to 'some giants' who 'laboured in that cloud to lift it from the world', above all his heroes Robert Louis Stevenson and Walt Whitman, this nightmare has ended (xxxix).

Crippled vices, giants ... Chesterton inhabits the landscape of mediaeval legend. And, in this context, it is the archetypal romantic figure of the wandering knight, battling with his moral enemies on foot, who promises to bring redemption.

In his *Autobiography*, Chesterton emphasized that during the early 1890s, when decadence was in its ascendancy, 'the whole mood was overpowered and oppressed with a sort of congestion of the imagination.' He admits that he too was briefly infected by this condition: 'As Bunyan, in his morbid period, described himself as prompted to utter blasphemies, I had an overpowering impulse to record or draw horrible ideas and images; plunging deeper and deeper as in a blind spiritual suicide.'[3] Chesterton suffered, that is, from something like the aesthetic equivalent of

Tourette's Syndrome, or that variant of it, at least, that is characterized by the tendency to blurt out blasphemies or obscenities.

The monstrous ideas and images of *The Man Who Was Thursday*, which Chesterton subtitled 'A Nightmare', are thus traces of
his apparent inability, at the *fin de siècle*, to repress the impulse
to represent a state of incipient spiritual suicide. But his time
at the Slade was not completely despondent. The 'dark side of
his undergraduate years', as William Oddie has recently noted,
'was the obverse of an intellectually more productive and generally more cheerful aspect of the same period', which pivoted on
the courses that he took in both French and English Literature.[4]
Most importantly, Chesterton attended the lectures of W. P. Ker,
one of the pioneering architects of English Literature as a university subject, who exercised an important intellectual influence
on him.

In the Introduction to Ker's *Collected Essays* (1925), Charles
Whibley observed that Ker was 'at once scholar and wanderer':
'The word "adventure" was always on his tongue or at the point
of his pen.'[5] And the *Oxford Dictionary of National Biography* confirms that he 'always kept the spirit of an adventurer,
wandering far afield when the spirit really prompted, carrying
his students with him by his power of mind and temper'. In
the *Autobiography*, Chesterton expresses his gratitude for 'the
extraordinarily lively and stimulating learning of Professor W. P.
Ker' (61). He attended his lectures so loyally, in fact, that on one
occasion he 'had the honour of constituting the whole of Professor Ker's audience' (62).

Ker was a polymath, but his most significant contribution to
scholarship was probably in the field of mediaeval literature.
His first book, *Epic and Romance* (1897), drawing in part on
material used in lectures he delivered at UCL, was a panoramic
survey of Teutonic, Icelandic and French epic that identified the
rise of mediaeval romance, and its 'wandering champions', with
the decline of the heroic age – 'a change involving the whole
world, and going far beyond the compass of literature and literary history'.[6]

In another of his lectures at UCL, Ker emphasized that 'the
enormous and unfair advantage over other writers' that Rabelais,

Shakespeare and Cervantes all possessed, apart from their literary abilities, was their relationship to the Middle Ages:

> They had the whole abandoned region of medieval thought and imagination to take over and appropriate. Of course they saw the absurdity of it, but that was only one charm the more in their inheritance. They had all the profusion and complexity, all the strength and all the wealth of the Middle Ages to draw upon.[7]

It is this image of the 'whole abandoned region of medieval thought and imagination' that interests me here, because just such an abandoned region interested Chesterton, too, in all its absurdity, complexity and strength. 'Mankind has not passed through the Middle Ages,' Chesterton admonished his readership in 1910; 'rather mankind has retreated from the Middle Ages in reaction and rout.'[8] Even more bluntly, in the introduction to *Alarms and Discursions*, also published in 1910, where he celebrates his love of the grotesque, he makes 'the high boast that I am a mediaevalist and not a modern'.[9]

Central to Chesterton's recourse to mediaevalism, and the premodern forms of epic and romance that he learned to love at UCL, were the 'wandering champions' that Ker had identified in his book. He saw these champions as a means of redeeming the damaging legacies of Enlightenment rationalism, as exemplified during his own time in the Impressionist ethics and aesthetics he associated with the *fin de siècle*. These wanderers are agents of the exception that at once negatively constitutes the logic of Enlightenment rationalism and positively escapes its regime.

'Chesterton's aim', Slavoj Žižek has commented, is 'to *save reason through sticking to its founding exception*: deprived of this, reason degenerates into a blind self-destructive skepticism – in short: into total *irrationalism*.' Chesterton thus pits the irrational, in the form of the spiritual, against the irrationalism implicit in the imperial intellectual project that is Enlightenment rationalism. This was his 'basic insight and conviction,' Žižek continues: 'that the irrationalism of the late nineteenth century was the necessary consequence of the Enlightenment rationalist attack on religion'.[10] He preferred to affirm the pre-Enlightenment spirit of the Middle Ages. It is in this that what might be called his counter-modernism consists.

Chesterton's prose and verse, shaped by Ker's visions of the past, consistently praised the ethical example of the chivalric champion. Knights errant, itinerant in their movements and vagrant in their imaginations, but implacably committed to the spiritual salvation of an embattled, fallen universe, seemed to him to represent agents of moral regeneration in a society beset by cynicism and scepticism. Wandering, then, especially in the conditions of metropolitan modernity, was for Chesterton shaped by a spiritual vocation. Wandering is, in the chivalric sense, a kind of erring. Wanderring.

Chesterton's first novel, *The Napoleon of Notting Hill* (1904), a thought experiment that, perhaps all too programmatically, imagines 'a revival of the arrogance of the old mediaeval cities applied to our glorious suburbs', offers a revealing instance of his mediaevalism.[11] In his *Autobiography*, Chesterton describes the incident that inspired this strange romance, which took place close to his family home:

> I was one day wandering about the streets in that part of North Kensington, telling myself stories of feudal sallies and sieges, in the manner of Walter Scott, and vaguely trying to apply them to the wilderness of bricks and mortar around me. I felt that London was already too large and loose a thing to be a city in the sense of a citadel. It seemed to me even larger and looser than the British Empire. (68)

The metropolis, like the imperial project of which it is the geopolitical centre, is impossibly incoherent. Chesterton therefore needs some device, one derived from the traditions of epic and romance, both for comprehending and redeeming the 'wilderness of bricks and mortar' that is the industrial city.

At this point, Chesterton continues, his eye was suddenly arrested by a block of 'lighted shops', and he fantasized that 'they contained the essentials of civilisation': a chemist's, a bookshop, a shop for provisions, a public house; and, at the end, in echo of his hero Dickens, 'a curiosity shop bristling with swords and halberds'. Finally, he looked up and glimpsed, 'grey with distance, but still seemingly immense in altitude', the Waterworks tower that overlooked Notting Hill and Holland Park (68).

'It suddenly occurred to me', he concludes with a final flourish of his mediaevalist imagination, 'that capturing the Waterworks might really mean the military stroke of flooding the valley; and with that torrent and cataract of visionary waters, the first fantastic notion of a tale called *The Napoleon of Notting Hill* rushed over my mind' (68). In this book's Dedication, to his friend Hilaire Belloc, Chesterton characterized it as the 'legend of an epic hour', dreamed up 'Under the great grey water-tower / That strikes the stars on Campden Hill'.[12]

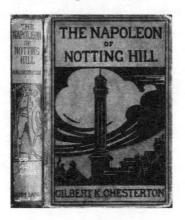

It is this industrial tower that, set against an apocalyptic sunset printed in red and black, illustrates W. Graham Robertson's imposing cover for the first edition of the novel. The Grand Junction Water Works Company, which had built a reservoir on the elevated ground at Campden Hill in the early 1840s, subsequently constructed both a pumping station and the tower to which Chesterton alludes. This tower, designed in a loosely Italianate style by Alexander Fraser in 1857 and 1858, played a significant part in the 'social landscape' of Chesterton's childhood, to use one of his formulations from the *Autobiography* (14).

This memoir opens with a reference to Chesterton's baptism, which took place 'in the little church of St. George opposite the large Waterworks Tower that dominated that ridge' (1). The church of St George's on Campden Hill, built in the so-called eclectic Gothic style with variegated patterns of brick and stone, was consecrated in 1864, as if to rebuke the hubristic Waterworks Tower. These two neo-mediaeval constructions – one religious, the other secular; one picturesque, the other an instance perhaps of the industrial sublime – were the totemic forms that shaped Chesterton's metropolitan imagination as an infant.

Chesterton confirms as much at the end of this chapter of the *Autobiography* when he explains how these structures imparted 'a visionary and symbolic character' to the cityscape of his childhood:

> In one way and another, those things have come to stand for so many other things, in the acted allegory of a human existence; the little church of my baptism and the waterworks, the bare, blind, dizzy tower of brick that seemed, to my first upward starings, to take hold upon the stars. Perhaps there was something in the confused and chaotic notion of a tower of water; as if the sea itself could stand on one end like a water-spout. Certainly later, though I hardly know how late, there came into my mind some fancy of a colossal water-snake that might be the Great Sea Serpent, and had something of the nightmare nearness of a dragon in a dream. And, over against it, the small church rose in a spire like a spear; and I have always been pleased to remember that it was dedicated to St. George. (14)

The emblematic image of a tower, symbolizing some sort of impossible spiritual quest, recurs again and again in Chesterton's writings during the 1900s. It is the point of the compass to which his knights errant angle their pennants. In *Orthodoxy*, for instance, in the course of what can be classified as an anti-Enlightenment defence of reason, he evokes a 'modern world' that, beset by rampant scepticism, is paradoxically 'at war with reason'; and concludes by declaring that 'the tower already reels'.[13] In 'The Advantages of Having One Leg', reflecting on the relationship between singularity and universality, Chesterton suggests rather more enigmatically that 'if you wish to symbolise human building, draw one dark tower on the horizon.' 'The poetry of art', he goes on, 'is in beholding the single tower.'[14]

In the 'wilderness of bricks and mortar' that are the streets around which he ambled when he dreamed up the narrative of *The Napoleon of Notting Hill*, an 'abandoned region' that lies open to the mediaevalist imagination, to paraphrase Ker's formulation, Chesterton is himself a kind of knight errant. That is, he is both a knight that travels or adventures and one that deviates or wanders. The adjective *errant*, as the *Oxford English Dictionary* indicates, originally comprised 'two distinct words, which, however, were to some extent confused in French'. The first of these words is derived from the Latin *errare*, meaning to stray; the second from the Old French *errer*, meaning to journey.

Chesterton, in effect, glorifies this confusion. For him, to travel is to deviate and to deviate is to travel. Indeed, the truth can only be attained by celebrating that which is subtly errant; the eccentric element that, in *Orthodoxy*, he characterizes as 'this silent swerving from accuracy by an inch that is the uncanny element in everything'. Nothing is absolutely symmetrical in the universe, and it is the slight deviations that matter to Chesterton. 'Everywhere in things there is this element of the quiet and incalculable,' he writes. 'It escapes the rationalists, but it never escapes till the last moment.'[15] The incalculable, the errant, is the basis of his critique of Enlightenment reason.

This is the Chestertonian dialectic. Reality lies in Elfland; and Elfland is to be located, like a second hidden city, in the streets of the modern metropolis. As the narrator of *The Napoleon of Notting Hill* comments, 'the boundary of fairyland runs through a crowded city.'[16] It is a sentiment the Swiss writer Robert Walser, Chesterton's almost exact contemporary, expressed in the voice of the eponymous narrator of *Jakob von Gunten* (1909): 'Often I go out onto the street, and there I seem to be living in an altogether wild fairytale.'[17]

The allegorical form of the chivalric quest, which appeared to Chesterton to encode the promise of spiritual emancipation, was for him one of the most significant legacies of Ker's 'abandoned region' of the Middle Ages. The knight's quest is a recurrent motif in Chesterton's work: 'But I, by God, would sooner be / Some knight in shattering wars of old', he writes in 'Vulgarised', a poem from 1900.[18] Under the influence of Robert Browning, one of his most important literary precursors, he attempts in his first published poems and in *The Man Who Was Thursday* to rethink the relevance of the quest to metropolitan modernity and to relocate its heroics to the terrain of the city's streets.

In a review of Chesterton's collection of stories entitled *The Man Who Knew Too Much* (1922), the anonymous critic of the *Observer* spotted that his detective fiction was indebted to Browning's poem 'Childe Roland to the Dark Tower Came' (1855). Chesterton's 'mind is so swift and sententious,' he remarked, 'his incidents are so apocalyptic, his characters such monstrous creatures of shadow, his scenery so reminiscent of Roland and the Dark Tower, that it is an intellectual adventure to follow the bewildering mazes of his imagination.'[19] Browning's dramatic monologue, one of the greatest poems of the nineteenth century, details the apprentice knight Roland's half-suicidal journey through a nightmarish landscape to the Tower, with its 'round squat turret, blind as the fool's heart'. Roland happens upon this tower, he tells us, 'in the very nick / Of giving up, one time more'.[20]

Browning's poems are studded with more or less minatory towers. A solitary tower, reclaimed by animal and vegetable life, is for instance all that remains of the barbaric warlord Alberic's castle in *Sordello* (1840). And there are a number of towers in his depictions of the Roman Campagna; one 'strange', another 'malicious', all of them enigmatic, resistant to meaning, and oddly threatening.[21] 'Love Among the Ruins' (1852), for example, a poem composed only two days before 'Childe Roland', features a solitary turret on the plains that 'Marks the basement whence a tower in ancient time / Sprang sublime'.[22] These ruined erections, traces of an imperial past, are suffixes of what Henri Lefebvre classified as 'the phallic formant', which is one of the basic permutations of abstract space: 'Metaphorically, it symbolizes force, male fertility, masculine violence.'[23]

Browning's towers, often in retreat from the profusion of organic life, are monuments to a regimen of political violence that, once omnipotent, has been fatally eroded by time. Bristling with abandoned towers, then, Browning's poems are built on 'ruined quests' as well as 'good moments', to use Harold Bloom's celebrated terms. The epiphanies he portrays are what Bloom calls 'vastations of quest'; and his 'darkest visions of failure', conversely, are 'celebrations'.[24]

'Childe Roland', with its enigmatic and ambiguous conclusion, is the supreme example of this. In Browning's treatment of the theme, the chivalric quest so closely resembles a desperate struggle simply to escape the spiritual horror of meaninglessness that it also appears to constitute the ruination of all quests. Only by confronting the failure of his quest, in the events narrated in the final stanzas, does Roland grasp the promise of success – although the fact that the final line of the poem loops the reader back to its title, 'Childe Roland to the Dark Tower Came', implies the possibility that this almost derelict knight is trapped in a cyclical structure from which he cannot ultimately escape. Perhaps, like the ancient Mariner, he is doomed endlessly to repeat a description of this pointless quest to anyone prepared to stop and listen to his guilt-ridden monologue.

Bloom argues that 'Childe Roland' is the supreme instance of the quest form emptying itself out. For Chesterton, implicitly, it is an example of the quest form being restored to its full significance. It is, according to him, a kind of test case of the reader's temperament or spiritual condition. When he discusses the poem in in his brilliant little biographical monograph on Browning, published in 1903, Chesterton pointedly expresses his frustration with readers who ask what it means. 'The only genuine answer to this', he expostulates, is 'What does anything mean?':

> Does the earth mean nothing? Do grey skies and wastes covered with thistles mean nothing? Does an old horse turned out to graze mean nothing? If it does, there is but one further truth to be added – that everything means nothing.[25]

For Chesterton, Browning's poem sets a sort of trap for the reader: if the reader assumes it is nihilistic, then they are themselves a nihilist, poised on the point of a spiritual suicide. Perhaps it is because rather than in spite of the fact that 'Childe Roland' superficially appears to be Browning's most pessimistic poem that it appealed to Chesterton. 'Childe Roland', for him, affirms the meaningfulness of the quest only by an abrupt and implausible leap of faith. 'All pessimism', Chesterton once wrote, 'has a secret optimism for its object.'[26]

In his concluding comments on 'Childe Roland', Chesterton praises it for being 'the hint of an entirely new and curious type of poetry, the poetry of the shabby and hungry aspect of the earth'. Chesterton effectively proposes that it represents the first truly post-Romantic poetry. For, unlike those poets who celebrated 'the poetry of rugged and gloomy landscapes', Browning 'insists upon celebrating the poetry of mean landscapes'.[27] The shift or displacement his poem describes is from the sublime to the grotesque.

Chesterton perceives in 'Childe Roland' the emergence of a poetics of the grotesque. Implicitly, the grotesque constitutes the first genuinely post-Romantic aesthetic. Standing in blunt contrast to Alfred Tennyson's contemporaneous Arthurian poems, with their idealization of imperial Britain, Browning's poem, festering as it is with images of corruption, triumphs in the demise of Romanticism. 'Childe Roland', Chesterton concludes with relish, is 'the song of the beauty of refuse; and Browning was the first to sing it'.[28] Here is a poetry of debris, rubbish and rejectamenta. And its characteristic landscape is a wasteland.

Perhaps Chesterton liked to think that he was the second to sing 'the beauty of refuse'. A number of the poems collected in *The Wild Knight and Other Poems* (1900) are indebted to 'Childe Roland'. Take 'The Pessimist', an intemperate attack on the ethics of the 1890s, which opens in these provocative terms: 'You that have snarled through the ages, take your answer and go –, / I know your hoary question, the riddle that all men know.'[29] The second of these lines alludes to the opening lines of 'Childe Roland': 'My first thought was, he lied in every word, / That hoary cripple ...'[30] Chesterton's poet is identified with Browning's knight; and this poet's pessimistic antagonist is implicitly identified with Browning's cripple, an accursed cynic standing at the roadside apparently attempting to deceive him and deter him from the quest.

In 'The Wild Knight', the volume's title poem, the poet is an embattled chivalric hero whose 'green, pale pennon', attached to

his spear, is a 'blazon of wild faith / And love of fruitless things'.
He journeys across an apocalyptic landscape where a cold wind
'blows across the plains, / And all the shrines stand empty'. The
object of this desperate knight's quest, it transpires, is not a
dark tower but a 'twisted path / Under a twisted pear-tree'. He
believes that there, precisely because of the 'strange-visaged blun-
ders' and 'mystic cruelties' he has suffered, he will finally come
to know God.

But, in the concluding lines, he admits for all his optimism that
this might be a dream: 'the grey clouds come down / In hail upon
the icy plains', and he rides 'Burning for ever in consuming fire'.[31]
Chesterton's poem finally seems to catalogue the poet's failure
both to redeem the darker ambiguities of Browning's dramatic
monologue and to affirm the Christian God to whom he longs to
accommodate himself.

'The Wild Knight' therefore charts some of the same territory
later mapped by T. S. Eliot's modernist epic *The Waste Land*
(1922) – a poem that is also shaped by the apocalyptic landscape
of 'Childe Roland'. The final section of Eliot's systematic critique
of the romance form offers febrile glimpses of 'the approach to
the Chapel Perilous', as the Notes to the poem summarize it,
in terms that recall both Browning's poem and, no doubt unin-
tentionally, Chesterton's. Eliot's 'empty chapel' itself, which is
discovered beside 'tumbled graves' where 'the grass is singing', is
in the end 'only the wind's home'.[32]

This section of *The Waste Land* is steepled with images of
shattered towers that stand out against the plains – from the
'Falling towers' of the great cities of ancient and modern civilization in the sixth stanza ('Jerusalem Athens Alexandria / Vienna
London'), to the towers that are 'upside down in air' and toll
'reminiscent bells' in the seventh. Ruined towers are one of Eliot's
central emblems for the collapse of contemporary Europe. The
final fragment of 'What the Thunder Said' quotes from Gérard de
Nerval's 'El Desdichado' (1854): '*Le Prince d'Aquitaine à la tour
abolie*', 'The Prince of Aquitaine, his tower in ruins'.[33]

If Chesterton is keen to demonstrate that 'Childe Roland' is
a 'new and curious type of poetry', then his interpretation of it
arguably renders it even newer and more curious; and it does so

by deliberately urbanizing it. The 'mean landscapes' that Chesterton has in mind are in the first instance those strange edgelands, in liminal regions of the city, that are neither picturesque nor sublime, and that don't as a result fit into the categories of aesthetics. Wastelands. 'That sense of scrubbiness in nature, as of a man unshaved,' Chesterton writes in relation to Browning's poem, 'had never been conveyed with this enthusiasm and primeval gusto before.'[34] This is an extraordinary and unexpected anthropomorphization. It brilliantly evokes the dishevelled, morally questionable atmosphere of the landscape described by Browning. And it has an oddly modernizing effect.

This becomes more apparent when Chesterton cites the twelfth stanza of 'Childe Roland':

> If there pushed any ragged thistle-stalk
> Above its mates, the head was chopped; the bents
> Were jealous else. What made those holes and rents
> In the dock's harsh swarth leaves, bruised as to balk
> All hope of greenness? 'tis a brute must walk
> Pashing their life out, with a brute's intents.[35]

Commenting on this stanza, with its tone of pinched, repetitious desperation, Chesterton notes that it is 'a perfect realisation of that eerie sentiment which comes upon us not so often among mountains and water-falls, as it does on some half-starved common at twilight, or in walking down some grey mean street'.[36]

Roland's landscape is a profoundly sinister but at the same time perfectly unsensational one; and it metamorphoses, in the course of Chesterton's comment, into a cityscape. Bloom perspicaciously notes that 'Roland describes his landscape like Zola describing an urban scene.'[37] Chesterton, too, brilliantly draws attention to the hidden urban dimension of 'Childe Roland', relocating its eponymous knight's quest to the nastier, more impoverished streets of the city, its torn and ragged outer edges. His interpretation of Browning thus experiments with the idea of transposing epic to a naturalist setting.

In the first half of *The Man Who Was Thursday*, an allegorical romance whose enigmatic goings-on unfold in the pubs and streets of a familiar London, Chesterton applies the same technique. In Chapter 4, Chesterton's hero, the poet and detective Gabriel Syme, boards a steamboat and travels up the Thames under moonlight that is like 'dead daylight'. The more conscious he becomes of the 'glittering desolation' of this cityscape, which is characterized by 'a luminous and unnatural discoloration' evocative of 'Childe Roland', 'the more his own chivalric folly glow[s] in the night like a great fire':

> Even the common things he carried with him – the food and the brandy and the loaded pistol – took on exactly that concrete and material poetry which a child feels when he takes a gun upon a journey or a bun with him to bed. The sword-stick and the brandy-flask, though in themselves only the tools of morbid conspirators, became the expressions of his own more healthy romance. The sword-stick became almost the sword of chivalry, and the brandy the wine of the stirrup-cup. For even the most dehumanised modern fantasies depend on some older and simpler figure; the adventures may be mad, but the adventurer must be sane. The dragon without St. George would not even be grotesque. So this inhuman landscape was only imaginative by the presence of a man really human.

The Man Who Was Thursday is an elaborate celebration, in a cultural climate poisoned by morbid conspirators, of healthy romance. It pits a solitary, sane and humane adventurer against the dehumanized modern fantasies that Chesterton associates with the 1890s – like Jack ranged against the Giant or St George against the Dragon. Or like Childe Roland confronting the Tower.

In 'A Defence of Detective Stories' (1901), Chesterton identified 'the agent of social justice', that is, the detective, as a romantic archetype whom he praises as 'the original and poetic figure'.[38] Syme, in The Man Who Was Thursday, is just such an emblematic figure of the romance tradition. He is a knight-errant reincarnated in the form of a detective desperately attempting to redeem the threat of damnation in the conditions of metropolitan modernity.

☙

'It is no use attempting to say what it is all about,' wrote Austin Harrison in his review of *The Man Who Was Thursday*; 'it is about everything, and that in curiously thrilling detective form.'[39]

Ostensibly at least, the book is about a battle to the death between anarchists and anti-terrorist detectives in London at the end of the nineteenth century – the 'boom of bomb throwing', as Orson Welles so deliciously put it in the comments with which he prefaced his radio recording of the novel in 1938.[40] But, in contrast to Joseph Conrad's *The Secret Agent* (1907), it is not about anarchists themselves, and the political and psychological destruction they may cause, so much as it is about the 'wandering champions' celebrated by Ker and the role these epic archetypes might play in the spiritual redemption of industrial modernity at the turn of the twentieth century.

The novel begins in a bohemian suburb of 1890s London, where Syme encounters another poet, the aesthete and self-professed anarchist Lucien Gregory. After a heated argument about the relationship between politics and aesthetics, one that Gregory hopes to clinch by offering Syme irrefutable proof that he is committed to anarchism in practice as well as in theory, the former takes the latter to a conspiratorial meeting in a subterranean chamber beneath a tavern, at which he expects to be selected for a post on the Central Anarchist Council.

Moments before they enter the chamber, however, after making a pact with Gregory that requires the anarchist to maintain strict secrecy, Syme reveals that he is a police detective. In the event, to Gregory's deepening horror, it is instead Syme whom the assembled anarchists elect to the Council. And it is Syme, consequently, who meets the other members of the Council, each of whom is named after one of the days of the week, at a bizarre breakfast party in Leicester Square where a plan to assassinate various European heads of state is being finalized. Syme thus becomes Thursday.

The president of the anarchists, a vast monument of a man 'like a statue carved deliberately as colossal', is Sunday (42). This mysterious, omniscient figure stages the dreamlike events that ensue, a succession of ominous and at the same time ludicrous social games conducted at breakneck pace, involving revelations of concealed identities, duels, pitched battles and crazed chases across London and France, all culminating, in the final chapter of the book, in a complicated religious masquerade.

In the course of these episodes, through a series of mesmerizing, artfully calculated narrative displacements, it successively emerges that, like Thursday himself, each of the anarchists on the Council is a detective in disguise. Indeed, it is eventually revealed that even Sunday, having appeared as the towering embodiment of pure evil, is none other than the police chief who, quite as imposing as the arch-anarchist he has mimicked and mirrored, is responsible for recruiting this team of anti-terrorists.

This does not make him the embodiment of pure good instead, though. The novel is not that simple. For the intricate dance that Sunday has choreographed, the elaborate metaphysical farce described by the book's plot, seems mystifyingly amoral. Chesterton half-helpfully intimated that Sunday was not so much God himself, as some commentators claimed, as 'Nature as it appears to the pantheist whose pantheism is struggling out of pessimism' (102). In spite of this, though, Sunday's identity, if the idea of an identity is not hopelessly inappropriate in relation to this super-human entity, remains the book's intractable, but at the same time oddly liberating, secret.

So is the plot an allegory, as a number of critics have suggested? No, not exactly. It is, perhaps, a plot. That is to say, the novel's plot, which apparently involves both the anarchists' plot to overthrow order and the detectives' plot to overthrow disorder, is itself a form of plot. It is a kind of conspiratorial campaign against the complacent reader expecting adventure fiction. The revelations of this metanarrative plot, however, pivot in the end not on the malign motives behind extraordinary events but the benign motivelessness of ordinary events.

In *Robert Browning*, Chesterton had praised the poet's commitment to the commonplace and even the superficial, and it is to this almost sublime state of superficiality that he himself aspired: 'To the man who sees the marvellousness of all things, the surface of life is fully as strange and magical as its interior; clearness and plainness of life is fully as mysterious as its mysteries.'[41] The fiendishly complicated plot of *The Man Who Was Thursday* is a deliberate attempt to bamboozle its readers and so leave them, at the novel's climactic conclusion, both amazed and relieved at the divine simplicity of the universe.

Chesterton's novel vibrates and reverberates like 'one incessant carnival of insane and inspired improvisation', as he himself once said of Dickens's life.[42] It comprises a riotously colourful patchwork of different genres, including the detective story, the metaphysical disquisition, the dream poem, the dystopia, the fairy tale, the dramatic farce, the gothic fantasia, the allegorical masquerade, the melodrama, the nonsense tale, the novel of ideas, the political fable, the religious allegory, the romance, the spy thriller and the theological treatise, among other things. It contains everything, in short, except the familiar qualities of the realist or naturalist novel.

On the contrary, it is gloriously, self-consciously 'irrealist'.[43] And, in this respect, it inhabits a tradition that Chesterton described in an essay entitled 'Dreams' (1901), a lineage of 'great works which mix up abstractions fit for an epic with fooleries not fit for a pantomime', and 'which present such a picture of literary chaos as might be produced if the characters of every book from *Paradise Lost* to *Pickwick Papers* broke from their covers and mingled in one mad romance'. Such books, this manifesto concludes, have 'the same unity that we find in dreams' – that is, 'an absolute unity of emotion'.[44]

The Man Who Was Thursday's subtitle is the important clue in this respect. In his *Autobiography*, Chesterton impatiently pointed out 'that hardly anybody who looked at the title ever seems to have looked at the sub-title; which was "A Nightmare", and the answer to a good many critical questions' (102). The novel is, moreover, as I have already intimated, a record of the dark night of the soul experienced by Chesterton in the 1890s. But, if it describes a nightmare, and a dark night of the soul, it also describes a nightwalk; a phantasmagorical ramble through the nocturnal streets.

In its Dedication, Chesterton describes himself and Bentley roaming through the night, deep in discussion, seeking to surmount their sense of spiritual displacement:

The doubts that were so plain to chase, so dreadful to withstand –
Oh, who shall understand but you: yea, who shall understand?
The doubts that drove us through the night as we two walked
    amain,
And day had broken on the streets e'er it broke upon the brain.
    (xl)

The novel's narrative is thus framed as a compulsive, if not obsessive walk through the suburban night. It begins at sunset, a sunset that looks 'like the end of the world' (2), when Syme first encounters Gregory in the streets of Saffron Park. And it ends when, after fifteen fantastical chapters, Syme gradually comes to full consciousness and realizes that he has been 'walking along a country lane with an easy and conversational companion', that is, Gregory again. Dawn is breaking, and Syme is surprised to discover 'rising all round him on both sides of the road the red, irregular buildings of Saffron Park' (158).

They are back where they began, after walking throughout the night. The entire feverish narrative, then, has been a sort of psychogenic fugue, one apparently unnoticed by Syme's companion. In freeing himself from it, he feels as if he is 'in possession of some impossible good news, which made every other thing a triviality, but an adorable triviality' (158). I too, at break of day, have experienced this euphoria, brought on by lack of sleep and utter physical exhaustion, after walking through the night.

Chesterton talks in the *Autobiography* about emerging from the pessimism of the *fin de siècle* and forging instead a philosophy of optimism:

When I had been for some time in these, the darkest depths of the contemporary pessimism, I had a strong inward impulse to revolt; to dislodge this incubus or throw off this nightmare. But as I was still thinking the thing out by myself, with little help from philosophy and no real help from religion, I invented a rudimentary and makeshift mystical theory of my own. It was substantially this: that even mere existence, reduced to its most primary limits, was extraordinary enough to be exciting. Anything was magnificent as compared with nothing. Even if the very daylight were a dream, it was a day-dream; it was not a nightmare. The mere fact that one could wave one's arms and legs about (or those dubious external objects in the landscape which were called one's arms and legs) showed that it had not the mere paralysis of a nightmare. Or if it was a nightmare, it was an enjoyable nightmare. (93–4)

In the concluding paragraphs of *The Man Who Was Thursday*, Chesterton depicts a daylight in which, metaphorically speaking, Syme cautiously but triumphantly waves his arms and legs about, supremely grateful for the mere fact of existence. 'Syme could only feel an unnatural buoyancy in his body and a crystal simplicity in his mind that seemed to be superior to everything that he said or did,' Chesterton writes (158). Syme has come out of the pessimism that he had slipped into like a coma; and finds himself susceptible at last to a spirit of optimism.

Chesterton defines the basis of this optimism in the *Autobiography* as 'a sort of mystical minimum of gratitude' (94). 'At the back of our brains,' he affirms, 'there [is] a forgotten blaze or burst of astonishment at our own existence,' and the 'object of the artistic and spiritual life [is] to dig for this submerged sunrise of wonder' (95). It is this that inspired Chesterton, from the end of the nineteenth century, 'to write against the Decadents and Pessimists who ruled the culture of the age' (95).

In *Orthodoxy*, composed at roughly the same time as *The Man Who Was Thursday*, Chesterton gives an important preliminary account of what he calls 'this elementary wonder', the principal function of which is to recall us, as in an artistic or spiritual epiphany, to a profound sense of being. In order to illustrate it, he sketches an archetypal subject – a modern, urban subject – who lives in an abysmal state of non-being:

We have all read in scientific books, and, indeed, in all romances, the story of the man who has forgotten his name. This man walks about the streets and can see and appreciate everything; only he cannot remember who he is. Well, every man is that man in the story. Every man has forgotten who he is. ... We are all under the same mental calamity; we have forgotten our names. We have all forgotten what we really are. All that we call common sense and rationality and practicality and positivism only means that for certain dead levels of our life we forget that we have forgotten. All that we call spirit and art and ecstasy only means that for one awful instant we remember that we forget.[45]

Who is the distinctly neurotic everyman, famous from 'scientific books' and romances alike, to whom Chesterton refers in this curious passage? I suspect that the 'story of the man who has forgotten his name', who roams the streets but cannot recall his identity, is that of the so-called 'mad traveller' that stalks in the background of Edward Bellamy's *Looking Backward* (1888).

In 1887, a preacher who had abruptly disappeared from his home in Rhode Island a couple of months previously reappeared in Pennsylvania under a different name. He had no memory of his former identity. In France, in the same year, another instance of 'ambulatory automatism', as some specialists named it, came to light; and as a result of interest from the medical establishment it quickly acquired the status of a specific mental disorder. This precipitated what Ian Hacking diagnoses as 'the fugue epidemic of the 1890s'.[46]

For Chesterton, traumatized as he had been in the 1890s, the man suffering from this apparently inexplicable form of amnesia is paradigmatic, because all individuals, in the times in which he lives, seem oddly inured to the environment they inhabit. In this anaesthetic condition, 'we have all forgotten what we really are'. Everyday life is a constant state of forgetting, and art or spiritual ecstasy alone can, according to a Freudian logic, make us forget for a moment that we have forgotten.

If Chesterton's Syme, who himself experiences a form of ambulatory automatism as he roams about the suburbs of London at night, can be seen as a mad traveller, then he too is finally made to forget that he has forgotten who he really is. The name Thursday is in this respect not simply the pseudonym he must adopt when, as he falls into the depths of the nightmare, he is forced to assume the identity of an anarchist. It is his real name. It is the magic formula that, as in an incantation, brings his real identity into being.

When Syme is forced to dress 'as Thursday' for the final biblical masquerade, at the end of the penultimate chapter, he experiences it as a relief, for 'though he affected to despise the mummer, he felt a curious freedom and naturalness in his movements as the blue and gold garment fell about him' (175). And his co-conspirators, from Monday through to Saturday, undergo the same epiphany, since 'these disguises did not disguise, but reveal' (175).

As Žižek has remarked of this passage, 'it is no longer "If you want to show your true self, tear off the mask!", but, on the contrary, "If you want to show your true self, put on the *right* mask!"'[47] In becoming Thursday, Syme becomes himself; and it is the consciousness that he is secretly Thursday that makes him feel he is 'in possession of some impossible good news' when he resurfaces from the nightmare on a country lane at first light. In the terms provided by *Orthodoxy*, he is residually conscious of the fact that for one awful instant he forgot that he had forgotten who he is; and this is in itself enough to transfigure his everyday life. The deeper irony of the novel's title, then, is that this man really is Thursday. He is not just called Thursday. It is not simply some disguise that he temporarily assumed; it is the originary identity that he managed to dig up. He is most himself when he finally becomes the man he pretended to be.

So, *The Man Who Was Thursday* is framed in the form of an episode of mad travelling, a dreamlike nocturnal tramp in which Syme adopts the false identity that is in fact his true identity. The scene of his epiphany – though the reader is made to forget this until the final paragraphs of the book – is the road along which he has been walking through the night. For Chesterton, it should be emphasized, the street is the supreme repository of poetry. 'Let us go through certain half-deserted streets,' he appeals to his reader, like Eliot's Prufrock. But Chesterton's streets do not 'follow like a tedious argument / Of insidious intent'.[48] They twist and gyrate with a mysterious, sometimes grotesque sense of joy. They are not meaningless but pregnant with spiritual significance.

In *The Napoleon of Notting Hill*, Chesterton's narrator describes in some detail a volume of poems by one of his main characters, Adam Wayne. The poems themselves are apparently rather poor, but they are nonetheless remarkable for channelling all the spiritual passion of Romanticism from the countryside into the city, and for positing London as the supreme poetic subject. In one of the finer love lyrics in the collection, according to the narrator, this poet, 'instead of saying that the rose and the lily contend in her complexion, says, with a purer modernism, that the red omnibus of Hammersmith and the white omnibus of Fulham fight there for the mastery!'[49]

The Man Who Was Thursday is itself an instance of this 'purer modernism', which jams the most incongruous urban images up against one another in order to evoke the glorious chaos of wandering through early twentieth-century London. The spectacular opening sight of the anarchists, 'all dressed in the insolence of fashion', boisterously eating breakfast on a balcony overlooking Leicester Square, in Chapter 5, is an exemplary instance of this, for it concentrates Syme's 'eerie sensation of having strayed into a new world' (41).

Chesterton's metropolitan city is an unstable, even at times explosive compound of the exotic and the everyday. Reality and Elfland. It is in the same spirit that, in the opening chapter of *The Man Who Was Thursday*, Syme insists that in so far as it embodies a kind of rapturous desire for order, the London Underground is 'the most poetical thing in the world' (4). Chesterton's modernism is a triumphant form of urban romanticism.

The narrator of *The Napoleon of Notting Hill* comments at one point that Wayne 'was perhaps the first to realise how often the boundary of fairyland runs through a crowded city'.[50] He was not of course the first to realize this. For Chesterton was conscious that Dickens had effectively been the poet laureate of the metropolitan city in the nineteenth century, and precisely because he possessed, 'in the most sacred and serious sense of the term, the key of the street':

Few of us understand the street. Even when we step into it, we step into it doubtfully, as into a house or room of strangers. Few of us see through the shining riddle of the street, the strange folk that belong to the street only … Of the street at night many of us know even less. The street at night is a great house locked up. But

Dickens had, if ever man had, the key of the street. His earth was the stones of the street; his stars were the lamps of the street; his hero was the man in the street.[51]

Chesterton too had the key of the street, especially in the dream-like conditions of the city at night, and the proof of this – evident especially in *The Man Who Was Thursday* – is that, as he said of Dickens, 'he saw all his streets in fantastic perspectives.'[52] Chesterton was capable, as almost none of the more famous modernists were, of defamiliarizing the mundane properties of the metropolitan city and making them seem miraculous.

The image of the streetlamp, to which Chesterton recurred again and again in his fictional and non-fictional prose, is characteristic of this, because it is an emblem of what, in *Orthodoxy*, he calls 'practical romance'. It combines 'something that is strange with something that is secure'; 'an idea of wonder and an idea of welcome'. Like other ordinary objects that only need to be estranged for a moment to seem extraordinary, it answers a 'double spiritual need, the need for that mixture of the familiar and the unfamiliar which Christendom has rightly named romance'.[53]

From its title on, then, *The Man Who Was Thursday* brings a fantastic perspective to bear on everyday life, and in particular the everyday life of the modern city. This fantastic perspective is of course informed by Chesterton's Christian faith, which became increasingly confident in the first years of the twentieth century (though he did not officially convert to Catholicism until 1922). I am however convinced that Samuel Hynes was correct when, some time ago, he claimed that notwithstanding the important scholarship on Chesterton by religious critics, 'above all, he needs secular attention.'[54] For Chesterton's commitment to estranging and transfiguring the commonplace is in literary terms consonant with the contemporaneous reaction against realism.

The Man Who Was Thursday is perhaps the supreme modernist romance. It uses the emergent techniques of modernism in order not to disenchant but to re-enchant everyday life. It takes the man who ambles about the streets but cannot remember who he is, and, in a gesture as anarchic as it is ecstatic, spins him about in order to recall him abruptly to himself. Suddenly, this man seems to inhabit a fairy tale in which, though nothing makes sense, everything makes sense.

Exemplary in this respect is one of the most sinister and darkly comic passages in *The Man Who Was Thursday*, where Syme discovers to his horror that the ancient, death-like anarchist Professor de Worms is stalking him through London's 'labyrinth of little streets' (61). Here, Chesterton's urban fairy tale acquires a particularly demented force. For, although the Professor appears to be decrepit, he displays an athletic capacity for keeping up with Syme that is deeply disturbing.

However much Syme accelerates, however much he loses himself in the maze of alleys and lanes that lead from the main thoroughfares, when he stops to catch his breath he continues to hear 'the clinking crutch and labouring feet of the infernal cripple' (62). Chesterton is in this chapter consciously rewriting 'The Man of the Crowd' (1840), reversing the terms of its narrative so that, rather than the narrator pursuing Poe's incomprehensible old man, the incomprehensible old man, even more unnervingly, pursues Syme.

Finally, in a state of desperation that is almost ecstatic, Syme has 'a new impulse to tear out the secret of this dancing, jumping and pursuing paralytic', and he determines to turn and confront his pursuer:

> Professor de Worms came slowly round the corner of the irregular alley behind him, his unnatural form outlined against a lonely gas-lamp, irresistibly recalling that very imaginative figure in the nursery rhymes, 'the crooked man who went a crooked mile.' He really looked as if he had been twisted out of shape by the tortuous streets he had been threading. He came nearer and nearer, the lamplight shining on his lifted spectacles, his lifted, patient face. (63)

The Professor thus comes closer and closer; and Syme, 'remembering all the nightmares he had ever known,' simply waits for him, 'as St. George waited for the dragon, as a man waits for a final explanation or for death' (63). In the Old English language, the word *wyrm* signified a serpent or dragon, so Chesterton deliberately identifies the Professor, a desiccated rationalist whose intellect alone resists 'the last dissolution of senile decay', with the legendary knight's monstrous antagonist (46).

It transpires, of course, that the Professor – his 'pale, grave' head grotesquely attached to a 'bounding body', 'like the head of a lecturer upon the body of a harlequin' (63) – is yet another police detective in elaborate disguise. The relief the reader feels at this revelation that he is not the hero's foe, however, does not efface the indelible creepiness of the chase that Chesterton has so brilliantly described. The metropolitan city itself, after this episode, appears to be fatally haunted. On its streets, criss-crossed by both satanic and angelic energies, identities are ceaselessly made and unmade.

Chesterton, the descendant of Dickens and Poe, is one of the great modernist poets of the city. And he is one of the great modernist poets of the city even though he is generally classified as neither a modernist nor a poet; even though, as a kind of counter-modernist, he insists on returning to the pre-modern form of the chivalric romance, with its wandering hero, in order to defamiliarize or estrange the modern metropolis. His epiphanies take place on pavements.

In the chapter on 'Browning in Later Life' in his monograph on the poet, Chesterton observes that 'Browning was one of those wise men who can perceive the terrible and impressive poetry of the police-news', before adding that 'a great many of his works might be called magnificent detective stories.'[55] 'Childe Roland' is one of these detective stories.

Indeed, I am almost tempted to claim that, according to Chesterton's interpretation, 'Childe Roland' anticipates the *noir* form. Chesterton is of course far from some proto-noir novelist himself, as the 'Father Brown' stories indicate clearly enough; but in his interpretation of 'Childe Roland' he implicitly identifies the configuration of generic influences that, half a century later, will shape the evolution of noir – epic, lyric and naturalism.

The unshaven man Chesterton pictures in trying to evoke the seediness of the landscape described in 'Childe Roland' – 'That sense of scrubbiness in nature,' he writes, 'as of a man unshaved' – is in the context of Browning's poem implicitly identified with the 'brute' that walks about 'pashing' the patchy, scrubby vegetation beneath its feet ('pashing', a rare word first recorded in the late fourteenth and early fifteenth centuries, means smashing or violently crushing).

The effect of this association, in Chesterton's deft *détournement*, is to evoke a rough-looking, unkempt man skulking about the mean streets of the city. Roland, according to the logic of Chesterton's reading, is thus effectively transposed to 'some grey mean street', where the brute confronts him as antagonist and double. In this interpretation, Roland is like no heroic or anti-heroic archetype so much as the noir detective that Raymond Chandler famously depicted in 'The Simple Art of Murder' (1944):

> But down these mean streets a man must go who is not himself mean, who is neither tarnished nor afraid. He is the hero; he is everything. He must be a complete man and a common man and yet an unusual man. He must be, to use a rather weathered phrase, a man of honor – by instinct, by inevitability, without thought of it, and certainly without saying it.

'The story', Chandler concludes, 'is this man's adventure in search of a hidden truth.'[56]

The detective that, picked out in chiaroscuro, features at the centre of noir movies and novels of the 1940s has long been regarded as an extremely belated chivalric knight, pursuing a perverse moral quest in the nocturnal city, attempting to vanquish evil.[57] In his reading of Browning, and in fragments of his own strange, uncategorizable fiction, Chesterton offers us an earlier, equally urgent glimpse of this tradition – that of the knight errant in the street. In a detective story, he reflected, 'the hero or the investigator crosses London with something of the loneliness and liberty of a prince in a tale of elfland.'[58]

It is this sort of chivalric romance that Chesterton excavated, above all in *The Man Who Was Thursday*, from what his former professor Ker had characterized as the 'abandoned region of medieval thought and imagination', re-embedding its 'wandering champions', who fight against the tyrannical forces of Enlightenment reason on foot, in the streets of the modern metropolis.

6

Collapsing

Ford Madox Ford's
Return to Yesterday

One day in late 1898 or early 1899, Ford Madox Ford came across Émile Zola seated on a bench in Hyde Park. Ford, still in his mid-twenties, was already a published biographer, novelist and poet. Zola was in his late fifties. He had fled to London after being convicted of criminal libel for his role in the Dreyfus Affair and sentenced to prison.

On Zola's previous visit to the city, in September 1893, he had been positively fêted: 'The Lord Mayor received him at the Guildhall; an elaborate firework display illuminated his portrait in the sky above the Crystal Palace; and editors and writers hosted soirées in his honour.'[1] At one point, he was conducted on a gruesome tour of the scenes of Jack the Ripper's crimes in Whitechapel. 'As to London, which I visited for the first time,' he told the *Manchester Guardian* on his return to Paris on that occasion, 'the big city made an indelible impression on my mind. Its beauty is not in its monuments, but in its immensity; the colossal character of its quays and bridges, to which ours are as toys.'[2]

What of the visit during which Ford encountered him? This time, exiled from his homeland, the city's immensity did not have the same exhilarating effect on him. He arrived at Victoria Station, with almost no possessions, in July 1898. Soon after, he left London on a series of 'suburban peregrinations' which his friends insisted would help him 'achieve total obscurity'.[3] He spent an anxious few months in England, sporadically afflicted by nervous seizures.

It is in his autobiographical memoir, *Return to Yesterday* (1931), that Ford recalls the occasion on which he happened upon Zola in Hyde Park. The fugitive 'had been gazing gloomily at the ground and poking the sand with the end of his cane'. 'No gloom could have ever been greater than his', he adds in a drily melancholic tone. According to Ford, Zola listlessly complained that on the ground beside the bench, over the course of the morning, he had found as many as eighteen hairpins carelessly dropped by negligent nursemaids: 'A city so improvident must be doomed.'[4] Ford, who appears to relish the precision of the number eighteen, implies that this behaviour was positively compulsive. 'He had, at any rate during that stay in London, many phobias,' he concludes (214).

So did Ford. Indeed, *Return to Yesterday* itself, not least in its mediations or representations of Zola, offers a rich opportunity to explore Ford's complicated, distinctly neurotic relationship to urban space, especially in the form of his agoraphobia. Ford's superstitious temperament, alongside his pathological fear of empty or open spaces, comprises another instance of the crisis of *flânerie*, of the unsustainability of the *flâneur*'s characteristic disposition, in the increasingly embattled conditions of industrial and metropolitan modernity in the second half of the nineteenth and first half of the twentieth centuries. It also provides important insight into Ford's Impressionist aesthetic.

In his anecdotal account of Zola in *Return to Yesterday*, Ford proceeds to describe another occasion, presumably at about the same time, when a mutual acquaintance asked him to convey the French novelist to some address in a hansom cab. Zola scarcely spoke during the journey, on the assumption that Ford couldn't speak French. 'But eventually I found that he was counting the numbers of the registration plates of the cabs that were in front of us,' Ford writes. 'If the added digits came to nine – or possibly to seven – he was momentarily elated; if they came to some inauspicious number – to thirteen I suppose – he would be prolongedly depressed' (214). Ford thus reads Zola reading the occult signs of the modern city.

The scattered hairpins that Zola had counted beneath the park bench, oddly intimate domestic detritus that has spilled out from the private recesses of the metropolis into its public space, seem potentially meaningful. They are both a kind of statistic, the indices of improvidence, and the residue of innumerable untold stories. In contrast, the number plates are merely random codes. The hairpins have narrative significance (even if they also perhaps signal the 'disintegration' of narrative into 'disconnected and autonomous details', as Georg Lukács might have argued[5]); the number plates do not. It is the difference, to put it schematically, between a naturalist and a modernist semiotics of the city.

The anecdote about the hansom cab is comic as well as tragic in its outline. It is amusing in particular to picture Ford silently attempting to infer Zola's numerological system – which is, in both the more and less strict senses of the term, idiotic – from his reactions to the number plates he sees in the traffic. Ford's eyes must have flickered incessantly between Zola's enigmatic face and the meaningless numbers on the hansom cabs themselves. In this respect, though, Ford's behaviour is quite as compulsive as Zola's.

Paradoxically, one can detect Ford's slightly obsessive investment in Zola's mental processes in the apparent imprecision with which he pinpoints the number that makes his companion elated: 'If the added digits came to nine – or possibly to seven –'. The presence of that 'possibly' signals that, for Ford, there is a difference. As the hesitant, ruminative syntax of this sentence indicates, it matters to him whether it is seven or nine. Indeed, it is as if, more than three decades later, he is still trying to crack the code. Ford too, in short, is secretly a numerologist. He is in this respect Zola's double. It might even be speculated, in fact, that Zola's numerological compulsion – one of several 'phobias' that this anecdote is intended to exemplify – is finally a fantastical projection of Ford's.

There is no positive evidence that the fleeting expressions of elation and depression inscribed on Zola's face had anything to do with the number plates. He might have been gazing into space and making purely introspective calculations. The exiled novelist might simply have been sifting through memories, thinking of his family or his mistress, or contemplating his return to Paris. Ford, then, is a distinctly unreliable narrator.

Of course, Impressionism, the literary aesthetic with which Ford was so closely associated in the early twentieth century, is all about unreliable narration. It is premised on the assumption that, in the act of representation, it is the subject as opposed to the object that is important; or, more specifically, that it is the relationship between them, the process of representation, that imparts meaning to a narrative, so that in the end, folded in on one another, subject and object cease to have independent significance. Impressionism hypostasizes the partial or unreliable narrator, as Ford's most celebrated novel, *The Good Soldier* (1915), makes creepingly apparent.

'The Impressionist author is sedulous to avoid letting his personality appear in the course of his book,' Ford once asserted. 'On the other hand, his whole book, his whole poem is merely an expression of his personality.'[6] *Return to Yesterday*, for its part, is an overtly impressionistic retrospective. In its 'Dedication', Ford explicitly describes it as 'a novel' rather than an autobiography: 'Where it has seemed expedient to me I have altered episodes that I have witnessed but I have been careful never to distort the character of the episode. The accuracies I deal in are the accuracies of my impressions' (4).

We should not be surprised, therefore, if these anecdotes about Zola in London tell us less about the French novelist than about Ford himself.

But, in addition to these external reasons, there is another reason, one internal to the text, for thinking that Ford is consciously or unconsciously projecting onto Zola. If he identifies the numbers that cause Zola to feel elated with an exactitude that is only underlined by his refusal definitely to commit to either nine or seven, he is unexpectedly casual when he comes to identify the numbers that cause Zola to feel depressed: 'if they came to some inauspicious number – to thirteen I suppose – he would be prolongedly depressed.'

This is an oddly imprecise assessment. Did he or didn't he

succeed in ascertaining the number that upset Zola? It is of course possible that, in spite of his manifest ability to recollect the positive numbers, he has simply forgotten the negative one. Yet the careless tone of the sentence – 'thirteen I suppose' – is suspect. It seems disingenuous.

But perhaps I, too, in reading Ford reading Zola reading the numbers, have been infected by the paranoiac hermeneutic that Umberto Eco has brilliantly analysed as 'over-interpretation'.[7] After all, the number thirteen is a proverbial object of superstition. Ford did not, however, cite the number thirteen merely because it is customarily assumed to be inauspicious. He himself suffered from a superstitious fear of the number thirteen; that is, from triskaidekaphobia.

Five years or so after his encounter with Zola, at the end of 1903, Ford moved from Sussex back to London. It is from this moment, when he was writing *The Soul of London* (1905), his attempt to explore the atmospherics of the metropolis, that the psychological crisis whose effects he would suffer throughout his life began to be manifest.

In both his professional and his domestic life, Ford was afflicted by problems at this time: he couldn't find a publisher for the book about London; his relations with Joseph Conrad, and the literary collaborations on which they were working, were severely affected by the senior novelist's depression; he felt acute guilt because of his affair with Mary Martindale; his marriage to his wife Elsie appeared, for this and other reasons, to be on the point of implosion; he caught the influenza then raging through London; and, as if all this was insufficiently dramatic, on one spectacular occasion, as he arrived home, Ford opened the front door to discover his eldest daughter Christina, aged six or seven, fleeing downstairs with her clothes and hair on fire. All of these factors no doubt contributed to the 'devastating mental breakdown' he experienced in 1904.[8]

'The move to London was for me the beginning of a series of disasters,' Ford writes in *Return to Yesterday*: 'That was perhaps because the year was 1903. Those digits added up to thirteen. No one should have done anything in that year' (174). This rather theatrical overstatement is undoubtedly comic, but Ford is deadly serious. The abrupt tone of these sentences, in an autobiography that, at some deep level, probes the parallels between his personal crisis of 1904 and the public crisis of 1914, is apocalyptic rather than mock-heroic: 'These were the early days of that mania that has since beset the entire habitable globe' (204). Ford declares later in the memoir, 'I have always been superstitious myself and so remain – impenitently' (226).

Ford defends his superstitious disposition on the grounds that everyone lives their daily lives under the influence of a sense of good or bad luck: 'The most rationalist of human beings does not pass his life without saying: "I am in luck today!"' It is thus a normal rather than deviant characteristic of human nature. He goes on to argue, convincingly enough, that this superstitious perception of whether one happens to be lucky or unlucky at a particular time, immaterial as it might appear, has a definite and measurable effect on one's psychology. When you feel lucky, 'you will be resolute, keen, active, awake to proper courses to pursue', and you thereby 'ensure luck' (226).

There is a similar circular logic to bad luck: 'When you are depressed by ill omens you are less resolute, you are despondent in the degree however small of the weight you attach to the beliefs of your fellow man' (226). Ford then gives two examples of runs of poor luck, and of psychological depression, that succeeded some inauspicious incident. He describes the first of these, involving a superstitious attempt to rid himself of an opal, which must have taken place in the opening months of 1904, in detail; and I want to examine it closely in a moment.

He alludes to the second one, which must have happened sometime in the late 1920s, more cursorily. Here, he recalls that he was driving in 'a closed automobile' in 'an open space' in Harlem when one of the car's female passengers suddenly exclaimed, 'Look at that immense crescent!' 'She was indicating the new moon,' he explains, 'which in consequence I saw through the front glass.' He concludes: 'From that day for a long time – indeed until about a year ago – I experienced nothing but disaster: in finances, in health, in peace of mind, in ability to work' (226). Indeed, the memory of that moon subsequently makes him incapable of working for several months. This phobia is the cause of a debilitating agraphia, an inability to write.

What interests me about this description is its emphasis on space: Ford was in a closed automobile in an open space in the city. A concern with the disposition of space, and with movement in it, is a consistent feature of his autobiographical memoir (as of his other writings). Indeed, Ford seems to have found it difficult to comprehend emotional states in abstraction from space. This is evident in *The Soul of London,* for example, where he repeatedly conceives the capital in terms of what he calls 'intimate London'.[9]

This highly personalized London, which as a committed Impressionist Ford believes is the only London it is possible for the individual to apprehend, not least because of the city's abstract immensity, consists of 'the little bits of it that witnessed the great moments, the poignant moods of his life; it will be what happened to be the backgrounds of his more intense emotions' (22). It is at all times a matter of affect. London and other cities are in this sense 'psychogeographical' entities for Ford. Guy Debord classically defined psychogeography, it will be recalled, as 'the study of the precise laws and specific effects of the geographical environment, whether consciously organized or not, on the emotions and behaviour of individuals'.[10]

Ford's spatial fixation is evident even from the 'Dedication' to *Return to Yesterday,* which addresses his friends, the poet Eileen Hall and her husband Dr Michael Lake. When Ford conceived his memoir, he was convalescing with them at their studio in New York. Ford was suffering from gout, and Michael Lake, known as 'Micky', had bandaged up his foot. 'My Dears,' the 'Dedication' begins, 'It was whilst looking up at the criss-cross beams in the roof of your tall studio that the form of this book was thought out.' Ford goes on to explain the formal analogy between the roof of the studio and the autobiography: 'So, as I go through these pages I seem to see that criss-cross in your gracious old house[,] and the literary form of the work is inextricably mingled with those Cubist intricacies' (3). This space, multi-faceted, intimate, is cosily familiar.

Here is a poetics of space comparable to the one that Gaston Bachelard famously devised, in which the individual's house is a 'universe, a real cosmos'.[11] I want however to suggest that, if Ford attempted in the form of his memoir to reproduce a comforting architectural space, then, less consciously perhaps, his writing from the early 1900s reproduced, or negotiated, an alien, alienating form of space. One might almost say that, in recasting his life until 1914 in the form of this comforting cubistic autobiography, Ford was redeeming the rather different poetics of space that shapes the earlier period.

That poetics of space can be glimpsed in the image of the house on Campden Hill in Holland Park – close to where G. K. Chesterton was born – that Ford and Elsie rented from friends at the end of 1903 and moved into in early January 1904. Initially, Ford ascribed the series of disasters that succeeded this move to the fact that the digits that constitute the year 1903 add up to thirteen. He does however propose an alternative interpretation:

> Or it was perhaps because the house I then took was accursed. It was a monstrous sepulchre – and not even whitened. It was grey with the greyness of withered bones. It was triangular in ground plan: the face formed the nose of a blunted redan [an arrow-shaped embankment in a fortified construction], the body tapered to a wedge in which there was a staircase like the corkscrew staircases of the Middle Ages. The façade was thus monstrous, the tail ignoble. It was seven stories in height in those days and in those days elevators in private houses were unknown. It was what housemaids call: 'A Murderer'. (174)

In contrast to the homely involutions of space in the Hall Lakes' house, the spatial disposition of this house is distinctly unhomely. Ford deliberately draws on a Gothic register in order to represent it, as in the image of the mediaeval staircase, which seems to have been transposed from the Castle of Udolpho. It is a haunted house. Even the housemaids' phrase for it, 'A Murderer', which refers colloquially to the murderous demands of the staircases they repeatedly had to climb in order to attend to their duties, assumes more sinister overtones – it is as if the house itself, with its violently angular features, takes on the anthropomorphic qualities of a psychopath.

Ford blames the house for 'the chain of disasters, suicides, bankruptcies and despairs that visited its successive tenants and owners' (174). The house is accursed. This is perhaps an instance, then, of the phenomenon that Anthony Vidler has called 'the architectural uncanny'.[12] And Ford manifestly suffers what might be characterized as a spatial phobia, or topophobic anxiety, in relation to it. The metropolis itself at this time he described as 'that London mausoleum of 1903' (208).

Ford was afflicted by a number of phobias in London. Of these, agoraphobia was by far the most prominent. 'From 1903 to 1906 illness removed me from most activities,' as he himself summarizes it in *Return to Yesterday*: 'I suffered from what was diagnosed as agoraphobia and intense depression.' While insisting that he 'had nothing specific to be depressed about', he admits nonetheless that these years, his 'lost years', represented 'uninterrupted mental agony' (202).

Ford's complaint, which in the autobiography he unconvincingly ascribes to intense fatigue, manifested itself in 'a slight fluttering of the heart' and a sudden faintness (204). 'This will naturally sometimes happen in the street,' he adds, and 'the result therefore a little resembles agoraphobia' (204). It happened in empty spaces other than the street, too, so his condition does more than simply resemble agoraphobia. It is a profoundly disabling 'movement inhibition', to use Paul Carter's deliberately unspecific, but nonetheless useful, definition of agoraphobia.[13]

In July 1904, to cite an incident that testifies directly to Ford's agoraphobia, his friend Olive Garnett set off with him on a walk across Salisbury Plain, close to a house that he and Elsie had rented; and found that he was suddenly incapable of proceeding. Garnett later offered a revealing description of this incident in a memorandum:

> Ford had an attack of agoraphobia, & said if I didn't take his arm he would fall down. I held on in all the blaze for miles, it seemed to me, but the town reached, he walked off briskly to get tobacco and a shave; and when I pointed this out to Elsie she said 'nerves'. He can't cross wide open spaces. She said he had

already consulted a local doctor. We explored further & went to
Stonehenge, but he got worse.[14]

Garnett also described him, while they walked together, 'sitting
down on every seat & putting a lozenge into his mouth against
agoraphobia'.[15] Here, too, Ford's susceptibility to superstition
appears to shape, even as it proposes a solution to, his agoraphobic anxiety about 'wide open spaces'.

Ford spent five months in Germany that same year in an
attempt to cure his condition, drifting unhappily from one
medical institution to another like some melancholic exile from
Thomas Mann's *Magic Mountain* (1924). 'Everyone diagnosed
my trouble as agoraphobia,' he reports with comic bitterness in
the autobiography; 'sixteen or seventeen of them attributed it to
sexual abnormalities and treated me for them' (204). Attempting
'a nerve cure on the Lake of Constance', for example, where the
treatment was principally hydropathic, he later admitted: 'I was
so weak that, even if the so-called agoraphobia had not inter-
fered with my walking I should hardly have been able to get
about' (202).

In the last of the sanatoria he attended, the Rhineland Kaltwasser-
Heilanstalt, he was put on a diet of pork and ice cream and forced
to take iced footbaths. 'There's such a lot of nervous breakdown
in the land,' he declared in a letter to Elsie, half in triumph, half
in defeat. 'They've a regular name for lack of walking power up
here: Platz Angst.'[16] In a letter to Garnett from Germany, Ford
told her that he was 'staggering along the streets'.[17]

The German psychologist Carl Otto Westphal first assigned the
name 'agoraphobia' to a fear of open or urban spaces in 1871. It
had however been identified as a distinct neuropathic phenomenon since at least the late 1860s, at the outset of what David
Trotter has called 'phobia's *belle époque*'.[18] In his *Die Agoraphobie* (1872), Westphal observed that 'for some years patients have
repeatedly approached me with the peculiar complaint that it is
not possible for them to walk across open spaces and through
certain streets and that, due to the fear of such paths, they are
troubled in their freedom of movement.'[19]

One example he offered was that of a salesman suffering from this complaint:

> For two years now a feeling of fear walking through the streets
> alone has been accompanying him; in the beginning such walks
> were almost impossible for him, now he at least tries, but a nib-
> bling feeling in the stomach area, a feeling of paralysis in his
> arms and legs, as if he could not move, as if he would fall to the
> ground[,] overcomes him.[20]

The feeling of falling. Of collapsing. This is the classic experience of the agoraphobic. As examined by Moritz Benedikt, Emil
Cordes and Henri Legrand du Saulle, in addition to Westphal
himself, agoraphobia was variously associated with epileptic,
melancholic and neurasthenic conditions, and with vertigo.
The psychiatrist Legrand du Saulle referred to it as '*la peur des
espaces*'.

In Britain in the late 1890s, some five years before Ford's acute
crisis, a physician to the Leicester Infirmary and Fever House
called J. Headley Neale insisted in the pages of the *Lancet* that
'the "agoraphobic" is a much more common individual than
you might be led to infer from the little which is said or written
about him.' In part so as to refute a 'West-end physician' who
had claimed that 'agoraphobia was all bosh and due to excess of
wine and venery', Neale offered his own experiences as forceful
testimony to its significance. These began, he relates, when he
was a medical student in Edinburgh:

> Walking briskly one evening down the slope [of Chalmers St] I
> have my first attack; and it is the suddenness and unexpectedness
> of the first attack that is so alarming – a feeling that something
> dreadful is going to happen, that the end of all my strivings and
> longings has come. I stop; the heart seems seized in an iron grip.
> I feel as though I were going down into the earth and the earth
> were coming up to meet me. There is no semblance of giddiness or
> faintness in these attacks, it is more a feeling of collapse as though
> one were being shut up like a crush hat or a Chinese lantern. I
> have a strong inclination to cry out and I feel that I must fall, so

I lay hold of, and steady myself by, the palings. A deep heaving
sigh, the breaking out of a cold sweat upon the forehead, and in
less time than it takes to describe (a few seconds only) the attack
has passed.

Neale associated agoraphobia both with 'fear of impending
death' and 'the dread of an open space' that is 'called up by a sensation of vastness, infinity, and solitude'.[21] In short, he concluded
that it was an existential condition rather than a moral one.

As the term's etymological root in the notion of *agora* or marketplace implied, agoraphobia was consistently associated with
cities. In France, for example, where cases of agoraphobia had
been documented since the late 1860s, Jean-Baptiste-Édouard
Gélineau, the discoverer of narcolepsy, refined the prevailing definition and insisted in 1890 on employing the term *kénophobie*,
on the grounds that the condition 'strikes only the inhabitant of
cities …, developing under the influence of that debilitating atmosphere of the big towns that has been called *malaria urbana*'.[22]

The empty spaces of the metropolis, especially large squares,
appear to have been a particular problem for agoraphobics.
'Nineteenth-century agoraphobics experienced the gigantic
squares and boulevards introduced into their cities as hostile
environments,' Kathryn Milun has stated. 'They perceived these
monumental spaces as "empty" and experienced intense anxiety
that caused them to retreat to the curb, to their homes, and even
to bed.'[23] (I am reminded of Ford's image of Zola marooned on
that park bench in London, oppressed perhaps by the 'immensity'
of a city whose 'colossal character' he had once admired.)

Agoraphobia is not exclusively an urban psychopathology, as
the example of Ford's collapse on Salisbury Plain itself demonstrates; but its emergence is arguably inseparable from a certain
experience of the city in the nineteenth and twentieth centuries.
'Once we recognise that the spaces which bring it on are not just
topographically open, but public, a social as well as a physical
expanse,' Trotter insists, 'we can surely agree that there is a great
deal in them to disable.'[24]

☞

Ford seems to have been conscious of this public, urban dimension. In *Return to Yesterday*, he writes that 'at the beginning of the [twentieth] century it would have taken you 247 years walking at four miles an hour to cover all the streets of London on foot' (notice here that the digits comprising the number 247 add up to thirteen). 'What it would take now goodness knows,' he adds – 'A thousand likely.' From this terrifying agoraphobic image, which evokes an inexhaustibly labyrinthine city, Ford infers an existential lesson he claims should be the first that artists learn, namely 'that you are merely an atom among vastnesses and shouldn't take yourself very seriously' (171).

This vision of an atom among vastnesses shapes a number of Ford's poems from the early 1900s, several of which have rural rather than urban settings. 'On a Marsh Road', for example, from *The Face of the Night* (1904), evokes 'infinite, glimpsing distances' and 'eternal silences'; 'infinite plains [which] know no wanderer's foot' and 'infinite distances where alone is rest'.[25] Ford's sense of isolation and insignificance, however, does seem to stem in particular from an alienated, psychopathological relationship to the streets of the metropolis. 'When you get out of the Paris train at Charing Cross,' he comments in *Return to Yesterday*, 'it feels as if you sink down like a plummet into dim depths and were at once lost to sight' (230).

He seems to have felt equally lost when arriving in Paris from London. In his Preface to Jean Rhys's collection *The Left Bank and Other Stories* (1927), he describes the Left Bank itself as 'a vast, sandy desert, like the Sahara ... but immense.' He concedes that, geographically, it hasn't altered since his childhood, but emphasizes that 'the mental image' has been dramatically altered by the passing of time. The Left Bank, which he boasts of knowing 'better than any other portion of the surface of the globe', is a place that nonetheless reminds him 'how minutely little one can know even of one street thickly inhabited by human beings'.[26] A densely populated place that is at the same time 'immense', like a 'desert', is a quintessentially agoraphobic one.

It is no surprise, then, that Ford goes on to talk about the ways in which the populous plains of the Left Bank have impeded his movements as a pedestrian in Paris, especially in the early evenings, when taxicabs are 'unprocurable' and 'it is impossible to get a place in a bus.'[27] (As one correspondent to the *Lancet* advised in 1885, 'should the symptom [of agoraphobia] be very aggravated, the patient should only (in London) walk in the open streets, where he can obtain a cab should he require one.'[28])

Ford is too delicate, of course, to refer to his agoraphobic condition in the context of this Preface. But he concludes nonetheless that 'the impression of infinitely long walks with the legs feeling as if you dragged each step out of sands ... remains.'[29] Impressions, obviously enough, are everything to the Impressionist, so this is a graphic testament – all the more vivid because of that ellipsis – to the inhibitive force of this psychopathology on his ability to move freely about the city on foot.

Certainly, the strikingly odd incident that seems in 1904 to have triggered Ford's agoraphobia, an incident in which superstitious and phobic behaviour are indissociable, is irreducibly urban. This is the first and most significant of the examples of poor luck that he offers in *Return to Yesterday*.

Ford explains that, after he had given Elsie an opal ring, for some reason they both became convinced that this precious stone was the cause of the series of disasters that befell them, including the most recent, his daughter's distinctly Gothic domestic accident. In consequence, having tried and failed to dispose of it in several improvised rites, he finally decided to neutralize its supernatural force by disposing of the ring in running water, through which, so he claims, witchcraft 'cannot operate' (227).

He therefore set out for the Thames at Hammersmith Bridge with the opal in his pocket: 'At once an indescribable lassitude fell on me. I was almost unable to drag my legs along and quite incapable of getting to the Thames' (227). He tells us that he thought of dropping the stone through a grating, but was unfortunate enough to meet a policeman every time he caught sight of one, and feared being accused of disposing of stolen property. The next day he decided to send the opal to a convent as a donation, having first apprised the Mother Superior of its malignant properties. But, in taking it to the post office, he found himself 'almost completely unable to walk': 'I could hardly drag my feet along,' he writes (227–8).

Ford derives a rather curious moral from this incident – one that, suspiciously perhaps, occludes its specifically spatial aspects. He claims that, if a novelist is superstitious, he will be at one with the ordinary people he represents in his fiction: 'A novelist had better share the superstitions of, than high-hat, humanity' (228). 'Superstitions, belief in luck, premonitions', he emphasizes, 'play such a great part in human motives that a novelist who does not to some extent enter into those feelings can hardly understand and will certainly be unable to render to perfection most human affairs' (229).

Ford's covertly elitist claim, here, is that a superstitious cast of mind, to the precise extent that it is a common, if not universal mentality, provides an effective means of identifying with the masses. He repeats an odd anecdote in support of this asseveration:

> I remember once dreadfully shocking Mr Edward Garnett. It was at the time when Limpsfield was disturbed by my wearing a cloth cap. I said it was my ambition to pass unobserved in a crowd. Mr Garnett never forgot that. Years after he advanced it against me as a proof of my bourgeois nature.
>
> And indeed it is so. Yet the novelist must pass unobserved in the crowd if he himself is to observe. And the crowd is his clay, of his observations of it he will build his monuments to humanity. The social reformer may – and usually does – render himself conspicuous by singular garments that express his singular personality. It does not matter how humanity reacts towards him. He will make capital out of persecution.
>
> But the first thing the novelist has to learn is self-effacement – that first and that always. (228)

The 'cloth cap' might unconsciously have functioned as a form of protection against Ford's agoraphobia. Interestingly, Carter has proposed that a hat 'introduce[s] a little distance between the walker and the street'; and moreover that, because 'no hat comes without its hatpeg, it implie[s] an imminent homecoming', and therefore acts as 'a thread through the day's labyrinth'.[30] But, in so far as this cap is a social disguise, even a cap of invisibility, it also speaks to the Baudelairean tradition of the artist remaining unseen in the city, the better to see the city.

The ambition to 'pass unobserved in the crowd' in order to observe the crowd is of course characteristic of that celebrated modernist archetype for the artist, the *flâneur*. Ford dreams, then, of being a *flâneur* of the kind described by Baudelaire; but, as an agoraphobic, he is congenitally, and almost comically, ill-equipped to perform the role. For the agoraphobic is in effect the antitype of the *flâneur*. In his famous commentary on the poetics of urban space in Baudelaire, Walter Benjamin states that 'the street becomes a dwelling for the *flâneur*; he is as much at home among the facades of houses as a citizen is in his four walls.'[31] An agoraphobic could not be less at home in the street. The spaces of the metropolis are profoundly alien to an individual such as Ford whose movement is pathologically inhibited.

'You are to remember', Ford had reminded his reader in a previous chapter of the autobiography, 'that my chief trouble was that I imagined that I could not walk' (206). He there implies that being at one with the common people whom the contemporary novelist must represent is simply a matter of putting on a proletarian cap. He assumes that it is impossible to 'high-hat' humanity if one is inconspicuous. A cloth cap, he hopes, like that of Perseus in the Greek myth, makes its wearer magically disappear in the metropolis. Ford is, in fact, concealing the extent to which his spatial phobia shaped his Impressionist aesthetic.

For, in representing the modern metropolis and its 'human affairs', Ford is forced into a compromise. He must attempt to grasp the dialectic of the fleeting and the infinite characteristic of modernity, as Baudelaire's example demands, but he is in practice capable of doing so only from outside the urban crowd that embodies it. This is a painful paradox for the ambitious modernist artist to find himself trapped in. He cannot be at the very centre of the world and at the same time unseen of the world. And it is in part because he cannot inhabit 'the multiplicity of life and the flickering grace of all the elements of life', as Baudelaire put it, that Ford's perception, his peculiar consciousness, is of paramount importance to his aesthetic.[32] His Impressionism, then, is among other things the product of his inability to participate in the life he is committed to representing. It is a half-vicarious means of experiencing the modernity that he is forced to observe from the margins of the city.

According to the psychoanalyst Adam Phillips, a phobia acts as an 'unconscious estrangement technique' because it constitutes the phobic object as an alien phenomenon.[33] Ford's agoraphobia estranges him from the life of the city, it might be concluded, because he cannot spontaneously or unselfconsciously partici-pate in it.

How did Ford's agoraphobia impinge on his writing? Max Saun-ders, his most authoritative biographer, has suggested that Granger, the narrator of *The Inheritors* (1901), a political romance Ford co-authored with Joseph Conrad, is his 'first fictional agoraphobic'.[34] I assume he is thinking of descriptions like this one from Chapter 5, in which Granger steps out into the city at night:

> All around me stretched an immense town – an immense black-ness. People – thousands of people hurried past me [–] had errands, had aims, had others to talk to, to trifle with. But I had nobody. This immense city, this immense blackness, had no interiors for me. There were house fronts, staring windows, closed doors, but nothing within: no rooms, no hollow places.[35]

Saunders's insight is persuasive, not least because it identifies this phobia as a problem for Ford even before it directly contributes to his breakdown in 1904. So is his hint that Dowell's vision, in *The Good Soldier*, of an 'immense plain' (like the one at Salisbury perhaps) that is 'the hand of God, stretching out for miles and miles, with great spaces above it and below it', is also informed by Ford's agoraphobia.[36]

Trotter, too, has briefly traced signs of agoraphobia in his fiction. In a characteristically sophisticated reading of Chapter 6 of *Some Do Not ...* (1924), the first volume of Ford's war tetral-ogy *Parade's End* (1924–28), he reflects on the incident in which Tietjens, Ford's protagonist, suffers a sudden agoraphobic attack on a road in the countryside. Agoraphobia, Trotter observes, 'is one of the various ways in which the two main protagonists think about, and move edgily towards, each other'.[37] It is also, perhaps, one of the various ways in which the psychopathologies associated with the spaces of the First World War, spaces of hitherto unimaginable devastation, are transposed to England.

But if Granger is Ford's first agoraphobic character, and Tietjens his final one, then *The Soul of London*, his most direct attempt to represent metropolitan modernity, is probably the first of his books to be shaped throughout by an agoraphobic aesthetic. It was after all composed at the time of his most acute phobic attack, in 1904. Indeed, it is tempting to propose that, in its calculated refusal to be 'encyclopaedic, topographical, or archaeological' in portraying the capital, and its insistence on filtering everything it reconstructs through the consciousness of its author, it is his first agoraphobic fiction (3).

The first chapter, 'From a Distance', captures the book's agoraphobic aesthetic from the opening. 'Thought of from sufficiently far,' Ford begins, 'London offers to the mind's eye singularly little of a picture' (7). London is not a unified phenomenon; it is instead comprised of the infinitely different perspectives with which individuals apprehend it: 'It remains in the end always a matter of approaches' (7). It depends, he argues, on one's preconceptions, on the point at which one enters the city, and innumerable other contingencies. It is impossible to gain a general impression of London, and for the provincial visiting it for the first time, for example, 'the dominant note of his first impression will be that of his own alone-ness' (9). Indeed, he 'will not ever have been so alone' (10).

London is, according to Ford, 'essentially a background, a matter so much more of masses than of individuals' (11). The individual that he subsequently idealized in *Return to Yesterday*, the suave novelist who actively dissolves his identity in the masses, is notably absent from this account of the metropolis. He is replaced by a neurotic or neurasthenic for whom 'an awakened sense of observation is in London bewildering and nerve-shattering, because there are so many things to see and because these things flicker by so quickly' (96). He is a broken kaleidoscope, to echo Baudelaire, endowed with consciousness.

In Ford's cityscape, the inhibited urban subject stands intimidated before 'the limitless stretches of roofs that you have never seen, the streets that you will never travel, the miles and miles of buildings, the myriads of plane-trees, of almonds, of elms – all these appalling regions of London that to every individual of us must remain unknown and untraversed' (102). Instead, the urban subject implicitly constructed in *The Soul of London* is far more fearful of what Ford identifies as the 'assimilative powers' of the city, its vast, indiscriminate appetite for effacing social difference (13).

London is a sublime phenomenon, and Ford's urban subject is almost completely overwhelmed by the fact that, 'if in its tolerance it finds a place for all eccentricities of physiognomy, of costume, of cult, it does so because it crushes out and floods over the significance of those eccentricities.' 'It is one gigantic pantheon of the dead level of democracy,' he concludes (12). In the context of this account, in which to pass unobserved in the city is by implication to capitulate to its death-like levelling of individuality, it seems positively defensive to ascribe London the identity of 'an incomparable background' (22).

In representing the metropolis as a background, 'with its sense of immensity that we must hurry through to keep unceasing appointments', or that we must simply hurry through in order to cope with this sense of immensity, Ford is engaged in a deliberate act of repression (10). He is stepping back from it, and pushing it to the edges of his consciousness, like an agoraphobic standing beside a chaotic road who cautiously retreats from the kerb.

Symptomatically, the vision of the city evoked by Ford in this book is often tangential or marginal to the life of its streets. For example, in the first chapter he describes an archetypal man looking down 'out of dim windows upon the slaty, black, wet misery of a squalid street' (22). And in the second chapter, he recalls the experience of arriving in London by train, which presents the capital as a series of unconnected glimpses, as 'so many bits of uncompleted life': 'I looked down upon black and tiny yards that were like the cells in an electric battery' (42). Ford repeatedly uses this word 'bits'. 'London', he declares at one point in Chapter 1, 'is a thing of these bits' (23).

The agoraphobic cannot see the city in its entirety, its immensity, for this panoramic perspective is overwhelming. He or she must instead glimpse it in the form of a series of 'fleeting impressions and chance encounters', as Siegfried Kracauer phrased it when capturing the aesthetics of the street in his *Theory of Film*.[38]

Far from being immersed in the mass of people, Ford's melancholic narrator is typically detached from it. This is the aesthetic of someone who loves the city but must preserve a safe distance from the life of its streets in order to protect his sense of identity. It is an Impressionist aesthetic, shaped by the contradictory imperative both to embrace the metropolis and to repudiate its oppressive advances. Ford's attempt to apprehend London in prose cannot in short be separated from the agoraphobic impulses that he was combating at the time of this book's composition. In the urban environment, Kracauer continues, 'the kaleidoscopic sights mingle with unidentified shapes and fragmentary visual complexes and cancel each other out'; it thus 'remains an unfixable flow which carries fearful uncertainties and alluring excitements'.[39]

It is these dynamics that Ford seeks to capture in *The Soul of London*, rejecting the apparent certainties of nineteenth-century realist narration, especially in its omniscient mode, and affirming an Impressionist form that, in its emphasis on 'bits', communicates both the kinetic, kaleidoscopic experience of being inside the city, or on its streets, and the psychopathological difficulty of comprehending it in its immensity.

Ford did half-overcome his agoraphobia. In *Return to Yesterday*, he recalls that, soon after his return from Germany in 1904, Conrad forced him to see a doctor called Tebb. Ford asked this doctor whether he thought it advisable, given his medical condition, to finish the biography of Holbein he had begun. The man peremptorily informed him, he records, that he might as well attempt it since he would be dead in a month.

According to Ford's triumphant account of this incident, as soon as Tebb was gone he dressed himself and leapt into a hansom cab that took him to Piccadilly Circus:

You are to remember that my chief trouble was that I imagined that I could not walk. Well, I walked backwards and forwards across the Circus for an hour and a half. I kept on saying: 'Damn that brute. I will not be dead in a month.' And walking across the Circus through the traffic was no joke. Motors are comparatively controllable but the traffic then was mostly horse-drawn and horses in motion are much more difficult to check than automobiles. (206–7)

Ford makes no further comment, but the reader is obviously intended to infer that, thanks to this cathartic treatment, he successfully cured himself.

Ford's condition unquestionably improved. From roughly 1906 to 1914, as he proudly reports in the final part of *Return to Yesterday*, 'The Last of London', he even became something of a *flâneur* – as if he continued to feel the need to demonstrate, in the most performative terms possible, that he was not an agoraphobic. 'You are to think of me then as rather a dandy,' he tells the reader. He describes himself issuing from the door of his London apartment wearing 'a very long morning-coat, a perfectly immaculate high hat, lavender trousers, a near-Gladstone collar and a black satin frock', and carrying 'a malacca cane with a gold knob' (270). Note that the cloth cap, mark of his former determination not to 'high-hat' humanity, has silently been replaced by a … high hat.

'As often as not,' Ford adds, 'I should be followed by a Great Dane' (270). This dog – like the lobsters or turtles that, according to the legend loved by Benjamin, accompanied the most fashionable Parisian *flâneurs* in 1840 – was obviously intended as a dandiacal accessory.[40] I suspect, though, that it also acted as one of those props that agoraphobics habitually employ to help them negotiate the fearsome open spaces of the metropolis.

In his intervention about agoraphobia in the *Lancet* at the turn of the century, Neale observed that the agoraphobic is recognizable, not only because of 'his sudden pausing to lay hold of a paling or to place his hand upon a wall', but because 'he will hardly ever be without a stick or umbrella, which you will notice he will plant at each step at some distance from him, in order to increase his base line of support'.[41] Freud, among later psychologists, confirmed that agoraphobics 'feel protected if they are accompanied by an acquaintance or followed by a vehicle, and so on'.[42] A dog offers an analogous means of increasing one's 'base line of support' when negotiating the city on foot. Ford had finally found a performance that, as Trotter puts it in his discussion of Tietjens's agoraphobic incident, 'enable[d] him to out-manoeuvre his anxiety'.[43]

Ford nonetheless remained haunted by his agoraphobic experiences. The Coda to *Return to Yesterday*, in which he describes Britain in 1914, revisits Piccadilly Circus, the scene of his therapeutic triumph a decade before. In this setting, Ford consciously or unconsciously uses an autobiographical image that is manifestly agoraphobic in order to explore a sense of imminent social cataclysm. Standing 'on the edge of the kerb' on 28 June, the date on which Archduke Ferdinand was assassinated, he confronts a Circus that is 'blocked and blocked and blocked again with vehicles' (311).

'I did not know it but I was taking my last look at the city – as a Londoner', Ford writes. 'And yet perhaps I did know it' (311). The kerb on which he stands symbolizes clearly enough the brink of war. 'I was feeling free and as it were without weight,' he continues, as if experiencing the vertiginous euphoria of a sudden suicidal impulse. Later in the Coda, after discussing his association with the Vorticists, he modifies the image slightly: 'So I stood on the kerb in the Circus and felt adrift' (317).

'The places are countless in the great cities where one stands on the edge of the void', Benjamin wrote in his 'Berlin Chronicle' (1932).[44] Ford's hesitation on the pavement stands in for a global paralysis. 'There's such a lot of nervous breakdown in the land,' he had written to Elsie. Piccadilly Circus implicitly opens up onto the terrifying expanses of the battlefields of France. He comes to terms with his phobia, then, in so far as this is possible, by universalizing it as an historical condition. Ford's agoraphobia and the mania that besets the 'entire habitable globe', as he phrases it in *Return to Yesterday*, are finally one.

7

Striding, Staring

Virginia Woolf's
Mrs Dalloway

In a scene from *Mrs Dalloway* (1925), Virginia Woolf's most sustained attempt to grasp the relationship of consciousness to the conditions of life in the modern metropolis, a solitary, middle-aged man, Peter Walsh, paces north along Whitehall, one of London's most monumental roads. If Walter Benjamin noted that, 'in his book on Dickens,' G. K. Chesterton 'masterfully captured the man who roams the big city lost in thought', then the same formulation might be applied to Woolf's novel, in relation both to Peter and, later in the narrative, his shell-shocked compatriot Septimus.[1]

The scene in which Peter circulates more or less aimlessly through central London is the one with which Woolf opened 'The Hours', the draft of *Mrs Dalloway* she composed in her notebooks in June 1923. It is in this respect the novel's inaugural or initiatory incident. Roaming the big city lost in thought, Peter is only half-conscious of his surroundings, which are the administrative centre of the British Empire, because he is preoccupied with clinging to the idea that he is still young. 'I am not old, he cried, and marched up Whitehall, as if there rolled down to him, vigorous, unending, his future.'[2]

Woolf's narrator describes him, pointedly, as 'striding, staring' (65). He is both at home in the imperial metropolis, supremely confident in his negotiation of its space, and oddly detached or displaced from it; not least perhaps because only the previous night he has returned from his colonial existence in India. Peter moves his limbs, he walks the streets, the narrator implies, principally because it stops him from 'feeling hollowed out, utterly empty within' – like Wells's Invisible Man in London (64). To 'stand', to 'stop', is to apprehend that 'the skeleton of habit alone upholds the human frame' (63).

In spite of Peter's sudden effusion about 'his future', it fails to roll down the road to him as he hopes. Instead, he hears behind him 'a patter like the patter of leaves in a wood' – a sound more like death than life. This unsettling, irregular sound is mingled with 'a rustling, regular thudding sound, which as it overtook him drummed his thoughts, strict in step, up Whitehall, without his doing' (65). The city's sounds infiltrate his consciousness; the rhythms of his consciousness reshape the city. As the thudding noise passes him, Peter glimpses a troop of soldiers:

> Boys in uniform, carrying guns, marched with their eyes ahead of them, marched, their arms stiff, and on their faces an expression like the letters of a legend written round the base of a statue praising duty, gratitude, fidelity, love of England. (65–6)

These uniformed youths, parading up Whitehall, have been commemorating the dead of the Great War, which ended some four and a half years earlier. They, too, are effectively 'striding, staring'. Marching 'with their eyes ahead of them', they collectively and ritualistically mimic, perhaps even mock, both Peter's appropriation of the city's streets and his alienation from them.

Disconcerted, Peter dismisses the boys in uniform. They are 'weedy for the most part', he thinks; the embodiment of an enfeebled empire. If the soldiers are youthful, then, they do not necessarily have a 'vigorous, unending' future before them either. 'Drugged into a stiff yet staring corpse by discipline,' the figures that form this troop are like the undead marching up behind him (66). But Peter cannot keep pace with them, and he admits to feeling a rueful sense of admiration for their order and mechanical precision.

I can't keep up with them, Peter Walsh thought, as they marched up Whitehall, and sure enough, on they marched, past him, past everyone, in their steady way, as if one will worked legs and arms uniformly, and life, with its varieties, its irreticences, had been laid under a pavement of monuments and wreaths … (66)

Hesitating on the edge of the pavement, Peter perceives that their gaze is like the 'marble stare' of those statues of heroic military leaders that stand sentinel along the roads lining the centre of London – 'the spectacular images of great soldiers [that] stood looking ahead of them' (66). Standing, staring. Peter respects the capacity of these recruits to renounce the contradictions of life in the metropolitan city, its varieties and – to underline the wonderful word that Woolf herself seems to have devised and first used in *Night and Day* (1919) – its 'irreticences'.[3]

Peter's admiration for the soldiers' freedom from responsibility has its limits, however, principally because he himself fears the loss of autonomy it seems to entail:

But the stare Peter Walsh did not want for himself in the least; though he could respect it in others. He could respect it in boys. They don't know the troubles of the flesh yet, he thought, as the marching boys disappeared in the direction of the Strand … (66–7)

Those who stare when they are negotiating the streets, especially if they lack the soldiers' excuse for gazing mechanically into the middle distance, implicitly align themselves not with the *flâneur*, the urbane stroller who appears to be effortlessly in control of his relationship to the city, but the *badaud*.

The *badaud* is an early nineteenth-century Parisian archetype defined by his gaping, gawping attitude to its spectacle. As the journalist and historian Victor Fournel explained in *Ce qu'on voit dans les rues de Paris* (1858), in a passage quoted by Benjamin, 'the simple flâneur [*sic*] is always in full possession of his individuality, whereas the individuality of the *badaud* disappears.' 'Under the influence of the spectacle,' Fournel continues, 'the *badaud* becomes an impersonal creature,' one who is 'no longer a human being'.⁴ No one wants this sort of stare for themselves in the least.

Reminded that he is alone and anonymous in London, Peter is suddenly suffused once again with a sense of excitement. 'The strangeness of standing alone, alive, unknown, at half-past eleven in Trafalgar Square overcame him. What is it? Where am I?' (67). These vertiginous questions induce not horror but a strange, fragile joy. He is overwhelmed by 'three great emotions', namely:

> understanding; a vast philanthropy; and finally, as if the result of the others, an irrepressible, exquisite delight; as if inside his brain, by another hand, strings were pulled, shutters moved, and he, having nothing to do with it, yet stood at the opening of endless avenues down which if he chose he might wander. (67)

Peter's sense of self, like that of the soldiers, whose actions are automatic, is cancelled out. Someone other than him appears to be controlling his consciousness – pulling the strings, moving the shutters. But at the same time his sense of self is affirmed, glorified. Rendered foreign to himself, he is freed. It is as if he stands at the centre of a city whose roads radiate out from him in the form of limitless possibilities.

Liberated for an instant from the need to find himself, Peter does for an instant find himself. He feels 'utterly free – as happens in the downfall of habit when the mind, like an unguarded flame, bows and bends and seems about to blow from its holding' (67). But this ecstasy cannot be maintained. At least, it is rapidly displaced into a hard, gem-like desire for an attractive young woman he happens to see crossing Trafalgar Square:

> Straightening himself and stealthily fingering his pocket-knife he started after her to follow this woman, this excitement, which seemed even with its back turned to shed on him a light which connected them, which singled him out, as if the random uproar of the traffic had whispered through hollowed hands his name, not Peter, but his private name which he called himself in his own thoughts. (68)

This is Peter as predator: Pete the Ripper. 'Stealthily fingering his pocket-knife', like an onanist or a potential rapist, he follows her along the Haymarket, up Regent Street, to Oxford Street, past all the shops (68). 'He was an adventurer, reckless, he thought, swift, daring, indeed (landed as he was last night from India) a romantic buccaneer, careless of all these damned proprieties' (69). This is a deeply disturbing fantasy of male sexual potency, potency that overrides precisely those proprieties on which, in a patriarchal society, it secretly depends.[5] And it cannot, frankly, be too reticent.

Finally, Peter pursues the young woman as far as Great Portland Street, where she enters a house in a side street, casts 'one look in his direction, but not at him', and is gone: 'It was over' (70). There has been no *échange de regards*. As Rachel Bowlby has pointed out, this passage constitutes a 'parody of the amorous clinch or climax that might have been expected', underlining the satirical role played by her glance back.[6] She has triumphed over him.

Peter is disappointed at the outcome of this game, which has sublimated what he called, in his reflections on the soldiers, 'the troubles of the flesh'; but he is not deflated. Certainly, he doesn't feel ashamed of his predatoriness, which is inseparable, so he unconsciously assumes with classic male complacency, from his playfulness. The libidinal after-effects of his epiphany persist, in fact, and he relishes the sense that, 'like the pulse of a perfect heart, life struck straight through the streets' (70). Life, then, is like the knife he fingers in his pocket. It is something he might use to strike straight through the streets, as he strides straight through the streets.

The female pedestrian on whom he has predated, flashing up in the form of a kind of after-image, is thus represented in coded form as the victim of a more or less frenzied, sexualized attack (the phrase 'struck straight through the streets' seems to echo a sensationalistic newspaper headline). Peter's unconscious, according to the dream-logic of displacement, substitutes 'life' for the 'knife' he has forgotten he is fingering; and it thus enacts the violence that his conscious thoughts merely brought him to the edge of imagining.

'Where should he go?' Woolf writes in free indirect style, as the episode ends:

> Where should he go? No matter. Up the street, then, towards Regent's Park. His boots on the pavement struck out 'no matter'; for it was early, still very early. (70)

The 'no matter' that his boots beat out on the stones like a tattoo is an unconscious abdication of precisely the responsibility and autonomy he had sought to preserve in the face of those soldiers who 'marched with their eyes ahead of them'. For Peter, too, it transpires, 'striding' and 'staring' are inseparable activities, for striding has spontaneously resulted in staring. And, like the *badaud* whose archetypal example he implicitly resisted, he has become, in the terms that Benjamin transcribed from Fournel, 'an impersonal creature,' one who is 'no longer a human being'.

This scene from *Mrs Dalloway*, initiating the action of 'The Hours', constitutes the novel's seminal scene. But it also constitutes what Marshall Berman characterizes, in a celebrated account of the dialectics of modernity, as a 'primal modern scene'.

Berman formulates the term during a discussion of Baudelaire's Paris after 1848, the time when Louis-Napoléon Bonaparte and Georges-Eugène Haussmann 'blast[ed] a vast network of boulevards through the heart of the old medieval city', creating a culture of spectacle in which, alongside the regimentation and reification of everyday life in the city, 'urban realities could easily become dreamy and magical.' But the notion of the 'primal modern scene' refers more generally to 'experiences that arise from the concrete everyday life' of the metropolis in capitalist society; experiences that 'carry a mythic resonance and depth that propel them beyond their place and time and transform them into archetypes of modern life'.[7] It is in anticipation of something like a 'primal modern scene', for example, that D. H. Lawrence's protagonist Paul Morel, disavowing both his mother and his lover, 'walk[s] towards the city's gold phosphorescence' in the final paragraph of *Sons and Lovers* (1913).[8]

It is above all in the street, the site where private and public experiences intersect, that these scenes are acted out. There, the dialectics of exterior and interior that are structural to the everyday conditions of modernity are constantly dramatized. 'The street', André Breton asserted in the formula that Benjamin liked to cite, is 'the only region of valid experience.'[9]

Alongside *Mrs Dalloway*, a series of significant European novels in the early twentieth century situated the relationship between the city and consciousness, or what the pioneering sociologist Georg Simmel typified as the metropolis and mental life, at the centre of their attempt to solve the representational problems thrown up by the social and cultural developments of the time: James Joyce's *Stephen Hero* (1904); Joseph Conrad's *The Secret Agent* (1907); Robert Walser's *Jakob von Gunten* (1909); Dorothy Richardson's *Pilgrimage* (1915–); Joyce's *Ulysses* (1922); Italo Svevo's *Zeno's Conscience* (1923); André Breton's *Nadja* (1928); Robert Musil's *Man Without Qualities* (1930–42); Djuna Barnes's *Nightwood* (1936); and Jean Rhys's *Good Morning, Midnight* (1939) – among others. These are novels in which, as Raymond Williams summarized it in relation to *Ulysses*, 'the forces of the action have become internal and in a way there is no longer a city, there is only a man walking through it.'[10] Or a woman. In Samuel Beckett's late-modernist fiction, for its part, from *Murphy* (1938) on, the social is internalized to a pathological extent, and 'the city becomes prolapsed', as one critic expressively puts it.[11]

The drama of Peter's epiphany on the roads of imperial London in Woolf's novel about the metropolis and mental life is of primal significance for both abstract and concrete reasons. In the concrete terms on which I propose to concentrate in the first instance, Peter's epiphanic experience dramatizes an encounter between the archetypal hero of modernity identified by Baudelaire in 'The Painter of Modern Life' (1863), namely the 'passionate spectator', and the representative forms of urban spectacle – here, the troop of soldiers and the female passer-by.[12] This relationship between spectator and spectacle finds its template in Paris, where Haussmann, driving boulevards through in order both to reinforce the counter-revolution and provide the optimum environment for the profit motive, and displacing some 350,000 people in the process, set out the geometries of commodity capitalism.

But it is not limited to Paris at this time; the concept of the 'primal modern scene' can be extended to describe some of the political and psychological effects of the monumental spaces of other cities, especially in the later nineteenth and early twentieth centuries, when an emergent culture of consumption, embodied most strikingly in the development of the department store, was superimposed onto the spatial order of the imperial metropolis.

The 'passionate spectator' sketched by Baudelaire is a middle- or upper-middle-class man who freely resides 'in the heart of the multitude, amid the ebb and flow of movement, in the midst of the fugitive and the infinite', as he puts it in 'The Painter of Modern Life' (9).

The function Baudelaire ascribed to this spectator was to act as an exquisitely tuned instrument for conducting and transmitting the contradictory energies of capitalist modernity, a state of permanent social and existential transformation. Women and working-class men were for the most part disqualified from performing the role of spectator due to the social restrictions that, in the class-divided, patriarchal conditions of capitalist society, determined their relations to the city. If the 'passionate spectator' defined modernity, because he had the requisite economic or social independence, then in an urban context he also marginalized these subaltern actors in relation to it.

For historical reasons, Williams observes, 'perception of the new qualities of the modern city had been associated, from the beginning, with a man walking, as if alone, in its streets.'[13] Perhaps the crucial phrase here, certainly in relation to Woolf's novel, is 'as if alone', for it hints at all those whose individual identities are erased in the streets in order to sustain the male, middle- or upper-middle-class spectator's sovereign subjectivity. Their reticences, to put it in Woolf's terms, sustain his irreticences.

The solitary man in the streets of the metropolis – a spiritual if not social aristocrat – is essentially a post-Romantic archetype. Baudelaire, like his hero Edgar Allan Poe in 'The Man of the Crowd' (1840), transposed the alienated but finally privileged individual crucial to Romantic ideology from the landscape to the cityscape. The modernists, of course, both extended and challenged this archetype. From Conrad to Barnes and Beckett, they variously displaced its social identity and delved deep into its existential one. In *Ulysses*, for example, Joyce located the life of the city in the consciousness of a lower-middle-class Jewish man, Leopold Bloom, whose vicambulations lead him on a tour of Dublin in the course of one day in June 1904. In *Mrs Dalloway*, Woolf centred it on the consciousness of an upper-class woman, Clarissa herself, whose own movements trace a path through central London on one day in June 1923. 'I love walking in London,' she declares the first time she speaks in the novel, adding for emphasis that 'it's better than walking in the country' (6).

'What else, after all, would Clarissa's surname have led us to expect,' Bowlby wryly comments, 'than the woman who likes to dally along the way, the *flâneuse* herself.'[14] *Mrs Dalloway* is one of Woolf's numerous affirmations, in articles, diary entries and letters, of her right as a female citizen, in spite of the social and moral restrictions historically imposed on women, freely to roam the streets of the city.

No doubt the richest of these declarations, aside from this novel, is the essay 'Street Haunting: A London Adventure' (1927), her distinctly Dickensian celebration of what she calls 'the greatest pleasure of town life in winter – rambling the streets of London'. Woolf's particular predilection, she admits, is for solitary walking on a cold, dark evening, because she relishes 'the irresponsibility which darkness and lamplight bestow': 'We are no longer quite ourselves.'[15] *Mrs Dalloway* is among other things an exploration of the ways in which we both are and aren't ourselves in the public spaces of the metropolis.

In *Mrs Dalloway*, in addition to asserting the rights of the *flâneuse*, Woolf deployed her principal male characters in ways that challenge the *flâneur*'s monopoly over representations of the modern metropolis. She uses Peter – whose shadowy form can be glimpsed in the penultimate paragraph of 'Street Haunting', where Woolf briefly portrays the city, in gendered language, as a 'forest where live those wild beasts, our fellow men' – to expose the social and sexual politics that have shaped the paradigm of the *flâneur*.[16] In his character, as Benjamin said of Poe's old man in 'The Man of the Crowd' (1840), she 'purposely blurs the difference between the asocial person and the *flâneur*'.

In the character of Septimus, with his psychotic, shell-shocked mind, Woolf presses the paradigm of the *flâneur* to the point of collapse. If for Poe, according to Benjamin once more, the *flâneur* is 'above all, someone who does not feel comfortable in his own company', then in Septimus this inability to feel at home in his own skin becomes pathological.[17] For Septimus, as for some of Beckett's characters, the city becomes prolapsed.

As an upper- or upper-middle-class man, Peter is an exemplary candidate for the role of *flâneur*, but his relationship to the metropolis is itself far from comfortable. In fact, Woolf identifies in him an immanent critique of this post-Romantic archetype; that is, she uses him to deconstruct it from the inside.

In Peter's stroll along Whitehall, she stages the ideological drama of the spectator's encounter with the concrete forms of metropolitan spectacle: the soldiers, who stand in for the culture of imperialism; and the female pedestrian, who stands in for the culture of consumerism. Woolf employs the phrase 'spectacular images' in reference to the military statues that Peter passes in Whitehall, but it applies to these other reified figures, too, frozen as they are by the gaze of the man walking, as if alone, in the streets (66). In the portrait of Peter, Woolf reveals the ways in which Baudelaire's 'passionate spectator' colludes – as Benjamin recognized when he spoke of the *flâneur* surrendering to 'the intoxication of the commodity immersed in a surging stream of customers' – in the culture of the spectacle.[18]

Alongside the dandy, both the soldier and the female passer-by play a privileged role in Baudelaire's poetics of modernity, a phenomenon he summarizes in terms of 'the *outward show of life*, such as it is to be seen in the capitals of the civilized world; the pageantry of military life, of fashion and of love' (24). The pageantries of military life and of fashion and love are spectacular expressions, respectively, of the cultures of imperialism and consumerism – the principal components of capitalist society in the European metropolis from the mid- to late nineteenth century. 'In many respects,' David Harvey has argued, 'imperial spectacle dovetailed neatly with commodification and the deepening power of the circulation of capital over daily life.'[19]

In addition to mobilizing support for imperial authority, the boulevards that Haussmann built in Paris, serving as sites of both production and consumption, created employment and 'facilitated circulation of commodities, money, and people'. Hence the 'sociality' of the people that inhabited their precincts 'was now as much controlled by the imperatives of commerce as by police power.' In this context, the soldier and the female passer-by both act as 'bearers of the spectacle'.[20]

First, then, the spectacle of the soldiers. Baudelaire comments that the painter and illustrator Constantin Guys, the artist who for him most conveniently embodies the aesthetics of metropolitan modernity, 'shows a very marked predilection for the military man, the soldier'. And he speculates that 'this fondness may be attributed not only to the qualities and virtues which necessarily pass from the warrior's soul into his physiognomy and his bearing, but also to the outward splendour in which he is professionally clad' (24).

Baudelaire appears to share his friend's predilection. In the most substantial section of 'The Painter of Modern Life', he glorifies Guys' love of 'the landscapes of the great city', his delight in its 'universal life', and imagines a military parade: 'A regiment passes, on its way, as it may be, to the ends of the earth, tossing into the air of the boulevards its trumpet-calls as winged and stirring as hope' (10). He pictures Guys' spontaneous artistic response to this sight, and evokes the alacrity with which, in his sketches, he examines and analyses 'the bearing and external aspect of that company' (11). Baudelaire mimes this rapid, poetic reaction in his own prose, which excitedly registers 'glittering equipment, music, bold determined glances, heavy, solemn moustaches' (11).

Baudelaire's description concludes in a paean to Guys' capacity for identifying with the phenomenon he represents, for collapsing subject into object: 'See how his soul lives with the soul of that regiment, marching like a single animal, a proud image of joy in obedience!' (11). It is an unsettling outburst. Berman has pointed out that 'these are the soldiers who killed 25,000 Parisians in June

3 and who opened the way for Napoleon III in December of 1851' – occasions when Baudelaire opposed the men whose militaristic glamour appears to thrill him a decade later.[21]

Uncomfortably, Baudelaire's celebratory image of troops marching through the roads of the capital, as if to the farthest reaches of the empire, carried cataclysmic implications for the proletarians of Paris (who were slaughtered in comparable numbers by Thiers's troops, it might be added, at the demise of the Paris Commune in 1871). Berman, in his account, underlines 'the tremendous importance of military display – psychological as well as political importance – and its power to captivate even the freest spirits'.[22]

But, if it captivates Baudelaire, it does not captivate Woolf. In the aftermath of the Great War, she strips away the pretensions of military spectacle. Peter perceives the 'stiff yet staring corpse' underlying the spectacular image of the marching soldier (66). Stiffening, staring. For this spectator, the thrill that Baudelaire had experienced is no longer possible. The horrors of history interrupt the spell of the imperial spectacle.

The second of Baudelaire's vectors of modernity as spectacle is the female passer-by. Baudelaire presents the spectacular image of this archetypal figure in a section of 'The Painter of Modern Life' entitled 'Women and Prostitutes'. He is especially interested in prostitutes.

'In that vast picture-gallery which is life in London or Paris,' he declares, 'we shall meet with the various types of fallen womanhood – of woman in revolt against society – at all levels', from courtesans to the 'poor slaves' of the stews (37). In classifying these types, and detailing their physiognomies, he insists that he is not trying 'to gratify the reader, any more than to scandalize him'; and he is adamant that, if anyone is intending to satisfy 'his unhealthy curiosity', 'he will find nothing whatever to stimulate the sickness of his imagination' (38).

In restaging the Baudelairean forms of the spectacle in *Mrs Dalloway*, Woolf hints that there is in fact an 'unhealthy curiosity' to Peter's interest in the woman he covertly tracks through the streets of central London. This is in part because, even as he idealizes her, he objectifies her body: 'she became the very woman he had always had in mind; young, but stately; merry, but discreet; black, but enchanting' (68). This scene is a feminist re-inscription, not only of 'The Painter of Modern Life' but of Baudelaire's famous poem 'À une passante' (1855), in which he describes a female passer-by dressed in mourning, 'stately yet lithe, as if a statue walked', investing this 'lovely fugitive' with his libidinal and spiritual longings.[23]

But Peter's curiosity is also implicitly unhealthy because, as he silently pursues the passer-by, he collapses her identity into the commodities amongst which, at the core of London's culture of consumption, she circumambulates:

> On and on she went, across Piccadilly, and up Regent Street, ahead of him, her cloak, her gloves, her shoulders combining with the fringes and the laces and the feather boas in the windows to make the spirit of finery and whimsy which dwindled out of the shops onto the pavement, as the light of a lamp goes wavering at night over hedges in the darkness. (69)

Here are the operations of 'fashion', which – in Benjamin's formulation – 'couples the living body to the inorganic world' in commodity society.[24] In an almost cubistic effect, the woman's body is broken up into discrete objects, including hands and shoulders. These then combine and intersect, in the reflective surfaces of the glass screening the shops or department stores, with the commodities on display. If the commodity itself, from the mid- to late nineteenth century, increasingly became the dominant form of the spectacle, then this anonymous woman, in acting as a 'bearer of the spectacle', is comprehensively colonized by it.

In Peter's consciousness, commodities are at the same time spiritualized, in the shape of the ethereal finery that spills onto the pavement, and eroticized. Bowlby, in her essay on Woolf and walking, revisits the journalist Louis Huart's *Le Flâneur* (1850) and emphasizes that 'the woman – the object *par excellence* of the *flâneur*'s interest – is in this regard analogous to the shop window'.[25] In this passage from *Mrs Dalloway*, it might be added, it is a relationship of identity as much as analogy.

Woolf uses Peter's predatory activities on the street to demonstrate, in Benjamin's compelling formulation from his essay on
'The Return of the *Flâneur*' (1929), 'how easy it is for the *flâneur*
to depart from the ideal of the philosopher out for a stroll, and
to assume the features of the werewolf at large in the social
jungle.'[26] Peter – a werewoolf, so to speak – is the 'passionate
spectator' as raptor; as one of those 'wild beasts, our fellow men',
the inhabitants of 'the heart of the forest' that is the city, whom
she mentions at the conclusion of 'Street Haunting'.[27]

Walking in the day, and stalking in the day, Peter recalls what
Baudelaire identifies, in a phrase from Rousseau that appears in
his account of Guys, as the '*depraved animal*' who is visible at
evening time in the city 'wherever the sun lights up [his] swift
joys' (10). In this primal modern scene, Woolf implicitly presents
a brutally unsentimental feminist critique of the Baudelairean
hero of modernity.

In the more abstract or formal terms that, before I looked at
Baudelaire's concrete instances of the soldiers and prostitutes,
I briefly invoked in order to identify the significance of Peter's
epiphany on the roads of London in *Mrs Dalloway*, it is important to underline that this character's perceptions of the city enact
what the artist and art theorist Victor Burgin has usefully referred
to as the 'imbrication of social and mental space'.[28]

This mutual interpenetration of inner and outer comprises an
exemplary experience, in the urban imaginary limned by modernist art and literature, of the reciprocal relationship between
spectacle and introspection. In this sense, too, the incident
involving Peter in central London revisits the site of some of
Baudelaire's meditations on the poetics of everyday life in Paris.
In the conditions of metropolitan modernity, private and public
forms of space are liable to open into and enfold one another.
For an instant, the multi-faceted forms of the individual's mental
and metropolitan lives, their shifting concavities and convexities,
connect and intersect.

At the moment of his epiphany in Whitehall, when he simultaneously experiences 'understanding', 'a vast philanthropy' and
'an irrepressible, exquisite delight', Peter feels his mind become

'flat as a marsh' and yet, at the same time, senses that he is suddenly standing 'at the opening of endless avenues' (67). In this dance of movement and stasis, surface and depth, of the interior and the exterior, the open and the closed, it is impossible to discriminate clearly between consciousness and the city. The contradictory effect of Woolf's composite image is, in this respect, comparable to the interpenetration of spaces explored by several of the modernist painters and poets of her generation, whose characteristic productions simultaneously compress and explode urban space, flattening it and fragmenting it.

Picasso's and Braque's 'analytical cubist' paintings from the first ten or fifteen years of the twentieth century, which used a monochromatic palette to intensify their multi-perspectival effects, provide a graphic illustration of the crisis of the old, apparently solid distinction between interior and exterior space, subject and object. Like the modernist literary experiments of the early twentieth century, they explore what Philip Fisher, writing about *Ulysses*, refers to as 'torn space' – 'a multiple, distracted, interrupted spatial experience that is related to "looking around" and derives from our everyday, usually overlooked experiences in the city street.'[29]

What about the poetics of the city in this period? Take Isaac Rosenberg's 'Fleet Street' (1912). Here, the poet carefully orchestrates the relations of inside and outside in his depiction of the individual embedded in the disorienting everyday life of the metropolis. He immerses the reader in the anarchic conditions of the 'shaking quivering street', which has a 'pulse and heart that throbs and glows / As if strife were its repose'. But, in spite of closing his ears to the chaotic metrics of this arterial road, he quickly capitulates to them:

> I shut my ear to such rude sounds
> As reach a harsh discordant note,
> Till, melting into what surrounds,
> My soul doth with the current float;
> And from the turmoil and the strife
> Wakes all the melody of life.

The poem's concluding stanza, in which both the buildings and passers-by that populate the street 'blindly stare' at its inhabitants, iterates the idea that the city is, in the end, repressive, secretive.[30] This cannot erase the impression, though, that the poet's private self has, for a moment, opened up to the public life of the metropolis, creating an almost miraculous harmony. The poet's reticence, it might be said, finally concedes to the varieties and irreticences of the city, which constitute the poem's very conditions of possibility.

Hope Mirrlees, to take another example, explores comparable territory, at once psychic and social, in *Paris* (1920). This remarkable, if often obscure poem about the interrelationship of metropolis and mental life, which Woolf edited for the Hogarth Press, is formally more experimental than Rosenberg's. As Sean Pryor notes, it is both 'a journey across the city, registering a speaker's encounters with people and places', and, at the same time, 'the interior monologue or phantasmagoria of a speaker ranging across Paris in her imagination'.[31] It intermingles fragments of script from the streets of the French capital, especially in the form of notices and shop signs, with apparently random, dreamlike phrases that seem to have floated from the poet's consciousness, like scraps of a torn-up notebook spilling from her pocket, as she wanders aimlessly through the city in the course of a single day.

Mirrlees' verse, endlessly inventive in its use of typography, like Braque's and Picasso's cubist paintings, is dense and hallucinatory: 'CONCORDE // I can't / I must go slowly.'[32] Here, too, in language that anticipates Beckett as well as Eliot, the city seems to have prolapsed into the poet's consciousness. 'Concorde' is both the Place de la Concorde, or the signage relating to it, and an ironic reference to the vision of a harmonious city that, in attempting to orchestrate the contradictions and cacophonies of the relations of consciousness and the street, the poet mocks. It is what Rosenberg identifies as 'the melody of life' that, if the poet can successfully orchestrate it, freely coalesces from 'the turmoil and the strife' of the metropolis.

ॐ

In 'The Painter of Modern Life', Baudelaire had sketched these kinds of complicated, constantly changing spatial dynamics between the inner and the outer when he compared the passionate spectator in the city 'to a kaleidoscope gifted with consciousness, responding to each one of [the crowd's] movements and reproducing the multiplicity of life and the flickering grace of all the elements of life'. Baudelaire adds: 'He is an "I" with an insatiable appetite for the "non-I"' (10).

For Baudelaire, as the philosopher Gaston Bachelard emphasized, 'immensity is an intimate dimension.' In his subtle phenomenological meditation on the role of the word 'vast' in Baudelaire's oeuvre, Bachelard quotes from the latter's *Journaux intimes* (first published two decades after the poet's death, in 1887): 'In certain almost supernatural inner states, the depth of life is entirely revealed in the spectacle, however ordinary, that we have before our eyes, and which becomes the symbol of it.' 'The exterior spectacle', Bachelard explains, 'helps intimate grandeur unfold.'[33]

Modernist literature pursues and plays out the Baudelairean dialectic of mental and metropolitan space, of the intimate and the spectacular, in multiple directions. Christopher Butler has typified this in terms of the tension, in the 'confrontation with the city' characteristic of the early twentieth-century avant-garde, 'between an introspective alienation and a celebration of the sheer energy and collective diversity of life.' This is the contrast, he adds, between *The Waste Land* and *Ulysses*, both published in 1922.[34]

In spite of their different forms and different emphases, both Eliot's poem and Joyce's novel explore the articulations of self and the city in a bid to apprehend the experience of metropolitan modernity (as do the poems by Rosenberg and Mirrlees). The former is a cracked collocation of voices that collectively evoke the consciousness of an imperial city in a state of terminal decline. The latter is a peregrination through the glorious, grimy life of a colonial city that, immersed in the present of its presiding consciousnesses, is filled with a sense of the future as well as the past.

In the representation of its principal male characters, Peter and Septimus, *Mrs Dalloway* explores both of the tendencies outlined by Butler – 'introspective alienation and a celebration of the sheer energy and collective diversity of life' – with notable clarity. During Peter's perambulation through central London, the city and his consciousness seem continuous, their spaces coterminous. But he remains within the orbit of the ordinary, the ostensibly rational. He is conscious, for instance, of 'the strangeness of standing alone, alive, unknown, at half-past eleven in Trafalgar Square' (67).

Empirical reality thus retains its ontological priority. It doesn't dissolve, however much it is transformed by being absorbed into Peter's consciousness. The shops, the statues, the streets, remain independent of him. It is only as he falls asleep beside an elderly children's nurse on a bench in Regent's Park that the real, for a time, seems spectral. Lapsing into this hypnagogic state, he toys with the idea that 'nothing exists outside us except a state of mind' (73).

Septimus, in contradistinction, does not remain within the orbit of the ordinary and ostensibly rational. For the shell-shocked soldier adrift in an indifferent metropolis, the exterior spectacle helps both an intimate grandeur and an intimate horror to unfold. Concrete reality is assimilated to his traumatized consciousness in a perpetual rush, at once exhilarating and terrifying. Exquisitely sensitive to his immediate environment, he feels as if his body has been 'macerated until only the nerve fibres were left':

> He lay back in his chair, exhausted but upheld. He lay resting, waiting, before he again interpreted, with effort, with agony, to mankind. He lay very high, on the back of the world. The earth thrilled beneath him. Red flowers grew through his flesh; their stiff leaves rustled by his head. Music began clanging against the rocks up here. (88–9)

The city itself is the cross on which Septimus is crucified. The sound of a motor horn, which reaches him from the road, cannons about in his consciousness, colliding in 'shocks of sound' that rise in 'smooth columns', and sliding in and out of his delirious fantasies (89).

These fantasies, which echo some of the imagery of *The Waste Land*, find him marooned on 'his rock, like a drowned sailor on a rock', struggling for air like a beached swimmer that the tide rips back and forth between the earth and the sea: 'and as, before waking, the voices of birds and the sound of wheels chime and chatter in queer harmony, grow louder and louder, and the sleeper feels himself drawing to the shores of life, so he felt himself drawing towards life, the sun growing hotter, cries sounding louder, something tremendous about to happen' (89–90).

Here, albeit in an accelerated form far more extreme than Peter's experience, is a dance of movement and stasis, surface and depth, of the interior and the exterior, the open and the closed, that makes it impossible to discriminate clearly between consciousness and the city. In contrast to Peter's hypnagogic state, though, Woolf portrays Septimus's thought in terms of a hypnopompic state; in other words, the state that precedes not falling asleep but awakening.

After his sleep, Peter passes the bench in Regent's Park on which Septimus happens to be sitting with his wife. This is one of those encounters or non-encounters characteristic of metropolitan modernity, which is daily defined by contingencies that seem both meaningful and meaningless. Seeing Peter approach, Septimus spontaneously identifies him with one of his dead comrades from the Front. In a horrifying moment, sensing 'legions of men prostrate behind him', he apprehends Peter as 'the dead man in the grey suit' (91, 92). His painful experience of the synaesthetics of the city – the chime of another motor horn 'tinkl[es] divinely on the grass stalks' – has in an instant opened out into a vision of London as a city of the dead (90).

This phantasmagoria provides a superimposition of two linked terrains: the prospect of urban modernity and the landscapes of technological war. 'So many,' as Eliot had intoned in an echo of Dante, 'I had not thought death had undone so many …'[35] The capital is suddenly a city composed not of streets encircling parks but of trenches bordering no-man's-land; not of endless avenues, to put it in terms of Peter's mental topography, but of marshland. A Waste Land.

In Lawrence's poem 'Town in 1917' (1918), an unsettling attempt to think through London's imperial inheritance, the poet glimpses an apocalyptic London consisting of 'Fleet, hurrying limbs, / Soft-footed dead'. Recalling Joseph Conrad's *Heart of Darkness* (1899), the nightmarish final stanzas of the poem, which evoke the imperial city's past as a colonized city, present the metropolis, in a time of cataclysmic war, as a place of primordial horror:

> London, with hair
> Like a forest darkness, like a marsh
> Of rushes, ere the Romans
> Broke in her lair.[36]

It is to this horrifying hinterland, the territory of brutal, senseless military conflict, that Whitehall secretly leads in *Mrs Dalloway*. Septimus's hallucination is the symptomatic expression of the imperial city's unconscious. It reveals the barbaric horror on which the grandeur of the capital is built, which Woolf subsequently evoked to such sudden, frightening effect in the image of 'the heart of the forest where live those wild beasts, our fellow men' in 'Street Haunting'.

This is the repressed topography of the 'landscapes of the great city' that Baudelaire's spectator gazes on, a city littered with the ghostly corpses of the 25,000 proletarians past which the regiment that thrills him have processed. It is the chaos and desolation that underlies 'the amazing harmony of life in the capital cities', which he glimpses in the fearful, infernal associations of the empty plain and the stony labyrinths of the metropolis (10).

In the terms famously developed by Simmel in 'The Metropolis and Mental Life' (1903), it might be said that Septimus fails 'to preserve the autonomy and individuality of his existence in the face of overwhelming social forces'. Or, more precisely, his autonomy and individuality are at once erased and intensified in the everyday conditions of the modern city. In his case, the organ that the 'metropolitan type of man' develops in order to protect himself 'against the threatening currents and discrepancies of his external environment which would uproot him' has degenerated.[37] It has atrophied on the battlefields of Europe.

The passion of Baudelaire's spectator becomes pathological in Septimus as he fails to cope with the 'myriad impressions' his mind attempts to assimilate. In 'Modern Fiction' (1925), Woolf pictures them as 'an incessant shower of innumerable atoms' – as if they are shrapnel.[38]

Septimus's kaleidoscopic consciousness rotates in uncontrollable motion. It cannot process what Simmel calls 'the psychological conditions which the metropolis creates' – 'the rapid crowding of changing images, the sharp discontinuity in the grasp of a single glance, and the unexpectedness of onrushing impressions.' Septimus is fatally susceptible to one of the 'great dangers of the metropolis' – 'indiscriminate suggestibility'. What Simmel identifies as 'the *intensification of nervous stimulation* which results from the swift and uninterrupted change of outer and inner stimuli' overwhelms him.[39] The partition that, however porous, preserves the distinction between interior and exterior, mental life and metropolitan life, collapses completely.

In this sense, inhabiting the city is itself like subsisting in a permanent state of combat. Septimus cannot keep the battlefield out of either his consciousness or the city. Woolf sees the war that produces this susceptibility as the constitutive condition of urban modernity. It is the barbarism that subsists beneath London's veneer of civilization; what Baudelaire, describing the Parisian courtesan in 'The Painter of Modern Life', calls 'the savagery that lurks in the midst of civilization' (36).

Peter, for his part, is far closer to an embodiment of Simmel's 'blasé attitude', and it might be claimed that the arc of his narrative traces his attempt to acquire, once again, the reserve, the self-protective disposition, needed to survive in the metropolis. This is the 'dissociation' that, for Simmel, is 'in reality' one of the 'elemental forms of socialization' in the city. Or, perhaps more precisely, it traces the failure of Peter's attempt to acquire this 'intellectualistic mentality'.[40] For at the end of the novel his state of mind is far from indifferent. 'What is this terror? What is this ecstasy?' he asks, filled with 'extraordinary excitement', as he sees Clarissa at her party in the final sentences (255).

Earlier in the narrative, however, his efforts to distance himself from the city seem to have been successful. He relishes 'the richness' of London, 'the greenness, the civilization,' in part presumably because he has just returned from India. He objectifies it. Indeed, passing Septimus in Regent's Park, in a moment of self-reflection for which he congratulates himself, he decides that, formerly, his 'susceptibility to impressions had been his undoing' (92).

This insight is more precarious than he suspects, as the ecstasy and terror he feels at the end of the day indicate. But it is more important to emphasize that, in spite of a certain unconscious kinship to Septimus, Peter can have no idea of what this susceptibility to impressions might mean for the anonymous working-class man he glimpses on the park bench: a psychotic who, at the highest pitch of ecstasy and terror, is on the point of killing himself (or being 'suicided by society', as Antonin Artaud might have put it[41]).

In the case of Septimus, in contrast to the Baudelairean hero, it is the 'non-I', teeming in the streets and parks of the city as on the battlefields of France, that has an 'insatiable appetite' for the 'I'. The non-I obliterates the I.

One of the gnomic but luminous equations that Benjamin jots down in his *Arcades Project* reads: 'The system of Parisian streets: a vascular network of imagination.'[42] The representation of Septimus's experience of inner and outer space in the modern city, which cannot be dissociated from the concatenations of solitude and multitude in the streets, violently collapses the arterial transport system and the vascular network of imagination in on each other. It requires that the relatively stable, static perspectives of nineteenth-century realist narrative are ruptured.

Woolf uses the double narrative perspective of indirect discourse, which is uniquely capable of exploring the dialectical relations of objective and subjective, to enact these tessellations and so rupture the realist paradigm:

> He had escaped! was utterly free – as happens in the downfall of
> habit when the mind, like an unguarded flame, bows and bends
> and seems about to blow from its holding. I haven't felt so young

for years! thought Peter, escaping (only of course for an hour or so) from being precisely what he was. (67–8)

In this sentence, the narrator and Peter speak simultaneously; and their voices weave in and out of one another. In spite of the grammatical differences between them – the different personal pronouns, the different tenses – the exclamation 'He had escaped!' is scarcely less Peter's own utterance, scarcely more the omniscient narrator's, than the succeeding one, 'I haven't felt so young for years!'

Like Joyce's narrative voice in *Ulysses*, Woolf's delicately mediates between exterior spectacle and the intimacies of her character's interior life. The distinction between inside and outside is delicately deconstructed in a displacement of the relations between the self and the city. Narrative voice, in Woolf's novel, unifies the disparate, sometimes competing individualities that comprise life in the metropolitan city. 'The omniscient narrator of *Mrs Dalloway*', as J. Hillis Miller observes, 'is a general consciousness or social mind which rises into existence out of the collective mental experience of the individual human beings in the story.'[43] The narrator's general language ingests the characters' particular languages.

Language itself is thus the means not only of representing the relations between inner and outer but healing the split between them. 'The most deeply known human community', Raymond Williams reminds us in his comments on *Ulysses*, 'is language itself.'[44] Form, in modernist art and literature, is the means not simply of presenting or performing the contradictions of content but of solving them.

Woolf's language attempts, too, both to unify and beautify the chaos of metropolitan life. This is the utopian dimension of modernist representations of the city – the dream of a form that, even as it reproduces the confusions of urban modernity, will assimilate and comprehend, in Simmel's words, 'the rapid crowding of changing images, the sharp discontinuity in the grasp of a single glance, and the unexpectedness of onrushing impressions'. In Rosenberg's terms, to cite them again, it is the dream of a form that will create 'the melody of life' from the city's 'turmoil and strife'. Modernist form is the imaginary resolution of those real contradictions, lived in the everyday metropolis, that it represents.

Metropolitan modernity in the early twentieth century entailed what Henri Lefebvre characterizes as a 'massive injection of discontinuity', as the older patterns in 'knowledge, behaviour, and consciousness itself' became more and more susceptible to the accelerating metabolism of commodity capitalism.[45] For modernists like Woolf, in this cultural climate, artistic form itself, especially when it mimicked these discontinuities, secretly represented the dream of a deeper continuity. This continuity, then, might ultimately dissolve the reified opposition between metropolitan and mental life, the politics of spectacle and the poetics of introspection, in a dialectic of the interior and the exterior that is adequately textured to the reality of that experience.

8

Beginning

Georges Bataille's
'Big Toe'

In a fascinating, fragmentary essay on the mouth, published in 1930, the surrealist philosopher Georges Bataille stated that 'man does not have a simple architecture like beasts, and it is not even possible to say where he begins.'[1]

As Roland Barthes understood, this is a statement of some philosophical importance. In 'Outcomes of the Text', Barthes noted that 'Bataille raises the question of the beginning where it had never been raised: "*Where does the human body begin?*"'[2] Bataille's claim is that the mouth is the beginning, or 'prow', of animals. Implicitly, then, the anus, which is sometimes politely concealed by a tail, is the 'end' of animals.

Bataille confronted this 'end', in the form of an ape's protuberant anus, which he characterized with typical expressiveness as an 'enormous anal fruit of radial and shit-smeared raw pink meat', on a visit to London Zoo in July 1927. In his article entitled 'The Jesuve', also written in 1930, Bataille identifies his obsession with the 'pineal eye', which he dates to the period in 1927 during which he wrote 'The Solar Anus' (1931), as 'an excremental fantasy'. He offers this autobiographical anecdote as a context for understanding it:

> It would have been impossible for me to speak explicitly of it, to express totally what I felt so violently in early 1927 (and it still

happens that I bitterly feel it) in any other way than by speaking
of the nudity of an ape's anal projection, which on a day in July
of the same year, in the Zoological Gardens of London, overwhelmed me to the point of throwing me into a kind of ecstatic
brutishness.[3]

This was an encounter that, because it seemed to him to violate
the discreet seclusion of the human anus, proved at the same
time horrific and epiphanic. 'What in human beings has, since
they have stood erect, withdrawn deep into the flesh and hidden
from sight,' as Bataille's biographer Michel Surya observes, 'in
the monkey juts out, "a beautiful boil of red flesh", in an obscene
and illuminating way.'[4]

Bataille insists that, in contrast to an ape's body, a man or
woman's body does not have a beginning or an end. But, reading
Bataille against Bataille, I want to argue that, as a bipedal species,
the human being begins with the big toe.

In 1929, the year before he published his essay on the mouth,
Bataille wrote his essay on the big toe. There, in a satirical attack
on André Breton's anti-materialist mode of surrealism, he contended that, although the big toe is routinely regarded as base,
if not contemptible, it is paradoxically the noblest part of the
human body.

Exploring the 'hideously cadaverous and at the same time loud
and defiant appearance of the big toe', which 'gives shrill expression to the disorder of the human body', Bataille there refers to
'the hilarity commonly produced by simply imagining *toes*'.[5] But
the big toe, in his view, is secretly responsible for giving 'a firm
foundation to the erection of which man is so proud' (87). 'The
big toe is the most *human* part of the human body,' he explains
from the outset, 'in the sense that no other element of this body is
so differentiated from the corresponding element of the anthropoid ape' (87).

In spite of this, though, or because of it, it is routinely bound,
hidden and treated as something shameful. The big toe is thus
both the most significant part of the human anatomy and the part
most neglected or denigrated in the cultural imagination. *Le gros*

orteil, as the big toe is called in France, is in a dual sense 'gross': it is at once excessively obtrusive and, quite simply, obscene. Disgusting. As Barthes pointed out, '*gros* is repulsive in a way that *grand* is not.'[6]

The phrase 'toe-rag', still occasionally used as an archaic-sounding insult in English today, can communicate a preliminary sense of this contradiction between the anatomical significance and the cultural insignificance of the big toe. Everyday language is a good guide to the semiotics of the big toe. 'How to make the body talk?' Barthes asks; and he responds that it is necessary, as Bataille did, 'to articulate the body not on discourse (that of others, that of knowledge, or even my own) but on *language*: to let idiomatic expressions intervene, to explore them, to unfold them, to represent their "letter" (i.e., their significance)'.[7]

'Toe-rag' is just such an idiomatic expression that articulates the politics of the body. It originated in the nineteenth century, as a contemptuous reference to tramps and vagrants who wrapped a piece of old cloth around their toes, especially their big toes, in order to prevent or alleviate blisters and corns. It therefore meant, and means, 'a despicable or worthless person', as the *OED* indicates; but, inadvertently, it also testifies to the heroic powers of endurance of the most immiserated sector of society, the lumpenproletariat; and, more concretely, to the heroic powers of endurance of the most oppressed (certainly, in the literal, physical sense, the most depressed) part of the body – the lumpy, lumpen big toe.

In terms of the politics of the body, as Shakespeare speculated, this makes the big toe analogous to the most strident representatives of the oppressed sections of society. In Act I, Scene I, of *Coriolanus* (c.1605–08), set in the Roman street, the patrician Menenius Agrippa characterizes the situation confronting the state in terms of the metaphor of the body politic. In his allegorical speech, he identifies the big toe as the leading figure in an insurrection of mutinous body parts against the belly, which stands in for the Senate, the locus of power. 'What do you think,' Menenius asks his interlocutor, the rebellious First Citizen, 'You, the great toe of this assembly?' 'I the great toe!' the Citizen responds indignantly, 'why the great toe?'

Menenius responds like this:

> For that, being one o' the lowest, basest, poorest,
> Of this most wise rebellion, thou go'st foremost:
> Thou rascal, that art worst in blood to run,
> Lead'st first to win some vantage.[8]

The big toe, according to Menenius's metaphor, is the last part of the body to receive the nutrition circulated through the bloodstream by the belly, which stores, processes and distributes energy. Hence it is the most disgruntled, cantankerous part of the body, the first to agitate for revolution. The lowest, most extreme part of the body – the big toe – will act as the vanguard of the insurrectionary body. The basest will go foremost.

It is as if Bataille were glossing this scene from *Coriolanus* when he wrote that 'the hideously cadaverous and at the same time loud and defiant appearance of the big toe … gives shrill expression to the disorder of the human body, that product of the violent discord of its organs' (92). As a consequence of this rebellion of the body parts, the *gros* will become *grand*. Bataille announces in 'The Solar Anus' that 'Communist workers appear to the bourgeois to be as ugly and dirty as hairy sexual organs, or lower parts.'[9] Among these lower parts he is surely thinking of the big toe.

Bataille adds, in a spirit of insurgency, that 'sooner or later there will be a scandalous eruption in the course of which the asexual noble heads of the bourgeois will be chopped off.'[10] If the etymological meaning of the word 'scandalous' is insecure, wobbly, or limping, as Barthes proposes in his commentary on Bataille, then the big toe must play a leading role in displacing the bourgeois regime of the human body in which the head is dominant. As in the citizens' rebellion in *Coriolanus*, it must give shrill expression to the disorder, the violent discord, of the various organs and parts that comprise the human body. Bataille, it might be said, calls for the dictatorship of the toeleprariat.

The big toe describes what Bataille, recalling a dream, characterized as a 'kind of ambivalence between the most horrible and the most magnificent'.[11] And it is on this dialectic of the magnificent and the horrible, the heroic and the pedestrian, the highest and the lowest, that my chapter on the biped concentrates. I should admit straight away, though, that it largely overlooks the idea of the big toe as a fetish – what Bataille, in a delightfully droll tone, calls 'classic foot fetishism leading to the licking of toes' (92).

Freud refers to the origins of this function in his comments on infantile sexuality from 1910, where he notes that, for the child, the lips, the tongue, the thumb 'and even the big toe' may be taken as objects for sucking, in spite of the fact that they offer no nourishment (as the mother's breast once did).[12] Barthes, silently leaning on Freud, summarized this dimension of the big toe in a note on its characteristic dynamics of desire: 'the toe is seductive-repulsive.'[13]

The 'seductive-repulsive' is very much the shifting, unstable terrain on which Bataille's thought operates: 'Extreme seductiveness is probably at the boundary of horror,' he observes in his essay on another bodily organ, the eye.[14] But Barthes, who seems to have been entranced but never finally satisfied by the interest he felt in Bataille, seduced but oddly repulsed perhaps, domesticates his compatriot's unruly philosophizing when he concludes his account of the fetishistic character of the big toe with this aphoristic verdict: 'fascinating as a contradiction: that of the tumescent and miniaturized phallus'.[15]

This is the aspect of the big toe explored a generation ago by the Japanese novelist Rieko Matsuura in *The Apprenticeship of Big Toe P* (1993). Matsuura's cult novel, which centres on the adventures of a young woman whose big toe, protruding at the end of her right foot, morphs suddenly one night into a tiny penis, exhaustively and rather predictably details the intriguing but finally rather reductive contradiction identified by Barthes.[16] Bataille himself, as Rosalind Krauss correctly emphasizes, 'does not work along the logic of the fetish'; and his essay on the big toe 'explicitly dismisses the play of substitutions. Of sublimations. Of foot = phallus'.[17]

In what follows, I largely neglect this phallic aspect of the big toe. I am concerned less with the big toe as a tumescent and miniaturized phallus than with its physical role in the fact that human beings are bipeds. And the symbolic implications of this. This chapter, then, is about beginning with the big toe in three senses: anatomical; anthropological; and iconographical. I will examine these associations in turn before going back to Bataille's philosophical reflections on the big toe.

'Isn't it really quite extraordinary to see that, since man took his first steps, no one has asked himself why he walks, how he walks, if he has ever walked, if he could walk better, what he achieves in walking?' This is the rhetorical question that Honoré de Balzac asks in his *Théorie de la démarche* (1833), 'Theory of Walking', which subsequently formed part of his incomplete *Pathology of Social Life* (1839). It is all the more extraordinary, Balzac underlines, because these questions 'are tied to all the philosophical, psychological, and political systems which preoccupy the world'.[18]

In examining the anatomical identity of the big toe, I am especially interested in the role it plays in the act of walking. 'A child learning to walk is engaged in attempting to make conscious material unconscious,' noted the British psychoanalyst Wilfred Bion (who counted Samuel Beckett among his patients); 'only when this is done can it walk.'[19] If one thinks about walking as one walks, if one looks down at one's feet and attempts to understand it while performing this most unthinking of everyday activities, one simply stops, topples over, or collapses – like Bion's infant, who cannot walk if she is conscious of learning to do so. In contrast to quadrupeds, bipeds are innately unstable. This is what Arthur Schopenhauer meant when, in a nicely balanced formulation from *The World as Will and Representation* (1818), slightly vertiginous in its rhetorical effect, he characterized walking as 'a continuously checked falling'.[20]

My aim is in one sense the opposite of the child's according to Bion, since in discussing walking in relation to the big toe I want to render the unconscious material conscious, and in so doing make this apparently spontaneous activity so self-conscious as to seem almost impossible to perform. It is a question of making the act of walking, and the apparatus of meaning on which it silently depends, limp. In 'Outcomes of the Text', Barthes points out that, in Bataille's article on the big toe, the apparatus of meaning is not destroyed but decentred and displaced: 'it is made *eccentric*, it is made insecure, wobbly' ['il est *excentré*, rendu boiteux'].[21] Meaning is made to limp by Bataille. And, just as a physical limp makes one conscious of the unconscious act of walking, so an epistemological limp might make one conscious of the unconscious meaning of walking.

When Walter Benjamin celebrated 'the unconscious optics' to which, as a technological medium, the camera introduces us, he used the example of walking: 'Even if one has a general knowledge of the way people walk, one knows nothing of a person's posture during the fractional second of a stride.'[22] In addition to the cinematic techniques of slow motion and the close-up, Benjamin is presumably thinking of the images produced by Eadweard Muybridge when, in the late nineteenth century, he developed the technology of motion photography in order to capture the movements of humans and other animals. The most ordinary of actions, like walking, suddenly seemed both more transparent than hitherto and more unfamiliar.

Focusing on the big toe, analogously, might momentarily make walking, and the philosophical, psychological, and political systems it sets in motion or embodies, to echo Balzac, seem both like a more and less conscious activity than it customarily is. And it might even provide glimpses of a kind of anatomical unconscious.

So, what do we know of a person's posture during the fractional seconds that, successively, comprise a stride? As Muybridge was compiling *Animal Locomotion: An Electro-Photographic Investigation of Connective Phases of Animal Movements* (1887), the French physician Georges Gilles de Tourette published an account of his clinical and physiological research at the Salpêtrière into the human gait, entitled *Études cliniques et physiologiques sur la marche* (1886).

Giorgio Agamben, who points out that Muybridge's and Tourette's experiments were almost exactly contemporaneous, has explained in his 'Notes on Gesture' that the latter's findings were based on the 'footprint method'. This involved smearing

the soles of those taking part in the experiment with iron sesqui-
oxide powder, then making them walk the length of a straight
line drawn on a seven- or eight-metre-long roll of white wall-
paper. 'The footprints that the patient left while walking along
the dividing line', Agamben observes, 'allowed a perfect measure-
ment of the gait according to various parameters (length of the
step, lateral swerve, angle of inclination, etc.)'.[23]

As a result of this research, Tourette summarized the dynamics
of the human step in these terms:

> While the left leg acts as the fulcrum, the right foot is raised
> from the ground with a coiling motion that starts at the heel and
> reaches the tip of the toes, which leave the ground last; the whole
> leg is now brought forward and the foot touches the ground with
> the heel. At this very instant, the left foot – having ended its revo-
> lution and leaning only on the tip of the toes – leaves the ground;
> the left leg is brought forward, gets closer to and then passes the
> right leg, and the left foot touches the ground with the heel, while
> the right foot ends its own revolution.[24]

In spite of the scientific method Tourette uses to anatomize the
human gait, he can finally offer only a narrative of the process,
and therefore a kind of fiction. Walking does not have a precisely
definable beginning and ending. I prefer a slightly different, no
doubt less scientific, fiction than Tourette's – one that is consistent
with the conviction that the human body begins with the big toe.

The action of walking, according to my mythology, begins
with the big toe. It is what provides the impetus needed to walk;
or at least to maintain bipedal motion. Certainly, it is crucial to
the physics of walking, and to an extent that is overlooked in the
passage from Tourette's book that I have cited. Before we raise
one foot completely off the ground, when we commence walking
from a standing position, we roll our body weight onto the toes
of the other foot.

More accurately, we transfer our body weight onto the toes of
one foot at the same instant that we raise the heel of the other
foot. The toes are in contact with the ground for about three
quarters of the walking cycle. And of all these toes, the big toe is

the most important. The big toe, which sustains approximately 40 per cent of our body weight when we walk, is what provides the crucial propulsive force needed to take a step.

The big toe is not absolutely indispensable in enabling us to walk, and people who have had it amputated are still generally able to move about on their feet; but it is probably more import-ant, proportionately, than any other component part of the foot's anatomy in this respect. 'Toe-off', as it is sometimes called, pro-vides the essential leverage needed to sustain bipedal motion.

A monograph on the human foot published in 1935 by Dudley J. Morton, the leading medical authority on the foot in the United States in the first half of the twentieth century, explains the pro-pulsive role of the big toe with some eloquence:

> [The] dorsal movement of the toes ... has the effect of increasing the tension of their muscles, and to such a degree that when the leverage effort of the foot against body weight has been com-pleted, the subsequent toe flexion is strong enough to add a final elastic impetus to body movement which gives it smoothness and grace. At this point the stresses have been swung toward the first metatarsal bone so completely that the most important digital effort is performed by the great toe. The phase of bipedal loco-motion undoubtedly accounts for the conspicuous size of that digit in man.[25]

This is eloquent, I think, partly because of its implicit or incipient sense of the aesthetics of walking. The big toe, Morton seems to say, is secretly responsible for the elegance of human ambulation. 'How do we actually move?" the neuroscientist Shane O'Mara has recently asked. 'The answer is rhythm,' he responds, 'which is intrinsic to walking.'[26]

In some literal sense, it is on the big toe that the rhythm and rhyme of walking depend.

Indeed, it seems a pity that, when Ancient Greek prosodists chose the term 'foot' to measure and calibrate the rhythms of poetic discourse (the name is commonly thought to allude to the movement of the foot as it beats time, though it is possible that it has something to do with the rhythm of walking too), they failed

to find a place in their technical vocabulary for the word 'toe'
too.[27] Here is a significant lacuna in the annals of rhetoric and
poetics. For the inner mechanics of the metrical foot might most
effectively be located in the metrical toe.

The 'sprung rhythm' sponsored by Gerard Manley Hopkins –
constructed from metrical feet in which the first syllable is
stressed, however many unstressed syllables succeed it – is for
example unimaginable without the energetic impetus of the metrical toe. This first, stressed syllable perhaps *is* the metrical toe.

Look at these lines from 'Hurrahing in Harvest' (1877), a
sonnet written after he had walked home alone from fishing
one afternoon at the end of summer beneath what, in a wonderful phrase for the currents along which clouds drift, he calls
the 'wind-walks'; lines marked with Hopkins's idiosyncratic and
often disconcerting diacritics:

> I wálk, I líft up, Í lift úp heart, éyes,
> Down all that glory in the heavens to glean our Saviour;
> And, éyes, héart, what looks, what lips yet gáve you a
> Rapturous love's greeting of realer, of rounder replies?[28]

Here, Hopkins's increasingly complicated, increasingly dynamic
rhythms ('I wálk, I líft up, Í lift úp heart, éyes') mimic not merely
the poet's movement forwards but his movement upwards – as
if this walker-watcher is using the metrical toe, with increasing emphasis or propulsive force, to dramatize an irrepressible momentum, in the face of Christ's palpable presence in the
countryside, that is both physical and spiritual.

One pictures Hopkins, in his ecstatic mental state, propelling
himself through the landscape on tiptoes, almost at a run, as if he
aspires impulsively and spontaneously to catch and get caught up
in those 'wind-walks' through which the clouds drift and dissolve
in the skies above him. The technical, Latin name of the big toe
is *hallux*, which is derived from the Greek *halmos*, meaning to
'spring or leap'. Sprung rhythm, then, is the poetic equivalent of
toe-off.

The big toe is habitually regarded as base, in spite of its heroic
labours. It is an ugly, clumsy-seeming, embarrassing part of the

human anatomy, perhaps the least celebrated part of all, one that is more often hidden as shameful than honoured; and yet it stops us from stumbling and makes the elastic grace of human perambulation, as mimed by Hopkins's use of metre, possible. Its 'digital effort', in Morton's formulation, its humble but titanic labour, is what guarantees the 'smoothness and grace' that is characteristic of walking in humans; yet it is despised. The languorous grace of the *flâneur*'s elegantly shod foot as he saunters along the pavement is secretly dependent on the hidden mechanics, the digital effort, of the big toe.

The foot, and the big toe in particular, gives 'a firm foundation to the erection of which man is so proud', as Bataille underlines, even though it is 'subjected to grotesque tortures that deform it and make it rachitic [or rickety]' (87).

If in a synchronic sense we begin with the big toe, because walking is reliant on 'toe-off', then there is also a diachronic sense in which, anatomically speaking, we begin with the big toe. This is the anthropological or palaeo-anatomical dimension of the physics of walking. For, in evolutionary terms, humanity itself, in so far as its history as a species traces what Bataille outlines in 'The Jesuve' as 'the progressive erection that goes from the quadruped to *Homo erectus*', can be said to begin with the big toe.[29]

That is, our identity as a species hinges, or pivots, on the development of the big toe – because it is cause or consequence, or both cause and consequence, of the fact that, to put it in simple pictorial terms, instead of climbing trees we walk across plains. It is responsible for the fact that we are bipedal. In short, it is what makes us human. In *The Descent of Man* (1871), Charles Darwin quoted his old antagonist Richard Owen, an opponent of the theory of evolution by natural selection, to precisely this effect: 'The great toe, as Prof. Owen remarks, "which forms the fulcrum when standing or walking, is perhaps the most characteristic peculiarity of the human structure".'[30]

The basic structure of our body is shared both with our evolutionary ancestors and our immediate relations, that is, chimpanzees and other apes. Obviously, there are quantitative differences between a human and a chimpanzee brain, and the left and right halves of the brain have developed differentially; but anatomically they are directly equivalent. To put it in terms of aesthetics, formally they are the same, even if they have different contents. And this is true of the eyes, the nose, the breasts, the penis and every other body part. The exception is the big toe.

For, in contrast to the innermost toe of both our ancestors and our genetic cousins, the big toe in humans is not, as the thumb is, opposable. We do not have a prehensile big toe. On the contrary, we have one that has evolved to enable us to walk rather than climb; and indeed, crucially, to develop tools. 'One cannot overemphasize the role of bipedalism in hominid development,' the archaeologist Mary Leakey, who discovered the Laetoli Footprints, argued; 'this unique ability freed the hands for myriad possibilities – carrying, tool-making, intricate manipulation.'[31]

The toe of the human foot is adducted: it is drawn inwards. The toe of the chimpanzee is abducted: it is drawn outwards. Or, to put it another way, if the chimpanzee's big toe is divergent, like our thumb, then the toes of the human foot are instead convergent (the big toe has aligned with the other toes, or vice versa). In addition, a human being's middle footbone is far more compact than that of the chimpanzee, making it less mobile and more stable; and these relatively dense, rigid, solid bones can be used to lever the body in walking.

So, even though it now seems that the earliest anatomical changes relating to bipedalism didn't in fact occur as a result of deforestation, there is no doubt that these features of the emergent human foot would have helped proto-humans to survive in the plains, perhaps giving them an evolutionary advantage over other primates, who were unable for instance to track migratory herds across the savannah. And research in fact suggests that bipedalism preceded distinctive and decisive brain development in humans.[32] Simplifying a little, it might be said that it is because the big toe became adducted that the brain expanded and, in consequence, humanity emerged as a distinct species.

The big toe, then, is the most peculiarly human part of our anatomy. And the one that guarantees our unique status in evolutionary terms. As the authors of a clinical textbook on the human foot summarize the point, anatomically modern humans, who emerged some 150,000 years ago, 'are the only living primate, indeed they are the only living mammal, that is an obligatory striding biped'.[33]

Obligatory bipeds are animals that rely solely on their hind-limbs for support and propulsion when walking on the ground. All other primates are characterized by optional bipedalism. Other primates have a mixed 'locomotor repertoire' – in other words, they use a range of means of mobility that includes, for example, balancing, hanging, jumping and quadrupedalism, as well as occasional bipedalism. For this reason they have a divergent *hallux*.

Humans are by contrast committed to a single locomotor mode – 'obligate bipedalism'. It is this that explains the other architectural features that, despite their anatomical similarity to the equivalent parts of primates, are characteristic of our bodies in particular: the long, straight legs; the protuberant buttocks (which, in contrast to those of the ape glimpsed by Bataille, conceal the anus); 'the flat stomach, the flexible waist, the straight spine, the low shoulders, the erect head atop a long neck.'[34]

The causes of the evolutionary shift to a flat, non-prehensile, in brief, modern human foot, are still debated; and the answers that scientists tend to volunteer only raise further questions. It might be the case, for example, that bipedal feet developed in humans as an adaptation enabling them to carry food or infants. It might be that they developed in order to minimize exposure to the tropical sun and so preserve energy in a hot habitat.

Conversely, it is possible that, for some reason, humans' forelimbs were used for purposes other than locomotion for prolonged periods, and that bipedalism came to be the most efficient means of locomotion as a result. For instance, some scientists claim that humans first learned to walk in trees, on an arboreal rather than terrestrial surface, using their arms to suspend and support themselves from higher branches. It is also possible that it was the development of an upright posture – perhaps in order to facilitate displays of aggression or virility – that created the evolutionary conditions for bipedal locomotion.[35]

The consequences, or coterminous developments, of bipedal locomotion, to which the quotation from Leakey alluded, are almost as debatable as its causes. Recently, for example, one group of anatomists and evolutionary biologists has argued for the co-evolution of human hands and feet, positing that 'evolutionary changes in the toes associated with bipedalism caused matching evolutionary changes in hand anatomy that may actually have facilitated the emergence and development of stone tool technology.'[36]

These biologists propose that when *Australopithecus afarensis*, a partly arboreal, so-called facultative biped, evolved into *Homo*, an obligate terrestrial biped which probably did a good deal of long-distance trekking, a change that occurred about two million years ago, the directional selection on the lateral toes for locomotion 'may have caused parallel changes in the fingers that provided further performance benefits for manipulation'.[37] According to this thesis, the morphological development of the toes, which became adapted for long-distance walking or running, increased the length and robusticity of the australopiths' thumbs, and so made it possible for humans to achieve the sophisticated, precise tool-making that gave them such an evolutionary advantage.

In a rather different register, of course, Freud speculated in *Civilization and Its Discontents* (1930) that what he rather cartoonishly calls 'man's decision to adopt an upright gait' led directly to 'the decline of the olfactory stimuli', and hence to the association of bodily dirt and smells with shame. 'The beginning of the fateful process of civilization, then,' he concludes, 'would have been marked by man's adopting an erect posture' – that is, by becoming an obligate biped.[38]

The emergence of the big toe is, according to this perspective, responsible for the beginnings of civilization, and for the history of repression that defines it. Hence the big toe is in effect the precondition of sexual fetishism as well as one of its privileged objects. It sets in motion the hierarchical opposition of high and low, head and foot, mouth and anus, 'beginning' and 'end' of the body, that imparts such libidinal force to the second, desublimated term in each of these pairs. This is an additional sense in which human beings could be said to begin with the big toe.

The peculiar type of primate locomotion known as obligate bipedalism, it can be concluded, probably first started to evolve between five and eight million years ago (although precise dating is difficult, largely because fossils of the foot are extremely rare: predators and scavengers having a predilection for the red marrow in the tarsal bones, they tended to eat the feet of their prey). We can however be fairly confident that early hominid species such as *Australopithecus* had predominantly grasping feet and relatively prehensile big toes until roughly 3.2 million years ago.[39]

The recent discovery of a fossilized foot in the Afar region of north-eastern Ethiopia, which has been dated to 3.4 million years ago, seems to confirm that pre-human ancestors were adapted at least partially to an arboreal existence, because the big toe juts out to the side like that of a gorilla or chimpanzee. This hominid species was probably a contemporary of *Australopithecus*, which had lost similar bone features in favour of other adaptations that committed it to walking on two feet – as the remains of 'Lucy', several hundred pieces of whose bones were found in the same region of eastern Africa in 1974, indicate.

Obligate bipedalism and the convergent big toe on which it depends developed rather belatedly, in evolutionary terms; and the human foot, with its everted rather than inverted posture, and its characteristic distribution of the metatarsals in a transverse arch configuration, is thus a comparatively recent anatomical structure. This might help to explain why our feet are so susceptible to signs of maladaptation and malfunction.

'Humanity has tortuously walked across the ages on two feet with a skeleton designed originally for four-legged travel,' as Joseph Amato has pointed out; 'flat feet, swollen feet, distorted toes, blisters, bunions, hammer toes, trick knees, herniated discs, and bad backs, not to mention hernias, hemorrhoids and other maladies associated with our bipedal locomotion, remain the price of standing proudly erect.'[40] Or, as Bataille puts it, in diction that characteristically combines the sacred and profane, the human foot, though it gives 'a firm foundation to the erection of which man is so proud', 'is stupidly consecrated to corns, calluses, and bunions, and … to the most loathsome filthiness' (87).

The malfunctioning of the foot – in evolutionary terms, its belatedness – may be one reason for the ignominious status of the big toe in the history of representations of the human body; for its iconographical insignificance. The big toe developed too hurriedly. It is a botched job, a strangely Frankensteinian touch. But, if it is belated, and far from perfect, it is also an advanced piece of technology, highly effective both at providing propulsive force and withstanding weight. It is a prosthesis that makes it possible to walk and to go on walking.

This contradiction is central to Bataille's interest in the big toe. The grossest, the ugliest, arguably the most alien-looking and least human-seeming part of the anatomy, is actually what makes us human. Conversely, the big toe is the part of our body that, despite its crucial role in enabling us to stand upright, and so transcend our brute past, most closely resembles a vestigial trace of that brute past, of some primitive, primeval, muddy origin. The big toe, to take a formulation from the philosopher Nick Land, 'protracts the trajectory of animality'; but it also projects beyond it.[41]

In order to defend this digit against its denigration, in iconographical terms, it is imperative to imagine reorganizing the entire history of art in relation not to the head (for long its privileged physical feature, especially in the form of the face), but to the big toe.

This is, in effect, what the Italian novelist Carlo Emilio Gadda proposed in his late modernist masterpiece, *That Awful Mess on the Via Merulana* (1957). At one point in this bizarre and brilliant novel, Gadda portrays Cocullo, the *carabiniere*, standing before a fresco of two saints attired in short cloaks that reveal 'four unsuspected feet'.[42] The two right feet, he specifies, are 'generously tentacled in toes'; toes that are 'stretched forward in their stride', and 'puncture the foreground' of the composition. Gadda goes on to rhapsodize as follows:

> With particular expressive vigor, in a remarkable adaptation to the mastery of the centuries, the big toes were depicted. In each of the two extended digits, the cross strap of otherwise unperceived footwear segregated and singled out the knuckled-toe in that august pre-eminence which is his, which belongs to the big toe,

and to that toe alone, separating it out from the flock of the toes of the lower rank, less suitable for the day of glory, but still, in the osteologues' atlases and in the masterpieces of Italian paintings, toes. The two haughty digits, enhanced by genius, were projected, hurled forward: they traveled on their own: they almost, paired off as they were, stuck in your eye; indeed, into both your eyes: they were sublimated to the central pathetic motif of the fresco, or alfresco, seeing as how it was plenty fresh. A bolt from heaven, a light of excruciated hours blanched them; however, when you came right down to it, the light seemed to rise from underground, since it struck them from below. (271–2)

The big toes project; are hurled forward. They stick in your eye. They belong, that is, to a different order of perspective to that of the rest of the composition. In their obtrusion from the picture plane, they acquire an almost anamorphic quality, like the smeared skull that is the peculiarly dynamic emblem of death in Hans Holbein's celebrated portrait of *The Ambassadors* (1533). They travel on their own, in Gadda's phrase, like entities from a different order of being. Gadda has excavated the distinct onto-logical space of the big toe.

The big toe in the painting described by Gadda, brilliantly refulgent, synthesizes Apollonian and Dionysian energies, the high and the low, the magnificent and the horrible. The theatrical extravagance of his ekphrastic digression seems unsurpassable. But Gadda's hymn to the big toe does not end at this point. He has only just begun. For he proceeds to make an even more osten-tatiously counter-intuitive claim:

The glorious history of our painting, in a part of its glory pays tribute to the big toe. Light and toes are prime ingredients, inef-fable, in every painting that aspires to live, that wants to have its say, to narrate, persuade, educate: to subjugate our senses, win hearts from the Malign One: insist for eight hundred years on the favorite images. (272)

Light and toes are prime ingredients. This is an elaborate pun on *la luce* (meaning 'light') and *l'alluce* (meaning 'big toe'). Both light and big toes, according to Gadda, are originary entities. They both lie at the very origins of being.

A couple of pages later, poring over 'the two big toes, the Pietrine and the Pauline', portrayed in a shrine to the *due santi*, Gadda brings the pun to its cosmic climax: 'The "creator"', he declares, apparently alluding both to the painter and to God ...: 'The "creator" couldn't bear another moment's delay, before creating. '"*Fiat lux!*" And there were toes. Plip, plop' (274–5). This is the divine command underlying Gadda's cosmology: Let there be toes! I mean – light! Too late ... In his absurdist theology, the universe has come into being not because light has split apart the darkness but because a gigantic big toe has irrupted into it. It is as if creation itself is a ridiculous, Beckettian accident caused by a slip of the tongue.

Gadda goes on to explore his thesis in relation to additional, more canonical paintings.[43] The first is Michelangelo's *Doni Tondo* (1504–06), a painting that, implicitly playing with its circular *tondo* form, he rotates, symbolically speaking, so as to pivot it on its representation of the big toe. There, in the exquisitely delicate tension between 'the inimitable big toe' of St Joseph and 'the little toe of the Bride', or Madonna, he perceives 'the Toe-Idea': 'a livid and almost surreal, or perhaps eschatological light, proposes the Toe-Idea, loftily incarnating – or inossifying [*sic*] – it, in the foreground of the contingent' (273).

The casual almost-contact between Joseph's big toe and Mary's little toe is nearly as significant as the far-from-casual, indeed the causal, almost-contact between God's index finger and Adam's in Michelangelo's painting of 'The Creation of Adam' (c.1512) on the ceiling of the Sistine Chapel. Raymond Tallis, who has argued for the quintessentially human quality of the index finger, admits in a reference to this fresco that he 'like[s] to think that the slightly awkward encounter between God and man through their index fingers depicted by Michelangelo ... was influenced by an intuition of the central role of the index finger in making us so different'.[44] I like to think that the slightly awkward, but infinitely tender, encounter between Joseph's big toe and Mary's little toe in the *Doni Tondo* was influenced by an intuition of the central role of the big toe in making human beings so different. Certainly, it is the index of these saints' humanity.

The other painting that Gadda reinterprets in relation to the big toe is Raphael's *Lo Sposalizio della Vergine* (1504), in the Brera, which depicts Mary and Joseph being married by a priest, in front of a temple, among assorted onlookers. Gadda's interest lies in Joseph's left foot, since it is there that, in order to symbolize his chastity, 'the same metatarsus protuberates, the foot's thumb':

> The divarication of the solitary, bony toe from the remaining herd of other toes is rendered prominent by the perspectively charming joints of the cleansed pavement, where there is no husk or skin, neither orange's nor chestnut's, nor has any leaf or paper settled there, nor has man urinated there, nor dog. And the master toe, though disjoined from the others, at its root is spurred and gnarled: and then it converges inwards, as if forced by gout or by the habitual constriction of a shoe momentarily removed, or I'd say *domum relapsa* as if too fetid for the hour of the wedding. (273–4)

On the beautifully clean surface of the pavement, the big toe so tenderly painted by Raphael displays both the holiness and the ordinariness, the spirituality and the physicality, of this saintly artisan. It is 'more than a toe of more than a barefoot carpenter', as Gadda puts it (274). It has been liberated from the stinking sandal that encased it and consecrated to a divinity who, one day shortly before his death, will advertise his humility and his ordinary humanity by washing the feet of his disciples. Gnarled, spurred and gouty – in short, horrible – Joseph's big toe is also magnificent.

In Gadda's baroque elaborations, it is thus possible to identify a profound grasp of the unity I have pointed to in this chapter between the sublime and bathetic aspects of the big toe. Elevating the big toe, in the form of the Toe-Idea, he glorifies the contingent, the basely material. *Fiat lux*. Plip, plop.

This Toe-Idea, with its violent collision of the spiritual and the basely material, is invoked again in a religious context, also to scurrilously satirical effect, in Thomas Pynchon's *The Crying of Lot 49* (1965). There, Oedipa Maas attends a performance of *The Courier's Tragedy*, a revenge tragedy by one Richard Wharfinger. In the second act of this parodic Jacobean drama, which centres on the 'protracted torture and eventual murder of a prince of the church' by the evil Duke Angelo, the cardinal in question is apparently 'forced to bleed into a chalice and consecrate his own blood, not to God, but to Satan':

> They also cut off his big toe, and he is made to hold it up like a Host and say, 'This is my body', the keen-witted Angelo observing that it's the first time he's told anything like the truth in fifty years of systematic lying.[45]

The amputated big toe is the central symbol of the satanic theology imagined by Pynchon. Its bleeding stump, consecrated to what Gadda calls the Malign One, is the sacred emblem of a materialist anti-religion.

The big toe once again asserts the animality and the humanity of humanity. Here is a metaphysics of the foot in all its messy materiality.

Bataille's article 'Le gros orteil' was first published in the sixth issue of *Documents*, the strange, crypto-anthropological journal that he edited, which he had set up as a materialist riposte to the idealist tendencies, as he regarded them, of Breton's brand of Surrealism.

As Surya notes in his biography, the article was an 'unrestrained parody of poetic idealism', and it was in this sense typical of *Documents*, which used its 'rancid' ideas to leave 'a doubtful taste in surrealism's mouth'.[46] The article on the big toe seems to have proved especially distasteful to Bataille's more conservative colleagues and acquaintances, and it was widely rumoured that its publication was the immediate cause of his demotion from a post in the Medal Department at the Bibliothèque Nationale, where he had worked for some six years, to one in the Printed Books Department.

Documents, according to Surya, 'created a great fuss right at the heart of the [library's] quiet establishment, especially over Bataille's article "The Big Toe"'; such a fuss, in fact, that the surrealist Michel Leiris, who himself sub-edited and contributed to *Documents*, 'speaks of a veritable "scandal".'[47] 'The Big Toe', in short, like the big toe celebrated by Bataille, thus gave 'shrill expression to the disorder of the human body' (92).

To illustrate 'The Big Toe', Bataille commissioned three photographs of that subject from Jacques-André Boiffard. Boiffard, who had taken the photographs that adorn Breton's *Nadja* (1928), was a relatively obscure and insignificant actor in the surrealist movement, but Breton nonetheless cited him in the first *Manifesto of Surrealism* as one of only two visual artists in a list of those who had 'performed acts of ABSOLUTE SURREALISM'.[48]

The remarkable photographs Boiffard took for Bataille, two of them of male and one of female big toes, were published in full page, so the digits themselves, shockingly, are several times larger than life-size. Disembodied, and dramatically lit against an ominous black background, these big toes are pungent in their detail: every stray hair, every striation of the skin, every bit of cracked nail varnish, is visible. As Michael Sheringham points out, 'the close-up, aided by spotlighting, blots out everything else, framing the big toe so that it emerges from a primal darkness.'[49]

Bataille's essay begins from the paradox that, though it is generally ignored and demeaned, associated with mud and darkness, 'the big toe is the most *human* part of the human body, in

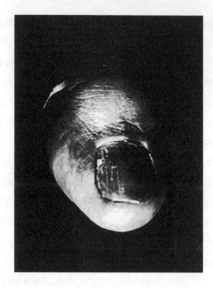

the sense that no other element of this body is so differentiated from the corresponding element of the anthropoid ape' (87). The big toe mocks or melodramatizes the constant, raging oscillation between ordure and the ideal, the ideal and ordure, which is characteristic of the confusion and frustration of human life.

The upright gait of which humanity is so proud, according to Bataille, is founded on the foot, 'but whatever the role the foot plays in his erection, man, who has a light head, a head raised to the heavens and heavenly things, regards it as spit, on the pretext that he has this foot in the mud' (87). More than contempt, though, the foot inspires a 'secret terror' in humans, according to Bataille, and it is this that explains their 'tendency to conceal, as far as possible, its length and form' (87). The big toe, 'hideously cadaverous and at the same time loud and defiant,' as Boiffard's photographs also insist, is the index both of our animality and our humanity (92).

Building on Bataille, we must press for nothing less than a philosophical reorientation of the human body. In order to understand the human being as a species that walks, a creature that is shaped in its species-being by walking, it is necessary to radically alter our perspective – as Gadda does before Michelangelo's and Raphael's paintings. We need to prostrate ourselves in the mud so as to gaze unflinchingly at this strange being's big toe, its crucial point of connection with matter itself.

We need to approach the big toe as we approach that anamorphic skull in *The Ambassadors*, a figure that forces us radically to reorient our relationship to its perspectival picture plane in the interest of comprehending an alternative ontology. An ontoelogy. Everything begins with the big toe, including being itself. It is by taking the big toe as its starting point, and as the point of contact with the world as brute matter, that we can best reorganize the semiotics of the body according to a materialist as opposed to an idealist paradigm. Marx famously announced that, inverting Hegel, he had set the dialectic back on its feet; I propose pivoting it on its big toe.[50] Or, again, adapting a Hegelian formulation, it might be claimed that the being of Spirit is a toe bone.[51]

The big toes in Boiffard's photographs stare at us – at once like 'an alien organism', as Adam Lowenstein has suggested, and like something all too human.[52] We must stare back at them unflinchingly, affirming our fear, horror and hilarity, to celebrate their humanity and inhumanity alike. And to celebrate our humanity and inhumanity alike.

In a fragment of his unpublished preface to *Le Mort* (published posthumously in 1964), Bataille described his experience as a tubercular patient in the autumn of 1942, when he happened upon the dead bodies of some German pilots shot down by an English fighter plane.

'The foot of one of the Germans was bared [*dénudé*],' he records, 'the sole of his shoe having been torn away.' In contrast to the heads of the dead, which had been torched into indistinctness, 'this foot alone was intact'. He stared at this 'diabolical', 'indecent', 'unreal' entity. He 'remained motionless for a long time', he recalls, 'for this naked foot was looking at me.' And this foot, he concludes, 'had the violence – the negative violence – of truth'.[53]

In this regard, one might also think of Andrea Mantegna's famous painting, from about 1480, of the Virgin's lamentation for the dead Christ.[54] In this violently foreshortened composition, Christ's feet, protruding over the edge of the marble slab on which he has been laid, are inertly thrust towards the spectator, their wrinkled, slightly leathery soles marked with the stigmata – which are like tiny, blackened mouths crying out in pain.

It is perhaps one of those rare Christian images in which the low, to take a formulation from Barthes, is not 'purely and scrupulously censured'.[55] Marcel Duchamp was surely thinking in part of the feet in Mantegna's painting when he constructed his *Torture-Morte* (1959), a sculpture of a dead foot pocked with flies. In art-historical terms, the latter is a deliberate *faux pas* or false step. Perhaps it's also both a testament and a rebuke to André Breton's celebrated claim, in *Nadja*, that 'il n'y a pas de pas perdus', there are no lost steps: here, Duchamp aggressively announces, is a lost step – a lost sole. In Mantegna's and Duchamp's *torture-mortes* alike the foot is the most pathetic part of the human anatomy – at once heroic and touchingly bathetic. Human dignity and vulnerability are both embodied in the foot.

A comparable image to that of the anonymous German pilot's foot, with its challenge to our humanity, emerges in the essay on the big toe, both in Bataille's prose and Boiffard's photographs. The big toe is the sign of a sort of zero-degree humanity, a reminder that we are always ultimately mired in a brutal struggle for subsistence. The big toe, then, as the stubby symbol of our bare, forked humanity. Perhaps this is the symbolic import of those identity tags that, because big toes can be conveniently lassoed and labelled, are tied to the big toes of corpses refrigerated in the morgue.

To scrutinize the big toe is to confront both our prehistoric past as an animal species and the dialectic of base and noble impulses, in our present, that determines our future. 'A return to reality', Bataille writes in a final poetic formulation in the article on 'The Big Toe', 'implies no new acceptance, but indicates that one is seduced basely, without transpositions and to the point of screaming, eyes wide open: open at the prospect of a big toe' (93).

9

Stumbling

Ray Bradbury's 'The Pedestrian'

'The Pedestrian' (1951) is a science-fiction short story by Ray Bradbury, only three or four pages long, about a man who, after nightfall, roams aimlessly and compulsively about the silent streets of a nameless metropolis.

It is set in a totalitarian society at the midpoint of the twenty-first century, roughly a hundred years after it was written. In Bradbury's dystopian parable – it is a satirical portrait of Los Angeles that, because of its bleak attack on urban alienation, continues to resonate – the supremacy of the automobile has made it impossible in practice to be a pedestrian. Indeed, the police state has in effect proscribed pedestrianism. So, in this far from distant future, no one travels by foot. Except, of course, the Pedestrian.

'To enter out into that silence that was the city at eight o'clock of a misty evening in November,' the story begins, 'to put your feet upon that buckling concrete walk, to step over grassy seams and make your way, hands in pockets, through the silences, that was what Mr Leonard Mead most dearly loved to do.'[1]

Mead, whose name gently reinforces the pastoral associations of those 'grassy seams' that furrow the pavement, generally begins his nightwalks at an intersection, because from there he can 'peer down long moonlit avenues of sidewalk in four directions, deciding which way to go'. But the point is that, 'alone in this world of A.D. 2053, or as good as alone,' it doesn't matter which direction he takes (569). So he relishes selecting a route at random, thinking of it as a 'path' rather than an avenue or road.

He is half-consciously creating what Paul Farley and Michael Symmons Roberts, in their celebration of the edgelands that characterize the uncertain border between cities and the surrounding countryside, have classified as 'desire paths'. These are 'lines of footfall worn into the ground' that transform the ordered, centralized spaces of the city into secret pockets; and that, in so doing, offer a 'subtle resistance to the dead hand of the planner'.[2]

Once he has decided on a direction, Mead strides off along his desire path, then, at once purposeful and purposeless. 'Sometimes he would walk for hours and miles and return only at midnight to his house.' Mead has never encountered another living creature on these nighttime walks. Nor has he so much as glimpsed another pedestrian in the daytime, because people travel exclusively by car. 'In ten years of walking by night or day, for thousands of miles, he had never met another person walking, not once in all that time' (569).

The proximate reason for the eerie solitude of the city at night is that everyone else has carefully secluded themselves in their living rooms in order to stare blankly and obediently at television screens. The silence of the city is an effect of what Theodor Adorno once called 'the unpeaceful spiritual silence of integral administration'.[3] If there is no political curfew in place in Bradbury's dystopian society, this is because a kind of cultural or moral curfew renders it superfluous.

Crossing and re-crossing the city at night on foot, aimlessly reclaiming the freedom of its streets from automobiles, Bradbury's Pedestrian is identifiable as the scion of a distinct tradition of urban rebellion or resistance, the dissident tradition of the nightwalker.

The distant origins of the so-called 'common night-walker' lie in late thirteenth-century England, when Edward I introduced the Statute of Winchester as a means of enforcing the curfew that prevailed at that time throughout the nation's towns and cities. This 'nightwalker statute', as it was known, then became central to the colonial law instituted in North America in the late seventeenth century.

In 1660, colonial law stipulated that the state's night watchmen should 'examine all Night Walkers, after ten of the clock at Night (unless they be known peaceable inhabitants) to enquire whither they are going, and what their business is'. If the individual accosted could not 'give Reasonable Satisfaction to the Watchman or constable' making this enquiry, they were liable to be arrested and taken before the magistrate, who would ask them 'to give satisfaction, for being abroad at that time of night'.[4]

In urban settlements throughout North America there was in the early modern period no right to the night, particularly for plebeians. Almost by definition, the poor could not 'give satisfaction for being abroad' after dark. In the streets at night the itinerant were an inherent threat to society. Today, as in the 1950s, residues of this situation persist. Indeed, in some places in the United States, the term 'common nightwalker' remains on the statute books, where it indicates a vagrant as well as a streetwalker or sex worker.

'An idle or dissolute person who roams about at late or unusual hours and is unable to account for his presence' is the definition of a nightwalker offered by two legal commentators who summarized a number of relevant statutes in the 1960s.[5] The ordinance against vagrants in Jacksonville, Florida, for instance, includes a reference to nightwalkers. The state, in its infinite leniency, doesn't construe a single night's wandering as necessarily criminal. 'Only "habitual" wanderers, or "common night walkers",' the authors of a legal textbook explain, 'are criminalized.' 'We know, however, from experience,' they rather drily add, 'that sleepless people often walk at night.'[6] The sleepless, the homeless and the hopeless, then, are all susceptible to this archaic charge.

It is against this legal background – and in view of the persistent suspicion about solitary people who inhabit the streets at night that, historically, it has sponsored – that Bradbury's portrait of a nocturnal pedestrian trapped in a dystopian cityscape demands to be interpreted. Despite the passage of more than 300 years since the origins of colonial law in North America, nightwalking remains a socially transgressive activity.

For Bradbury, writing in the 1950s, it potentially also has political implications. 'The Pedestrian' is an affirmation of the heterodox politics of the night, which 'has always been the time for daylight's dispossessed,' as Bryan Palmer writes, '– the deviant, the dissident, the different.'[7] The Pedestrian's footsteps, echoing on empty, darkened pavements, interrupt the ominous silence of the totalitarian city, which insists that its inhabitants remain visible but inaudible at all times.

'The Pedestrian' was written at a time when domestic life in North America was being dramatically altered, not only by the rise of the automobile but also the rise of television. The number of TV sets in the US leapt from 7,000 in 1946 to 50 million in 1950. Bradbury was evidently deeply troubled by these developments; and his dystopian dream of an oppressive society that uses television to ensure a docile, depoliticized population is comparable to Adorno's contemporaneous critique of the 'culture industry'.

'The total effect of the culture industry is one of anti-enlightenment,' so the German philosopher argued, 'in which enlightenment, that is the progressive technical domination of nature, becomes mass deception and is turned into a means for fettering consciousness.'[8] Adorno, who had lived in Los Angeles throughout the 1940s, contended in 'How to Look at Television' (1954) that this particular technology had already become a crucial medium of psychological control. 'The repetitiveness, the selfsameness, and the ubiquity of modern mass culture,' he insisted, 'tend to make for automatized reactions and to weaken the forces of individual resistance.'[9]

More recently, in his powerful critique of 'the 24/7 control society', Jonathan Crary includes a diatribe – manifestly influenced by the Frankfurt School – against the sedative and immobilizing effects of the 'mass diffusion of television in the 1950s'. Applied like a medicinal balm to a population made febrile by the traumatic experience of World War II, he claims, television 'was the omnipresent antidote to shock'. It insinuated masses of people into 'extended states of relative immobilization': 'Hundreds of millions of individuals precipitously began spending many hours of every day and night sitting, more or less stationary, in close proximity to flickering, light-emitting objects.'[10]

Crary's retrospect of the psychic and social impact of the new technology in this epoch itself reads like science fiction. But his insights are penetrating. 'In spite of more uprooted and transient lifestyles following the war,' he notes, 'television's effects were anti-nomadic: individuals are fixed in place, partitioned from one another, and emptied of political effectiveness.'[11] This is the immediate context for 'The Pedestrian'. Strolling in the streets at night becomes a means of reclaiming, for a moment, a sense of autonomy in an administered world.

In Bradbury's story, the city is a cemetery, its houses like tomb-stones that, as Mead ambles past them, are sometimes troubled by 'sudden gray phantoms' – the cold, cathode images flickering in rooms that as yet have not been curtained off from the street. Despite the stupefied state of these citizens, Mead is careful not to make a noise outside their homes. Indeed, 'long ago he had wisely changed to sneakers when strolling at night, because the dogs in intermittent squads would parallel his journey with bark-ings if he wore hard heels, and lights might click on and faces appear and an entire street be startled by the passing of a lone figure, himself, in the early November evening' (569). He has to be surreptitious, as those sneakers indicate. He is conscious that nightwalking is unacceptable because – semi-criminalized as it is in this society – it constitutes an act of what might be called 'excarceration'.[12]

If the television shows to which other citizens have become addicted are escapist, the Pedestrian's nightwalking instead rep-resents, simply, a form of escape. It is a flight; a fugue, at once psychogenic and sociogenic. But its affirmation of the nomadic is also, implicitly, a critique of the static, desiccated and depolit-icized culture of the United States in the 1950s. It is a refusal of reification.

On the particular evening narrated by Bradbury in 'The Pedes-trian', Mead heads in the direction of 'the hidden sea' (569). It is a crisply cold autumnal night; and, as he passes their houses, he whispers his contempt for the people watching comedies and cowboy movies behind closed doors: 'Time for a dozen assorted murders? A quiz? A revue? A comedian falling off the stage?' (570).

Occasionally, Mead catches at a leaf, 'examining its skeletal pattern in the infrequent lamplights' and 'smelling its rusty smell' (570). He is acutely sensitive to the faint residues of a non-mechanized existence that can still be found amid the city's alienated conditions. This is evidently one of the reasons the Pedestrian repairs to the streets at night. It reminds him he is alive. Nightwalking de-alienates Mead's perception of the quotidian world, which in contradistinction to that of the other citizens has not been relentlessly deadened, either by the automated routines of the daytime or the anaesthetic effects of television.

In one sense, then, 'The Pedestrian' is a celebration of – the pedestrian. It affirms the ordinary, insignificant details of existence that, like the leaf, have been discarded by this increasingly attenuated, if not skeletalized society, and left to rust. 'The future', André Breton once wrote in a mysterious but suggestive sentence, 'is a beautiful striated leaf that takes on colorings and shows remarkable holes.'[13]

In his minatory reflections on television, Adorno warned that 'people may not only lose true insight into reality, but ultimately their very capacity for life experience may be dulled by the constant wearing of blue and pink spectacles.'[14] Reality, according to Adorno, was in danger of becoming a kind of 3D illusion in California in the 1950s. In the solitude of the city at night, Mead's experience of the physical life about him, no matter how debased and deformed, can momentarily be made to seem disalienated. His nightwalk transforms the metropolis into a sort of biosphere.

By night the city is immediate. It is no longer seen from afar – mediated by television, which literally means sight at a distance – but from close to. For the Pedestrian, nightwalking effectively participates in what the Russian Formalists called the poetic function. In a famous article from 1917, Viktor Shklovsky wrote that it is the point of art 'to return sensation to our limbs' – 'to make us feel objects, to make a stone feel stony.'[15] Encountering the remnants of physical life alone at night, Mead experiences them as if for the first time. He grasps the leaf, suddenly alive to its skeletal pattern and its rustiness. The leaf feels leafy.

In the night, the metropolis itself appears magically estranged to the Pedestrian. It comes to seem so alien that it no longer feels alienated. Its dystopian landscape paradoxically adumbrates the faint promise of a utopian future. At one point, he stops in a street that is 'silent and long and empty' and fantasizes that the city too has been silenced and emptied. Indeed, that it is no longer a city at all: 'If he closed his eyes and stood very still, frozen, he could imagine himself upon the center of a plain, a wintry, windless American desert with no house in a thousand miles, and only dry riverbeds, the streets, for company' (570).

This prophetic vision – not simply of a deserted city, but of a city that, perhaps after the collapse of civilization itself, has been reduced to no more than the desert that, at its foundation, it originally reclaimed – can be found as far back as the Hebrew Bible: 'Thy holy cities are a wilderness, Zion is a wilderness, Jerusalem a desolation' (Isaiah 64:10).

It is a cataclysmic dream that shapes a number of important precursors to the dystopian fiction of the twentieth century, from Daniel Defoe's *Journal of the Plague Year* (1722), via Mary Shelley's *The Last Man* (1826), to Richard Jefferies' *After London* (1885). It appears, for example, to unsettling effect in Oliver Goldsmith's *The Citizen of the World* (1760–61), a collection of letters about contemporary England purportedly sent by 'a Chinese philosopher' corresponding with 'his friends in the East'. In one of these letters, the celebrated author of *The Deserted Village* (1770) – a poem about the brutal dispossession, in the late eighteenth-century English countryside, of the labouring class – describes walking about in the emptied streets of London at 2 a.m.

Here is The Deserted City. 'There will come a time', Goldsmith comments, when the 'temporary solitude' of the metropolis at night 'may be made continual, and the city itself, like its inhabitants, fade away, and leave a desert in its room.'[16] For Mead, as for Goldsmith's Chinese philosopher, the depopulated metropolis at night (the deserted city) anticipates a post-apocalyptic future in which civilization itself, hopelessly corrupt, has been almost completely effaced (the desert city).

∂

Setting off again, the Pedestrian momentarily loses his footing on a jagged piece of paving stone. 'He stumbled over a particularly uneven section of sidewalk,' Bradbury writes (570).

The pavement has been displaced, incipiently, by the subterranean presence of plant life. Weeds, as Richard Mabey has reminded us, 'green over the dereliction we have created' and 'insinuate the idea of wild nature into places otherwise quite shorn of it'.[17] Bradbury's narrator observes that the city's endless plains of cement appear already to be eroding – 'vanishing under flowers and grass' (570). He scrutinizes the ruderals secretly reappearing on the roadsides of the totally administered city. This is the nocturnal equivalent – it is a strikingly literal as well as political one – of what Walter Benjamin famously characterized as 'botanizing on the asphalt'.[18]

In the 'grassy seams' of the nighttime streets, in those signs of irrepressible organic life gradually erupting through the surface of the neglected city, Mead glimpses the ecology of an emergent apocalypse (569). The first phase of the city's apocalyptic destruction, or dissolution, is perhaps a creeping pastoral collapse. Organic life will corrode the manmade forms, the concrete and steel, in which the city is encased. 'The Pedestrian', therefore, is a vengeful fantasy of what Mike Davis has called 'the monstrous vegetative powers of feral nature'.[19]

The final phase of the apocalypse implicit in the Pedestrian's dream of the future is no doubt the kind of cataclysmic destruction that, as in the case of an atomic bomb, might reduce the city to little more than a 'wintry, windless American desert' (570). In this image, Bradbury evokes what Fredric Jameson has called the 'pleasures of dystopia'.[20]

The pleasures of dystopia can be sensed in the surreptitious, almost unacceptable thrills to be derived from the images of depopulation that accompany the representation of a catastrophe. Jefferies gives satisfying expression to them in *After London*, where his unsentimental narrator, reflecting on the implosion of the capital after a natural disaster, records that it 'was after all only of brick, and when the ivy grew over and trees and shrubs sprang up, and, lastly, the waters underneath burst in, this huge metropolis was soon overthrown'.[21] Bradbury's destructive or self-destructive hopes for the dystopian metropolis he describes in 'The Pedestrian' are comparable to those of Jefferies. After Los Angeles ...

'The more rational, productive, technical, and total the repressive administration of society becomes,' Adorno's friend Herbert Marcuse wrote in *One-Dimensional Man* (1964), 'the more unimaginable the means and ways by which the administered individuals might break their servitude and seize their liberation.'[22] It is only by imagining total social and ecological destruction that an alternative to the rational administration of totalitarian society can be envisaged.

For the Pedestrian, Bradbury suggests, this destruction, this alternative, only becomes imaginable because, in stumbling over the uneven paving stone, he is suddenly made conscious of the subterranean operation of a force that cannot be administered. Nature itself – notwithstanding the potentially terminal impact of climate change, under the impact of industrial capitalism, that has been discerned since the 1950s – cannot be administered out of existence.

But in Bradbury's narrative there is after all a political curfew, as well as the cultural or moral one enforced by the addiction of the masses to television. Mead's apocalyptic imaginings as he steals across the city under the partial protection of the dark – his ecological fugue – are suddenly interrupted by the appearance of a car that flashes 'a fierce white cone of light upon him' (570). It is a police car. No logo or slogan is stencilled on the side of the police car; but, if there had been, it might have read 'We Own the Night' – the tagline of the NYPD's Street Crimes Unit, disbanded after the brutal shooting of an unarmed immigrant in 1999.

The vehicle recalls John Rechy's description of a 'copcar driving along the streets' of Los Angeles in his novel *City of Night* (1963), like 'a slowly moving hearse'.[23] Mead stands 'entranced' before it, 'not unlike a night moth, stunned by the illumination, and then drawn toward it' (570). In fact, this is the only one in existence in Bradbury's city of the future. 'Crime was ebbing,' the narrator explains; 'there was no need now for the police, save for this one lone car wandering and wandering the empty streets' (570–1).

Meandering along the roads at night, the police car is Mead's mechanical double. It mimics his aimless movements, cruelly mocking the limits of his freedom.

In a 'metallic whisper' – which makes it clear that it is automated and contains no policemen – the vehicle interrogates the Pedestrian. It asks him first for his profession. Mead is a writer, as he confesses. The machine's phonographic voice offers a clinical, if laconic, response: 'No profession' (571). By 2053, television has rendered books all but redundant. The disembodied voice of the state proceeds to question Mead further:

> 'What are you doing out?'
> 'Walking,' said Leonard Mead.
> 'Walking!'
> 'Just walking,' he said simply, but his face felt cold.
> 'Walking, just walking, walking?'
> 'Yes, sir.'
> 'Walking where? For what?'
> 'Walking for air. Walking to see.' (571)

Dissatisfied with this reason that is no reason at all – Mead's statement is a tautological one that constitutes an affront to a society defined, as Herbert Marcuse might have put it, by 'the rational character of its irrationality' – the police machine coerces him into the back seat of the vehicle.[24] He will be transported in this 'little cell', he is informed, 'to the Psychiatric Center for Research on Regressive Tendencies' (572). In the totalitarian state imagined by Bradbury, then, to walk in the city at night is not only to transgress; it is to regress. Nightwalking, according to this logic, is intrinsically deviant, even atavistic. It transpires that the Pedestrian's final nightwalk is a flight that concludes, as psychogenic fugues often do, in a psychiatric institution.[25] The act of excarceration ends in incarceration.

So, the narrative ends – abruptly: 'The car moved down the empty riverbed streets and off away, leaving the empty streets with the empty sidewalks, and no sound and no motion all the rest of the chill November' (572). Indeed, for all time, it is to be presumed. For Leonard Mead, who has carefully tried to curate the remaining residues of the alienated city's humanity, is effectively its Last Man. Only the unevenness of the pavement, secretly undermined by feral plants, gives cause for hope.

At the end of 'The Pedestrian', it still seems possible that Nature itself, at some far-distant date, in the form of an ecological apocalypse, might be a stumbling block to the totally administered society of the twenty-first century. If only for the reader, those empty streets that in the dark look like cracked, dried riverbeds are, potentially, desire paths.

In the story of Lazarus in St John's Gospel, Jesus observes that 'if any man walk in the day, he stumbleth not, because he seeth the light of this world', adding that, if instead 'a man walk in the night, he stumbleth, because there is no light in him' (John 11:9–10). Mead stumbles when he takes the aimless walk in the night described by Bradbury, not because there is no light in him but for precisely the opposite reason. He stumbles because, alone in this totalitarian conurbation, he does contain an inner light.

The other citizens are bathed in the feverish half-light that leaks from the television sets in front of which they lifelessly sit; Mead seeks illumination in the darkness. In this respect, he is like one of those persecuted sixteenth-century mystics who were driven by the surveillance operations of the post-medieval Church to find spiritual consolation in the night, and who valued not simply light in the dark but 'the darkness that illuminates'. This phrase is taken from St John of the Cross, perhaps the most famous of these mystics, who was forced by his experiences as a prisoner in an almost lightless cell to identify faith, in an apophatic inversion of traditional theological assumptions, with the darkness of midnight rather than the light of midday. 'The more the soul is darkened,' John affirmed, 'the greater is the light that comes into it.'[26] For Mead, as for the theologians of the night, the dark has become a place of refuge and a site of possible redemption.

Obversely, illumination is associated with oppression, as when he is immobilized by the beam of the police car that arrests him. The 'light of this world' (John 11:9), in Christ's formulation, is an agent of post-Enlightenment oppression. By contrast, the absence of light – in the sort of fully enlightened, highly technologized society that, according to Adorno and Horkheimer, 'radiates disaster triumphant' – offers a form of freedom.[27] Strolling through the streets of Los Angeles after dusk is, for Mead, a spiritual, if not religious, ritual. Reclaiming the city at night, when no one else is about, he redeems it; and in so doing he retains a fragile hold on his humanity.

He is the post-contemporary equivalent of a *benandante*, or 'good walker', one of those medieval Italian peasants who set out at night to do battle with witches. In the eyes of the authorities these benign walkers were malign walkers. Mead's sacred walks, like those of the *benandanti*, who claimed their nighttime activities took place in a dream-like state between sleeping and waking, are finally punished as satanic.[28]

Mead's humanity consists in being, mere being – not a state of subsistence, like that of the numbed citizens connected to their screens as if to life-support machines, but being for its own sake. The nightwalker walks because he likes to breathe, as he admits, and because he likes to see; but he also walks because he likes to walk. He just walks. The nightwalker does not walk from one point to another in order to reach a destination. Hence it does not matter which direction he takes when he stands at the crossroads at the commencement of the night. He simply walks, opening himself up to the empty city.

In the night, Bradbury indicates, the Pedestrian likes to stands at a silent intersection, the junction at which the city's main roads meet, precisely because in the day it is 'a thunderous surge of cars, the gas stations open, a great insect rustling and a ceaseless jockeying for position as the scarab-beetles, a faint incense puttering from their exhausts, skimmed homeward to the far directions'. At nighttime, this intersection becomes a somnambulist's dream space. The roads are 'like streams in a dry season, all stone and bed and moon radiance' (570). This is the landscape of the 'moonlit enchanted night' celebrated by the German Romantic poet Ludwig Tieck. It is the realm of 'irrealism' in which Michael Löwy has discovered 'a critical attitude towards the disenchanted modern world, illuminated [as it is] by the blinding sun of instrumental rationality'.[29]

The Pedestrian does not commute, then, unlike the other citizens of this future, because commuting, travelling directly from one place to another, far from commuting him or transforming his identity, reinforces his sense of sameness. The commuter, as Rachel Bowlby observes, is 'a traveller along straight, known lines, not an aimless, curious drifter'.[30] It is precisely in order to be commuted, or spiritually transmuted, that the Pedestrian does not commute. His routes through the city are the opposite of a commute; they are a more or less conscious indictment of its instrumental regime. Mead's pedestrianism, at once calculated and spontaneous, defies the metrics of the commute. The nightwalker sets himself against the rhythms of the city's traffic, the frenetic movements of its commodities and people. He is a romantic anti-capitalist who nonetheless remains passionately in love with the modern metropolis. He refuses the city in the name of the city.

In this context, nightwalking is a radical activity, in both the political and more literal senses of the term (it brings to light the root of his being). Or, to put it in the terms of the police state depicted by Bradbury, it is both a transgressive and a regressive tendency. It is inherently countercultural, as Mead's ultimate incarceration demonstrates; but it is also an activity that, to the scandal of an automated, mechanized culture, goes back to the root of what it is to be human.

Walking in its countercultural mode can in this latter sense be identified with what Marx called men and women's 'species-being', or 'species-life', the fundamental properties of their physical and spiritual existence that define their humanity.[31] It is not constituted by exchange-value but by use-value. Nightwalking, for Mead, is not instrumental; it is an end in itself. Something like a negative dialectics of the nightwalk is thus made visible in Bradbury's narrative. As in Samuel Beckett's universe, according to Adorno, the empty nocturnal cityscape of 'The Pedestrian' is 'the negative imprint of the administered world'.[32]

Nightwalking constitutes a rejection, conscious or unconscious, of the tedious logic of the diurnal city. It renounces the predictable trajectories, the teleologies, of what William Blake, in his poem 'London' (1794), called its 'chartered streets'; and it does so in the name of what Blake called 'midnight streets'.[33] It glories in the contingent, the tangential. Walking, for Mead, satisfies a human need. And it is this that renders it unacceptable to a society like the one portrayed by Bradbury, where human needs have become so attenuated that they can be satisfied, for almost all of the population, by automobiles and TV comedies.

In so far as it is an allegory of oppression, 'The Pedestrian' was probably influenced by 'The Revolt of the Pedestrians' (1928), a short story first published in *Amazing Stories*, under the editorship of Hugo Gernsback, by the popular science-fiction writer David H. Keller. Far more reactionary than Bradbury's fantasy, Keller's dystopian fable centres on a hyper-mechanized society in which the so-called Automobilists, humans whose legs have progressively atrophied because they are so dependent on motorized transport, oppress an embattled minority of enlightened Pedestrians whom they are encouraged by the state to exterminate.[34]

But 'The Pedestrian' was also the product of a psychological obsession reaching back into Bradbury's childhood. Aged sixteen, some three years after his family had moved to Los Angeles, he witnessed a car crash involving several fatalities, and became traumatized. 'I walked home holding onto walls and trees,' as he put it, like someone describing an acute attack of agoraphobia. He subsequently elaborated his almost pathological opposition to the automobile into a political position, writing an anonymous editorial for his high-school magazine, when he was no more than eighteen, entitled 'Pedestrian becomes Freak among Modern Inventions'. Bradbury recapitulated the theme of this article on numerous later occasions: 'I would replace cars wherever possible with buses, monorails, rapid trains – whatever it takes to make pedestrians the center of our society again, and cities worthwhile enough for pedestrians to live in.'[35] He never held a driving licence.

'The Pedestrian' was however more immediately precipitated by Bradbury's Kafkaesque encounter with the LAPD one night in 1949. He and a friend happened to be walking along Wilshire Boulevard in Los Angeles, deep in conversation, 'when a police car pulled up and an officer stepped out to ask what we were doing'. Bradbury responded: 'Putting one foot in front of the other.' This did not impress the policeman, so Bradbury added, 'Breathing the air, talking, conversing, walking.' The officer remained mystified. 'Walking, eh? Just walking?' Eventually, after giving it some thought, he dismissed the two nightwalkers, telling them not to do it again. It was this 'Alice in Wonderland encounter', as Bradbury characterized it, that provided the impetus for 'The Pedestrian'.[36]

Bradbury had undergone similar experiences several times before this date, as he subsequently testified: 'I had been stopped on numerous occasions for walking at night, for being a pedestrian.' As far back as 1941, for example, the police had accosted him and another friend sometime after midnight in Pershing Square. He extrapolated 'The Pedestrian' from these experiences, developing a sort of politics of pedestrianism in the process. As Bradbury's biographer has argued, he 'had come to see the pedestrian as a threshold or indicator species among urban dwellers – if the rights of the pedestrian were threatened, this would represent an early indicator that basic freedoms would soon be at risk.'[37]

'The Pedestrian', for its part, sparked the composition of *Fahrenheit 451* (1953), probably Bradbury's most famous dystopian fiction (not least because François Truffaut adapted it for the cinema in 1966). Soon after finding a publisher for the short story, as Bradbury has explained, he decided to take his 'midnight criminal stroller out for another job around the city'.[38]

Fahrenheit 451 describes a totalitarian society – its population, too, is pacified if not completely sedated by television – in which literature is forbidden. In this future, it is the function of firemen not to extinguish fires but to burn books. The protagonist of Bradbury's humanist fable, Montag, is a fireman who, after meeting an enlightened, quietly incendiary young woman, starts to rebel against this regime.

In the end he escapes from the city, where he has become a fugitive, and joins a community of exiles who, living like hobos or tramps, have memorized the contents of classic books in order to preserve the remnants of civilization from the authoritarian interventions of the state. At the close of the novel, in a far-off cataclysm, the metropolis from which Montag has escaped, along with other American cities, is abruptly flattened by atomic bombs; and he imagines the 5 a.m. bus 'on its way from one desolation to another', its destination suddenly 'meaningless', 'its point of departure changed from metropolis to junkyard'.[39]

Originally entitled 'Long After Midnight', traces of the night-walking episode that constitutes 'The Pedestrian' can be discerned in *Fahrenheit 451*. The novel begins with a commute – though in this case one that has a genuinely transformative effect. Changing out of his protective clothing after a routine shift spent torching a house that contains books, Montag leaves the fire station in which he works, walks out 'along the midnight street' that leads to the metro, and takes a train back to the suburbs (12).

Recently, when returning home from the station, Montag has sensed someone else's presence on the street at night; but, on checking, he has seen 'only the white, unused, buckling sidewalk' (12). As in 'The Pedestrian', which also includes images of buckling sidewalks, this is a city that by night is almost as uninhabited as a lunar landscape. On this occasion, though, he encounters a girl, aged seventeen, called Clarisse – her name is emblematic of the role she plays in enlightening and hence radicalizing Montag. In a calculated attempt to meet him, Clarisse is strolling apparently casually along the 'moonlit pavement' (13). This is the domain, once again, of the enchanted city at night, though in this case the street is also the site of a kind of political or spiritual conversion.

Intrigued, Montag asks the girl what she is doing 'out so late wandering around'; and she tells him, with a simplicity that charms him, that it is 'a nice time of night to walk': 'I like to smell things and look at things, and sometime stay up all night, walking, and watch the sun rise' (14). Like Leonard Mead, she invokes the city's poetic function at night. They walk together on the 'silvered pavement', with 'the faintest breath of fresh apricots and strawberries in the air', and she gives him a detailed account of her family, made up of booklovers and intellectuals – i.e., deviants (14). In particular, she relates that her uncle has twice been arrested, once for driving too slowly on a highway ('He drove forty miles an hour and they jailed him for two days'), and once 'for being a pedestrian' (16–17).

Clarisse disappears shortly after this episode, and the reader assumes that she has either been detained or murdered by the authorities. But by this time the clandestine nightwalks that Montag shared with her, which have been unimpeachably chaste, have had the requisite effect on his political consciousness. As the fire chief later contemptuously puts it, she appeared in his life 'like the midnight sun', upsetting the natural order (121). She concentrated or reflected the darkness that illuminates, to formulate it in mystical terms.

In the central section of the novel, Bradbury charts his protagonist's deepening disaffection with the barbaric regime of which he has hitherto been an obedient agent. A disaffection that can be measured by the number of books that, instead of destroying, he secretly accumulates at home.

It is once his cache of books has been discovered that the state ruthlessly pursues him. At this point, the moonlit city that had opened up to him on his perambulations with Clarisse is transformed into an obscure labyrinth from which he must desperately escape. 'Watch for a man running,' the police announce to vigilant citizens, 'watch for the running man … watch for a man alone on foot' (132). The nightwalker has been forced to go on the run.

As the narrative of *Fahrenheit 451* starts to accelerate to its conclusion, Montag furtively enters a gas station in order to wash himself ('Men as a rule do not visit gas stations at night on foot,' as the authors of an article in an American journal of criminology wryly remarked in the mid-1930s, in the course of their reflections on a case concerning 'night prowlers'[40]). Then he steals out 'into the darkness' and stands in silence looking onto a vast, empty boulevard. He must traverse this road in order to elude his pursuers, even though it will make him highly visible (not least because of streetlamps that seem 'as bright and revealing as the midday sun' [133–4]). He has to reach the safety of a dark alley he can see across the road.

It is a richly dramatic scene taken straight from the noir cinema of the 1940s and 1950s, and it offers a reminder that Truffaut's mistake, when he filmed the novel in the mid-1960s, was to disregard this noir element and instead set all the exterior action in the daytime. If only *Fahrenheit 451* had looked more like *Alphaville* (1965) ... In Jean-Luc Godard's far more atmospheric science-fiction film, the eponymous futuristic city constitutes the centre of a technocratic society that is supposedly entering 'the Civilization of Light', one in which emotions have been criminalized and citizens have been made the 'slaves of probability'. But Godard's cinematographer, Raoul Coutard, deliberately portrays it as a city of darkness. He dramatizes this irony – this noirony, as it might be called – in a series of cool, cynical shots of slickened, crepuscular streets in a dystopian Paris of the night.

After leaving the gas station, Bradbury's protagonist begins 'his little walk' across the deserted road, which looks like a 'vast concrete river': 'He put his right foot out and then his left foot and then his right. He walked on the empty avenue' (134). But Montag is aware that he can be seen by a half-concealed vehicle with its headlights on, three blocks distant from him. The car accelerates in his direction and he starts to run. Then he abruptly reduces his pace so as not to attract attention: 'Walk, that's it, walk, walk' (134).

The car continues to hurtle closer and closer, a hostile emissary of the technological culture from which he has recently exiled himself.

> He began to shuffle idiotically and talk to himself and then he broke and just ran. He put out his legs as far as they would go and down and then far out again and down and back and out and down and back. God! God! He dropped a book, broke pace, almost turned, changed his mind, plunged on, yellowing in concrete emptiness, the beetle scuttling after its running food, two hundred, one hundred feet away, ninety, eighty, seventy, Montag gasping, flailing his hands, legs up down out, up down out, closer, closer, hooting, calling, his eyes burnt white now as his head jerked about to confront the flashing glare, now the beetle was swallowed in its own light, now it was nothing but a torch hurtling upon him; all sound, all blare. Now – almost on top of him! (135)

Montags's increasingly panicked motions, as the thumping syncopations of the second of these sentences in particular indicate, are reduced to their basic mechanical components. In 'The Pedestrian', it will be recalled, travelling by foot is classified as a 'regressive tendency'. Here, in this skilfully written passage, with its breathless rhythms, it describes a process almost of terminal collapse.

Montag plunges on across the road; and, as Mead had done, stumbles. And falls. But, at the last moment, the car misses him. Instead of the police, it contains thrill-seekers: 'children out for a long night of roaring five or six hundred miles in a few moonlit hours' (136). They must, he thinks, have accidentally seen a 'very extraordinary sight' – 'a man strolling' – and decided to 'get him' just for the hell of it (136).

They failed to kill him because he happened to fall. A fortunate fall, then. *Felix culpa.* Montag speculates, though, that it might have been kids like this, and not the police, that killed Clarisse simply because she liked to walk at night. Perhaps she was not a political martyr after all. Perhaps she was just another senseless victim of a mechanized society careering out of control.

Montag staggers onto the far kerb, 'telling each foot to go and keep going' (136). Then he hides 'in the safety of the dark alley for which he had set out', standing 'shivering in the night' as the youths in the car circle back for him (137). Soon he has to move. The state continues to track him as a fugitive, instructing all citizens to leave their television sets in order to stand at their front doors and identify his fleeing outline: 'He couldn't be missed! The only man running alone in the night city, the only man proving his legs!' (146).

Montag manages to escape, of course; first up the river, then along a desire path that takes the form of a forgotten train track. In the end, he finds the other refugees from this totalitarian society – exiled intellectuals who have adopted the identities of the books they have memorized ('I am Plato's *Republic*', etc. [158]). One of them has a portable television, so the former fireman is able to see a triumphant live broadcast of his own death, dramatized by the state for the benefit of the docile masses sitting semi-comatose in their homes.

How is this spectacle possible? It transpires that the authorities have targeted 'some poor fellow [who] is out for a walk' in the night, and persuaded the audience, through some deft manipulations of the camera, that he is Montag (156). Any social outcast will do. 'Don't think the police don't know the habits of queer ducks like that,' he is told by one of the other fugitives, 'men who walk mornings for the hell of it, or for reasons of insomnia' (156). This innocent pedestrian – perhaps it is Leonard Mead – is tracked down and exterminated on screen. In Bradbury's dystopian imagination, once again, the nightwalker, a 'midnight criminal stroller', is the quintessential heroic outcast.

The anonymous nightwalker made to stand in for Montag by the state when it stages its retribution as a television spectacle is, like the protagonist of Wells's *The Invisible Man*, a scapegoat. Montag is a scapegoat, too. And so is Mead. In Bradbury's totalitarian future, these nightwalkers are like the *pharmakoi*, the scapegoats of ancient Greek religion: criminalized but nonetheless sacred outsiders whose social function is to incarnate the guilt of the community from which they have been emblematically excluded.

In the dystopian narratives in which they feature, they are therefore innately double, at once sanctified and accursed; the 'symbol of both transgression and redemption', in Terry Eagleton's terms. As such, they represent a homeopathic form of hope. At the end of 'The Pedestrian', the reader pities Mead when the police deport him in silence to the Psychiatric Center for Research on Regressive Tendencies (which functions as an ancient zone of exclusion that has been relocated inside the city's precincts).

As Eagleton has argued, compassion for the *pharmakos* is a form of identification that has the effect of displacing feelings of outrage and disgust onto the social order that has victimized him:

> The scapegoat, itself beyond speech and sociality, becomes a judgement on that order in its very being, embodying what it excludes, a sign of the humanity which it expels as so much poison. It is in this sense that it bears the seeds of revolutionary agency in its sheer passivity; for anything still active and engaged, however

dissidently, would still be complicit with the *polis*, speaking its language and thus unable to put it into question as a whole. Only the silence of the scapegoat will do this.⁴¹

When Mead closes his eyes and stands stock-still in the street at night, picturing the city as a desert plain, he is this scapegoat. At the end of the story, 'the empty streets with the empty sidewalks', which are disturbed by 'no sound and no motion', represent a materialization of his mute, passive protest (572). The city itself, in its silence and through its cracked sidewalks, constitutes a concrete refusal of the totalitarian logic that has deformed it. It has been reduced to a state of Beckettian resistance. But the nocturnal city's bare life, and the one man who inhabits the night, haunting it like the undead, points beyond itself to an apocalypse from which it might ultimately be rebuilt.

Perhaps the most significant moment in 'The Pedestrian', as I have already implied, is when Mead misses his step on the warped or buckled pavement: 'He stumbled over a particularly uneven section of sidewalk' (570). If there are no lost steps, as Breton's *Nadja* professes, then there are no missed steps either.⁴² Every misstep is significant. 'The walker who stumbles', Paul Carter writes in his book on the aesthetics of agoraphobia, 'invalidates the modern city,' because he or she fails to conform to its accelerationist logic.⁴³

Mead's stumble momentarily points to the utopian remainder embedded or hidden in this dystopia. The loose stone, a token of both past and future that juts into the present, is the *skandalon*, meaning a stumbling block, one which will become the cornerstone of some new social order.

In the language of Adorno's friend Ernst Bloch, it is a utopian surplus or excess, symbolic of the 'Not Yet'.⁴⁴ It marks the site from which this apparently indestructible totalitarian society will start to undermine itself and collapse. The nightwalker also marks a point of deconstruction. He too is a scandal.

According to St John's Gospel, to walk in the night is by definition to stumble, to admit to having fallen or lapsed: 'But if a man walk in the night, he stumbleth, because there is no light in him.' The verb 'to stumble' comes from Old Norse, meaning to grope or trip in the dark. To walk in the night is to be benighted, morally blinded. Only those who have no light in them walk at night. But in spite of stumbling, or because of it (it is another fortunate fall), Bradbury's Pedestrian finds in the night, in the darkness that illuminates, an inner light.

In this sense, over and above his incarceration at the end, Mead embodies hope. Excluded from the diurnal city, like the sixteenth-century mystics who reclaimed the dark for spiritual purposes, he is forced to find redemption in the night. In this respect, the Pedestrian himself, in his stubborn refusal of the rules of Bradbury's totalitarian society, dramatized in his nightwalking, is this society's stumbling block or *skandalon*.

Nightwalking is, in a dual sense, scandalous: the rambling and stumbling of the nightwalker is socially unacceptable; but, if he has been scapegoated, historically, then his aimless activity is, potentially at least, the cornerstone of a different kind of society.

10

Not Belonging

On the Architectural Logic of
Contemporary Capitalism

There is in Jean Rhys's novel *Good Morning, Midnight* (1939) a powerful account of what it feels like to walk about the streets of a city when one has no money and no status. Rhys's female narrator, Sasha, an alcoholic leading a penurious, fairly peripatetic existence in Paris in the 1930s, describes the animosity and hostility of the buildings past which, as in some urban fairy tale, she must venture on foot in order to return at night to the dreary, flea-bitten hotel where she is a restless and reluctant tenant.

'If you have money and friends,' Sasha points out, houses 'stand back respectfully'. But if you don't, if you are penniless and rootless, then they intuit this – 'they know' – and they adopt a far less respectful, indeed a demeaning, insulting attitude:

> Then they step forward, the waiting houses, to frown and crush. No hospitable doors, no lit windows, just frowning darkness. Frowning and leering and sneering, the houses, one after another. Tall cubes of darkness, with two lighted eyes at the top to sneer. And they know who to frown at. They know as well as the policeman on the corner, and don't you worry …[1]

At our most vulnerable, perhaps we have all experienced this paranoid relationship to the built environment. Perhaps, as individuals, we have all felt persecuted and victimized by the 'waiting

houses' that stare and sneer at us as we sidle past them on foot, as
in some ritual of humiliation. Walking in the city, especially when
our lives are precarious, entails a perpetual struggle to resist the
intimidating permanence and stability of the built environment;
the sense that it is home to others but not to us.

Do we feel at home in the cities we inhabit? This, then, is the
question. There are, of course, innumerable ways in which ordinary people, especially the poor and those from marginalized
social groups, experience an almost permanent sense of displacement in the urban environments in which they live, even if the
consolations of belonging to a particular, more or less organic,
community can at times alleviate this fragile state of being. There
are forms of economic exclusion, political exclusion and social
exclusion – competing and overlapping in complex, shifting patterns – that determinately shape the everyday lives of individuals
in cities, especially in so far as these are also defined by gendered,
racial and religious identities.

   The built environment actively contributes to these modes of
displacement; and in the early twenty-first century it is probably more aggressive in prosecuting or reinforcing this politics of
exclusion than ever before. As Margit Mayer has written, 'cities
have transformed into gated communities and privatized public
spaces, where wealthy and poor districts are increasingly separated by invisible barriers, and access of the poor to the amenities
and infrastructures that cities once held for all have become more
and more restricted.'[2]

   The specifically urban forms of alienation and exclusion to
which I have alluded are perhaps most acutely experienced by
those classified by the state, for transparently ideological purposes, as illegal immigrants. But there is also a chronic and
pervasive sense of unease that, whoever we are, from wherever
we have come, is virtually constitutive of our experiences of living
in cities. No doubt it was this existential as well as social condition that theorists of the metropolis, from at least the advent of
the industrial European city in the nineteenth century, diagnosed
in their accounts of its intrinsically alienating effects.

   The individual's need for 'self-preservation in the face of the large city', as Georg Simmel famously expressed it in 'The Metropolis and Mental Life' (1903), requires as its prerequisite a 'mental attitude' that he designated in terms of 'reserve'.[3] The reserved disposition that the individual self-protectively adopts in relation to the urban environment he or she inhabits presupposes – and at the same time compounds – a state of dissimilation that perpetually vitiates his or her sense of assimilation. Perhaps cities, at least in the alienated conditions of capitalist society, are precisely those social collectives in which, as a matter of definition, no one ever feels completely at home. The fundamental, if not predominant, phenomenological experience of the built environment, from this perspective, is one of discomfort.[4]

Here, I want to explore some aspects of the role that buildings play in reinforcing the concrete and the more abstract forms of this feeling of not being at home in the urban environment. Of not belonging. I am inspired in part by the novelist China Miéville's article 'The Conspiracy of Architecture', a brilliantly imaginative but at the same time rigorously materialist analysis of what he calls 'the *animate, alien building*'.[5]

To put it in phenomenological terms, I am interested not simply in how we relate to buildings, as sentient beings, but in how buildings, as effectively animate entities, relate to us (Bruno Latour, in his Actor-Network Theory, has pioneered the assumption that buildings 'act', not least because they arouse 'a sense of wellbeing or an impulse to flee').[6] To put it in psychopathological terms, so to speak, I am interested not only in how we look at buildings but, more significantly still, in how buildings look at us; that is, in how we internalize the gaze of buildings.

Applying Slavoj Žižek's fertile notion of the 'architectural parallax', in addition to other theoretical resources, I use this chapter to examine the ways in which, moving through the contemporary city on foot, buildings negotiate us just as we negotiate buildings; and I explore the ways in which, in some fundamental sense, they reinforce a sense of the city's uncanniness, its unhomeliness. I go on to detail some of the ways in which a specific type of contemporary architecture, which I characterize in terms of its 'visored' façades, dramatizes the intrusive, even offensive, relation to the individual I initially outline.

In developing the concept of the visor, I revisit some of the ideas and tropes explored by Jacques Derrida in his *Specters of Marx* (1994), especially in his suggestive interpretation of the opening scenes of *Hamlet*. Finally, I propose a symptomatic, or more precisely homeopathic, solution to the pathological relation in which these visored buildings, indeed urban buildings in general, situate us. What Alejandro Zaera Polo has pursued in the shape of a 'politics of the envelope' lies behind my reflections, throughout this chapter, on what I call the politics of the visor.[7]

These reflections, it can be added, also comprise a contribution to recent debates about the 'right to the city'. Peter Marcuse has helpfully reminded us that this Lefebvrian slogan, which dates from the late 1960s, articulates both a 'demand' and a 'cry' – the demand of 'those who are excluded' and the cry of 'those who are alienated'. 'The demand is for the material necessities of life,' he elaborates, 'the aspiration is for a broader right to what is necessary beyond the material to lead a satisfying life.'[8]

It seems to me that this aspirational or even spiritual dimension of the right to the city, absolutely inseparable from the material dimension, should among other things entail the right to feel at home in the built environment in which we live. Certainly, as the architect and architectural theorist Christian Norberg-Schulz once put it, 'one gets along without feeling "at home".'[9] But why should we accept this state of permanent displacement? Why should we have to learn to live with a habitual feeling of not being at home?

This chapter, which thinks about cities in philosophical terms but also as a pressing political problem at the present time, investigates the unhomeliness of the urban environment, for diagnostic purposes, in terms of the spectral gaze, or 'visor effect', that is encoded in individual buildings. It does so in the belief that belonging in the city should be a necessary corollary to being in the city.

The intervention on architecture in Žižek's *Living in the End Times* consists of a fascinating 'interlude' in which he develops the concept of the 'architectural parallax'.[10] The word 'parallax', derived from the Greek verb *parallassein*, meaning 'to alternate', is in its ordinary sense the apparent difference in an object, or the position of an object, when it is viewed from different perspectives.

Cubist painting, to develop an example at which Žižek merely hints, could be productively characterized as a sustained and elaborate attempt to capture a 'parallax view' of the object. A painting like Picasso's *Violin Hanging on the Wall* (1912–13), to pick one almost at random, reconstitutes the image of the instrument itself, and its relation to the wall on which it hangs, as if the painter is repeatedly shifting his perspective. It apprehends the violin not simply as a three-dimensional object but a four-dimensional one; that is, an object situated in time as well as space. The painter's dynamic, unstable point of observation compels the shapes, planes and angles of the composition to intersect with one another as if conducting an elegant, complicated dance in time. And in addition, the parallax form of the cubist aesthetic folds the viewer herself into the dynamics of the picture, collapsing subject into object. This is not a still life so much as an unstill one.

But Žižek, who is leaning on the Japanese philosopher Kojin Karatani's account of the antinomies in Kant's thought, emphasizes that, philosophically speaking, this apparent difference in an object when it is viewed from alternative perspectives is more than simply subjective; it is, in effect, objective. 'An "epistemological" shift in the subject's point of view', he writes, 'always reflects an "ontological" shift in the object itself.'[11] Picasso's violin, to return to that example, is constitutively transformed by the dynamic decomposition that is the result of the painter's shifting perspectives.

There is, then, something objectively as well as subjectively unsettling about this process, so to speak. The object, in the shifting perspective of the parallax, is both itself and not itself. It is non-identical with itself. The parallax view therefore renders the object uncanny. It imparts a kind of alien life to it. Think of a photograph in which, because the camera has been accidentally moved during exposure, the object or person captured is not only blurred but visible from two slightly distinct angles (Michel de Certeau refers with some elegance to 'the way a tremulous image confuses and multiplies the photographed object').[12] This ghostly,

monstrous effect registers the inscription of what Žižek calls the
'parallax gap', the interval or passage between changing, competing perspectives.

How does this relate to architecture? Žižek underlines his
point that, in this context, the parallax gap is 'not just a matter
of shifting perspective (from one standpoint, a building looks a
certain way – if I move a bit, it looks different)'. For it also marks
a radically destabilizing shift in the building's very identity, its
individuality (in the literal sense of its indivisibility). 'Things get
interesting,' he suggests, 'when we notice that the gap is inscribed
into the "real" building itself – as if the building, in its very
material existence, bears the imprint of different and mutually
exclusive perspectives.' He continues:

> When we succeed in identifying a parallax gap in a building, the
> gap between the two perspectives thus opens up a place for a
> third, virtual building. In this way, we can also define the creative
> moment of architecture: it concerns not merely or primarily the
> actual building, but the virtual space of new possibilities opened
> up by the actual building. Furthermore, the parallax gap in archi-
> tecture means that the spatial disposition of a building cannot be
> understood without reference to the temporal dimension: the par-
> allax gap *is* the inscription of our changing temporal experience
> when we approach and enter a building.[13]

When we walk about the city in our everyday lives, approaching,
circling, entering buildings, we relate to them as animate, alien
entities. All houses, from the parallax perspective, are spectral;
they haunt us.

The virtual building invoked or provoked by these encounters with the material building in time as well as space is then,
apparently, an instance of what Anthony Vidler, extrapolating
from Freud, has called 'the architectural uncanny'.[14] But, if this
is the case, it is an iteration of it that, significantly, is not the contingent or circumstantial property of a particular home, or even
a particular style of architecture such as the postmodern, but is
in fact positively structural to the built environment. For, if the
urban fabric is grasped in Žižek's terms rather than Vidler's, the

uncanny is effectively constitutive of architecture as it is encountered by pedestrians negotiating the city streets.

Freud's influential notion of the *unheimlich*, the unhomely or uncanny, which he identified as a 'special class of the frightening', centres on the disconcerting obtrusion of the unconscious into conscious existence. Published in 1919, his essay was an attempt to overcome the theoretical limitations of the only previous essay on the topic, by the German psychologist Ernst Jentsch, who had argued in 1906 that a sense of the uncanny is invariably generated in the subject by the sudden appearance of an alien or unexpected object.

The *unheimlich* was for Jentsch associated with the characteristic moment of uncertainty experienced by the human intellect as it half-reluctantly tries to assimilate an unfamiliar phenomenon to its 'ideational sphere', as when a wax model momentarily seems to be animate. He reassured his readers, however, that this '*lack of orientation*' could be overcome by sheer intellectual mastery.[15] Freud disputed Jentsch's complacent rationalist assumption: he insisted that his predecessor's interpretation was incomplete because, according to its logic, 'the better oriented in his environment a person is, the less readily will he get the impression of something uncanny in regard to the objects and events in it.'[16]

Freud argued instead that it is precisely when one feels at home in an environment that one is most susceptible to the uniquely subversive influence of the uncanny. 'The uncanny', he stated at the outset, 'is that class of the frightening which leads back to what is known of old and long familiar.'[17] Freud buttressed the central claim of his article with an etymological examination of the term *heimlich*, which on the one hand means 'what is familiar and agreeable, and on the other, what is concealed and kept out of sight'.[18] The uncanny marks the moment at which, according to Freud, the familiar becomes unfamiliar, and the unfamiliar, at the same time, comes to seem all too familiar.

The house is for this reason the *locus classicus* of the uncanny, as Freud concedes when he observes that the example of 'a *haunted* house' is 'perhaps the most striking of all, of something uncanny'.[19] The entity that people most take for granted, where they supposedly most feel at home, the house, is peculiarly uncanny when it is revealed to be secretly hostile to those that inhabit it. The *heim* is, in both an etymological and a phenomenological sense, the root of the *unheimlich*.

The built environment is, then, especially susceptible to the logic of the uncanny. We presume in our everyday lives, as we traverse the pavements of the city on foot, that it is hospitable to us, because it is the product of our collective labours; but it is in fact secretly opposed to us. Buildings, as numerous horror movies have testified, watch us with suspicion. We feel ourselves observed by them and, as in the example of the 'dread of the evil eye', which Freud adduces as another classic instance of the uncanny, we fear 'a secret intention of doing harm'.[20] All houses, in a sense, are haunted, because they are susceptible to the dynamics of the architectural parallax. They are both themselves and not themselves.

In his book on the architectural uncanny, Vidler reconstructs a kind of archaeology of the trope, running from early nineteenth-century Romanticism through to early twentieth-century avant-gardism, in order to understand the unhomely aspect of domestic buildings as this has impinged historically both on literature and the built environment itself. His inspiration is historically proximate, as the book's suitably baroque opening sentence indicates:

> Intrigued by the unsettling qualities of much contemporary architecture – its fragmented neoconstructivist forms mimetic of dismembered bodies, its public representation buried in earth-works or lost in mirror reflection, its 'seeing walls' reciprocating the passive gaze of domestic cyborgs, its spaces surveyed by moving eyes and simulating 'transparency,' its historical monuments indistinguishable from glossy reproductions – I have been drawn to explore aspects of the spatial and architectural uncanny, as it has been characterized in literature, philosophy, psychology, and architecture from the beginning of the nineteenth century to the present.

Vidler traces a fascination, inherited from Freud, both with 'the hidden terrors of the house', as an architectural space, and with what he identified as the 'dedomesticated subject' that inhabits it.[21]

But for Vidler, as I have implied, the uncanny implicitly remains an alien fragment lodged in the familiar fabric of the building, as opposed to an irreducible, indeed 'ontological', dimension of its form. Žižek's concept of the 'virtual building' – which is necessarily precipitated by the interaction between the individual subject, moving through space and time, and the building's architectural form – seems to me an important development (albeit one that is ultimately susceptible to the charge of ahistoricism).

I propose to refine it a little here, or perhaps to displace it slightly, by situating it more explicitly in relationship to the trope of the uncanny; and, specifically, by reconceptualizing the virtual building in terms of the idea of the spectral building. I intend to refine or displace it, too, by rethinking the building's ontology in terms of what Derrida, in a neat pun of characteristically serious intent, calls 'hauntology'.

The concept of hauntology is Derrida's relatively late attempt, as part of his relentless deconstruction of the metaphysical tradition, to think the 'logic of haunting' as opposed to the logic of being. Ontology 'speaks only of what is present or what is absent; it cannot conceive of what is neither,' as Warren Montag has argued.[22] Hauntology speaks of the neither, and the both, that is the spectral. Here, I want to insist on the hauntology of architecture; that is, on the hauntological house, and not merely, as Vidler does, the haunted house. Derrida talks in *Specters of Marx* of 'the virtual space of spectrality', and what I am positing here, with respect to Žižek's virtual building, is simply the obverse of that, the spectral space of virtuality.[23]

Offering a kind of paranoid reading of the city, my reflections here are centred on how buildings look at us quite as much as on how we look at buildings. They focus on how buildings look at us when, approaching them on foot, we look at them; on how they look at us both when we participate in what Alberto Pérez-Gómez called architecture's 'space-matter' and when we enter into their field of social, and political, relations.[24] The dynamics of this force field, which is necessarily constituted and reconstituted not in the abstract but in the historical conditions of time and space, as David Harvey's studies of 'relational space' have amply demonstrated, are of course extremely complicated.[25]

After all, 'architecture is rarely experienced as an isolated autonomous object'; urban space, in fact, is 'encountered as being connected, made up by interrelations between buildings rather than the impact of buildings on their own'.[26] But my specific claim, despite the risk of simplification, is that the parallax gap that, when we experience it as a pedestrian, opens up between two or more competing, interpenetrating perspectives on a particular building – when, for example, we turn a corner in a city and approach it – is, precisely, the spectral architectural point from which the building *looks back at us*. It is the ghostly site at which its hauntology materializes or momentarily becomes visible.

As we move about in their spatio-temporal orbit, all buildings look back at us from some virtual vantage point. 'Our changing temporal experience when we approach and enter a building,' to borrow Žižek's words again, animates this building and imparts a kind of life to it. And that life, finally, is an alien one. The building is a Thing, in so far as it embodies the gaze of a Subject but at the same time does not subjectivize itself. In this way the individual is trapped in the logic, imprisoned in the perspective, of the Other-Thing.[27]

A classic example might be Mother's house, perched above the Bates Motel, in Hitchcock's *Psycho* (1960), which from the moment it is first seen trains its uncanny gaze on the events that take place on the concourse beneath it. And on the camera. Paradoxically, it is the antiseptic motel, and not the crumbling gothic mansion, that is the haunted house in this movie, for the simple reason that the former is haunted by the latter. Both are virtual buildings, in that they occupy the parallax gap between the competing perspectives that Hitchcock's camera traces, but Mother's house is also a spectral building. *Psycho* is a movie about a haunting house, a house that haunts, as much as a haunted one.

But there is a fundamental historical sense in which every building is always-already haunting, as Miéville demonstrates in his persuasive attempt 'to show that the image of the animate, alien building is explicable as an aesthetic response to the peculiar alienated relation between humanity and architecture under capitalism'.[28] For the alienness, the non-humanness, of buildings is at root social and economic. It is a structural effect of alienation, of the alienated relations that prevail under capitalism; that is, a mode of production in which, as Marx's theory of commodity fetishism in *Capital* (1867) indicates, producers are ruled by their products, and these products, including buildings, which are profoundly implicated in the capitalist marketplace, consequently come to seem animate, autonomous and endowed with an independent power.

All buildings, all houses, are in this sense alien. To overstate the matter a little, we might say of the built environment, as Sartre said of the world, that it is 'human but not anthropomorphic'.[29] It remains at some fundamental level resistant to the attempt to domesticate it. And the alien life of buildings, their alien gaze, is a structural effect of this. The parallax gap is thus historically, as well as ontologically, inscribed in buildings.

So, the commodity status of a building in capitalist society renders it intrinsically haunted, intrinsically other than itself (like Marx's dancing table in Volume One of *Capital*). But there is of course an additional, rather more ordinary sense in which 'the alienation of building from dweller is the result of the mediation of the market'; and inevitably this too is relevant.[30] Most producers, as consumers, do not own the house they inhabit. Moreover, they are excluded from the vast majority of buildings, in so far as these are privately rather than publicly owned.

For this reason, a person's home, like the buildings that surround it, is necessarily what Marx, in the *Economic and Philosophical Manuscripts* of 1844, characterizes as

> a hostile dwelling, an 'alien, restraining power which only gives itself up to him in so far as he gives up to it his blood and sweat' – a dwelling which he cannot regard as his own home where he might at last exclaim, 'Here I am at home,' but where instead he finds himself in *someone else's* house, in the house of a *stranger* who daily lies in wait for him and throws him out if he does not pay his rent.[31]

We live in hostile dwellings; we live surrounded by hostile buildings. If, as Freud once said, the ego is not master in its own house,
then neither is – the master.

Under capitalism, it might be said, all buildings embody an
alien, restrictive power, and people are in consequence engaged
in a perpetual, if largely unconscious, attempt to tame and
domesticate them, to force them to surrender. On the other
hand, consciously and unconsciously, people are forever trying
to accommodate and assimilate themselves to the built environment. This is both a material process, as Marx implied, and a
spiritual process.

In relation to the latter, de Certeau has speculated that, at the
level of the streets through which the pedestrian is impelled to
walk, the city represents 'an immense social experience of lacking
a place', one in which people are ceaselessly searching for opportunities, either real or ideal, to feel temporarily at home. The city
in which, in the face of this fundamental experience of homelessness, the passer-by finds a provisional sense of security and
significance, is thus what he calls 'a network of residences temporarily appropriated by pedestrian traffic'.[32]

It is as part of this ceaseless struggle between buildings and
pedestrians that the former look at the latter defensively, even
offensively. Frowning and leering and sneering, as Rhys puts it. In
hosting us, in apparently accommodating us, buildings function
as an enemy host; they are hostile. The 'complementary relation'
that Arnold Berleant has identified 'between building and site
and between both of these and the human user' is, at root, antag-
onistic too.[33]

But buildings also function in ways that are ghostly – as the
etymological tangle of 'host', 'guest' and 'ghost', all of which
probably have a common root in the West Aryan word *ghosti-s*,
suggests.[34] Perhaps, then, buildings are not simply potentially
but constitutively inhospitable. Perhaps, in spite of their obdu-
rate materiality, they are not only innately alien but intrinsically
ghostly. Here, again, is the house as a hauntological entity.

'Do not trust houses,' the French-Egyptian poet Edmond Jabès
once remarked; 'they are not always hospitable.'[35] The gaze of

buildings is hostile, armed. My concrete interest here is in those buildings that, because and not in spite of the fact that they half-conceal, half-reveal their alien stare, exhibit with peculiar clarity the spectral logic I have invoked. Specifically, I mean buildings that are, as I characterize them, visored.

The word 'visor' seems to me to be a useful term for thinking about the appearance of buildings in part because it is closely related to the word 'façade'. Just as the latter is derived from the French *face*, the former is etymologically related to the French *visage* – both signifying the facc. But where the word 'façade' connotes a building's openness to the world on which it looks (the street or garden or whatever), the word 'visor' connotes its closedness, its defensiveness.

Lefebvre observes that the façade has often been viewed 'as a face or countenance perceived as expressive, and turned not towards an ideal spectator but towards the particular viewer'; but he also points out that, to the extent that it is the basis for an 'organic analogy' – or, it might be added, an organicist ideology – there is something 'fraudulent' about it. The façade 'implies a front and a back – what is shown and what is not shown – and thus constitutes a seeming extension into social space of an asymmetry which arose rather late in the evolution of living organisms as a response to the needs of attack and defence'.[36]

The façade is armoured; it is part of the struggle through which buildings force us to surrender to them. Zaera Polo comments in 'The Politics of the Envelope' that 'the power of architecture is not just iconographic but also organizational.'[37] I would add, more specifically and more pointedly, that the power of the façade is not just iconographic and organizational, but also territorial, martial. If the façade is a face, it is a visored face.

In English, according to the *OED*, the Anglo-Norman word 'visor', which came into use in the fourteenth century, signifies 'the front part of a helmet, covering the face but provided with holes or openings to admit of seeing and breathing, and capable of being raised and lowered'. To put it metaphorically, it is a form of facial fortification; and its design, which features apertures, slits and even a sort of portcullis, is indeed not unlike the front elevation of a castle.

For obvious reasons, in the Middle Ages the word visor also came to mean 'a mask to conceal the face'; a vizard. And by the sixteenth century it was being used figuratively to signify, on the one hand, 'a face or countenance, an outward aspect or appearance'; and, on the other, a disguise, 'an outward appearance or show under which something different is hid'. In these two senses it was cognate with the word façade, which also means both an outward appearance and an artful deceit.

How, then, do we defamiliarize our relationship to the buildings we encounter in an everyday urban context? How do we both analyse and estrange the political logic of architecture? More precisely, how do we restore a political dimension to our relationship to the city in such a way that we do justice to those who, perhaps because they are homeless or jobless, experience the built environment as a site of exclusion? To those who experience it as a labyrinth; a labyrinth, on the one hand, in which they feel trapped, and, on the other, from which they feel expelled? In response to these questions, we might start by deliberately displacing the term 'façade' from our architectural vocabulary and replacing it with the term 'visor'. It is imperative to unmask the façade. And to expose it as a visor.

Žižek, in his reflections on architecture, notes that the 'basic issue' he is addressing can be condensed in this question: 'How does an ideological edifice (real architectural edifices included) deal with social antagonisms?'[38] It is surely in this sense, among others, that 'the fate of capitalist society is not at all extraneous to architectural design', as Manfredo Tafuri formulated it in *Architecture and Utopia*.[39] In so far as ideology is inscribed in the façade of an architectural edifice – and the façade is a privileged site in this regard – it makes sense to think of all buildings as having visors.

It seems especially appropriate, though, in the context of a contemporary metropolis like London, where – as Maria Kaika and Korinna Thielen confirm – a 'new generation of private shrines', in the shape of corporate buildings that compete with older civic monuments, 'stand like self-assured and self-sufficient fortresses, neither needing nor desiring to engage with public space'. 'Despite making a loud public statement,' they continue, these buildings 'nevertheless look inwards and more often than not even try to "protect" themselves from the public realm, by blocking access to the public, or by making access excessively expensive.'[40]

It only needs to be added that the business of protecting themselves from the public domain, as outlined by Kaika and Thielen, involves these private buildings in a look outwards as well as inwards; but one that is, as I see it, visored. It entails seeing, in an intrusive sense, without being seen to do so.

In class society, all buildings, but especially corporate or state-sponsored buildings, are effectively in a state of siege, however innocent or hospitable they purport to be – not only in relation to the environment but to people. Zaera Polo, discussing 'an increase in the complexity of the *faciality* of buildings', argues that power, corporate capitalist power for example, however abstracted it has become, is still necessarily inscribed in buildings: 'the building envelope will still be required to fulfill a complex set of performances, as the primary regulator between public and private, inside and outside.'[41]

The façades of all buildings are engaged in the irreducibly political business of negotiating social antagonisms; that is to say, of reinforcing them as well as neutralizing or attempting to resolve them. In the contemporary metropolis, so-called iconic buildings, in spite of their implicit claims to transcend the politics of the urban environment, are profoundly and problematically invested in the reordering of urban space along these lines.[42] Their infantilizing nicknames – the Cheese-Grater, the Gherkin, the Walkie Talkie, etc. – serve to domesticate them, and to render them semi-comic, so obscuring this investment in the production and politics of space.

Every building must be able at the same time both to admit and to reject those that approach it; to attract and repel. Every building must be able to assimilate some people and to intimidate and dissimilate others. To give a simple example, numerous buildings, including many hotels and shops, will either overtly or covertly embrace the economically and socially privileged and block access to the under-privileged. All buildings, through their form as well as their social function, privilege one sort of person over another. The façade of every building 'interpellates' the individual subjects that encounter it, hailing some and ignoring or deterring others.[43] Policing them. This, again, is the implication of Rhys's description, in *Good Morning, Midnight*, of the attitude of buildings to the poor and precarious: 'They know as well as the policeman on the corner, and don't you worry ...'

All buildings watch us without being seen to do so. The underpaid private security guards that patrol so many buildings both in the daytime and the night, as well as the CCTV cameras with which their façades bristle, are in this respect only emblems of the hidden logic of all contemporary urban architecture.

Every building is visored. But, if every façade is a visor, some buildings exhibit this fact with particular clarity. I am thinking of visored buildings in a concrete as well as an abstract sense, an explicit as well as an implicit one.

Visored buildings are those structures that, almost spitefully refusing the paradigm of transparency central to modernist architecture, angle their gaze at us through shutters or slats that make it impossible for us to see into their interior. In this way, through windows that are not windows, they objectify the subject, forcing him or her to internalize a sense of being observed, watched; to live with a feeling of not being at home.

Of course, there is always a rationale for these designs, often an admirably benign one, based on the materials and aesthetics of these buildings, and on the local climatic and cultural conditions. In hot countries, for instance, slatted or screened façades can of course be efficient mechanisms for controlling heat and light. But I am interested, from a phenomenological point of view, in the politics encrypted in these exteriors and their surrounding spaces. For the concrete appurtenances or attributes of the architectural visor exemplify what Paul Jones has described as 'the role of architecture in providing the material symbols connected to capital accumulation'.[44]

I am interested, then, in the uncanny effects of the visor. Let me briefly give some examples. Perhaps the grandest and most monumental of them is the Onassis Cultural Centre in Athens, by the French practice Architecture Studio, a vast, rather impressive

Figure 1: Grimshaw, UCL Roberts Building, London
Photo: Matthew Beaumont

rectangular block that veils its exterior with marble bands. More open, more porous in relation to its immediate urban surroundings, is the façade of concrete blocks and slatted metal blinds which comprises the elevation of the 906 School in Sabadell, outside Barcelona, designed by H Arquitectes. Less interesting, and far more aggressive in its use of the visor effect, as seems appropriate for a building with an explicitly commercial as opposed to educational function, is the headquarters of Banca Sella in Biella, Italy, which uses the terracotta colour of the slats to mitigate its intrusive, high-rise intervention in the local area.

In London, the same terracotta effect is used for the slatted front extension to the University College London Engineering Building, which I pass on foot every morning in order to enter my office on Torrington Place in Bloomsbury. It is designed by Grimshaw, whose website used to boast that this 'distinctive outward-looking façade' is their response to a brief which prioritized the need for 'a striking public face for the university'.

The façade is 'outward-looking', though, only in the sense that a visor, surmounted by a grille, is outward-looking. It creates the impression of closedness rather than openness. The effect is of a private rather than public face for what Grimshaw describes as 'the university's renowned Centre for Enterprise and Management

Figure 2: Rogers Stirk Harbour, World Conservations
and Exhibitions Centre, London
Photo: Matthew Beaumont

in Industry'. Here, the language of 'faciality', in Zaera Polo's terms, seems especially hypocritical. It is indeed noticeable that, like both this university facility and the Onassis Cultural Centre, several of the buildings that deploy these visored façades occupy the borderland between private and public architecture.

At the opposite end of Malet Street from the UCL Engineering Building, to take another example, the discreet new extension to the British Museum is visible. Designed by Rogers Stirk Harbour and Partners, the World Conservations and Exhibitions Centre, as it is named, has been slid like the flat side of a blade between two wings of the original building.

There, with cool, clinical precision, it plunges twenty metres below ground. From the back of the British Museum, where it is sited, only one of its four modular pavilions is visible, and the effect of its silver-grey façade – which Rowan Moore evocatively characterizes in terms of 'slats of milky cast glass and pale stone'[45] – is oddly secretive for a public building. Perhaps this is no accident. Richard Rogers's partner Graham Stirk, who built the 'luxury residential fortresses' of One Hyde Park, Neo Bankside and Riverlight in Nine Elms, led the design for the British Museum extension, and it 'shares these projects' ruthless efficiency and slick finish', as Oliver Wainwright astutely commented in a piece for the *Guardian* when it was unveiled in 2014.[46]

In short, this is a private-sector aesthetic, consonant with the ascendancy in London of a culture dominated by the super-rich, one that is inclined to conceal and sequester its accumulated wealth, whether this consists in financial or cultural capital. In place of the aesthetic of transparency with which modernist architecture signalled its ostensible commitment to a democratic politics, buildings like the British Museum extension, in spite of their provenance in the public sector, institute an aesthetic of opacity consistent with a metropolis in which real power, even in a parliamentary context, is increasingly undemocratic in its structures, increasingly subordinate to the private sector.

City Hall, the distinctive building which houses the Greater London Authority, on the South Bank of the Thames, is in some respects even more exemplary in this respect. For, in spite of the fact that it is the official headquarters of a publicly elected body, namely the London Assembly, this building and the land on which it stands are privately owned. In 2013, its original owners, More London, sold a thirteen-acre stretch of the South Bank to a Kuwaiti property company called St Martins in an enormously lucrative, and secretive, deal.

Today, St Martins rents the land to the city's mayor and the various businesses that occupy the surrounding office blocks. More London Estates Management, which continues to coordinate and control this 'privately owned public space' (POPS), has not only installed an extensive CCTV and security personnel system but banned numerous vital urban activities, including begging, busking, demonstrating, loitering and skateboarding. All kinds of pedestrian activity, in other words, that fail or refuse to conform to the regime of briskness, busy-ness, and business.

Moreover, City Hall itself, which was opened in 2002, exhibits the characteristic logic of visored architecture. Designed by Foster and Partners, which claims on its website, without irony, that City Hall expresses 'the transparency and accessibility of the democratic process', the building resembles nothing so much as an armoured helmet. If its aesthetic has something of the Space

Age about it, because it evokes an astronaut's helmet, it also has something of the Middle Ages about it, for its form recalls, for example, the rounded skull of a visored bascinet from the fourteenth or fifteenth centuries. Like these helmets, it secretes an invisible and almost existentially disquieting gaze. City Hall thus hides in plain sight its hostility to the transparency and accessibility both of public space and the democratic process.

What is the phenomenological effect of these visored buildings? It is, I think, to feel unsettled by the presence of an alien gaze. Here, we can return to Derrida's discussion of 'hauntology', and in particular the metaphor he devises for his reading of Shakespeare's *Hamlet* (c.1602) – the metaphor of the visor.

In the opening pages of *Specters of Marx*, Derrida explores the disconcerting effect that Hamlet's late father's spectral presence has, at the start of the play, on Horatio, Marcellus and the protagonist himself. It will be remembered that in the first scene of the play the ghost of old Hamlet assumes a 'warlike form' (I, i, 45). He is a 'portentous figure' that 'comes armèd through [the] watch' (I, i, 108–9). 'A figure like your father, / Armèd at point exactly, cap-a-pe,' Horatio tells Hamlet in the third scene of the play, has been stalking the battlements, wearing its beaver, the lower part of the helmet's face guard, raised (I, iii, 199–200). It is this image that Derrida (relying on a French translation by the late Yves Bonnefoy) reconfigures as a visor.

Derrida's interpretation of the gaze of the armed apparition – which he identifies, interestingly, as a Thing – is uncanny: 'This Thing meanwhile looks at us and sees us not see it even when it is there. A spectral asymmetry interrupts here all specularity.' 'We will call this the *visor effect*,' he states: 'we do not see who looks at us.'[47] This 'visor effect', he further explains, evokes a protective helmet into which 'slits are cut' so as to permit Hamlet's father 'to see without being seen':

> For the helmet effect, it suffices that a visor be *possible* and that one play with it. Even when it is raised, *in fact*, its possibility continues to signify that someone, beneath the armor, can safely

see without being seen or without being identified. Even when it is raised, the visor remains, an available resource and structure, solid and stable as armor, the armor that covers the body from head to foot, the armor of which it is a part and to which it is attached. This is what distinguishes a visor from the mask with which, nevertheless, it shares this incomparable power, perhaps the supreme insignia of power: the power to see without being seen.[48]

The visor effect is what makes us 'feel ourselves seen by a look which it will always be impossible to cross'. 'This spectral *someone other looks at us*,' Derrida concludes, italicizing his reference to the other in order to reinforce its uncanny associations; 'we feel ourselves being looked at by it.'[49]

This sense of uncanniness, of feeling ourselves seen by a look that it is impossible to cross, to counteract or cancel out, not least because it cannot be directly returned or reciprocated, embodied as it is in the building-as-Thing, this sense of uncanniness is structural to the phenomenological effect of the visored buildings I have identified. For them, the visor functions, in Derrida's language, as 'an available resource and structure, solid and stable as armor,' which instigates, and in an everyday context ceaselessly enacts, the supreme form of power, 'the power to see without being seen'.

In this respect, visored buildings paradoxically display precisely the relations of power that secretly obtain in all buildings, which can be characterized in terms of what Derrida calls 'a spectral asymmetry' that interrupts 'all specularity'. In arming their gaze, and thus ensuring that it cannot be returned, mirrored, reflected back, they reveal that every façade inscribes an aggressive, offensive orientation to those that inhabit its immediate environment, especially when they are on foot. 'The mask does not hide the face, it *is* the face,' Deleuze and Guattari write in their discussion of 'faciality'.[50] The visor does not hide the face, it *is* the face; but it encodes the gaze.

The visored building thus constitutes an insignia, to use Derrida's term, for the disposition of power in the contemporary metropolis. Its armed gaze is symptomatic of the developments that have for some time been taking place in metropolitan cities such as London, where spaces are not only increasingly privatized but shaped at all levels by the technological apparatus of a surveillance system deployed to consolidate, police and reinforce this relentless process of privatization.

It is also symptomatic, perhaps, of an architectural practice that is currently being reshaped by 'the increasing facelessness of the client'.[51] The visored building – profoundly implicated in what Mike Davis once called 'the archisemiotics of class war'[52] – thus exhibits the architectural logic of contemporary capitalism. It is a monumental but at the same time everyday embodiment of an urban society that, in both its state and corporate forms, interpellates pedestrians as atomized individuals subject to an insidious system of surveillance.

We are not at home in the streets of our cities. How then do we respond to this situation? Critics such as Tal Kaminer have rightly insisted on the importance of contemporary citizens' active participation in the politics of architecture.[53] So this conclusion represents a response to that challenge.

I propose that, dystopian as this scenario might sound, we adopt our own masks, our own visors, in relation to what Walter Benjamin once called 'the masks of architecture'.[54] Only in this way, as inhabitants of cities who are committed to a culture of openness and transparency, to the notion of public space, can we neutralize the uncanny gaze inscribed in an architecture that is persistently private, secretive, subtly intimidating.

Simmel, with typical perspicacity, grasped the significance of this homeopathic logic in his seminal essay on the 'Sociology of the Senses' in 1907. There, exploring the power relationship that is inscribed in the interaction between people's eyes, the intersection of their looks, he recognizes that when one's eyes are seen by other eyes, not least in the context of urban life, one is known, and one is therefore disempowered. This can be avoided, though, or at least mitigated – in the interests of what, in 'The Metropolis and Mental Life', he had called 'self-preservation in the face of the large city' – if one withdraws one's gaze, if one screens one's eyes.[55]

'Lowering my gaze', he argues, 'deprives the other of the possibility of finding out about me.' Simmel characterizes this defensive response, which he insists has 'an actual practicality in this directly sensory and sociological relationship', as the 'ostrich tactic'. And he concludes that 'whoever does not look at the other party really does remove him or herself to a certain extent from being seen.'[56]

The Occupy movement, with its appropriation of the distinctive Guy Fawkes masks that featured in the 2005 film adaptation of David Lloyd and Alan Moore's graphic novel *V for Vendetta* (1988), has been pioneering in this respect (even if it has also, inadvertently, lined the pockets of Time Warner, the corporation that owns the copyright). For it has developed an affordable, uniform device that, rendering the activist resistant to 'being seen', and therefore evading state surveillance, neatly but also theatrically deploys or implements the 'ostrich tactic'. Perhaps these masks should not merely be reserved for demonstrations or protests against finance capital but worn as an everyday uniform, as a form of protective armour, in the dwindling public spaces we traverse in our cities as pedestrians.

But the 'hoodie', a ubiquitous garment on contemporary city streets, not least because it provides partial shelter from the intrusive gaze of CCTV cameras, probably already functions as this everyday uniform. The fact that, like other security companies, More London Estates Management has banned hoodies from the stretch of the South Bank it polices points to precisely this. Certainly, on urban protests and demonstrations, at least since those against the World Trade Organization in Seattle in 1999, hoodies have functioned, in practical terms, as a means of eluding the more primitive systems of surveillance; and, in symbolic terms, as a reciprocal response to the armoured and visored helmets adopted by a more or less militarized urban police force.

'Who are those hooded hordes?' T. S. Eliot demands in 'What the Thunder Said', the final section of *The Waste Land* (1922), as he invokes apocalyptic images of 'cracks and reforms' that burst in 'the violet air', and of 'falling towers': 'Jerusalem Athens Alexandria / Vienna London / Unreal.'[57] Let us collectively embrace our identity as hooded hordes among the plains, mazes and chasms of cement and glass and steel and stone that structure the metropolitan cities we inhabit on foot in the twenty-first century. In this way, by blocking and reversing its gaze, we might at least refuse, if not cancel out, the coercive logic of the visored building.

Here, in other words, is the germ of a politics of the visor, productively paranoiac, that we might use to resist the politics of the visor.

Afterword

Walking in London and Paris at Night

I. Marble Arch, London, 2012

The plaque commemorating London's most prominent site of execution, the Tyburn Tree, where criminals and political prisoners were hanged in public from the late twelfth century to the late eighteenth century, isn't easy to identify amid the lifeless chaos of Marble Arch. I visited it at about midnight one night in June 2012, on a short nightwalk that, though it began and ended in Kilburn, traced a route from Marble Arch to the Old Bailey, the site of what was once Newgate Prison.

The point of the walk was to re-enact the final journey taken by the victims of Tyburn's 'Fatal Tree' in the eighteenth century, but in reverse. A 'resurrection walk', a friend called it. At midnight the night before a hanging day or 'hanging fair', which generally took place on a Monday, the bellman of St Sepulchre-without-Newgate recited verses to the men and women who were due to be executed. 'All you that in the condemn'd Holds do lie, / Prepare you, for to Morrow you shall die,' he began ... The next morning, between 9 a.m. and 10 a.m., a procession left the prison, to the deafening sound of church bells, first those of St Sepulchre, then of other churches along the route.

The condemned, whose irons were first struck off in the prison's press yard in front of their friends and relations, climbed into a horse-drawn cart that eventually rumbled off along the cobbled streets on its protracted two- or three-hour journey to the gibbet. In the spirit of clemency, the carter might stop at a series of taverns, starting in Holborn, to enable those about to be executed to inebriate and so anaesthetize themselves.

The three-mile route, which snaked through St Giles before proceeding along Tyburn Road, today's Oxford Street, was dense with curious, sometimes riotous spectators, who packed the streets and pressed up against the windows of buildings that adjoined the road. Some handed measures of ale or gin to the condemned, others lobbed orange or apples to them.

At Tyburn itself, fifty or one hundred thousand people might be in attendance, jostling one another for standing room, teetering on ladders, sitting precariously along the wall that enclosed Hyde Park, or crowding into 'Mother Proctor's Pews', the grandstand on the western side of the Edgware Road (originally Watling Street) – all of them competing for a glimpse of the moment when the condemned man or woman, who would die of strangulation, dangled from the gallows and 'danced the Paddington frisk'. 'The whole vagabond population of London,' wrote the diarist Francis Place, 'all the thieves, and all the prostitutes, all those who were evil-minded, and some, a comparatively few curious people made up the mob on those brutalizing occasions.'

From the late sixteenth century, the infamous scaffold at Tyburn took the distinctive form of a 'Triple Tree' design. This consisted of three wooden posts, in a triangular formation, connected across the top by three beams. In addition to ensuring almost indestructible stability, this design facilitated mass executions, since each beam could accommodate up to eight bodies, and on occasion as many as twenty-four people were hanged at once.

The original gallows, in the Middle Ages, were made from the elms that stood beside Tyburn Brook (a tributary not of the River Tyburn but the River Westbourne, which today runs as an underground stream into the Serpentine). Tyburn was a bucolic site of execution when its first victim, William Longbeard, was hanged in 1196. And even in the mid- and later eighteenth century, when on hanging days a temporary scaffold was erected, before being dismantled until needed for the next execution, the area around Tyburn felt like rough countryside.

This entire area, some of it farmed, was open land that belonged to the Bishop of London's Paddington estate. The only building

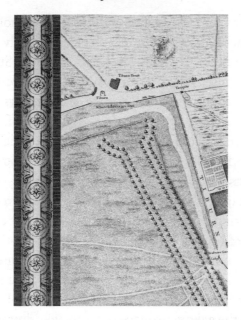

nearby, at least until the 1760s, was Tyburn House, which stood at the junction of Tyburn Road and Watling Street and probably had something to do with the gallows it overlooked. This was the western edge of the capital, with Hyde Park to its south and open land to its north. The outer limits of Georgian London were demarcated by Tyburn Lane, now Park Lane, which ran south-east to Hyde Park Corner; and Tyburn Road, which ran east in the direction of the City.

In John Rocque's detailed map of London, first published in 1746, the Triple Tree is starkly marked – printed onto the crook between the roads running west and north like a crude symbol tattooed onto the webbing between index finger and thumb on a prison inmate's hand. Immediately to its south, along the northern fringe of the park, is the legend, 'Where Soldiers are Shot'. These are killing fields.

The last execution at Tyburn, that of one John Austen, took place in November 1783, in part because of the risks of social disorder in an increasingly respectable region of the city. 'The gradual spread of gentility to the west meant that the old tribal route from Newgate to Tyburn began to impinge upon the fashionable quarters close to Oxford Street,' as Peter Ackroyd puts it. Thereafter, those sentenced for capital offences were hanged at the Debtors' Door, Newgate – a mercifully short journey from the condemned's cell.

At Marble Arch, I threaded through the rapid stream of late-night cars and taxis, which at this time still had to be cautiously forded, to one of the traffic islands at the junction of Bayswater Road and the Edgware Road; then found myself already standing on the memorial to the site of execution. I hadn't noticed it. (In the sump at the bottom of the Edgware Road, where the Middle-Eastern restaurants peter out, I had seen a pub called The Tyburn, part of the Wetherspoon's chain – 'shit, brown dollops of establishments smeared incontinently across our cities', as Will Self has daubed them).

The plaque, embedded in this piece of pavement in 1964, is a cracked, circular piece of stone, the inside perimeter of which is engraved with fine bronze lettering that reads: 'THE SITE OF TYBURN TREE'. Apart from a mysterious cross that seems to rotate or spiral silently at its centre, this is it. No doubt most of those who do notice it assume that it is the site of – a tree.

There is at Marble Arch not a single reference to the victims of these infamous gallows, who might in total have numbered as many as 50–60,000 people. This regime of terror reached a climax in the late seventeenth and eighteenth centuries, when

Britain became a 'thanatocracy', in Peter Linebaugh's term, 'a government that ruled by the frequent exercise of the death penalty'. In fact, the application of the death penalty declined in this period; but the state nonetheless used the spectacle of the scaffold, with increasing efficiency and intensity, to terrorize people tempted to challenge or infringe a legal and socio-political system to which the protection of property was of more and more totemic importance.

Right up until the early nineteenth century, England lacked a public police force – in spite of the founding of Henry and John Fielding's Runners, who were little more than 'a gang of professional thief takers, with a reputation for brutality and corruption', in London in 1749. Moreover, unlike France, the British state did not rely on a network of spies and informers to control its subjects (though in the early 1790s, Jacobins such as John Thelwall, shadowed by government agents at meetings of the London Corresponding Society, used to lecture on the 'moral tendency of spies and informers'). 'In place of police, however,' as Douglas Hay confirms, 'propertied England had a fat and swelling sheaf of laws which threatened thieves with death.' Approximately 49,000 offences were tried before a jury at the Old Bailey in the course of the eighteenth century, and almost 95 per cent of them were property-related. Through the courts the ruling elite prosecuted a pitiless class war against the poor. This exacerbated the cruelty of a society built on ever more brutal economic inequalities.

In an essay for the *Rambler* in 1750, Samuel Johnson provided a powerful critique of capital punishment and the eighteenth-century state's business of 'investing lawful authority with terror, and governing by force rather than persuasion'. He grimly conceded that 'rapine and violence are hourly encreasing', but complained that few law-makers question the efficacy of 'capital inflictions'. 'Of those who employ their speculations upon the present corruption of the people,' as he sarcastically put it, 'some propose the introduction of more horrid, lingering and terrifick punishments; some are inclined to accelerate the executions; some to discourage pardons; and all seem to think that lenity has given confidence to wickedness, and that we can only be rescued from the talons of robbery by inflexible rigour, and sanguinary justice.'

Johnson was acutely sensitive to the contradictions of the criminal justice system, and to the hypocrisies both of the elite that sentenced people to death and the masses that relished the spectacle of their execution. He cited the authority of the Dutch humanist Herman Boerhaave, who related 'that he never saw a criminal dragged to execution without asking himself, "Who knows whether this man is not less culpable than me."'

On the days when 'the prisons of this city are emptied into the grave,' Johnson added in a pungent image, 'let every spectator of the dreadful procession put the same question to his own heart.' 'Few among those that croud in thousands to the legal massacre, and look with carelessness, perhaps with triumph, on the utmost exacerbations of human misery, would then be able to return without horror and dejection,' he concluded; 'for, who can congratulate himself upon a life passed without some act more mischievous to the peace or prosperity of others, than the theft of a piece of money?'

Tyburn Tree was in the eighteenth century the symbol not of some crude, outdated order of justice, a remnant of feudal times, but of a legal system engineered and rebuilt by the capitalist bourgeoisie. Most of those executed at Tyburn were ordinary men and women who had been reduced by economic circumstances to a state of desperation – apprentices, ill-paid servants, unemployed labourers, vagrants. As Roy Porter points out, 'those committing crimes – notably the 1,200 Londoners hanged in the eighteenth century – were less hardened professionals than servants and seamstresses and the labouring poor, down on their luck or out of work, starving, or just fatally tempted.'

Among them were female nightwalkers, although these were executed not for prostitution but because they had committed crimes against property. Mary Young, for instance, a seamstress from Northern Ireland who became a celebrated thief, was gibbeted at Tyburn in 1741. She had been confined to Bridewell, along with other 'loose idle and disorderly persons & comon Street Walkers', in 1737; and was imprisoned there again in 1738, on this occasion with one other woman, both of them

'Night Walkers'. Nineteen others died at Tyburn alongside Mary Young the day she hanged, and all of them were executed for crimes against property.

No doubt it is predictable enough that the obscurest, most desperate members of London's poor population, condemned for committing trifling crimes against property, should remain uncommemorated at Marble Arch. But even the more notorious victims of the Tyburn regime, including Mary Young, who arrived at the gallows in a mourning coach, are unnamed. There is no mention, for example, of Jack Sheppard, the most famous and popularly celebrated thief of the eighteenth century, who twice escaped from Newgate, and whose execution in 1724 drew admiring crowds of as many as 200,000 people.

There is, furthermore, no testament at Marble Arch to Oliver Cromwell – a reminder that Britain continues to be a monarchy, and organizes its heritage accordingly. The remains of his body, along with those of two other regicides, were disinterred in 1661, after the Restoration, before being carried in coffins by cart from Westminster to Holborn, then dragged on to the Fatal Tree at Tyburn. There, in an undignified posthumous execution, the three were hanged before a large crowd, and beheaded. According to John Evelyn, their battered carcasses were 'then buried under that fatal and ignominious monument in a deep pit'. It is possible that Cromwell's bones still lie beneath Marble Arch. The turf at the north-eastern corner of Hyde Park, that looks so serene and calm beside the congested, agitated roads that encircle it, should still be soaked in blood.

The plaque commemorating the Fatal Tree is today lost beneath the feet of teenagers and tourists milling about among the night buses and the pointless, elephantine sculptures that have been deposited, in a passive-aggressive gesture of benevolence and public-spiritedness, at Cumberland Gate. On the cool night I was there these optimists appeared to be trying to persuade themselves that the desolate roundabout on which they were marooned, in a thin mist of carbon monoxide, was in fact a continental piazza in which they might meaningfully congregate.

Instead, resurfacing at the end of the day as the tide subsides, Marble Arch is a little island of alienated social life that looks as if it has been cut adrift from the end of Oxford Street – the shops and department stores of which, disgorging pedestrians into the road at closing time, stretch like a line of cliffs to the east in the artificial half-light of the night. The arch itself is a picturesque but pointless geological stack around which commuters and shoppers surge.

In a poem written for a BBC documentary in 1968, John Betjeman lamented that Marble Arch is a place of martyrdoms that is 'trodden by unheeding feet'. But the 'greatest crime' of all, he continued, standing on the roof of the Arch and speaking in the voice of a polite, if irritable prophet, is 'the martyrdom of London': 'For here, where once were pleasant fields, / And no one in a hurry, / Behold the harvest Mammon yields / Of speed and greed and worry ...'

The clock-like face of the commemorative plaque looks as if it has been carefully but pitilessly stamped into the ground by the nearby Arch's vast and trunkless legs of stone. Marble Arch was originally designed by John Nash, in the later 1820s, as a triumphal entrance for Buckingham Palace; then relocated to Hyde Park, where Thomas Cubitt rebuilt the royal home in 1851. But – not least because Nash's plans for reliefs commemorating English victories against France in the Napoleonic conflict were never fully executed – the triumph it celebrates is an oddly blank one.

After it had been 'islanded' in 1908, G. K. Chesterton remarked that, 'in its new insular position, with traffic turning dizzily all about it,' the Marble Arch seemed 'a placid monstrosity'. It is a 'massive symbol of the modern mind', he added; 'a door with no house to it; the gigantic gate of Nowhere'. For all its pretensions to imperial grandeur, it is a portal into empty space, empty time. In this respect, it is the imperturbable, self-important Arch, not the shame-faced and secretive plaque, which makes the most fitting memorial to the Tyburn Tree. In its arrogant, impassive refusal to contemplate the scene of destruction on which it has been silently founded, the Arch stands like a sentinel protecting London from a confrontation with the tradition of violent oppression on which the British state is built.

From 1851, the upper chambers of the Arch were used as a police observation post, with room for a hundred officers if necessary, as Betjeman noted during his tour of its interior – all 'ready to rush out' if there were civil disturbances. During the mass demonstration against the Sunday Trading Bill in 1855 – which Karl Marx, who was in attendance, excitedly identified as the beginning of the English Revolution – a detachment of police leapt out from beneath the hollow thighs of the Arch and ambushed protestors.

During the Reform League's demonstrations for universal male suffrage in 1866, Marble Arch was once again the scene of scattered battles with police on horseback. And at the riot in 1994 against the Criminal Justice Bill, a raft of measures that targeted ravers, Roma, travellers and young black people who were already susceptible to discriminatory stop-and-search procedures, mounted police repeatedly charged at demonstrators, in a panicky clatter of hooves, from the adamantine precincts of the Arch.

On that occasion, Marble Arch seemed to have been restored to its secret identity as a monument that, belying its placid appearance, boasted of Britain's history of state oppression, but at the same time obliterated the memory of it. Perhaps its inner cavities are still used for tactical surveillance.

If this is the case, Marble Arch makes for a peculiarly short-sighted, or perhaps long-sighted, panopticon. Approximately three hours after I had sloped off from the traffic island in which the Tyburn plaque is roughly embedded, in order to pursue my walk to Newgate through the emptying streets, police who had been called to Marble Arch found a man in his mid-forties lying dead on the central concourse, directly beneath one of the arches. This man was Mark Morrison, a Scot who, though he had formerly worked as a chef, had for some time been homeless. He had been strangled with a strip of green tent fabric. An engineer working for London Underground caught sight of a man stooping over the murder victim at around 3 a.m., but this man ran off when challenged.

A week later, an Afghan asylum-seeker, Ghodratollah Barani, then in his mid-twenties, was charged with Morrison's murder. Like the victim of this crime, he was of no fixed address. Psychiatric doctors at both St Thomas's and the Gordon Hospitals had examined Barani prior to the murder, because he had repeatedly tried to gain entry to Buckingham Palace, claiming voices had informed him that, in order to become the rightful king of England, he needed to kill someone; but he had been discharged. Police officers at the palace, for their part, had ignored his threats on the assumption that they were a ruse to secure asylum. Eventually, in March 2013, Barani pleaded guilty to manslaughter on the grounds of diminished responsibility. He was detained under the Mental Health Act and recommended for deportation on his release.

The violent climax of this drama encoded a sickly irony: it is as if the horrors of old Tyburn, with its countless, near-anonymous victims of strangulation, many of them itinerant and unemployed, had irrupted beneath the empty portal of Marble Arch in the shape of this corpse. The tomb of the forgotten vagrant.

II. Eiffel Tower, Paris, 2012

The picturesque lightshow that, once the sun has set, takes place on the hour, every hour, when the Eiffel Tower is lit up for five minutes by thousands of coruscating bulbs, stops with a final spasm at 1 a.m. It was unlit when I reached it at 3 a.m. on a damp Monday morning. The surrounding streets were deserted.

The Tower had proved oddly, eerily difficult to find in the darkness. Pursuing it along the left bank of the Seine, in insistent rain, it kept escaping me. In spite of its immense, brutal outline, it seemed to be able to conceal itself behind the solemn buildings that overlook the river. Each time it reappeared, rearing suddenly above me, I experienced a slight sense of shock. Its presence in the darkness was oppressive. I felt as if I'd been trapped in a malign game – like the one Umberto Eco describes in *Foucault's Pendulum* (1988), where the narrator stumbles into the Eiffel Tower at night and finally understands that this 'foul metal spider' is the symbol and instrument of his enemies' diabolical power.

I entered the landscaped park at the base of the Tower, the section of the Champ de Mars closest to the Seine, from the tapered end of the Rue de l'Université. A few streetlamps emitted a sickly gleam. It was almost completely silent. The light rain blanketed the sound of occasional cars on the Quai Branly. For a moment I stood still, faintly disturbed by the scaffold of heavy, shadowy forms in front of me; slabs of cold metal that no longer had the tensile delicacy that characterizes the Tower's tracery from a distance, especially when it is artificially lit. In the darkness, close up, it resembled the sort of enigmatic, minatory structure that, by accident or design, some alien species might have deposited on our planet.

When I set off across the Champ de Mars in order to stand beneath the Tower, my footsteps disturbed several rats that had been eating from the ruined litterbins full of tourists' droppings. The rats loped across the path in front of me and disappeared into the dirty pools of darkness beneath the nearby trees. It reminded me of the repulsive landscape described by Robert Browning in his dream-like quest-poem, 'Childe Roland to the Dark Tower Came', where the grass grows 'as scant as hair in leprosy', and rats shriek like babies.

I felt a little frightened. If I'd seen anyone else standing or walking in the precincts of the Tower, I'd have panicked and run. There was no one. Perhaps that was more ominous. In Eco's novel, a taxi driver admits to the narrator that at night he always feels compelled to accelerate past the Eiffel Tower, because it scares him. Why? *Parce que … parce que ça fait peur, c'est tout.* I too felt that fear – and couldn't remain an instant longer. So I rapidly retraced my steps to the rue de l'Université, spooked by the thought of the Tower rearing up implacably behind me. I felt as if a layer of skin had been coolly scraped from my back beneath my neat, black rucksack and thick clothes.

Turning into the Avenue de La Bourdonnais I slid into a dark dreamscape. A handgun lay on the doorstep of a building to my left: solid-looking, geometric, shocking. It must have been dropped on the stone step by someone running up the avenue; or tossed from a passing car. I tried to remember the emergency number as I pictured the man who had left it; then imagined him returning for it and finding me. Perhaps it was one of the young men who, an hour or so earlier, had almost run me down at a junction, hip-hop pumping from their car as they shouted unintelligible abuse.

As I peered more closely at the gun I realized with a creeping sense of the ridiculous that it looked ... plastic. Bending lower, I saw it didn't have a trigger, and must have been bought in one of those shops retailing things, stuff, crap for €1.50 a pop. Behind me, sagging in the rain, a cardboard box filled with broken toys and kids' clothes had been abandoned on a bench.

Although steeped in noir clichés, my conspiratorial delusion wasn't implausible. In April 2012, a forty-three-year-old homeless Bulgarian man had found a cache of weapons discarded near the Place Stalingrad. Sifting through rubbish bins in search of food, he came across one that contained a 6.35-calibre automatic pistol, four grenades, sixteen rounds of ammunition, and a shell designed for the sort of armoured vehicle used by the French army. Beside a dump truck nearby was a wooden box full of grenades.

The police ascertained soon enough that these arms belonged to a local 'collector' – the term sounded euphemistic to me – who had recently died. But it wasn't entirely clear why the man's relatives, however desperate to get rid of them, had dumped the weapons in public bins in a densely populated part of Paris. 'This was a completely inconsiderate act,' a police spokesman commented humourlessly, 'because the weapons were still operational and could have fallen into the wrong hands.'

In Paris, during the fourth year of an economic recession used by both centre-left and centre-right administrations to punish the poorest sections of the population, homeless Bulgarian men who rummage through bins in the city centre are not often thought to possess the right hands. Theirs are dirty, grasping, thieving hands. According to the authorities and the right-wing press, the Roma who have arrived in France in increasing numbers over the last five years, migrating from Bulgaria and Romania, are beggars, pimps, prostitutes and petty criminals.

As many as 20,000 *Romanichels*, or *Gitans*, as they're known in France, subsist in abject conditions in makeshift camps on the suburban margins of the capital and other cities. There they are often the victims of vigilante attacks by local residents, like the one that ended the life of a sixteen-year old Roma known as Darius near the A1 motorway in June 2014. They are also the target of violent expulsions by the police. The forcible clearing of these camps and the repatriation of their inhabitants commenced under Nicolas Sarkozy, prompting one EU commissioner to compare it to the persecution of Jews during the Occupation. It was continued, even extended, under François Hollande. Amnesty International claims that more than 10,000 Roma were evicted from temporary camps in the first half of 2013.

The pavements of central Paris are currently home to several hundred Roma. In the course of the night I spent traversing the city on foot I felt I glimpsed most of them, their features distinctive among the scattered forms of the white and black homeless people that also populate the streets. Some slept alone. At 1 a.m., on the Place des Vosges, where Cardinal Richelieu lived in the early seventeenth century, four or five of them were huddled under the arcades in frayed sleeping bags. At 4 a.m., on Boulevard Haussmann, single Roma men slept in the entrances of department stores, their bodies heaped beneath blankets, clothes and rags, their grimy faces often encircled by scarves. Some were stretched out beside the road – in spite of the rain – on mattresses and even battered wooden doors that had been removed from their frames. They looked as if they had been washed up on life rafts.

Other Roma slept together. Couples had crammed themselves into phone booths dotted along the main avenues and boulevards. In one booth the woman sat huddled at the feet of the man, who stood to attention and stared blankly at me as I passed. In another, the woman's body was contorted into a V-shape. Her head, at waist height, was wedged in one corner; her naked feet were wedged in the opposite corner. There was something so intimate about the sight of the woman's calloused soles, pressed up against the Perspex surface of the booth, that I felt as if simply in glancing at their flattened form I had intruded on her.

Most unnerving of all were the Roma families, who face a struggle to find accommodation in emergency shelters originally designed for single men (many of these hostels have in any case been forced to close down because of government cuts). Sometimes three or four children slept in the entrance of a shop beside their mother and father. These doorways were so heaped with small sleeping bodies, thick clothes and faded quilts that, perversely, they communicated a sense of cosiness. The unhappy faces of their parents as they watched over the children dispelled this illusion.

So did the presence of others condemned to remain on the street at night. A hundred feet from where the Roma families squatted, I came across six or seven sex workers. It was 4:30 a.m., and they seemed mystified by the grim determination with which I marched through the rain. Five minutes later, sheltering from the downpour in a doorway, I watched two men of North African origin fighting one another. They threw hard, slippery punches, and one of them knocked the other to the ground, sending him skidding along the slick surface of the pavement. A bottle shattered. '*Ta mère! Ta mère!*' – 'Motherfucker!' – the man who was still standing screamed.

Roma were the most striking presence on the street that night, but innumerable other destitute or desperate people became visible in the city after dark. At about 2 a.m., close to the Musée d'Orsay, I leaned over the parapet above the Seine because of a commotion. Three young men were scrawling something on the embankment while a security guard looked on in bemusement. One of the men hurled himself at the stone wall and smashed his forehead against it repeatedly. When he finally rolled back onto the ground, rocking on his spine with a strangely acrobatic elegance, then staggered to his feet again, the guard reluctantly lifted a mobile phone to his ear.

I had begun my *noctambulisme* shortly before 9 p.m. on Sunday, walking northeast from the Place de la République to the *périphérique*. After a coffee I climbed the hill to Belleville. At the entrance to the Couronnes metro station a black man in his fifties and a white man in his twenties sifted through a tangled stack of broken furniture, like nineteenth-century ragpickers, and poked at the rotten vegetables spilling out of crates that had been dumped there. On the Rue des Couronnes, an elderly, bearded man slept heavily on the pavement in a foetal position, piss leaking from his trousers and forming a runnel as it snaked down the steeply sloping street.

On the terrace above the Parc de Belleville – where I watched the shivering lights of the Eiffel Tower signal 10 p.m. in the far distance – there were forty or fifty people standing around some trestle tables waiting for something to happen. Africans, Arabs, Eastern Europeans, Roma; and, looking cheerfully incongruous, two dilapidated white men on crutches. Almost everyone clutched shopping trolleys or carried empty bags and holdalls. The rain was only falling lightly, and there was a companionable, if not festive, atmosphere. Some young people were drinking and smoking and listening to a tinny radio. Kids ran around squealing. Everyone was talking, in a riot of different languages.

Then a van arrived, and several men unloaded its contents onto the tables, lit by a string of bare bulbs. Suddenly the terrace resembled a market: precarious piles of fresh fruit and vegetables; boxes filled with biscuits and pasta; neat stacks of school exercise books, kids' rucksacks; nappies, tampons. A food bank. Everyone crowded round the trestle tables, but they behaved with generosity, a lack of urgency, in waiting to receive things. Emblazoned on the organizers' T-shirts was the name of their charity, 'La Main de l'autre'.

The *bobos* – the bohemian-bourgeois class that cultivates what Eric Hazan calls a 'superficial non-conformism' – have in recent years moved into Belleville in droves, driving up rents and pushing out immigrants, marginals and the poor. But there was no sign of them this Sunday night. Once the bars and cafés have closed, Paris stubbornly resists gentrification. In the night the Roma and other poor and homeless people – those whom the streets have claimed – reclaim the streets. Only the Eiffel Tower, emblem of the city of light, encompasses a completely lifeless space.

Acknowledgements

For encouragement or editorial advice of one kind or another in producing the chapters that comprise this book, I'd like to thank Pushpa Arabindoo, Kasia Boddy, Rachel Bowlby, Peter Boxall, Ben Campkin, Bob Catterall, Gregory Dart, Mark Ford, Tom Gretton, Andrew Hemingway, Phil Horne, Matthew Ingleby, Tom Keymer, Judith Luna, Colin MacCabe, Josephine McDonagh, Clare Melhuish, China Miéville, Florian Mussgnug, Victoria Noel-Johnson, Jordan Rowe, Vincent Sherry, Iain Sinclair, William Sharpe, Christophe Soligo, Hugh Stevens, Allan Wallach, Martin Willis, and David Young. Special thanks are due to Nick Papadimitriou and Will Self. In terms of production, I am grateful to Mark Martin and Lorna Scott Fox. As ever, I am deeply indebted to my exemplary editor, Leo Hollis.

The Walker consists of more or less heavily revised versions of the following essays: 'Urban Convalescence in Lamb, Poe and Baudelaire', in *Transatlantic Romanticism: British and American Art and Literature, 1790–1860*, eds Andrew Hemingway and Allan Wallach (Amherst, MA: University of Massachusetts Press, 2015), pp. 67–80; 'The Mystery of Master Humphrey: Dickens, Nightwalking and *The Old Curiosity Shop*', *Review of English Studies* 65: 268 (2014), pp. 118–36; 'The Bourne Identity: On Utopian Psychopathology', in *The Good Place: Comparative Perspectives on Utopia*, eds Florian Mussgnug and Matthew Reza (Bern: Peter Lang, 2014), pp. 53–68; 'Introduction,' *The Invisible Man*, ed. Matthew Beaumont (Oxford: Oxford World's Classics, 2017), pp. vii–xxxiii; 'The Knight Errant in the Street:

Chesterton, Childe Roland and the City', in *G. K. Chesterton, London and Modernity*, eds Matthew Beaumont and Matthew Ingleby (London: Bloomsbury, 2013), pp. 93–112; 'Ford Madox Ford: Autobiography, Urban Space, Agoraphobia', *Journal of Literature and Science* 3 (2010), pp. 37–49; 'Modernism and the Metropolitan Imaginary: Spectacle and Introspection', in the *Cambridge History of Modernism*, ed. Vincent Sherry (Cambridge: Cambridge University Press, 2017), pp. 220–34; 'In the Beginning Was the Big Toe: Bataille, Base Materialism, Bipedalism,' *Textual Practice* 29: 5 (2015), pp. 869–83; 'Stumbling in the Dark: Ray Bradbury's Pedestrian and the Politics of the Night', *Critical Quarterly* 57: 4 (2015), pp. 71–88; 'The Politics of the Visor: Looking at Buildings Looking at Us', *CITY: Analysis of Urban Trends, Culture, Theory, Policy, Action* 22: 1 (2018), pp. 63–77; 'Short Cuts', *London Review of Books* 35: 12 (20 June 2013), p. 22; 'Paris at Night', *The White Review* (September 2014).

The Mystery and Melancholy of a Street, by Giorgio de Chirico on p. 25: Private Collection/the Bridgeman Art Library Copyright DACS.

Gros orteil (Sujet masculin, 30 ans), by Jacques-André Boiffard on p. 208: Musée national d'art moderne, Centre Pompidou, Paris. Centre de création industrielle. Photo © Centre Pompidou, MNAM-CCI, Dist. RMN-Grand Palais/Philippe Migeat.

Notes

Introduction

1 André Breton, *Nadja*, trans. Richard Howard (Harmondsworth: Penguin, 1999), p. 72.
2 Marshall Berman, *Modernism in the Streets: A Life and Times in Essays*, eds David Marcus and Shellie Sclan (London: Verso, 2017).
3 André Breton, 'The Disdainful Confession', in *The Lost Steps*, trans. Mark Polizzotti (Lincoln, NE: University of Nebraska Press, 1996), p. 4.
4 Ibid.
5 Breton, *Nadja*, p. 113. Cited in Walter Benjamin, 'Marseilles', in *Reflections: Essays, Aphorisms, Autobiographical Writings*, trans. Edmund Jephcott (New York: Schocken, 1986), p. 131.
6 Michael Sheringham, *Everyday Life: Theories and Practices from Surrealism to the Present* (Oxford: Oxford University Press, 2006), p. 73.
7 Alejo Carpentier, *The Lost Steps*, trans. Harriet de Onís (London: Minerva, 1991), p. 250. For Auden's image, see W. H. Auden, 'In Memory of W. B. Yeats', in *Selected Poems*, ed. Edward Mendelson (London: Faber & Faber, 1979), p. 81.
8 See André Breton, 'The New Spirit', in *The Lost Steps*, p. 73.
9 See Paul Celan, 'Speech on the Occasion of Receiving the Literature Prize of the Free Hanseatic City of Bremen', in *Collected Prose*, trans. Rosemarie Waldrop (Manchester: Carcanet, 1986), p. 34 – though note that, disappointingly, Waldrop translates *unverloren* not as 'unlost' but as 'secure'.
10 Guy Debord, 'Theory of the *Dérive*', in *The Situationists and the City*, ed. Tom McDonough (London: Verso, 2009), pp. 77–85.

11 Samuel Beckett, *The Lost Ones*, trans. Samuel Beckett (Calder & Boyars, 1972), p. 7. See Mark Nixon, *Samuel Beckett's German Diaries, 1936–1937* (London: Continuum, 2011), p. 17; and Samuel Beckett, *Watt*, ed. C. J. Ackerley (London: Faber & Faber, 2009), pp. 200f. The settings of both *Waiting for Godot* (1953) and *Endgame* (1957) might also be usefully identified as *salles des pas perdus*.

12 Breton, *Nadja*, p. 71.

13 Henry Miller, *Black Spring* (New York: Grove Press, 1963), p. 3.

14 Ibid.

15 Walter Benjamin, 'The Paris of the Second Empire in Baudelaire', in *Selected Writings, Vol. 4: 1938–1940*, trans. Harry Zohn and Edmund Jephcott, eds Howard Eiland and Michael W. Jennings (Cambridge, MA: Harvard University Press, 2003), p. 44.

16 T. S. Eliot, *The Waste Land*, in *The Complete Poems and Plays of T. S. Eliot* (London: Faber & Faber, 1969), p. 62. John Carey, in *The Intellectuals and the Masses: Pride and Prejudice among the Literary Intelligentsia, 1880–1939* (London: Faber & Faber, 1992), p. 10, rather drily observes that, 'largely through Eliot's influence, the assumption that most people are dead became, by the 1930s, a standard item in the repertoire of any self-respecting intellectual.'

17 Marshall Berman, *All That is Solid Melts into Air: The Experience of Modernity* (London: Verso, 1983).

18 See Walter Benjamin, 'The Work of Art in the Age of Its Technological Reproducibility (Third Version)', in *Selected Writings, Vol. 4*, p. 269. For a fine essay on the complexities of Benjamin's evolving understanding of the dialectical relationship between attention and distraction, see Carolin Duttlinger, 'Between Contemplation and Distraction: Configurations of Attention in Walter Benjamin', *German Studies Review* 30: 1 (2007), pp. 33–54.

19 Howard Eiland, 'Reception in Distraction', *boundary* 2 30: 1 (2003), p. 60.

20 T. S. Eliot, *The Four Quartets*, in *The Complete Poems and Plays of T. S. Eliot*, p. 174.

21 Benjamin, 'The Paris of the Second Empire in Baudelaire', p. 41.

22 Georg Simmel, 'The Metropolis and Mental Life', in *Simmel on Culture: Selected Writings*, eds David Frisby and Mike Featherstone (London: Sage, 1997), pp. 175, 178.

23 Ibid., p. 179.

24 See: nsc.org/home-safety/safety-topics/distracted-walking.

25 Jun-Ming Lu and Yi-Chin Lo, 'Can Interventions Based on User Interface Design Help Reduce the Risks Associated with Smart-

phone Use While Walking?' in *Proceedings of the 20th Congress of the International Ergonomics Association (IEA 2018)*, vol. 2, eds Sebastiano Bagnara et al. (Cham: Springer, 2018), p. 269.

26 Guy Debord, *The Society of the Spectacle*, trans. Black & Red (London: Notting Hill Editions, 2013), p. 17.

27 Siegfried Kracauer, *The Mass Ornament: Weimar Essays* (Cambridge, MA: Harvard University Press, 1995), p. 325.

28 Charles Baudelaire, 'The Painter of Modern Life', in *The Painter of Modern Life and Other Essays*, trans. Jonathan Mayne (London: Phaidon, 1995), p. 10.

29 Adam Greenfield, *Radical Technologies: The Design of Everyday Life* (London: Verso, 2017), p. 79.

30 Ibid.

31 See Jane Jacobs, *The Death and Life of American Cities* (New York: Vintage, 1992), p. 35.

32 See Benjamin, 'The Paris of the Second Empire in Baudelaire', pp. 41, 83.

33 Greenfield, *Radical Technologies*, pp. 48–9.

34 Setha Low, 'How Private Interests Take Over Public Space: Zoning, Taxes, and Incorporation of Gated Communities', in *The Politics of Public Space*, eds Setha Low and Neil Smith (New York: Routledge, 2006), p. 82.

35 Michel de Certeau, *The Practice of Everyday Life*, trans. Steven Rendall (Berkeley: University of California Press, 1984), p. 93.

36 de Certeau, *The Practice of Everyday Life*, pp. 96, 105, 107, 108.

37 Virginia Woolf, 'Street Haunting: A London Adventure', in *Selected Essays*, ed. David Bradshaw (Oxford: Oxford World's Classics, 2008), pp. 177–87.

38 Susan Sontag, 'Foreword: Walser's Voice', in Robert Walser, *The Walk and Other Stories*, trans Christopher Middleton et al. (London: Serpent's Tail, 2013), p. ix.

39 Raymond Williams, *The Country and the City* (London: Hogarth Press, 1993), p. 233.

40 Lauren Elkin, *Flâneuse: Women Walk the City in Paris, New York, Tokyo, Venice and London* (London: Chatto & Windus, 2016), p. 11.

41 For pioneering work in this field, see for example Deborah Epstein Nord, *Walking the Victorian Streets: Women, Representation, and the City* (Ithaca: Cornell University Press, 1995); Deborah L. Parsons, *Streetwalking the Metropolis: Women, the City and Modernity* (Oxford: Oxford University Press, 2000); and Judith Walkowitz, *City of Dreadful Delight: Narratives of Sexual Danger in Late-Victorian London* (Chicago: University of Chicago Press, 1992).

42 Erika Diane Rappaport, *Shopping for Pleasure: Women in the Making of London's West End* (Princeton: Princeton University Press, 2000), pp. 7, 116.

43 For this quotation from Victor Fournel's *Ce qu'on voit dans les rues de Paris* (1867), see Anke Gleber, *The Art of Taking a Walk: Flanerie, Literature, and Film in Weimar Culture* (Princeton: Princeton University Press, 1999), p. 3. See Tom Gretton, 'Not the *Flâneur* Again: Reading Magazines and Living the Metropolis around 1880', in *The Invisible Flâneuse: Gender, Public Space, and Visual Culture in Nineteenth-Century Paris*, eds Aruna D'Souza and Tom McDonough (Manchester: Manchester University Press, 2008), p. 95.

44 Benjamin, 'The Paris of the Second Empire in Baudelaire', p. 27.

45 Charles Baudelaire, 'The Sun', in *Les Fleurs du Mal*, trans. Richard Howard (London: Picador, 1987), p. 88.

46 For a recent theory of walking, one that oddly doesn't cite Balzac's, see Frédéric Gros, *A Philosophy of Walking*, trans. John Howe (London: Verso, 2014).

47 James Joyce, *Portrait of the Artist as a Young Man*, ed. Seamus Deane (Harmondsworth: Penguin, 2000), p. 10.

48 Roland Barthes, 'The Kitchen of Meaning', in *The Semiotic Challenge*, trans. Richard Howard (Berkeley: University of California Press, 1994), p. 157.

49 For this translation, see Anna Fuchs, 'Modernist Perambulations through Time and Space: From Enlightened Walking to Crawling, Stalking, Modelling and Street-Walking', *Journal of the British Academy* 4 (2016), p. 204.

50 Dennis J. Schmidt, 'Translator's Introduction: In the Spirit of Bloch', in Ernst Bloch, *Natural Law and Human Dignity*, trans. Dennis J. Schmidt (Cambridge, MA: MIT Press, 1986), p. xvi.

51 Ernst Bloch, 'The Marxist Distance to Right and Even to Natural Right; the Problem of a Classless Quintessence of "The Upright Path" in Natural Right', in *Natural Law and Human Dignity*, p. 208.

1. Convalescing

1 Giorgio de Chirico, 'Meditations of a Painter', trans. Louise Bourgeois and Robert Goldwater, in *Theories of Modern Art: A Source Book by Artists and Critics*, ed. Herschel B. Chipp (Berkeley: University of California Press, 1969), pp. 397–8.

2 Ibid., p. 397.

3 Ibid., p. 398.

4 Marshall Berman, *All That Is Solid Melts into Air: The Experience of Modernity* (London: Verso, 1983), p. 148.

5 Walter Benjamin, 'Little History of Photography', in *Selected Writings, Vol. 2: 1927–1934*, trans. Rodney Livingston, eds Michael W. Jennings, Howard Eiland and Gary Smith (Cambridge, MA: Harvard University Press, 1999), p. 519.

6 John Ashbery, 'Introduction: The Decline of the Verbs', in Giorgio de Chirico, *Hebdomeros*, trans. John Ashbery et al. (Cambridge: Exact Change, 1992), p. x.

7 Walter Benjamin, 'The Paris of the Second Empire in Baudelaire', pp. 101–2. I have been unable to locate this concept in Marx's writings; but this might not matter, for the formulation in any case seems more Benjaminian than Marxian. Benjamin himself, however, uses it rather enigmatically. He invokes it in relation to some lines from Baudelaire about an old woman who, because she is excluded from 'the large, closed parks' of Paris, sits alone and pensive on a bench in a public garden, 'at that hour when the setting sun / Bloodies the sky with bright red wounds.' The only other use of the phrase 'socially empty space' I have been able to find is in an article by J. B. Harley, 'Maps, Knowledge, and Power', which argues that maps '"desocialize" the territory they represent', and so 'foster the notion of a socially empty space'. See Denis Cosgrove and Stephen Daniels, eds, *The Iconography of Landscape: Essays on the Symbolic Representation, Design and Use of Past Environments* (Cambridge: Cambridge University Press, 1988), p. 303. See also Matthew Beaumont, *The Spectre of Utopia: Utopian and Science Fictions at the Fin de Siècle* (Bern: Peter Lang, 2015), pp. 97–120.

8 De Chirico, 'Meditations of a Painter', p. 400.

9 Walter Benjamin, 'Central Park', in *The Writer of Modern Life*, p. 134.

10 De Chirico, 'Meditations of a Painter', p. 397.

11 Ara H. Merjian, *Giorgio de Chirico and the Metaphysical City: Nietzsche, Modernism, Paris* (New Haven: Yale University Press, 2014), p. 1.

12 Friedrich Nietzsche, *Twilight of the Idols* and *The Anti-Christ*, ed. Michael Tanner, trans. R. J. Hollingdale (Harmondsworth: Penguin, 1990), p. 54.

13 Friedrich Nietzsche, *Human, All Too Human*, ed. and trans. Marion Faber (Harmondsworth: Penguin, 2004), p. 8.

14 Friedrich Nietzsche, *Thus Spoke Zarathustra*, ed. and trans. R. J. Hollingdale (Harmondsworth: Penguin, 2003), pp. 233, 235–6.

15 De Chirico, 'Some Perspectives on My Art', trans. Mark Polizzotti, in *Hebdomeros*, p. 252.

16 De Chirico, *Hebdomeros*, p. 109.

17 De Chirico, 'Some Perspectives on My Art', p. 248.

18 Virginia Woolf, *Jacob's Room*, ed. Kate Flint (Oxford: World's Classics, 1992), p. 162.

19 D. H. Lawrence, *Sons and Lovers*, ed. Keith Sagar (Harmondsworth: Penguin, 1986), p. 107.

20 Walter Benjamin, 'On Some Motifs in Baudelaire', in *The Writer of Modern Life*, p. 201.

21 Lawrence, *Sons and Lovers*, p. 107.

22 See for example Walter Benjamin, *Understanding Brecht*, trans. Anna Bostock (London: Verso, 1983), p. 12.

23 Michael Löwy and Robert Sayre, 'Figures of Romantic Anti-Capitalism', *New German Critique* 32 (Spring/Summer 1984), p. 58. See also Michael Löwy and Robert Sayre, *Romanticism Against the Tide of Modernity*, trans. Catherine Porter (Durham: Duke University Press, 2001).

24 Walter Benjamin, *Charles Baudelaire: A Lyric Poet in the Era of High Capitalism*, trans. Harry Zohn (London: Verso, 1983), p. 69.

25 Fredric Jameson, *The Modernist Papers* (London: Verso, 2007), p. 76.

26 S. C. Lowry, *Convalescence: Its Blessings, Trials, Duties and Dangers: A Manual of Comfort and Help for Persons Recovering from Sickness* (London: Skeffington, 1845), p. 1.

27 Athena Vrettos, *Somatic Fictions: Imagining Illness in Victorian Culture* (Stanford: Stanford University Press, 1995), pp. 1, 19.

28 These studies might be seen as related to the pervasive interest in intermediate states of being, such as somnambulism and mesmeric trance, that Tony James has identified in France in the early nineteenth century – see *Dream, Creativity, and Madness in Nineteenth-Century France* (Oxford: Clarendon Press, 1995).

29 Hyacinthe Dubranle, *Essai sur la convalescence: Thèse* (Paris: Rignoux, 1837), p. 5. Translation mine.

30 Charles Lamb, 'The Convalescent', in 'Elia and the Last Essays of Elia', in *The Works of Charles and Mary Lamb*, vol. 2, ed. E. V. Lucas (London: Methuen, 1903), p. 186.

31 E. P. Thompson, 'Time, Work-Discipline and Industrial Capitalism', in *Essays in Social History*, eds Michael W. Flinn and T. C. Smout (Oxford: Clarendon Press, 1974), p. 43.

32 Benjamin, 'The Paris of the Second Empire in Baudelaire', p. 104.

33 See Natalie Bell Cole, 'Attached to Life Again: The "Queer Beauty" of Convalescence in *Bleak House*', *Victorian Newsletter* 103 (Spring 2003), pp. 17–19.

34 Lamb, 'The Convalescent', p. 185.
35 On Marx's concept of 'disalienation', see Henri Lefebvre, *Critique of Everyday Life, Vol. 2: Foundations for a Sociology of the Everyday*, trans. John Moore (London: Verso, 2002), p. 207.
36 Lamb, 'The Convalescent', p. 185.
37 Ibid., p. 186.
38 Ibid.
39 Ibid., p. 185.
40 Jacques Lacan, 'The Mirror Stage as Function of the I as Revealed in Psychoanalytic Experience', in *Écrits: A Selection*, trans. Alan Sheridan (London: Routledge, 1977), p. 4.
41 Ibid.
42 George Eliot, *Middlemarch*, ed. David Carroll (Oxford: World's Classics, 1988), p. 230.
43 Lowry, *Convalescence*, pp. 3, 33, 42, 42–3.
44 Ibid., p. 33.
45 Ibid., p. 11.
46 Samuel Taylor Coleridge, *Biographia Literaria, or Biographical Sketches of My Literary Life and Opinions*, vol. 1, eds James Engell and W. Jackson Bate, in *The Collected Works of Samuel Taylor Coleridge*, vol. 7 (London: Routledge & Kegan Paul, 1983), p. 81.
47 Ibid. Note that William Morris subsequently transmutes the Romantic tradition initiated by Coleridge, lending the idea of convalescence a utopian, anti-capitalist impetus in his lecture on 'The Society of the Future' (1887): 'I remember, after having been ill at once, how pleasant it was to lie on my bed without pain or fever, doing nothing but watching the sunbeams and listening to the sounds of life outside; and might not the great world of men, if it once deliver itself from the struggle for life amidst dishonesty, rest for a little while after the long fever and be none the worse for it?' See Matthew Beaumont, *Utopia Ltd.: Ideologies of Social Dreaming in England, 1870–1900* (Chicago: Haymarket, 2009), p. 183.
48 Charles Baudelaire, 'The Painter of Modern Life', in *The Painter of Modern Life and Other Essays*, trans. Jonathan Mayne (London: Phaidon Press, 1995), pp. 7–8. Hereafter, page references appear in parenthesis after the quotation.
49 It might be added that the prolific American writer Nathaniel Parker Willis – of whom Poe was at this time especially critical, but whose accounts of central London, published in *The Romance of Travel* in early 1840, are a plausible influence on 'The Man of the Crowd' – subsequently de-urbanized and de-modernized the

convalescent, perhaps deliberately, in a collection published in 1855. See Nathaniel Parker Willis, *Romance of Travel, Comprising Tales of Five Lands* (New York: Colman, 1840); and *The Convalescent* (New York: Scribner, 1859).

50 Edgar Allan Poe, 'The Man of the Crowd', in *Selected Tales*, ed. David Van Leer (Oxford: Oxford World's Classics, 1998), p. 84. Hereafter, page references appear in parenthesis after the quotation.

51 Benjamin, 'On Some Motifs in Baudelaire', p. 188.

52 Ibid., p. 191.

53 Charles Baudelaire, 'Edgar Allan Poe: His Life and Works', in *The Painter of Modern Life and Other Essays*, p. 90.

54 Paul de Man, *Blindness and Insight: Essays in the Rhetoric of Contemporary Criticism*, revised edition (Minneapolis: University of Minnesota Press, 1983), p. 157.

2. Going Astray

1 Charles Dickens, 'Night Walks', in *On London* (London: Hesperus Press, 2010), p. 71. Hereafter, page references appear in parenthesis after the quotation.

2 Rachel Bowlby, 'Commuting', in *Restless Cities*, eds Matthew Beaumont and Gregory Dart (London: Verso, 2010), pp. 47, 45.

3 For a preliminary sense of this historical context, see Paul Griffiths, 'Meanings of Nightwalking in Early Modern England', *The Seventeenth Century* 13 (1998), pp. 212–38. See also Matthew Beaumont, *Nightwalking: A Nocturnal History of London, Chaucer to Dickens* (London: Verso, 2015).

4 Walter Benjamin, *Charles Baudelaire: A Lyric Poet in the Era of High Capitalism*, trans. Harry Zohn (London: Verso, 1983), p. 55.

5 Dickens, 'The Heart of London', in *On London*, pp. 5–6.

6 Dickens, 'Gone Astray', in *On London*, pp. 7–19.

7 Benjamin, *Charles Baudelaire*, p. 53. The Tramp's mode of ambulation might be called a concrete instance of the Kantian notion of 'purposiveness without purpose'.

8 George Eliot, *Romola*, ed. Andrew Brown (Oxford: Oxford World's Classics, 1998), pp. 202–3.

9 Benjamin, *Charles Baudelaire*, p. 54.

10 Adam Smith, *An Inquiry into the Nature and Causes of the Wealth of Nations,* ed. Edwin Cannan (Chicago: University of Chicago Press, 1976), pp. 12–13.

11 J. S. Mill, cited in Norman Feltes, 'To Saunter, to Hurry: Dickens, Time, and Industrial Capitalism', *Victorian Studies* 20: 3 (1977),

pp. 251–2. I have relied extensively on pp. 250–2 of Feltes's excellent article in this paragraph, though it should be pointed out that he is interested in time-discipline as opposed to walking per se.

12 Theodor W. Adorno, 'Trying to Understand *Endgame*', in *Notes to Literature*, vol. 2, trans. Shierry Weber Nicholsen, ed. Rolf Tiedemann (New York: Columbia University Press, 1991), p. 255.

13 Quoted in Joseph A. Amato, *On Foot: A History of Walking* (New York: New York University Press, 2004), p. 1.

14 See E. P. Thompson, 'Time, Work-Discipline and Industrial Capitalism', *Past and Present* 38: 1 (1967), pp. 56–97.

15 Charles Dickens, 'The Street – Morning', in *Dickens's Journalism: Sketches by Boz and Other Early Papers 1833–39*, ed. Michael Slater (London: Phoenix, 1996), p. 54.

16 Quoted in Michael Slater, 'Introduction', in *Dickens's Journalism*, p. xvi. These sentences were subsequently omitted from collected editions of the *Sketches*.

17 Thomas Hood, unsigned review of *Master Humphrey's Clock* in the *Athenaeum* of 7 November 1840, in *Charles Dickens: The Critical Heritage*, ed. Philip Collins (London: Routledge & Kegan Paul, 1971), p. 97. Note that Hood's apparently misleading assessment of Swiveller, who eventually evolves into something close to the novel's moral hero, reflects his characterization in the first issue of the periodical.

18 Paul Carter, *Repressed Spaces: The Poetics of Agoraphobia* (London: Reaktion, 2002), p. 39.

19 Charles Dickens, 'His General Line of Business', in *The Uncommercial Traveller and Reprinted Pieces*, ed. Leslie C. Staples (Oxford: Oxford University Press, 1958), pp. 1–2.

20 'Cash Payment the sole nexus: and there are so many things which cash will not buy!' See Thomas Carlyle, 'Chartism', in *Selected Writings*, ed. Alan Shelston (Harmondsworth: Penguin, 1987), p. 199.

21 Dickens, 'His General Line of Business', pp. 1, 2.

22 Charles Dickens, 'Shy Neighbourhoods', in *The Uncommercial Traveller*, p. 95.

23 John Bowen, *Other Dickens: Pickwick to Chuzzlewit* (Oxford: Oxford University Press, 2000), p. 133.

24 Charles Dickens, *The Old Curiosity Shop*, ed. Elizabeth M. Brennan (Oxford: Oxford World's Classics, 1998), p. 5. Hereafter, page references appear in parenthesis after the quotation. Note that the first issue of *Master Humphrey's Clock* sold 70,000 copies but that within a fortnight its circulation had dropped to 50,000.

25 See Elizabeth M. Brennan, 'Introduction', in *The Old Curiosity Shop*, p. xxvi.

26 Peter Ackroyd, *Dickens* (London: Minerva, 1991), p. 335. Michael Hollington has underlined the fact that throughout his life walking in streets functioned for Dickens as an outlet for tension when he was labouring especially hard on a book – see 'Dickens the Flâneur', *The Dickensian* 77: 2 (1981), pp. 71–87.

27 John Forster, *The Life of Charles Dickens*, vol. 1 (London: J. M. Dent, 1966), p. 121.

28 Audrey Jaffe, '"Never Be Safe but in Hiding": Omniscience and Curiosity in *The Old Curiosity Shop*', *Novel: A Forum on Fiction* 19: 2 (1986), p. 130.

29 Sheridan Le Fanu, 'The Familiar', in *In a Glass Darkly*, ed. Robert Tracy (Oxford: Oxford World's Classics, 1999), p. 70.

30 For example, Michael Hollington does not mention him in his discussion of *The Old Curiosity Shop* in his *Dickens and the Grotesque* (London: Croom Helm, 1984), pp. 79–95.

31 Bowen, *Other Dickens*, p. 141.

32 James Joyce, *Finnegans Wake*, ed. Seamus Deane (Harmondsworth: Penguin, 2000), p. 434. Loralee MacPike invokes Joyce's phrase, but makes little more than cosmetic use of it, in *Dostoevsky's Dickens: A Study of Literary Influence* (London: George Prior, 1981), p. 19.

33 Alfred Tennyson, *Maud*, in *Tennyson: A Selected Edition*, ed. Christopher Ricks (London: Longman, 1989), p. 575.

34 Edgar Allan Poe, 'The Man of the Crowd', in *Selected Tales*, ed. David Van Leer (Oxford: Oxford World's Classics, 1998), p. 85. On relevant aspects of the complicated, rather elusive literary relations between Dickens and Poe, who reviewed the first volume of *Master Humphrey's Clock* for *Graham's Magazine*, see Gerald C. Grubb, 'The Personal and Literary Relationships of Dickens and Poe, Part One: From "Sketches by Boz" through "Barnaby Rudge"', *Nineteenth-Century Fiction* 5: 1 (1950), pp. 1–22; and Laurence Senelick, 'Charles Dickens and "The Tell-Tale Heart"', *Poe Studies* 6: 1 (1973), pp. 12–14.

35 Benjamin, *Charles Baudelaire*, p. 48.

36 Charles Dickens, *Master Humphrey's Clock*, ed. Derek Hudson (Oxford: Oxford World's Classics, 1958), p. 5. Hereafter, page references appear in parenthesis after the quotation.

37 Charles Baudelaire, 'The Painter of Modern Life', in *Baudelaire: Selected Writings on Art and Artists*, trans. P. E. Charvet (Cambridge: Cambridge University Press, 1972), pp. 397–8.

38 Ibid., pp. 399–400.

39 Catherine Robson, *Men in Wonderland: The Lost Girlhood of*

the Victorian Gentleman (Princeton: Princeton University Press, 2001), p. 87.

40 Judith Walkowitz, *City of Dreadful Delight: Narratives of Sexual Danger in Late-Victorian London* (London: Virago, 1992), p. 22.

41 See Brennan, 'Introduction', p. xxviii.

42 Charles Dickens, 'The Prisoners' Van', in *Dickens's Journalism*, p. 272.

43 Henry Mayhew, *London Labour and the London Poor*, ed. Victor Neuberg (Harmondsworth: Penguin, 1985), p. 475.

44 Robert Louis Stevenson, *The Strange Case of Dr Jekyll and Mr Hyde and Weir of Hermiston*, ed. Emma Letley (Oxford: Oxford World's Classics, 1998), pp. 9, 19. 'Compared most often to an ape, a monkey, or a child', Nina Auerbach has observed, 'the dwarfish Mr Hyde is less vividly present than was Dickens' Quilp, from whom he seems to have derived' – see *Woman and the Demon: The Life of a Victorian Myth* (Harvard: Harvard University Press, 1982), p. 102.

45 See Rosemary Mundhenk, 'Creative Ambivalence in Dickens's *Master Humphrey's Clock*', *Studies in English Literature* 32: 4 (1992), p. 652, where she calls Quilp 'a grotesquely inverted parody of Humphrey'. Matthew Rowlinson, in 'Reading Capital with Little Nell', *Yale Journal of Criticism* 9: 2 (1996), p. 359, has observed that Master Humphrey and Nell's grandfather, both of whom take walks at night, are also doubles,. Incidentally, I am convinced that G. K. Chesterton was correct to argue, in an essay on *The Old Curiosity Shop*, that 'the function of criticism, if it has a legitimate function at all, can only be one function – that of dealing with the subconscious part of the author's mind which only the critic can express, and not with the conscious part of the author's mind, which the author himself can express. Either criticism is no good at all (a very defensible position) or else criticism means saying about an author the very things that would have made him jump out of his boots.' See *Criticisms and Appreciations of the Works of Charles Dickens* (London: J. M. Dent, 1933), pp. 51–2.

46 See Dickens, *The Old Curiosity Shop*, p. 79: 'the dwarf being one of that kind of persons who usually make themselves at home, he soon cast his eyes upon a chair, into which he skipped with uncommon agility, and perching himself on the back with his feet upon the seat, was thus enabled to look on and listen with greater comfort to himself, besides gratifying at the same time that taste for doing something fantastic and monkey-like, which on all

occasions had strong possession of him. Here, then, he sat, one leg cocked carelessly over the other, his chin resting on the palm of his hand, his head turned a little on one side, and his ugly features twisted into a complacent grimace.'

47 Joyce, *Finnegans Wake*, p. 433.

48 Ibid., p. 33. In *Stephen Hero* (1903–05), Stephen mentions *The Old Curiosity Shop* during a discussion of *The Wild Duck* with his mother. She has been moved by it, but Stephen is keen not 'to encourage her to an open record of her feelings', so he pre-empts her by saying: 'I hope you're not going to mention Little Nell in *The Old Curiosity Shop*.' See James Joyce, *Stephen Hero*, ed. Theodore Spencer (London: Panther, 1977), p. 80. Joyce also parodies Little Nell's death in 'The Oxen of the Sun' section in *Ulysses* – for a discussion of this, consult Matthew Bolton, 'Joycean Dickens/Dickensian Joyce', *Dickens Quarterly* 23: 4 (December 2006), p. 245.

49 See Thomas Karshan, *Vladimir Nabokov and the Art of Play* (Oxford: Oxford University Press, 2011), p. 178. Note too that the name of Humbert's antagonist Quilty recalls that of Quilp.

50 Vladimir Nabokov, *Lolita* (Harmondsworth: Penguin, 1990), p. 62.

51 Ibid., p. 115.

3. Disappearing

1 Quoted in Greg Olsen, *David Lynch: Beautiful Dark* (Lanham, Maryland: Scarecrow Press, 2008), p. 436.

2 See David Lynch, *Lynch on Lynch*, ed. Chris Rodley, revised edition (London: Faber & Faber, 2005), pp. 238–9, 289.

3 American Psychiatric Association, *Diagnostic and Statistical Manual of Mental Disorders*, 5th edition (Washington: American Psychiatric Association, 2013), pp. 293, 299.

4 Iain Sinclair, *London Orbital: A Walk Around the M25* (London: Granta, 2002), pp. 120–1.

5 Ibid., p. 121. See also Iain Sinclair, 'The Pilgrim Painter', *Tate Etc.* 45 (2019), pp. 70–81.

6 Edward Bellamy, *Looking Backward: 2000–1887*, ed. Matthew Beaumont (Oxford: Oxford World Classics, 2007), p. 197. Hereafter, page references appear in parenthesis after the quotation. For a fuller account of *Looking Backward*, see Matthew Beaumont, *The Spectre of Utopia: Utopian and Science Fictions at the* Fin de Siècle (Bern: Peter Lang, 2015), Chapters 1 to 5.

7 William Morris, '"Looking Backward"', in *Political Writings: Contributions to Justice and Commonweal, 1883–1890*, ed. Nicholas Salmon (Bristol: Thoemmes Press, 1994), p. 420.

8 Krishan Kumar, *Utopia and Anti-Utopia in Modern Times* (Oxford: Blackwell, 1987), p. 151.

9 Edward Bellamy, 'Why I Wrote "Looking Backward"', in *Edward Bellamy Speaks Again! Articles, Public Addresses, Letters* (Kansas City: Peerage Press, 1937), p. 202.

10 Kumar, *Utopia and Anti-Utopia*, p. 151.

11 I am of course echoing Adorno's limpid assessment of the dialectical relationship between high and low art, in a letter to Walter Benjamin of 18 March 1936: 'Both are torn halves of an integral freedom to which, however, they do not add up.' See Theodor W. Adorno and Walter Benjamin, *The Complete Correspondence 1928–1940*, trans. Nicholas Walker (Cambridge: Polity Press, 1999), p. 130. The essay and romance forms are, respectively, expressions of precisely this cultural divide.

12 Franklin Rosemont, almost the only critic to have taken Bellamy seriously as a psychologist, has gone so far as to eulogize him as 'a relentless explorer of his own mind' who 'advanced to the threshold of psychoanalysis and even of surrealism'. See 'Bellamy's Radicalism Reclaimed', in *Looking Backward: 1988–1888*, ed. Daphne Patai (Boston: University of Massachusetts Press, 1988), p. 149.

13 Edward Bellamy, *Miss Ludington's Sister* (London: William Reeves, 1893), pp. 96, 98.

14 The formulation 'Go West, young man, and grow up with the country' was used by John B. L. Soule as the title of an editorial for the *Terre Haute Express* in 1851. Subsequently, in the abbreviated form of 'Go west, young man', it came to be associated with Horace Greeley, founding editor of the *New York Tribune*, who was famous in the mid-nineteenth century for his criticism of the consequences of monopolization and land speculation. In 1870, Greeley publicly supported a Fourierian utopian colony, called Greeley, which the agricultural editor of the *Tribune*, Nathan Meeker, set up in Colorado.

15 Edward Bellamy, 'The Blindman's World', in *Apparitions of Things to Come: Edward Bellamy's Tales of Mystery and Imagination*, ed. Franklin Rosemont (Chicago: Charles H. Kerr, 1990), p. 45.

16 Tom H. Towers, 'The Insomnia of Julian West', *American Literature* 47: 1 (1975), pp. 56, 53.

17 Philip E. Wegner, *Imaginary Communities: Utopia, the Nation, and the Spatial Histories of Modernity* (Berkeley, CA: University of California Press, 2002), p. 90.

18 Kathryn Milun, *Pathologies of Modern Space: Empty Space, Urban Anxiety, and the Recovery of the Urban Self* (London: Routledge, 2006), p. 2.

19 Edward Bellamy, *Talks on Nationalism* (Chicago: Peerage Press, 1938), pp. 98–9.

20 Edward Bellamy, 'A Midnight Drama', in *Apparitions of Things to Come*, p. 102.

21 Edward Bellamy, 'The Old Folks' Party', in *Apparitions of Things to Come*, p. 54.

22 Ibid., p. 62.

23 Samuel Haber, 'The Nightmare and the Dream: Edward Bellamy and the Travails of Socialist Thought', *Journal of American Studies* 36: 3 (2002), p. 435.

24 Marshall Berman, *All That Is Solid Melts into Air: The Experience of Modernity* (London: Verso, 1983), p. 18.

25 Michael G. Kenny, *The Passion of Ansel Bourne: Multiple Personality in American Culture* (Washington: Smithsonian Institution Press, 1986), p. 77.

26 Richard Hodgson, 'A Case of Double Consciousness', cited in Frederic W. H. Myers, *Human Personality and Its Survival or Bodily Death* (London: Longmans Green, 1903), vol. 1, p. 309.

27 Kenny, *The Passion of Ansel Bourne*, p. 67.

28 Jessica Catherine Lieberman, 'Flight from Haunting: Psychogenic Fugue and Nineteenth-Century American Imagination', in *Spectral America: Phantoms and the National Imagination*, ed. Jeffrey Andrew Weinstock (Madison: University of Wisconsin Press, 2004) p. 150.

29 William James, *The Principles of Psychology*, vol. 1 (Cambridge, MA: Harvard University Press, 1981), p. 371.

30 Ibid.

31 In the medical literature, Albert Dadas is often referred to as 'Albert X' – appropriately, perhaps, because since at least the late eighteenth century the letter 'X' has signified an indeterminate identity, or, in mathematical terms, an unknown quantity.

32 Ian Hacking, *Mad Travelers: Reflections on the Reality of Transient Mental Illnesses* (Cambridge, MA: Harvard University Press, 1998), p. 7.

33 Ibid., p. 12.

34 Ibid., p. 32.

35 Ibid., pp. 28, 78.

36 Ian Hacking, '*Automatisme Ambulatoire*: Fugue, Hysteria, and Gender at the Turn of the Century', *Modernism/Modernity* 3: 2 (1996), p. 41.

37 W. H. Hudson, *A Crystal Age* (London: Fisher Unwin, 1887); and Mrs George Corbett, *New Amazonia: A Foretaste of the Future* (London: Tower, 1889). On the latter, see Matthew Beaumont, 'The New Woman in Nowhere: Feminism and Utopianism at the *Fin de Siècle*', in *The New Woman in Fiction and Fact: Fin de Siècle Feminisms*, eds Angelique Richardson and Chris Willis (London: Palgrave, 2001), pp. 212–23; and Matthew Beaumont, *Utopia Ltd.: Ideologies of Social Dreaming in England 1870–1900* (Leiden: Brill, 2005), pp. 120–8.

38 Robert Louis Stevenson, *The Strange Case of Dr Jekyll and Mr Hyde & Weir of Hermiston*, ed. Emma Letley (Oxford: Oxford World's Classics, 1998), p. 67.

39 William Morris, *News from Nowhere*, in *Three Works by William Morris*, ed. A. L. Morton (London: Lawrence & Wishart, 1986), pp. 400–1.

40 Hacking, *Mad Travelers*, p. 37.

41 H. G. Wells, *The Time Machine*, ed. John Lawton (London: Everyman, 1995), p. 81.

42 Hacking, *Mad Travelers*, p. 115.

43 See Beaumont, *Utopia Ltd.*, pp. 1–5.

44 In 1881, the physician George Miller Beard published *American Nervousness*. In it he defined neurasthenia as the 'American disease', locating its origins in the mechanics of metropolitan life at the *fin de siècle* – in particular, technological developments such as steam power and the telegraph, and social developments such as the periodical press and the women's movement. Beard also argued that, although forethought or 'foreworry', as he termed it, makes civilization possible, 'this forecasting, this sacrifice of the present to the future, this living for our posterity', also causes anxiety and increased nervousness. See George M. Beard, *American Nervousness, Its Causes and Consequences; A Supplement to Nervous Exhaustion (Neurasthenia)* (New York: G. P. Putnam's Sons, 1881), p. 129. Bellamy's utopian vision offers to redeem the neurasthenic consequences of 'forecasting' by transforming anticipation of the future into an inspiriting activity, collective rather than individual, active rather than passive.

45 Bellamy, 'The Blindman's World', p. 33.

46 Edward Bellamy, 'Plots for Stories', in *Apparitions of Things to Come*, p. 175.

47 Kenny, *The Passion of Ansel Bourne*, p. 69.

48 See Lieberman, 'Flight from Haunting', pp. 149–50.

49 Ibid., pp. 151–2.

50 On 'social dreaming', see Lyman Tower Sargent, 'The Three Faces

of Utopianism Revisited', *Utopian Studies* 5 (1994), pp. 1–37; and Beaumont, *Utopia Ltd.*, passim.

51 Fredric Jameson, *Archaeologies of the Future: The Desire Called Utopia and Other Science Fictions* (London: Verso, 2005), p. 339.

52 Morris, *News from Nowhere*, p. 400.

53 Robert Philmus, 'H. G. Wells's Revisi(tati)ons of *The Time Machine*', *English Literature in Transition 1880–1920* 41: 4 (1998), pp. 427–52.

54 Making a rather different point, Jameson writes that the fiction of Philip K. Dick 'is a virtual "art of the fugue" of storytelling, narrative pyrotechnics that unravel themselves in delirium and can stand as a critique of representation itself' – see *Archaeologies of the Future*, p. 348.

4. Fleeing

1   H. G. Wells, *The Invisible Man*, ed. Matthew Beaumont (Oxford: Oxford World's Classics, 2017), p. 114. Hereafter, page references appear in parenthesis after the quotation.

2   Herman Melville, *Moby Dick*, ed. Tony Tanner (Oxford: Oxford World's Classics, 1998), p. 171. For some additional comments on Griffin's albinism, see David J. Lake, 'The Whiteness of Griffin and H. G. Wells's Images of Death', *Science Fiction Studies* 8: 1 (1981), pp. 12–18.

3   Friedrich Nietzsche, *The Genealogy of Morals: A Polemic*, ed. Douglas Smith (Oxford: Oxford World's Classics, 1998), p. 22. Nietzsche was first translated into English in 1896, but David S. Thatcher has noted that 'Nietzschean motifs appear in Wells's work long before Nietzsche was available in English – certainly before his ideas began to make themselves felt' – see *Nietzsche in England, 1890–1914: The Growth of a Reputation* (Toronto: University of Toronto Press, 1970), p. 82. John Batchelor claims that 'Wells may not have read [Nietzsche] but was certainly aware of him – see *H.G. Wells* (Cambridge: Cambridge University Press, 1985), p. 5. On *ressentiment*, see too Paul A. Cantor, '*The Invisible Man* and the Invisible Hand: H.G. Wells's Critique of Capitalism', *The American Scholar* 68: 3 (1999), p. 99.

4   H. G. Wells, *The History of Mr Polly*, ed. Simon J. James (Harmondsworth: Penguin, 2005), pp. 8, 9.

5   Fyodor Dostoevsky, *Notes from the Underground and The Gambler*, trans. Jane Kentish, ed. Malcolm Jones (Oxford: Oxford World's Classics, 1991), p. 14.

6   Nietzsche, *The Genealogy of Morals*, p. 22.

7   On the optical science behind Griffin's experiments, see Philip Ball, *Invisible: The Dangerous Allure of the Unseen* (London: Bodley Head, 2014), pp. 172–9. 'The invisibility of H. G. Wells,' Ball later concludes, 'in which light is not deviated by a substance because it has a refractive index equal to that of air, is possible in principle but not in practice, at least for an ordinary material' (p. 257).

8   These suggestive phrases are taken from Louis Althusser, *Philosophy and the Spontaneous Philosophy of the Scientists*, ed. Gregory Elliot (London: Verso, 1990), p. 250.

9   H. G. Wells, *The Holy Terror* (London: Michael Joseph, 1939), pp. 229, 242.

10 Terry Eagleton, *Sweet Violence: The Idea of the Tragic* (Oxford: Blackwell, 2003), p. 278.

11 W. T. Stead, in *H. G. Wells: The Critical Heritage*, ed. Patrick Parrinder (London: Routledge & Kegan Paul, 1972), p. 61.

12 Eagleton, *Sweet Violence*, p. 279.

13 Clement Shorter, in *H. G. Wells: The Critical Heritage*, pp. 58, 59.

14 For further details, see Ball, *Invisible*, pp. 92–3, 124–7. As Ball observes, *Pearson's Weekly* printed an interview with Röntgen in April 1896, fourteen months before the same periodical began its serial publication of *The Invisible Man*.

15 See Allen W. Grove, 'Röntgen's Ghosts: Photography, X-Rays, and the Victorian Imagination', *Literature and Medicine* 16: 2 (1997), p. 169.

16 Karl Marx and Friedrich Engels, *The Manifesto of the Communist Party*, in *Karl Marx: Selected Writings*, ed. David McLellan (Oxford: Oxford University Press, 1977), p. 226.

17 See Mary Shelley, *Frankenstein, or, The Modern Prometheus*, ed. Marilyn Butler (Oxford: Oxford World's Classics, 1998). On Wells's 'mad scientists', see Anne Stiles, *Popular Fiction and Brain Science in the Late Nineteenth Century* (Cambridge: Cambridge University Press, 2012), pp. 119–55.

18 John Sutherland, 'Introduction', in H. G. Wells, *The Invisible Man*, ed. David Lake (New York: Oxford University Press, 1996), p. xvii.

19 H. G. Wells, *Experiment in Autobiography: Discoveries and Conclusions of a Very Ordinary Brain (Since 1866)* (London: Victor Gollancz, 1834), vol. 1, p. 138.

20 Plato, *The Republic of Plato*, trans. and ed. Francis Macdonald Cornford (Oxford: Oxford University Press, 1941), p. 45. See also Philip Holt, 'H. G. Wells and the Ring of Gyges', *Science Fiction Studies* 57 (July 1992), pp. 236–47.

21 Christopher Marlowe, *Doctor Faustus*, III. ii. 11–13, in *The Complete Plays*, ed. J. B. Steane (Harmondsworth: Penguin, 1986), p. 300. See also Roslynn D. Haynes, *H.G. Wells: Discoverer of the Future* (Basingstoke: Macmillan, 1979), p. 203.

22 Charles Baudelaire, 'The Painter of Modern Life', in *The Painter of Modern Life and Other Essays*, trans. Jonathan Mayne (London: Phaidon, 1995), p. 9.

23 Georg Simmel, 'The Metropolis and Mental Life', in *Simmel on Culture: Selected Writings*, eds David Frisby and Mike Featherstone (London: Sage, 1997), pp. 174–5, 177.

24 Ibid., p. 176.

25 The reference here is to George M. Beard, *American Nervousness, Its Causes and Consequences: A Supplement to Nervous Exhaustion (Neurasthenia)* (New York: G.P. Putnam's Sons, 1881).

26 Wells, *Experiment in Autobiography*, vol. 1, pp. 311–17.

27 H. G. Wells, *Tono-Bungay*, ed. Patrick Parrinder (Harmondsworth: Penguin, 2005), p. 105.

28 Michael Sherborne, *H. G. Wells: Another Kind of Life* (London: Peter Owen, 2010), p. 124.

29 Simon J. James, *Maps of Utopia: H. G. Wells, Modernity, and the End of Culture* (Oxford: Oxford University Press, 2012), p. 72.

30 Robert Louis Stevenson, *The Strange Case of Dr Jekyll and Mr Hyde and Other Tales*, ed. Roger Luckhurst (Oxford: Oxford World's Classics, 2006), pp. 52, 7. On this scene as an echo of Dickens's *The Old Curiosity Shop*, see Chapter 2 above.

31 On Griffin and the Professor, see Martin Ray, 'Conrad's Invisible Professor', *The Conradian* 11: 1 (May 1986), pp. 35–41.

32 Joseph Conrad, letter, in *H. G. Wells: The Critical Heritage*, p. 60.

33 Joseph Conrad, *Heart of Darkness and Other Tales*, ed. Cedric Watts (Oxford: Oxford World's Classics, 1998), pp. 241, 221. Linda Dryden notes that other descriptions of Kurtz – as 'very little more than a voice', for example, and 'indistinct like a vapour exhaled by the earth' – are also 'suggestive of Griffin's insubstantiality' – see 'H. G. Wells and Joseph Conrad: A Literary Friendship', in *H. G. Wells's Fin de Siècle: Twenty-First-Century Reflections on the Early H. G. Wells*, ed. John S. Partington (Frankfurt: Peter Lang, 2007), pp. 103–4.

34 Marcia Ian, 'Henry James and the Spectacle of Loss: Psychoanalytic Metaphysics', in *Cultural Politics at the* Fin de Siècle, eds Sally Ledger and Scott McCracken (Cambridge: Cambridge University Press, 1995), p. 122.

35 Rachel A. Bowser, 'Visibility, Interiority, and Temporality in *The Invisible Man*', *Studies in the Novel*, 45: 1 (2013), p. 22.

36 Wells, *The History of Mr Polly*, pp. 120, 154.

37 See Patrick A. McCarthy, '*Heart of Darkness* and the Early Novels of H. G. Wells: Evolution, Anarchy, Entropy', *Journal of Modern Literature* 13: 1 (1986), p. 49.

38 T. S. Eliot, 'The Hollow Men', in *Collected Poems, 1909–1962* (London: Faber & Faber, 1963), p. 89.

39 Bernard Bergonzi, *The Early H. G. Wells: A Study of the Scientific Romances* (Manchester: Manchester University Press, 1961), p. 119.

40 Northrop Frye, *Anatomy of Criticism: Four Essays* (Harmondsworth: Penguin, 1990), p. 148.

41 Mladen Dolar, *A Voice and Nothing More* (Cambridge, MA: MIT Press, 2006), p. 69.

42 Wells, *The History of Mr Polly*, p. 127.

43 William Shakespeare, *The History of King Lear*, ed. Stanley Wells (Oxford: Oxford World's Classics, 2001), p. 191.

44 Grégoire Chamayou, *Manhunts: A Philosophical History*, trans. Steven Rendall (Princeton: Princeton University Press, 2012), pp. 1–2.

45 See Giorgio Agamben, 'A Self-Annihilating Nothing', in *The Man Without Content*, trans. Georgia Albert (Stanford, CA: Stanford University Press, 1999), pp. 52–8.

46 See H.G. Wells, *The Invisible Man: A Grotesque Romance, A Critical Text of the 1897 New York First Edition, with an Introduction and Appendices*, ed. Leon Stover (Jefferson, NC: McFarland, 1998), p. 208.

47 Eagleton, *Sweet Violence*, p. 278.

48 Franco Moretti, 'Dialectic of Fear', in *Signs Taken for Wonders: Essays in the Sociology of Literary Forms*, trans. Susan Fischer, David Forgacs and David Miller (London: Verso, 1997), pp. 84, 107.

49 Jorge Luis Borges, 'The First Wells', in *Other Inquisitions, 1937–1952*, trans. Ruth L. C. Simms (Austin: University of Texas Press, 1964), p. 86.

50 Ibid., p. 87.

51 See Jorge Luis Borges, 'H. G. Wells, *The Time Machine; The Invisible Man*', one of his 'Prologues to *A Personal Library*', in *Selected Non-Fictions*, ed. Eliot Weinberger (New York: Penguin, 2000), p. 516.

52 W. S. Gilbert, 'The Perils of Invisibility', in *More Bab Ballads* (London: Macmillan, 1925), pp. 149–53. For an excellent brief overview of the Victorian short stories and novels that make use of the invisibility motif, see Sutherland, 'Introduction', p. xvii.

53 H. G. Wells, 'Under the Knife', in *Selected Stories of H. G. Wells*, ed. Ursula K. Le Guin (New York: Modern Library, 2004), pp. 61–2.

5. Wandering

 1 G. K. Chesterton, *The Man Who Was Thursday: A Nightmare*, ed. Matthew Beaumont (Harmondsworth: Penguin, 2011), p. 108. Hereafter, page references appear in parenthesis after the quotation.
 2 Matthew Arnold, 'Dover Beach', in *Selected Poems and Prose*, ed. Miriam Allott (London: Everyman, 1978), p. 89.
 3 G. K. Chesterton, *Autobiography* (Cornwall: Stratus, 2001), pp. 49, 57. Hereafter, page references appear in parenthesis after the quotation.
 4 William Oddie, *Chesterton and the Romance of Orthodoxy: The Making of GKC, 1874–1908* (Oxford: Oxford University Press, 2008), p. 94.
 5 Charles Whibley, 'Introduction', in *Collected Essays of W. P. Ker*, vol. 1, ed. Charles Whibley (London: Macmillan, 1925), p. ix.
 6 W. P. Ker, *Epic and Romance: Essays on Medieval Literature* (London: Macmillan, 1897), pp. 6–7. See also W. P. Ker, *English Literature: Medieval* (London: Williams and Norgate [1912]).
 7 This passage, reproduced by B. Ifor Evans, another of Ker's students, in *W. P. Ker as a Critic of Literature* (1955), is cited in Oddie, *Chesterton and the Romance of Orthodoxy*, p. 94.
 8 G. K. Chesterton, *What's Wrong with the World?* (New York: Dover, 2007), p. 29.
 9 G. K. Chesterton, *Alarms and Discursions* (London: Methuen, 1910), p. 7.
10 Slavoj Žižek, *The Puppet and the Dwarf: The Perverse Core of Christianity* (Cambridge, MA: MIT Press, 2003), p. 47.
11 G. K. Chesterton, *The Napoleon of Notting Hill*, ed. Bernard Bergonzi (Oxford: Oxford University Press, 1994), p. 39.
12 Ibid., p. 4.
13 G. K. Chesterton, *Orthodoxy* (London: Filiquarian, 2007), p. 34.
14 G. K. Chesterton, 'The Advantages of Having One Leg', in *Tremendous Trifles* (London: Methuen, 1909), p. 40.
15 Chesterton, *Orthodoxy*, pp. 97, 98.
16 Chesterton, *The Napoleon of Notting Hill*, pp. 122, 131.
17 Robert Walser, *Jakob von Gunten*, trans. Christopher Middleton (New York: New York Review of Books, 1999), p. 36.
18 G. K. Chesterton, '"Vulgarised"', in *The Wild Knight and Other Poems*, Fourth Edition (London: J. M. Dent, 1914), p. 104.

19 See *G. K. Chesterton: The Critical Judgments*, ed. D. J. Conlon (Antwerp: Antwerp Studies in English Literature, 1976), p. 402.

20 Robert Browning, *Selected Poems*, ed. Daniel Karlin (Harmondsworth: Penguin, 2004), pp. 98, 99.

21 See Daniel Karlin, *Browning's Hatreds* (Oxford: Oxford University Press, 1993), pp. 119–20n., 241.

22 Browning, *Selected Poems*, p. 50.

23 Henri Lefebvre, *The Production of Space*, trans. Donald Nicholson-Smith (Oxford: Blackwell, 1991), p. 287.

24 Harold Bloom, *Poetry and Repression: Revisionism from Blake to Stevens* (New Haven: Yale University Press, 1976), p. 175.

25 G. K. Chesterton, *Robert Browning* (Middlesex: Echo Library, 2006), pp. 81–2.

26 Chesterton, 'The Advantages of Having One Leg', p. 42.

27 Chesterton, *Robert Browning*, p. 81.

28 Ibid.

29 Chesterton, 'The Pessimist', in *The Wild Knight and Other Poems*, p. 83.

30 Browning, 'Childe Roland', in *Selected Poems*, p. 93.

31 Chesterton, 'The Wild Knight', in *The Wild Knight and Other Poems*, pp. 115–17.

32 T. S. Eliot, *The Waste Land*, in *The Complete Poems and Plays of T. S. Eliot* (London: Faber & Faber, 1969), p. 73.

33 Eliot, *The Waste Land*, p. 75; see Gérard de Nerval, *Selected Writings*, trans. Richard Sieburth (Harmondsworth: Penguin, 1999), p. 363.

34 Chesterton, *Robert Browning*, p. 81.

35 Browning, 'Childe Roland', p. 95.

36 Chesterton, *Robert Browning*, p. 81.

37 Bloom, *A Map of Misreading*, p. 110.

38 G. K. Chesterton, 'A Defence of Detective Stories', in *The Defendant* (London: R. Briley Johnson, 1901), p. 123. 'The whole noiseless and unnoticeable police management by which we are ruled and protected', he adds in the concluding sentence of the article, in a slightly different proposition, 'is only a successful knight-errantry.'

39 Conlon, ed., *G. K. Chesterton*, p. 145.

40 This is available at cse.dmu.ac.uk.

41 Chesterton, *Robert Browning*, p. 57.

42 G. K. Chesterton, *Charles Dickens* (Ware: Wordsworth Editions, 2007), p. 108.

43 On 'irrealist' literature, see Michael Löwy, 'The Current of Critical Irrealism: A Moonlit Enchanted Night', in *Adventures in Realism*, ed. Matthew Beaumont (Oxford: Blackwell, 2007), pp. 193–206.

44 G. K. Chesterton, 'Dreams', in *The Coloured Lands* (London: Sheed & Ward, 1938), pp. 81–2.

45 Chesterton, *Orthodoxy*, pp. 80–1.

46 See Ian Hacking, *Mad Travelers: Reflections on the Reality of Transient Mental Illnesses* (Cambridge, MA: Harvard University Press, 1998), p. 12.

47 Slavoj Žižek, 'Hegel – Chesterton: German Idealism and Christianity', in *The Symptom*, available at lacan.com/zizhegche.htm.

48 T. S. Eliot, 'The Love Song of J. Alfred Prufrock', in *The Complete Poems and Plays*, p. 13.

49 Chesterton, *The Napoleon of Notting Hill*, p. 68.

50 Ibid., p. 70.

51 Chesterton, *Charles Dickens*, pp. 23–4.

52 Ibid., p. 144.

53 Chesterton, *Orthodoxy*, pp. 3–4.

54 Samuel Hynes, 'The Chesterbelloc', in *Edwardian Occasions: Essays on English Writing in the Early Twentieth Century* (London: Routledge & Kegan Paul, 1972), p. 80.

55 Chesterton, *Robert Browning*, p. 63.

56 Raymond Chandler, 'The Simple Art of Murder: An Essay', in *The Simple Art of Murder* (New York: Vintage, 1988), p. 18. Chandler's essay does not refer to Chesterton, but it does refer to his friend E. C. Bentley, author of *Trent's Last Case* (1913) and, as I have noted, the dedicatee of *The Man Who Was Thursday*.

57 On the disenchantment of this ideal in Chandler's fiction, see Ernest Fontana, 'Chivalry and Modernity in Raymond Chandler's *The Big Sleep*', in *The Critical Responses to Raymond Chandler*, ed. J. K. Van Dover (Westport, CT: Greenwood Press, 1995), pp. 159–75.

58 Chesterton, 'A Defence of Detective Stories', pp. 119–20.

6. Collapsing

1 Anthony Cummins, 'Émile Zola's Cheap English Dress: The Vizetelly Translations, Late-Victorian Print Culture, and the Crisis of Literary Value', *Review of English Studies* 60 (2009), p. 130.

2 *Guardian*, 3 October 1893, From the Archives, guardian.co.uk/books/2004/jan/03.

3 Frederick Brown, *Zola: A Life* (London: Macmillan, 1996), p. 752.

4 Ford Madox Ford, *Return to Yesterday*, ed. Bill Hutchings (Manchester: Carcanet, 1991), p. 214. Hereafter, page numbers from this edition are cited in parenthesis in the text.

5 Georg Lukács, 'Narrate or Describe? A Preliminary Discussion of Naturalism and Formalism', in *Writer and Critic and Other Essays*, trans. Arthur D. Kahn (New York: Grosset and Dunlap, 1971), p. 132.

6 Ford Madox Ford, 'On Impressionism', in *The Good Soldier*, ed. Martin Stannard (New York: Norton, 1995), p. 265.

7 See Umberto Eco, *The Limits of Interpretation* (Bloomington: Indiana University Press, 1994); and, for a fictional account of a paranoiac hermeneutic, *Foucault's Pendulum*, trans. William Weaver (New York: Harcourt Brace, 1989).

8 Max Saunders, *Ford Madox Ford: A Dual Life*, vol. 1 (Oxford: Oxford University Press, 1996), p. 164.

9 Ford Madox Ford, *The Soul of London: A Survey of a Modern City*, ed. Alan G. Hill (London: Everyman, 1995), p. 22. Hereafter, page numbers are cited in parenthesis in the text.

10 Guy Debord, 'Introduction to a Critique of Urban Geography', trans. Ken Knabb, in *Critical Geographies: A Collection of Readings*, eds Harald Bauder and Salvatore Engel-Di Mauro (Kelowna, BC: Praxis Press, 2008), p. 23.

11 Gaston Bachelard, *The Poetics of Space*, trans. Maria Jolas (Boston: Beacon Press, 1992), p. 4.

12 See Anthony Vidler, *The Architectural Uncanny: Essays in the Modern Unhomely* (Cambridge, MA: MIT Press, 1992); see also China Miéville, 'The Conspiracy of Architecture: Notes on a Modern Anxiety', *Historical Materialism* 2 (1998), pp. 1–32.

13 See Paul Carter, *Repressed Spaces: The Poetics of Agoraphobia* (London: Reaktion, 2002), p. 9 and *passim*. Carter does not mention Ford in this perceptive, if speculative, account of modernism and agoraphobia.

14 Quoted in Thomas C. Moser, *The Life in the Fiction of Ford Madox Ford* (Princeton: Princeton University Press, 1980), pp. 54–5.

15 Quoted in ibid., p. 56.

16 Quoted in Saunders, *Ford Madox Ford*, p. 176.

17 Quoted in Moser, *The Life in the Fiction*, p. 56.

18 David Trotter, 'The Invention of Agoraphobia', *Victorian Literature and Culture* 32 (2004), p. 463. See also David Trotter, 'Ford against Joyce and Lewis', in *The Uses of Phobia: Essays on Literature and Film* (Oxford: Blackwell, 2010), pp. 113–22; and, for a fine introduction to Ford, 'Ford's Impressionism', in *Paranoid Modernism: Literary Experiment, Psychosis, and the Professionalization of English Society* (Oxford: Oxford University Press, 2001), pp. 187–219.

19 Carl Otto Westphal, *Westphal's 'Die Agoraphobie'*, *with*

Commentary: The Beginnings of Agoraphobia, eds. Terry J. Krappi and Michael T. Schumacher (Langham: University Press of America, 1988), p. 59.

20 Ibid., p. 86.

21 J. Headley Neale, 'Agoraphobia', *The Lancet* (19 November 1898), pp. 1322–3.

22 Cited in Anthony Vidler, 'Psychopathologies of Modern Space: Metropolitan Fear from Agoraphobia to Estrangement', in *Rediscovering History: Culture, Politics, and the Psyche*, ed. Michael S. Roth (Stanford: Stanford University Press, 1994), p. 15.

23 Kathryn Milun, *Pathologies of Modern Space: Empty Space, Urban Anxiety, and the Recovery of the Public Self* (London: Routledge, 2007), p. 2. See also Shelley Z. Reuter, *Narrating Social Order: Agoraphobia and the Politics of Classification* (Toronto: University Press of Toronto, 2007).

24 Trotter, 'The Invention of Agoraphobia', p. 465.

25 Ford Madox Ford, *Selected Poems*, ed. Max Saunders (Manchester: Carcanet, 1997), p. 35.

26 Ford Madox Ford, 'Preface', in Jean Rhys, *The Left Bank and Other Stories* (London: Jonathan Cape, 1927), p. 10.

27 Ibid.

28 Henry Sutherland, letter, *The Lancet* (17 January 1885), p. 131.

29 Ford, 'Preface', pp. 10–11.

30 Carter, *Repressed Spaces*, p. 69.

31 Walter Benjamin, *Charles Baudelaire: A Lyric Poet in the Era of High Capitalism*, trans. Harry Zohn (London: Verso, 1983), p. 37. Of Benjamin, T. J. Clark laconically remarks that 'agoraphobia was not his thing' (see 'Should Benjamin Have Read Marx?' in *boundary 2* 30 [2003], p. 47).

32 Baudelaire, 'The Painter of Modern Life', p. 10.

33 Adam Phillips, 'First Hates: Phobias in Theory', in *On Kissing, Tickling and Being Bored: Psychoanalytic Essays on the Unexamined Life* (London: Faber & Faber, 1993), p. 16.

34 Saunders, *Ford Madox Ford*, p. 132. Trotter notes, incidentally, that the Professor in Conrad's *The Secret Agent* (1907) 'suffers from an intense dread of the "mass of mankind in its numbers" which looks a lot like agoraphobia' – see 'Introduction', in *The Uses of Phobia*, p. 12.

35 Joseph Conrad and Ford Madox Ford, *The Inheritors: An Extravagant Story*, ed. David Seed (Liverpool: Liverpool University Press, 1999), p. 35.

36 Ford Madox Ford, *The Good Soldier*, ed. Thomas C. Moser

(Oxford: Oxford World's Classics, 1999), p. 82. See Saunders, *Ford Madox Ford*, p. 434.

37 See Trotter, 'The Invention of Agoraphobia', pp. 471–2.

38 Siegfried Kracauer, *Theory of Film: The Redemption of Physical Reality* (Oxford: Oxford University Press, 1960), p. 72. See Carter, *Repressed Spaces*, p. 168.

39 Kracauer, *Theory of Film*, p. 73.

40 Walter Benjamin, 'The Paris of the Second Empire in Baudelaire', in *Selected Writings, Vol. 4: 1938–1940*, ed. Michael W. Jennings (Cambridge, MA: Harvard University Press, 2003), p. 31.

41 Neale, 'Agoraphobia', p. 1323.

42 Sigmund Freud, *Introductory Lectures on Psychoanalysis*, trans. James Strachey (Harmondsworth: Penguin, 1991), p. 310.

43 Trotter, 'The Invention of Agoraphobia', p. 471.

44 Walter Benjamin, 'A Berlin Chronicle', in *One-Way Street and Other Writings*, trans. Edmund Jephcott and Kingsley Shorter (London: Verso, 1997), p. 301.

7. Striding, Staring

1 Walter Benjamin, 'The Paris of the Second Empire in Baudelaire', in *Selected Writings Vol. 4: 1938–1940*, ed. Michael W. Jennings (Cambridge, MA: Harvard University Press, 2003), p. 41.

2 Virginia Woolf, *Mrs Dalloway*, ed. Claire Tomalin (Oxford: Oxford University Press, 1992), p. 65. Hereafter, page references appear in parenthesis after the quotation.

3 See Virginia Woolf, *Night and Day*, ed. Suzanne Raitt (Oxford: Oxford World's Classics, 1999), p. 209.

4 See Benjamin, 'The Paris of the Second Empire in Baudelaire', p. 83, n. 189.

5 The word 'buccaneer', which evokes the activities of imperial plunderers, is derived from the French term for a kind of barbecue on which, following the practices of the colonized people of Saint-Domingue in the seventeenth century, flesh is dried or roasted. Peter's consciousness, in this scene, is itself a kind of rude frame on which he heats and cooks his erotic fantasies.

6 Rachel Bowlby, 'Walking, Women and Writing', in *Feminist Destinations and Further Essays* (Edinburgh: Edinburgh University Press, 1997), pp. 205–6. See also Deborah L. Parsons, *Streetwalking the Metropolis: Women, the City and Modernity* (Oxford: Oxford University Press, 2000), pp. 73–4.

7   Marshall Berman, *All That Is Solid Melts into Air: The Experience of Modernity* (London: Verso, 1983), pp. 148, 150, 152.

8   D. H. Lawrence, *Sons and Lovers*, ed. Keith Sagar (Harmondsworth: Penguin, 1988), p. 492.

9   André Breton, *Nadja*, trans. Richard Howard (Harmondsworth: Penguin, 1999), p. 113.

10 Raymond Williams, *The Country and the City* (London: Hogarth Press, 1993), p. 243.

11 Richard Lehan, *The City in Literature: An Intellectual and Cultural History* (Berkeley: University of California Press, 1998), p. 121.

12 Charles Baudelaire, 'The Painter of Modern Life', in *The Painter of Modern Life and Other Essays*, trans. Jonathan Mayne (London: Phaidon, 1995), p. 9. Hereafter, page references appear in parenthesis after the quotation.

13 Williams, *The Country and the City*, p. 233.

14 Bowlby, 'Walking, Women and Writing', p. 206. See also Lauren Elkin, *Flâneuse: Women Walk the City in Paris*, New York, Tokyo, Venice and London (London: Chatto & Windus, 2016), pp. 69–93.

15 Virginia Woolf, 'Street Haunting: A London Adventure', in *Selected Essays*, ed. David Bradshaw (Oxford: Oxford World's Classics, 2008), p. 177.

16 Ibid., p. 187. It is impossible, I think, not to suspect that Woolf intended the phrase 'fellow men', for all its superficial universalism as a euphemism for 'human beings', to be gendered specifically as male.

17 Benjamin, 'The Paris of the Second Empire in Baudelaire', p. 27.

18 Ibid., p. 31.

19 David Harvey, *Paris, Capital of Modernity* (London: Routledge, 2006), p. 212.

20 Ibid., pp. 212, 221.

21 Berman, *All That Is Solid Melts into Air*, p. 137.

22 Ibid.

23 Charles Baudelaire, 'In Passing', in *Les Fleurs du Mal*, trans. Richard Howard (London: Picador, 1987), pp. 97–8.

24 Walter Benjamin, 'Paris, the Capital of the Nineteenth Century', in *The Writer of Modern Life: Essays on Charles Baudelaire*, trans. Howard Eiland, Edmund Jephcott, Rodney Livingston and Harry Zohn (Cambridge, MA: Harvard University Press, 2006), p. 37.

25 Bowlby, 'Walking, Women and Writing', p. 198.

26 Walter Benjamin, 'The Return of the *Flâneur*', in *Selected Writings, Vol. 2, 1927–1934*, trans. Rodney Livingstone et al. (Cambridge, MA: Harvard University Press, 1999), p. 265.

27 Woolf, 'Street Haunting', p. 187.

28 Victor Burgin, *In/Different Spaces* (Berkeley: University of California Press, 1996), p. 28.

29 Philip Fisher, 'Torn Space: James Joyce's *Ulysses*', in *The Novel: Volume 2, Forms and Themes*, ed. Franco Moretti (Princeton: Princeton University Press, 2006), p. 668.

30 Isaac Rosenberg, 'Fleet Street', in *London: A History in Verse*, ed. Mark Ford (Cambridge, MA: Harvard University Press, 2012), p. 519.

31 Sean Pryor, 'A Poetics of Occasion in Hope Mirrlees's *Paris*', *Critical Quarterly* 61: 1 (2019), p. 43.

32 Hope Mirrlees, 'Paris: A Poem', in *Collected Poems*, ed. Sandeep Parmar (Manchester: Carcanet: 2011), p. 3.

33 Gaston Bachelard, *The Poetics of Space*, trans. Maria Jolas (Boston: Beacon Press, 1994), pp. 194, 192.

34 Christopher Butler, *Early Modernism: Literature, Music and Painting in Europe, 1900–1916* (Oxford: Oxford University Press, 1994), p. 137.

35 T. S. Eliot, *The Waste Land*, in *Collected Poems, 1909–1962* (London: Faber & Faber, 1974), p. 65.

36 D. H. Lawrence, 'Town in 1917', in *The Complete Poems of D. H. Lawrence*, eds Vivian de Sola Pinto and Warren Roberts (Harmondsworth: Penguin, 1977), p. 171.

37 Georg Simmel, 'The Metropolis and Mental Life', in *Simmel on Culture: Selected Writings*, eds David Frisby and Mike Featherstone (London: Sage, 1997), pp. 174–5.

38 Virginia Woolf, 'Modern Fiction', in *The Essays of Virginia Woolf*, vol. 4, ed. Andrew McNeillie (London: Hogarth Press, 1994), p. 160.

39 Simmel, 'The Metropolis and Mental Life', p. 179.

40 Ibid., pp. 177, 180.

41 See Antonin Artaud, 'Van Gogh: The Man Suicided by Society', trans. Mary Beach and Lawrence Ferlinghetti, in *Artaud Anthology*, ed. Jack Hirschman (San Francisco: City Lights Books, 1965), pp. 135–63.

42 Walter Benjamin, *The Arcades Project*, trans. Howard Eiland and Kevin McLaughlin (Cambridge, MA: Harvard University Press, 1999), p. 901.

43 J. Hillis Miller, '*Mrs Dalloway*: Repetition as the Raising of the Dead', in *The J. Hillis Miller Reader*, ed. Julian Wolfreys (Stanford: Stanford University Press, 2005), p. 171.

44 Williams, *The Country and the City*, p. 245.

45 Henri Lefebvre, *Introduction to Modernity*, trans. John Moore (London: Verso, 1995), pp. 179–80.

8. Beginning

1   Georges Bataille, 'Mouth', in *Visions of Excess: Selected Writings, 1927–1939*, trans. and ed. Allan Stoekl (Minneapolis: University of Minnesota Press, 1985), p. 59.

2   Roland Barthes, 'Outcomes of the Text', in *The Rustle of Language*, trans. Richard Howard (Berkeley: University of California Press, 1989), pp. 240–1.

3   See Georges Bataille, 'The Jesuve', in *Visions of Excess*, p. 78. The ape, it might be said, is the ultimate anti-bourgeois.

4   Michel Surya, *Georges Bataille: An Intellectual Biography*, trans. Krzysztof Fijalkowski and Michael Richardson (London: Verso, 2002), pp. 109–10.

5   Georges Bataille, 'Big Toe', in *Encyclopaedia Acephalica: Comprising the Critical Dictionary and Related Texts*, trans. Iain White (London: Atlas Press, 1995), pp. 90, 92. Hereafter, page references appear in parenthesis after the quotation.

6   Barthes, 'Outcomes of the Text', p. 245. Note that Barthes also mentions Bataille's essay on the big toe in relation to his definition of 'obtuse meaning' in 'The Third Meaning: Research Notes on Some Eisenstein Stills', in *Image, Music, Text*, ed. Stephen Heath (London: Fontana, 1977), pp. 59–60.

7   Barthes, 'Outcomes of the Text', p. 244.

8   William Shakespeare, *Coriolanus*, I, i, 154–8, in *The Alexander Text of the Complete Works*, ed. Peter Alexander (London: Collins, 1951), p. 829.

9   Georges Bataille, 'The Solar Anus', in *Visions of Excess*, p. 8.

10 Ibid.

11 Georges Bataille, '[Dream]', in *Visions of Excess*, p. 4.

12 Sigmund Freud, *Three Essays on the Theory of Sexuality*, in *On Sexuality: Three Essays on the Theory of Sexuality and Other Works*, trans. James Strachey, ed. Angela Richards (Harmondsworth: Penguin, 1977), p. 96.

13 Barthes, 'Outcomes of the Text', p. 245.

14 Georges Bataille, 'Eye', in *Visions of Excess*, p. 17.

15 Barthes, 'Outcomes of the Text', p. 245.

16 See Rieko Matsuura, *The Apprenticeship of Big Toe P*, trans. Michael Emmerich (Tokyo: Kodansha International, 2009).

17 Rosalind E. Krauss, *The Optical Unconscious* (Cambridge, MA: MIT Press, 1993), p. 184. Patrick French confirms – in '*Documents* in the 1970s: Bataille, Barthes and "Le gros orteil"', *Papers of Surrealism* 7 (2007), p. 8 – that 'Bataille's fiction of the body … is posed alongside the psychoanalytic semiotics of fetishism, not against it.'

18 Quoted in Joseph A. Amato, *On Foot: A History of Walking* (New York: New York University Press, 2004), p. 1.

19 Wilfred Bion, *Cogitations*, ed. Francesca Bion (London: Karnac, 1992), p. 71.

20 Arthur Schopenhauer, *The World as Will and Representation, Volume 1*, eds Judith Norman, Alistair Welchman and Christopher Janaway (Cambridge: Cambridge University Press, 2010), pp. 337–8.

21 Barthes, 'Outcomes of the Text', p. 246.

22 Walter Benjamin, 'The Work of Art in the Age of Mechanical Reproduction', in *Illuminations*, trans. Harry Zohn (London: Fontana, 1992), p. 230.

23 Giorgio Agamben, 'Notes on Gesture', in *Means without End: Notes on Politics*, trans. Vincenzo Binetti and Cesare Casarino (Minneapolis: University of Minnesota Press, 2000), p. 50.

24 Quoted in ibid.

25 Dudley J. Morton, *The Human Foot: Its Evolution, Physiology, and Functional Disorders* (New York: Columbia University Press, 1935), p. 140.

26 Shane O'Mara, *In Praise of Walking: The New Science of How We Walk and Why It's Good for Us* (London: Bodley Head, 2019), p. 72.

27 A dactyl, incidentally, is a metrical foot consisting of a long syllable followed by two short ones, probably derived from Latin *dactylus*, Greek δάκτυλος, meaning a finger, a date, a dactyl (from its three joints).

28 Gerard Manley Hopkins, 'Hurrahing in Harvest', ll. 5–8, in *The Major Works*, ed. Catherine Phillips (Oxford: Oxford World's Classics, 2002), p. 134. It seems strange that there is no reference to Hopkins in Marc Shell, *Talking the Walk and Walking the Talk: A Rhetoric of Rhythm* (New York: Fordham University Press, 2015).

29 Bataille, 'The Jesuve', p. 75.

30 Charles Darwin, *The Descent of Man: Selection in Relation to Sex*, eds Adrian Desmond and James Moore (Harmondsworth: Penguin, 2004), p. 28.

31 Quoted in Rebecca Solnit, *Wanderlust: A History of Walking* (London: Verso, 2001), p. 41.

32 Dean Falk et al., 'Metopic suture of Taung (*Australopithecus africanus*) and its implications for hominin brain evolution', *PNAS* 109: 22 (2012), pp. 8467–70.

33 Leslie Klenerman and Bernard Wood, *The Human Foot: A Companion to Clinical Studies* (London: Springer, 2006), p. 9. Note

that I am grateful to Christophe Soligo, of the Department of Anthropology at University College London, for his generosity in teaching me the anatomical and anthropological significance of the big toe.

34 Solnit, *Wanderlust*, p. 35.

35 For the range of hypotheses, see ibid., p. 40.

36 Campbell Rolian, Daniel E. Lieberman, and Benedikt Hallgrimsson, 'The Coevolution of Human Hands and Feet', *Evolution* 64: 6 (2010), p. 1565.

37 Ibid., p. 1566.

38 Sigmund Freud, *Civilization and Its Discontents*, trans. David McLintock (Harmondsworth: Penguin, 2002), pp. 41–2.

39 Carol V. Ward, William H. Kimbel and Donald C. Johanson, 'Complete Fourth Metatarsal and Arches in the Foot of *Australopithecus afarensis*', *Science* 331 (11 February 2011), p. 753.

40 Amato, *On Foot*, p. 22.

41 Nick Land, 'Spirit and Teeth', in *Fanged Noumena: Collected Writings, 1987–2007*, eds Robin Mackay and Ray Brassier (New York: Sequence Press, 2011), p. 188.

42 Carlo Emilio Gadda, *That Awful Mess on the Via Merulana*, trans. William Weaver (New York: New York Review Books, 2007), p. 271. Hereafter, page references appear in parenthesis after the quotation.

43 Incidentally, Gadda's revisionist account of Renaissance art, in which he seizes on the most insignificant feature of its iconography, iconicizing the irreducibly non-iconic or anti-iconic, is also a guide to his own innovations – at once literary and philosophical – as a writer. For, as Italo Calvino underlined, in addition to forging an extraordinarily original use of language, in which the erudite and the popular are freely, energetically intermingled, Gadda developed a form of narrative composition 'in which minimal details take on giant proportions and end up by occupying the whole canvas and hiding or obscuring the overall design'. See Italo Calvino, 'Carlo Emilio Gadda, the *Pasticciaccio*', in *Why Read the Classics?* trans. Martin McLaughlin (Harmondsworth: Penguin, 2009), p. 201.

44 Raymond Tallis, *Michelangelo's Finger: An Exploration of Everyday Transcendence* (London: Atlantic Books, 2010), p. xvii.

45 Thomas Pynchon, *The Crying of Lot 49* (London: Vintage, 2000), p. 46.

46 Surya, *Georges Bataille*, pp. 122–3. For an excellent account of Bataille's materialism, see Pierre Macherey, 'Georges Bataille: Materialism Inverted', in *The Object of Literature*, trans. David Macey (Cambridge: Cambridge University Press, 1995), pp. 112–31.

47 Surya, *Georges Bataille*, p. 146.

48 André Breton, 'Manifesto of Surrealism', in *Manifestos of Surrealism*, trans. Richard Seaver and Helen R. Lane (Ann Arbor: University of Michigan Press, 1972), p. 26.

49 Michael Sheringham, *Everyday Life: Theories and Practices from Surrealism to the Present* (Oxford: Oxford University Press, 2006), p. 96.

50 Karl Marx, 'Postface to the Second Edition', in *Capital, Volume One*, trans. Ben Fowkes (Harmondsworth: Penguin, 1990), p. 103.

51 G. W. F. Hegel, *Phenomenology of Spirit*, trans. A. V. Miller (Oxford: Oxford University Press, 1977), pp. 200–2.

52 Adam Lowenstein, 'The Surrealism of the Photographic Image: Bazin, Barthes, and the Digital Sweet Hereafter', *Cinema Journal* 46: 3 (2007), p. 6.

53 A translation of the fragment, from which these quotations are taken, appears in Lucette Finas, 'Reading Bataille: The Invention of the Foot', *diacritics* 26: 2 (Summer 1996), pp. 97–8. For a probing, richly illustrated discussion of the role that feet played in the iconography of the First World War, and of Modernism more generally, see Maud Ellmann, 'More Kicks than Pricks: Modernist Body-Parts', in *A Handbook of Modernism Studies*, ed. Jean-Michel Rabaté (Oxford: Oxford University Press, 2013), pp. 255–80; see also the hint contained in Trudi Tate, *Modernism, History and the First World War* (Manchester: Manchester University Press, 1998), p. 78, where she briefly refers to 'the grey feet of the Crucified' in Mantegna's painting.

54 See Finas, 'Reading Bataille', p. 104.

55 Barthes, 'Outcomes of the Text', p. 239.

9. Stumbling

1 Ray Bradbury, 'The Pedestrian', in *Stories*, vol. 2 (London: Harper-Collins, 2003), p. 569. Hereafter, page references appear in parenthesis after the quotation.

2 Paul Farley and Michael Symmons Roberts, *Edgelands: Journeys into England's True Wilderness* (London: Jonathan Cape, 2011), p. 23.

3 Theodor W. Adorno, *Negative Dialectics*, trans. E. B. Ashton (London: Routledge, 1990), p. 205.

4 William Henry Whitmore, *The Colonial Laws of Massachusetts. Reprinted from the Edition of 1660, With the Supplements to 1672* (Boston: City Council of Boston, 1889), pp. 198–9. On the

history of the nightwalker, see Matthew Beaumont, *Nightwalking: A Nocturnal History of London, Chaucer to Dickens* (London: Verso, 2015).

5   Quoted in Martha Grace Duncan, *Romantic Outlaws, Beloved Prisons: The Unconscious Meanings of Crime and Punishment* (New York: New York University Press, 1996), p. 172.

6   David C. Brody, James R. Acker and Wayne A. Logan, *Criminal Law* (Gaithersburg, MD: Aspen, 2001), p. 63.

7   Bryan D. Palmer, *Cultures of Darkness: Night Travels in the History of Transgression* (New York: Monthly Review Press, 2000), pp. 16–17.

8   Theodor W. Adorno, 'Culture Industry Reconsidered', in *The Culture Industry: Selected Essays on Mass Culture*, ed. J. M. Bernstein (London: Routledge, 1991), p. 92.

9   Theodor W. Adorno, 'How to Look at Television', in *The Culture Industry*, p. 138. Incidentally, in a larger political context, I agree with Terry Eagleton that 'the dystopian view that the typical citizen of advanced capitalism is the doped telly viewer is a myth, as the ruling class itself is uncomfortably aware.' See *Ideology: An Introduction* (London: Verso, 1991), p. 42.

10   Jonathan Crary, *24/7: Late Capitalism and the Ends of Sleep* (London: Verso, 2013), pp. 79, 80.

11   Ibid., p. 81.

12   I take this formulation from Peter Linebaugh, *The London Hanged: Crime and Civil Society in the Eighteenth Century*, 2nd edition (London: Verso, 2006), p. 23.

13   André Breton, 'Jacques Vaché', in *The Lost Steps*, trans. Mark Polizzotti (Lincoln, NE: University of Nebraska Press, 1996), p. 42.

14   Adorno, 'How to Look at Television', p. 147.

15   Viktor Shklovsky, 'Art as Device', in *Theory of Prose*, trans. Benjamin Sher (Champaign, IL: Dalkey Archive Press, 1990), p. 6.

16   Oliver Goldsmith, *The Citizen of the World: or, Letters from a Chinese Philosopher, Residing in England, to His Friends in the East* (London, 1782), pp. 216–17.

17   Richard Mabey, *Weeds: How Vagabond Plants Gatecrashed Civilization and Changed the Way We Think about Nature* (London: Profile, 2010), p. 20.

18   Walter Benjamin, *The Arcades Project*, trans. Howard Eiland and Kevin McLaughlin (Cambridge, MA: Harvard University Press, 1999), p. 372.

19   Mike Davis, *Dead Cities* (New York: New Press, 2002), p. 370.

20   Fredric Jameson, 'Then You Are Them', *London Review of Books* 31: 17 (10 September 2009), p. 7.

21 Richard Jefferies, *After London: or, Wild England* (Oxford: Oxford University Press, 1980), p. 36.

22 Herbert Marcuse, *One-Dimensional Man:* (London: Sphere, 1972), p. 20.

23 John Rechy, *City of Night* (London: Souvenir Press, 2009), p. 136.

24 Marcuse, *One-Dimensional Man*, p. 21.

25 On psychogenic fugue, see the chapter on Edward Bellamy in this volume; and, for a fuller sense of the historical background, Ian Hacking, *Mad Travelers: Reflections on the Reality of Transient Mental Illnesses* (Cambridge, MA: Harvard University Press, 1998).

26 See Craig Koslofsky, *Evening's Empire: A History of the Night in Early Modern Europe* (Cambridge: Cambridge University Press, 2011), pp. 59, 79. For further thoughts on this theological tradition, see Matthew Beaumont, 'R. S. Thomas's Poetics of Insomnia', *Essays in Criticism* 68: 1 (2018), pp. 74–107.

27 Theodor W. Adorno and Max Horkheimer, *Dialectic of Enlightenment*, trans. John Cumming (London: Verso, 1986), p. 3.

28 See Carlo Ginzburg, *The Night Battles: Witchcraft and Agrarian Cults in the Sixteenth and Seventeenth Centuries*, trans. John and Anne Tedeschi (Baltimore: Johns Hopkins University Press, 1983).

29 Michael Löwy, 'The Current of Critical Irrealism', in *Adventures in Realism*, ed. Matthew Beaumont (Oxford: Blackwell, 2007), p. 198.

30 Rachel Bowlby, 'Commuting', in *Restless Cities*, eds Matthew Beaumont and Gregory Dart (London: Verso, 2010), p. 52.

31 See Karl Marx, *Economic and Philosophical Manuscripts* (London: Lawrence & Wishart, 1977), pp. 67–9.

32 Theodor W. Adorno, *Aesthetic Theory*, eds Gretel Adorno and Rolf Tiedemann, trans. Robert Hullot-Kentor (London: Athlone Press, 1997), p. 31.

33 William Blake, 'London', in *The Complete Poetry and Prose of William Blake*, revised edition, ed. David V. Erdman (New York: Anchor Books, 1988), pp. 26–7.

34 David H. Keller, 'The Revolt of the Pedestrians', in *The Road to Science Fiction: From Wells to Heinlein*, ed. James E. Gunn (New York: Signet, 1979), pp. 168–97.

35 See 'Playboy Interview: Ray Bradbury', *Playboy* 43: 5 (May 1996), pp. 47–56, 149–50.

36 Ray Bradbury, 'Burning Bright: An Afterword', in *Fahrenheit 451*, anniversary edition (London: HarperCollins, 2003), p. 177.

37 Jonathan R. Eller, *Becoming Ray Bradbury* (Urbana, IL: University of Illinois Press, 2011), p. 239. No doubt Bob Dylan would understand Bradbury's alarm. In 2009, he was arrested late one

afternoon while wandering alone in the rain, some distance from his tour bus. A local resident reported 'an eccentric-looking old man' behaving suspiciously. As this incident demonstrates, the isolated, slightly tattered individual on the street embodies a spontaneous refusal of the suburban values that prevail in tightly curtained interiors.

38 Bradbury, 'Burning Bright', p. 178.

39 Bradbury, *Fahrenheit 451*, p. 166. Hereafter, page references appear in parenthesis after the quotation.

40 Andrew A. Bruce and Shurl Rosmarin, 'The Gunman and His Gun', *Journal of Criminal Law and Criminology (Northwestern)* 24 (1933–4), p. 537.

41 Terry Eagleton, *Sweet Violence: The Idea of the Tragic* (Oxford: Blackwell, 2003), p. 279.

42 André Breton, *Nadja*, trans. Richard Howard (Harmondsworth: Penguin, 1999), p. 72.

43 Paul Carter, *Repressed Spaces: The Poetics of Agoraphobia* (London: Reaktion, 2002), p. 45.

44 See Ernst Bloch, *The Principle of Hope*, vol. 1, trans. Neville Plaice, Stephen Plaice and Paul Knight (Cambridge, MA: MIT Press, 1995), p. 144.

10. Not Belonging

1 Jean Rhys, *Good Morning, Midnight* (Harmondsworth: Penguin, 2016), p. 23.

2 Margit Mayer, 'The "Right to the City" in the Context of Shifting Mottos of Urban Social Movements', *City* 13: 2–3 (2009), p. 367.

3 Georg Simmel, 'The Metropolis and Mental Life', in *Simmel on Culture: Selected Writings*, eds David Frisby and Mike Featherstone (London: Sage, 1997), p. 179.

4 On the phenomenological interpretation of architecture, which comprises an extensive literature of course, see for example Kent C. Bloomer and Charles W. Moore, *Body, Memory, and Architecture* (New Haven: Yale University Press, 1977); Christian Norberg-Schulz, *Genius Loci: Towards a Phenomenology of Architecture* (London: Academy Editions, 1980); and, more recently, M. Reza Shirazi, *Towards an Articulated Phenomenological Interpretation of Architecture: Phenomenal Phenomenology* (London: Routledge, 2014).

5 China Miéville, 'The Conspiracy of Architecture: Notes on a Modern Anxiety', *Historical Materialism* 2: 1 (1998), p. 1.

6 See Silke Steets, 'Taking Berger and Luckmann to the Realm of Materiality: Architecture as a Social Construction', *Cultural Sociology* 10: 1 (2016), p. 99.

7 Alejandro Zaera Polo, 'The Politics of the Envelope: A Political Critique of Materialism', *Volume* 17 (2008), pp. 76–105.

8 Peter Marcuse, 'From Critical Urban Theory to the Right to the City', in *City* 13: 2–3 (2009), p. 190. See Henri Lefebvre, 'The Right to the City', in *Writings on Cities*, ed. and trans. Eleonore Kofman and Elizabeth Lebas (Oxford: Blackwell, 1996), pp. 147–59; also, David Harvey, *Rebel Cities: From the Right to the City to the Urban Revolution* (London: Verso, 2012).

9 Norberg-Schulz, *Genius Loci*, p. 20.

10 Slavoj Žižek, *Living in the End Times* (London: Verso, 2011), pp. 244–78.

11 Ibid., p. 244. See Kojin Karatani, *Transcritique: On Kant and Marx* (Cambridge, MA: MIT Press, 2003).

12 Michel de Certeau, *The Practice of Everyday Life*, trans. Steven Rendall (Berkeley: University of California Press, 1984), p. 100.

13 Žižek, *Living in the End Times*, pp. 244–5.

14 Anthony Vidler, *The Architectural Uncanny: Essays in the Modern Unhomely* (Cambridge, MA: MIT Press, 1992).

15 Ernst Jentsch, 'On the Psychology of the Uncanny', trans. Roy Sellars, *Angelaki* 2 (1995), p. 8. I have written about what I call the 'historical uncanny' in 'Red Sphinx: The Mechanics of the Uncanny in *The Time Machine*', in *The Spectre of Utopia: Utopian and Science Fictions at the Fin de Siècle* (Bern: Peter Lang, 2012), pp. 221–52.

16 Sigmund Freud, 'The "Uncanny"', in *Art and Literature*, trans. James Strachey, The Penguin Freud Library, vol. 14, ed. Albert Dickson (Harmondsworth: Penguin, 1990), p. 341.

17 Ibid., p. 340.

18 Ibid., p. 345.

19 Ibid., p. 364.

20 Ibid., p. 362.

21 Vidler, *The Architectural Uncanny*, pp. ix–x.

22 Warren Montag, 'Spirits Armed and Unarmed: Derrida's *Specters of Marx*', in *Ghostly Demarcations: A Symposium on Jacques Derrida's Specters of Marx*, ed. Michael Sprinker (London: Verso, 1999), p. 71.

23 Jacques Derrida, *Specters of Marx: The State of the Debt, the Work of Mourning, and the New International*, trans. Peggy Kamuf (London: Routledge, 1994), p. 11.

24 Alberto Pérez-Gómez, A. (2006) 'The Space of Architecture:

Meaning as Presence and Representation', in *Questions of Perception: Phenomenology of Architecture*, eds Steven Holl, Juhani Pallasmaa and Alberto Pérez-Gómez (San Francisco: William Stout, 2006), p. 23.

25 David Harvey, *Social Justice and the City*, revised edition (Athens: University of Georgia Press, 2009).

26 Monika Grubbauer, 'Architecture, Economic Imaginaries and Urban Politics: The Office Tower as Socially Classifying Device', *International Journal of Urban and Regional Research* 38: 1 (2014), p. 340; see also Monica Degen and Gillian Rose, 'The Sensory Experiencing of Urban Design: The Role of Walking and Perceptual Memory', *Urban Studies* 49: 15 (2012), pp. 3271–87.

27 See Slavoj Žižek, 'In His Bold Gaze My Ruin Is Writ Large', in *Everything You Always Wanted to Know about Lacan* (London: Verso, 1992), p. 252.

28 Miéville, 'The Conspiracy of Architecture', p. 2.

29 Jean-Paul Sartre, *What Is Subjectivity?* trans. David Broder and Trista Selous (London: Verso, 2016), p. 114.

30 Miéville, 'The Conspiracy of Architecture', p. 18.

31 Karl Marx, *Economic and Philosophical Manuscripts of 1844*, trans. Martin Milligan (New York: International Publishers, 1964), pp. 155–6.

32 De Certeau, *The Practice of Everyday Life*, p. 103.

33 Arnold Berleant, 'The Environment as an Aesthetic Paradigm', *Dialectics and Humanism* 15: 1–2 (1988), p. 97.

34 J. Hillis Miller, 'The Critic as Host', in *Modern Criticism and Theory*, ed. David Lodge (London: Longman, 1988), p. 281.

35 Edmond Jabès, *The Book of Questions*, vol. 1, trans. Rosmarie Waldrop (Hanover: Wesleyan University Press, 1991), p. 368.

36 Henri Lefebvre, *The Production of Space*, trans. D. Nicholson Smith (London: Routledge, 1991), p. 273.

37 Zaera Polo, 'The Politics of the Envelope', p. 78.

38 Žižek, *Living in the End Times*, p. 253.

39 Manfredo Tafuri, *Architecture and Utopia: Design and Capitalist Development*, trans. B. Luigia La Penta (Cambridge, MA: MIT Press, 1976), p. 179.

40 Maria Kaika and Korinna Thielen, 'Form Follows Power', *City* 10: 1 (2006), p. 63.

41 Zaera Polo, 'The Politics of the Envelope', p. 80.

42 See, for example, Leslie Sklair, 'Iconic Architecture and Capitalist Globalization', *City* 10: 1 (2006), pp. 21–47.

43 See Louis Althusser, 'Ideology and Ideological State Apparatuses (Notes Towards an Investigation', in *Lenin and Philosophy*, trans.

Ben Brewster (New York: Monthly Review Press, 2001), pp. 85–126.

44 Paul Jones, 'Putting Architecture in its Social Place: A Cultural Political Economy of Architecture', in *Urban Studies* 46: 12 (2009), pp. 2525.

45 Rowan Moore, 'British Museum Extension', *Observer*, 29 June 2014, available at: theguardian.com/artanddesign.

46 Oliver Wainwright, 'British Museum's £135m Extension for Care and Collection of World Treasures', *Guardian*, 8 July 2014, available at: theguardian.com/artanddesign.

47 Derrida, *Specters of Marx*, pp. 6–7.

48 Ibid., p. 8.

49 Ibid., p. 7.

50 Gilles Deleuze and Félix Guattari, *A Thousand Plateaus: Capitalism and Schizophrenia*, trans. B. Massumi (London: Continuum, 2004), p. 127.

51 Zaera Polo, 'The Politics of the Envelope', p. 79.

52 Mike Davis, *City of Quartz: Excavating the Future in Los Angeles* (London: Verso, 1990), p. 231.

53 See Tal Kaminer, *The Efficacy of Architecture: Political Contestation and Agency* (London: Routledge, 2017).

54 Walter Benjamin, *The Arcades Project*, trans. Howard Eiland and Kevin McLaughlin (Cambridge, MA: Harvard University Press, 1999), p. 151.

55 Georg Simmel, 'Sociology of the Senses', in *Simmel on Culture*, p. 112.

56 Ibid.

57 T. S. Eliot, *The Waste Land*, in *The Complete Poems and Plays* (London: Faber & Faber, 1969), p. 73.

Index